ATTICA—MY STORY

ATTICA – MY STORY

Russell G. Oswald

Commissioner, Department of Correctional Services
State of New York

EDITED BY RODNEY CAMPBELL

1972
Doubleday & Company, Inc., Garden City, New York

Acknowledgment is gratefully made for permission to reprint from the following material:

Excerpts from an editorial broadcast by WCBS-TV, September 14, 1971. Reprinted by permission.

Excerpts from an editorial broadcast by WAST-TV, September 16, 1971. Reprinted by permission of WAST Television 13, Albany, New York.

Excerpt from "letter to the editor," October 20, 1971, issue of Batavia *Daily News*. Reprinted by permission.

Excerpts from Max Lerner's editorial in September 15, 1971, and Harriet Van Horne's editorial in September 17, 1971, issues of the New York *Post*. Copyright © 1971, Los Angeles Times. Reprinted by permission.

Excerpts from Pete Hamill column entitled "Slaughter," September 15, 1971 issue of New York *Post*. Copyright © 1971, New York Post Corporation. Reprinted by permission of New York *Post*.

Excerpt from article "An Attica Graduate Tells His Story" by William Roo Coons, October 10, 1971, issue of New York *Times* Magazine. Copyright © 1971 by New York *Times*; excerpt from Tom Wickers column September 16, 1971, and from editorial "The Prisoners" from September 20, 1971, issue of the New York *Times*. Copyright © 1971 by The New York Times Corporation. Reprinted by permission.

Excerpt from editorial, September 21, 1971 issue of *The Saratogian* of Saratoga Springs, New York. Reprinted by permission.

Excerpt from editorial, September 14, 1971, issue of The Syracuse *Post-Standard*. Reprinted by permission.

Excerpt from editorial as it appeared in the London *Daily Telegraph*. Reprinted by permission.

Excerpt from "Of Attica and the Alamo" by Clark Whelton, September 23, 1971, issue of *The Village Voice*. Reprinted by permission of *The Village Voice*. Copyrighted © by The Village Voice, Inc., 1971.

Excerpt from editorial roundup, September 15, 1971, issue of *The Wall Street Journal*. Reprinted by permission.

Excerpt from editorial "That's Telling Em, Your Honor" appearing in October 15, 1971, issue of the New York *Daily News*. Reprinted by permission of the New York *Daily News*.

ISBN: 0-385-08199-5
Library of Congress Catalog Card Number 72-77002
Copyright © 1972 by R. Oswald and R. Campbell
All Rights Reserved
Printed in the United States of America
First Edition

TO JANE AND KURT
WHO LIVE WITH ME THROUGH THIS TRAGEDY

AUTHOR'S NOTE

The purpose of this book is to tell what I know about the terrible events that took place in September of 1971 in and about the New York State Correctional Facility at Attica, New York.

First of all, I have an obligation to the American people to help set the record straight. Rarely has so much propaganda, emotion, untruth, half-truth, and journalistic naïveté competed so massively with the valiant efforts of serious reporters and objective investigators. All who reported from the scene labored under the most difficult of circumstances. I feel a deep responsibility to report the facts in detail and in perspective—from my special vantage point at Attica and in the light of what we have been able to learn since Attica. This book undertakes that assignment.

Next, I have an obligation to the cause to which I have devoted my professional lifetime—that of finding more effective means of fighting crime by changing criminals. The loss of life at Attica must not be compounded by a loss of momentum in the progress we have been making toward genuine prison reform. It therefore is crucial to expose the extremism at both poles of the Attica story.

On the one hand, there are the leftist militants in and out of prison who couldn't care less about the reality of prison reform. They seek to turn America's correctional system into a revolutionary battleground by capitalizing on the very real issue of prison reform. They led the Attica rebellion and made a peaceful settlement impossible. Yet these are the very people who level the horrendous cries of "murder" at public officials, myself included, who did their best to save lives and prevent anarchy. On the other hand, there is the "keep-them-in-their-place" school of penology—typified, alas, by the few of my own correctional officers who reviled me to my face at Attica for even attempting to negotiate a peaceful settlement—and who subsequently petitioned for my removal. Attica must not be made an excuse for a new era of rightist repression. Both the leftists and the rightists are impediments to progress toward a more useful and humane correctional system.

I learned many things from the Attica experience, but my faith in the correctibility of most criminal behavior remains unshaken. I will not give up on the human beings in my charge: I must fight for more public understanding and support so correction personnel everywhere can do a better job in an atmosphere of mutual respect—not of fear and mortal danger. This, too, is a major reason for writing this book.

I feel a deep personal obligation to the families of those who died to tell what I know of those terrible last days. I take comfort in the fact that we saved many lives. Hostages and inmates alike, those who lost their lives at Attica were victims of tragic circumstances offering nothing but tragic choices. I can only say that I did what all my experience and all my most careful and prayerful consideration convinced me that I had to do.

Finally, a few expressions of great gratitude that I hope will serve as an indication of my sentiments to the many, many others who deserve my thanks:

To my wife, Jane, for love and understanding beyond measure —and for faithfully compiling and preserving the files and memorabilia which jogged my memory and illuminated my account of the eventful years that went before Attica;

To Rodney Campbell, whose professional skills as editor and literary adviser made the writing of this volume possible;

And to Nelson A. Rockefeller, for his unswerving faith and stanch support through the darkest days of my life—the days recounted, in much heretofore untold detail, in the pages that follow.

—R.G.O.

Albany, New York

CONTENTS

Author's Note   vii

PART I

CHAPTER 1 *The Revolution That Failed*   3

CHAPTER 2 *The Rise of the Militants*   21

CHAPTER 3 *How to Take a Maximum-Security Prison in
           Thirty Minutes*   45

CHAPTER 4 *My Decision to Negotiate*   71

CHAPTER 5 *Out of Chaos Came the Twenty-eight Points*   95

PART II

CHAPTER 6 *Wisconsin—Years of Struggle*   127

CHAPTER 7 *"With Our Imperfect Knowledge of Twisted
           Minds"*   140

CHAPTER 8 *Massachusetts: One Damned Crisis After
           Another*   155

CHAPTER 9 *The Cliff-Hangers, the Heartbreaks, the Hu-
           mane Victories of Parole*   173

CHAPTER 10 *The Eve of the Storm*   194

PART III

CHAPTER 11 *"Let Them Give Their Agenda of Death"*   213

CHAPTER 12 *"We Want the Governor Here, Now!"*   230

CHAPTER 13 *The Battle of Attica I: Attack—with Minimal Force*   254

CHAPTER 14 *The Battle of Attica II: Victory—at a Tragic Cost*   271

PART IV

CHAPTER 15 *"The State Is Guilty of Murder!"*   301

CHAPTER 16 *Three Secret Meetings*   320

CHAPTER 17 *On with Prison Reform*   342

APPENDIXES

APPENDIX A *Letters to the Commissioner from Prisoners at Attica*   361

APPENDIX B *The Hostages Who Died*   369

APPENDIX C *The Hostages Who Survived*   375

APPENDIX D *The Prisoners Who Died*   379

APPENDIX E *Members of the Citizens Observer Committee*   391

APPENDIX F *General Rules of Parole in New York State*   395

APPENDIX G *Report of the Goldman Panel Investigation of the Aftermath of Attica*   399

ATTICA—MY STORY

PART I

"Why should there not be a patient confidence in the ultimate justice of the people?"

ABRAHAM LINCOLN

CHAPTER 1

The Revolution That Failed

Attica before the massacre offered us a sleeping but graphic glimpse of the monumental feats attainable by men and women moving along a revolutionary course . . . In a figurative sense, it evoked visions of the Paris Communes, the liberated areas of pre-revolutionary Cuba, the free territories of Mozambique.

Angela Y. Davis

There are four Third World and African country people across the street from this prison, prepared to provide asylum for everyone who wants to leave this country for this purpose . . . (Shouts and pandemonium from the inmates.)
The gringos talk about "Remember the Alamo!!"
Remember Attica!

William M. Kunstler

Bobby Seale was here because my secretary sent him a prepaid ticket. The Young Lords were here because my secretary sent them a prepaid ticket . . . We are mad, and we are with you one thousand, one hundred thousand per cent. (Shouts and applause from inmates.)
We want complete amnesty . . . And we want the governor here now . . . Now!

New York State Assemblyman
Arthur O. Eve

Look at this, Pig, go ahead and pray, Pig. You're going to die.
Attica Inmate "Executioner"
to a Hostage

My executioner combed my hair and gave me a Tum and a cigarette and said he wanted me to look pretty to die.
Hostage Ronald Kozlowski
After Rescue with His Throat Cut

*The order came. Stand the hostages up. They kept me up. They
were all around my legs. Then somebody pulled me down. "Kill the
pigs! Kill the pigs!" Somebody said "Don't kill 'em." A stick at my
throat. Gas. Blindfold off. Stick came off my throat. I heard somebody
saying "I'm stabbed." State troopers arrived. Said lay down with your
hands on your head. I identified myself. I saw Red Whalen lying there.
I thought he was dead. His mouth was open, blood coming out.*

Hostage Dean Stenschorn
After Rescue

I was the man in charge at Attica.

My name is Russell George Oswald. I am sixty-four years old,
and have been Commissioner of Correctional Services for the
State of New York since January 1, 1971. For the previous twelve
years I was chairman of the New York State Parole Board. I came
to New York from Massachusetts, where I was Commissioner of
Corrections, and, originally, from my home state of Wisconsin,
where I was Director of Corrections.

I am a prison reformer by profession—with a relevant record as
an advocate of humane change in the treatment of offenders and
the wiping out of prison brutality. I am a law-and-order man in
the most affirmative sense, as a specialist in the rehabilitation of
lawbreakers.

I am also a patriotic citizen who believes that the current crime
wave has become an almost unbelievably serious threat to the
quality of life for millions of our people.

As a political realist—with ideals and, hopefully, without naïveté—I believe we must arrest the present revolutionary trends in
the United States—not by repression, but by working toward
higher levels of justice for all Americans. We must do this if we
value America as we have known it, if we wish to survive as a free,
moderate, and progressive nation, if we intend to continue to
offer opportunity and dignity to all our people. But we *must* en-
trust our passion for justice to our tested rule of law.

It was in this frame of reference that I finally gave the order to
the New York State Police, on the dark, rainy morning of September 13, 1971, to put an end to a four-and-a-half day rebellion
at the Attica Correctional Facility in upstate New York. I thereby
became the man who has been acclaimed and vilified for termi-
nating the bloodiest prison uprising and one of the most blatant
and bizarre episodes of political anarchy in our history.

The Attica rebellion began on the morning of Thursday, September 9, 1971, when many of the 2,243 inmates of the Attica Correctional Facility won control of most of the maximum-security institution in a skilled, well-planned, well-armed, sudden, and savage attack. At that time, the rebel inmates fatally fractured the skull of one of our corrections officers and brutally injured almost all of the forty-nine other corrections officers and civilian employees they took hostage. Later that day, a scratch force of approximately 100 State Police troopers and corrections officers recaptured sections of the prison, helped rescue nine of the hostages, and regained control of 962 inmates who had not been involved in the uprising.

From Thursday until the following Monday we attempted, with the help of an outside Citizens Observer Committee, formed of nominees of the prisoners and the state government, to negotiate the release of the hostages. We tried to work out a speed-up of prison reforms that, before the outbreak, I was beginning to put into effect. But even as negotiations went forward, the rebels secretly murdered three dissident fellow inmates—stabbing each victim more than twenty times—in addition to the fatal bludgeoning of the corrections officer. Then at the critical moment on that Monday morning, eight of the hostages were brought out in full view, blindfolded and bound, with knives held at their throats by designated inmate "executioners." Our four and a half days of negotiations had narrowed down to this brutal challenge. I had no further choice.

Attica Correctional Facility, the scene of this historic confrontation, is one of seven maximum-security institutions in New York State. It was built between 1929 and 1930 on a fifty-five-acre plot at a cost of some $9 million. With its individual cell capacity of 2,466, not quite fully occupied before the uprising, Attica is the receiving institution for newly committed criminals and parole violators from the Fifth, Sixth, Seventh, and Eighth Judicial Districts, or the thirty-two counties of Western New York State.

The prison is set in the midst of the village of Attica, with a population of 2,911, a rural community less than an hour's drive east of Buffalo and less than half an hour's drive southwest of Batavia on the New York Thruway. Many of the corrections officers live or lived in Attica, including twenty-seven of the hostages. The mayor of Attica, Richard W. Miller, works eight hours a day as a corrections officer. He also drives a school bus and operates an oil-burner installation and repair business with the deputy mayor, Angelo Corcimiglia.

"We never considered our jobs real dangerous," Mr. Miller said during the uprising. "There were very few assaults on officers. But there have been more in the last year and a half than in all my ten years on the job before. It just didn't use to happen."

The Attica Correctional Facility consists of four main cell blocks, A, B, C, and D, formed around a five-acre quadrangle. This was divided into four quarters by long, intersecting, built-up corridors, approximately one story in height, with tunnels inside and catwalks along the roofs. The quarters were termed A, B, C, and D Yards. The junction of the corridor-tunnels was nicknamed "Times Square." Off to one side, behind the rectangle of the main cell blocks, there was a fifth cell block, E, and also a disciplinary block for the segregation of rule violators, known as Housing Block Z, or HBZ.

Behind A Block on the rectangle, where the rebellion was to begin, the superintendent and his staff worked in the Administration Building. Here were up to two dozen women secretaries and aides and here also was the prison arsenal. It was in cubbyhole offices on the second floor of the Administration Building that we were to set up our headquarters.

Behind C Block, proceeding clockwise around the rectangle, there were HBZ, the hospital and dispensary, the main mess hall, the laundry and bath, and E Block. Behind B Block, still moving clockwise, were the all-important industrial building, metal shops, the commissary, and the powerhouse. Behind D Block, which was to become the center of rebel resistance, was located the paint shop and also the chapel, auditorium and schoolhouse.

A towering concrete wall, almost thirty inches thick, studded with observation and guard towers, surrounded the facility. It formed the secure perimeter during the crisis.

Approximately 90 per cent of the prisoners at Attica had been sent there for murder, manslaughter, felonious assault, burglary, robbery, grand larceny, dangerous drugs offenses, or sex crimes. The remaining 10 per cent were miscellaneous offenders. These approximate percentages are based on 1968 statistics, which hold good today:

Murder in the first or second degree (life imprisonment)	8%
Manslaughter and felonious assault	17%
Robbery and burglary	35%
Grand larceny	13%
Dangerous drugs offenses	9%
Sex offenses	8%
Miscellaneous offenses	10%

Twenty-eight per cent of the prisoners were serving sentences of twenty years imprisonment or longer. Of these men, 35 per cent were between twenty-one and twenty-nine years, and 34 per cent were between thirty and thirty-nine years. One hundred and eighty-one men were serving life sentences.

All subsequent attempts at romanticization to the contrary, most of the men inside Attica were hardened criminals. No fewer than 89 per cent had previous adult criminal records—and 58 per cent had previously served time in federal and/or state institutions.

All subsequent attempts to brush off society's failure to the contrary, the men inside Attica showed indisputably that conviction for major crime is linked to a lack of education. No fewer than 80 per cent had not graduated from high school.

Later I shall denote the racial composition of the population —it is similarly surprising and at variance from many of the myths that sprang up during and after the rebellion.

At Attica an authorized force of 380 corrections officers, in addition to civilian employees, was assigned to guard and tend the 2,243 prisoners. At the time of the uprising we had a full complement of uniformed officers except for four vacancies—but it was a fair question whether the authorization was adequate. Because of shift scheduling, there were never more than one third of the corrections officers on duty at any one time, and this feeling of being undermanned and exposed in dangerous work was damaging to staff morale. On the one hand, the state budget for all arms of government had never been more stringent, and the taxpayers had never been so tax-conscious. On the other hand, the inmates

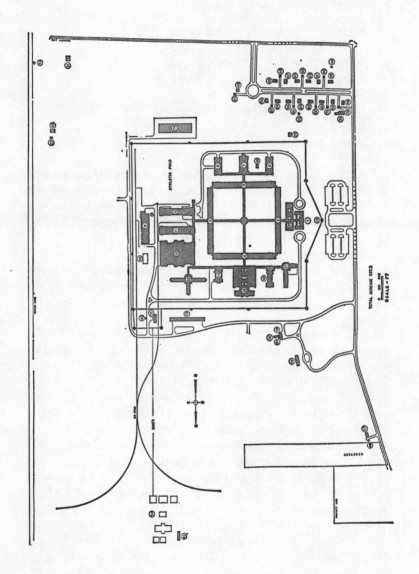

BUILDING INDEX

		Year Built
1.	Administration Building	1932
2.	West Cell Block ''A''	1931
3.	East Cell Block ''B''	1932
4.	North Cell Block ''C''	1934
5.	South Cell Block ''D''	1938
6.	School Building	1934
7.	Auditorium & Chapel	1934
8.	State, Carpenter & Paint Shop	1933
9.	Power House	1931
10.	Maintenance Storehouse & Garage	1932
11.	Industrial Building, Metal Shop #1	1932
12.	Metal Shop #2 & Garment Shop	1932
13.	Electric Eye — Front Gate	1940
14.	Laundry & Bath	1932
15.	Dining, Kitchen & Bakery	1931
16.	Hospital Building	1933
17.	Reception & Disciplinary	1933
18.	Warden's Residence	1934
19.	Warden's Garage	1935
20.	Dairy Barn #1	1935
21.	Head Farmer's Residence	1890
22.	Barn #2	1962
23.	Root Cellar	1936
24.	Barn #3	1890
25.	Farm Manager's Residence	1900
26.	Farm Machinery & Tool Shed	1945
27.	Deputy Warden s Residence	1935
28.	Utility Gang Shelter & Tool House	1937
29.	House over Meter Pit	1950
30.	Chicken House	1939
31.	Shooting Range Shelter	
32.	Cell Block ''E''	1966
33.	Transformer Building	1937
34.	Sewage Disposal Plant	1931
35.	Slaughter House & Piggery	1937
36.	Sewage Pump Station	1935
37.	Transformer Building	1935
38.	Village Filter Plant	
39.	Two Family Residence	1900
40.	Office — Lock Gates	1937
41.	Sewage Plant Office & Laboratory	1936
42.	Greenhouse	1938
43.		
44.	Tool & Bulb Shed Storage, Warden's Grounds	1936
45.	Maple Sugar House	1933
46.	Gas Chamber	1938
47.		
48.	Deputy Warden's Garage	1935
49.	Catholic Chaplain's Residence	1939
50.	Water Storage Tank	1955

51.	Barn #4	1880
52.	Farm Manager's Garage	1936
53.	Hose House	1936
54.	Head Farmer's Garage	1934
55.	Hose House	1936
56.	Officer's Cottage	1935
57.		
58.	Officer's Cottage	1935
59.	Officer's Cottage	1935
60.	Officer's Cottage	1935
61.	Officer's Cottage	1935
62.	Officer's Cottage	1935
63.	Officer's Cottage	1935
64.	Officer's Cottage	1935
65.	Officer's Cottage	1935
66.	Officer's Cottage	1935
67.	Officer's Cottage	1935
68.	Officer's Cottage	1935
69.	Officer's Cottage	1935
70.	Officer's Cottage	1935
71.	Lumber & Cement Storage	1937
72.		
73.	Medical Defense Storage Building	1957
74.	Medical Defense Storage Building	1966
75.	Visitors, Correspondence & Package Building	1966
76.	Maintenance Building (Future)	
77.	Milk House	1935
78.	2 Car Garage	1935
79.	2 Car Garage	1935
80.	2 Car Garage	1935
81.	2 Car Garage	1935
82.	2 Car Garage	1935
83.	Catholic Chaplain's Garage	1939
84.	2 Car Garage	1935
85.	2 Car Garage	1935
86.	2 Car Garage	1935

in the maximum-security institutions had rarely seemed more dangerous.

In addition to Attica, the state maximum-security institutions in New York are Auburn (built in 1816); Ossining, or Sing Sing (1825–28); Clinton, in the village of Dannemora (1845); Elmira (1876); Great Meadow, at Comstock (1911); and Green Haven, near Poughkeepsie (1941; used by the federal government during the war; a state prison since 1949). All of these were powder kegs in the fall of 1971—and, before Attica, we did not know which one, or which ones, would be ignited. There are also fifteen other types of medium- or minimum-security institutions dotted about the state. The New York City prison system is separate.

All in all, I am in charge of approximately 40,000 criminal offenders—some 13,000 of whom are in the correctional facilities and the remainder out on parole. In this endeavor, I am assisted by 3,340 members of our professional custodial staff, given a full complement, and by 400 parole officers in eleven area offices. In our state we have merged our prison and parole functions into an integrated Department of Correctional Services, and I am the first commissioner of the new organization.

Attica in the fall of 1971 was also one of the twenty-one prisons in the United States with more than 2,000 inmates. There are more than 400 prisons in the country, with some 25,000 men and women in federal prisons, almost 200,000 in state prisons, and almost another 200,000 in local jails and workhouses. Four state prisons have an astonishing population of 4,000 inmates or more apiece—San Quentin Prison in California, the Illinois State Penitentiary complex at Joliet-Stateville, the State Prison of Southern Michigan at Jackson, and the Ohio Penitentiary at Columbus.

For many years after the Second World War, the associate warden at San Quentin was a tough-minded advocate of prison reform named Walter B. Dunbar. He was later promoted to Deputy Director of Corrections for California and subsequently to Director. Then he became chairman of the Federal Board of Parole. Only a few months before the Attica rebellion, I was fortunate to be able to obtain Mr. Dunbar's services as my executive deputy commissioner in New York State. Walter Dunbar would serve throughout the crisis at my right hand.

Altogether, there are more than 120,000 correctional workers in the United States, of whom 63,000 are supervisors and custodial officers, 33,000 technicians and maintenance men and women, 17,000 caseworkers and managers involved directly in rehabilitation, and some 10,000 specialists. These last include psychologists, academic and vocational training instructors, medical personnel, researchers, and others with pinpoint professional qualifications.

Attica was, in a sense, the pressure point at the heart of a massive, national complex that could be broken apart. As George Jackson put it—he was the famous "Soledad Brother" who had been shot while trying to escape from San Quentin less than three weeks before Attica:

"I'll reiterate that I feel that the building of the revolutionary consciousness of the prisoner class is paramount in the over-all development of a hard-core left revolutionary cadre."

On the eve of Attica, then, the disinherited and the villainous, the alienated and the pawns, the flotsam and jetsam of society, and a new generation of revolutionary leaders focused on the prisons as their point of leverage. Here was where the Establishment could be made to buckle and the class issue could be most clearly defined.

On the eve of Attica, also, the Establishment was moving toward its own intramural test. Almost all the governors of almost all of the states watched the growth of organized militancy in the prisons, anticipating trouble but unable to mobilize the tens of thousands of police and troops that would have been needed to contain all the correctional institutions. When the first prison "blew," how would we react? With instant repression, instant grants of inmate demands, or with a professional "sorting out" of legitimate grievances from revolutionary ultimata? The real test would be to extend the steady momentum of prison reform itself —to turn our correctional services into *an asset* of our society in which all of our citizens can participate and take pride.

In the crisis at Attica, caught in revolution and holding off repression, I chose reform.

It was in this reformer's spirit that I made five decisions, that is, five major decisions at Attica between Thursday, September 9, and Monday, September 13. All of them led up to the sixth decision, the one to recapture the correctional facility. I summarize these decisions here briefly and will give my essential reasoning in later chapters.

I was at Attica almost from the start of the crisis until after the finish. I will admit to occasional distractions, in fact torment, because my wife, Jane, was in a hospital in Albany for treatment of a serious spinal condition, and I could not be with her. I was distracted also by the personal vilifications—as unexpected as I think they were unwarranted—from the radicals on the Citizens Observer Committee and the rightists among the corrections officers.

Yet, I *did* make the decisions at Attica and we *are* still full speed ahead for prison reform.

FIRST DECISION
THURSDAY, SEPTEMBER 9
APPROVE THE RECAPTURE OF AS MUCH OF THE PRISON AS POSSIBLE WITH THE LIMITED POLICE FORCES AVAILABLE

Shortly after 8:50 A.M., the first force of rebel prisoners won control of A Block. They were led by inmate Company 5, formed from known troublemakers and political militants. Second forces won control of B, D, and E Blocks, sweeping through Times Square, the intersection of the four corridor-tunnels that quadrisected the prison yard. The rebels were armed in advance with knives, spears, clubs, swords, steel and metal pipes, pickaxes, shovels, straight razors, wire bolos, and baseball bats with extended spikes. They took their objectives within twenty minutes.

Then the rebels attacked the commissary, metal shops, industrial building, and they set fires in the auditorium, chapel, and schoolhouse. A forklift truck was used to batter down heavy doors. After a sharp struggle, the rebels then took C Block. They had won control of most of the maximum-security institution within thirty minutes. They had also seized and brutalized forty-nine hostages and mortally wounded Corrections Officer William E. Quinn.

Superintendent Vincent Mancusi reported to us that he intended to attempt to regain control of the institution, block by block. He had retaken as much as he could and had chosen to await reinforcements before proceeding further. My deputy, Walter Dunbar, told him, "Good luck." We encouraged Mr. Mancusi

to keep on going, to recapture as much of the facility as possible
with the limited forces at his disposal.

SECOND DECISION
THURSDAY, SEPTEMBER 9
HOLD OFF FURTHER ACTION, START NEGOTIATIONS
WITH THE PRISONERS, AND TRY TO OBTAIN THE
PEACEFUL RELEASE OF THE HOSTAGES

At 2:15 P.M. I arrived at Attica and reviewed the situation with
Mr. Mancusi and with Major John W. Monahan, commanding
the State Police on the scene. My second decision—and a controversial one—was to hold off further police action for the time
being to seek a conference with the rebel leaders. These men had
already told Superintendent Mancusi that they would no longer
speak with anyone except Governor Rockefeller or me. I made
this decision even though I knew many of the corrections officers
would disapprove. Understandably, many wanted to storm right
in and rescue their comrades, whatever the risk, whatever the cost
—and some of them vilified me to my face for negotiating. But I
felt the prisoners were volatile and dangerous; furthermore, I
wanted to hear what the inmates had to say. I therefore entered
D Yard three times for direct negotiations with the rebel leaders
—at grave risk of being held hostage myself.

THIRD DECISION
FRIDAY, SEPTEMBER 10
FORM THE CITIZENS OBSERVER COMMITTEE, AP-
POINT RESPONSIBLE LEADERS TO BALANCE THE
RADICAL NOMINEES OF THE PRISONERS; WORK
THROUGH THE COMMITTEE FOR THE RELEASE OF
THE HOSTAGES

From late on Friday, September 10, we had the capability to
recapture the prison. The state Commissioner of General Services, Almerin C. "Buzz" O'Hara, formerly commanding general
of the New York Army National Guard, was now on the scene,
along with Chief Inspector John C. Miller of the State Police,
who had come to Attica with me, and we had adequate supplies of
CS gas and National Guard helicopters with gas-drop mechanisms.

But I decided to press my negotiations for a peaceful settlement through the medium of a Citizens Observer Committee. The rebels had nominated several well-known radical leaders, including William M. Kunstler, the attorney who had defended the "Chicago 7," and representatives from the Black Panther party and the Young Lords. I also decided to bring in responsible leaders to whom the rebels might relate—these would include United States Congressman Herman Badillo; Clarence B. Jones, publisher of the *Amsterdam News* in Harlem and a former counsel to Dr. Martin Luther King, Jr.; and Alfredo Mathew, Jr., superintendent of Community School District No. 3 in New York City. Influential state legislators would serve on the committee, including State Senators John Dunne and Thomas F. McGowan, and Assemblymen James L. Emery and Arthur O. Eve. Mr. Eve brought in another key member of the committee, Tom Wicker, a man requested by the prisoners, a columnist of the New York *Times*.

The committee was doomed from the outset. Its mission was confusing to its members: they could reach no consensus whether they were intermediaries attempting to facilitate a settlement, or whether they were the prisoners' advocates, or even an element of the movement at Attica against the state. It is possible to conclude that the committee did more harm than good and stiffened the rebel resistance, especially since its majority later criticized our recapture of the facility once the talks had broken down and the committee failed to achieve a peaceful settlement. In addition, some of the corrections officers were given another opportunity to slur me—now I was said to be turning over the fate of the hostages to the likes of Mr. Kunstler, the Black Panthers, and the Young Lords.

But I took this major decision to negotiate through the committee—as I took other decisions—because I thought it might offer us another way to obtain the release of the hostages, to save lives. In a truly fruitful middle ground, we might be able to negotiate the demands for improved conditions in the prisons while exposing the revolutionary moves for "structural change" in society.

FOURTH DECISION
SATURDAY, SEPTEMBER 11–SUNDAY, SEPTEMBER 12
APPROVE TWENTY-EIGHT POINTS OF PRISON RE-
FORM NEGOTIATED THROUGH CITIZENS OBSERVER
COMMITTEE; TAKE STAND AGAINST THE REBELS'
NON-NEGOTIABLE DEMANDS

Through most of the weekend I worked with the Citizens Observer Committee, with moderates, and with radicals to hammer together a list of "traditional" prison reforms that might be acceptable to the prisoners.

My fourth major decision at Attica was to accept this complete twenty-eight-point proposal and to convey my acceptance to the prisoners, while opposing what I considered to be their non-negotiable demands for complete criminal amnesty, freeing the leaders and trans-shipping them to "non-imperialistic" countries, and the removal of the superintendent.

FIFTH DECISION
SUNDAY, SEPTEMBER 12–MONDAY, SEPTEMBER 13
RECOMMEND THAT GOVERNOR ROCKEFELLER
COME TO ATTICA IN PERSON

On Sunday morning—my negotiations with the rebels having failed, the observers' negotiations having failed, the twenty-eight points having failed, and with nobody wanting to admit defeat—the observers recommended that the governor come to Attica.

This was, admittedly, based on nothing more than a last-ditch hope that something might happen. Except for such radicals as William Kunstler, Arthur Eve and some lesser known, everyone frankly recognized that we could make no further concessions to the prisoners and still preserve the fundamentals of a free society. I did not then, and do not now, believe that the governor could have accomplished anything if he had come to Attica. Nonetheless, I joined in the recommendation of the Citizens Observer Committee because I was concerned about the governor's reputation as a humanitarian. I felt it might be damaging for him in this context if he seemed in the public mind to be standing to one side. I felt I had to put to him my deep concern for his public image, if you like, in the nation and the world.

SIXTH DECISION
MONDAY, SEPTEMBER 13
GIVE THE ORDER TO THE NEW YORK STATE POLICE,
WITH CORRECTIONS OFFICERS IN THE BACKUP
FORCE AND NATIONAL GUARDSMEN IN RESERVE,
TO RECAPTURE THE ATTICA CORRECTIONAL FA-
CILITY.

In the aftermath of these decisions I am aware that not only
the so-called "people's courts," but respected citizens as well have
thought of or accused me of launching more than a minimal-
force rescue mission against rebellious, hostage-holding convicts
—more than leading men in a showdown against murderous an-
archists. I find myself accused, in effect, of firing the first shots in
a new civil conflict between whites and blacks in the United
States. I am told I am guilty of "unmitigated racist oppression,"
of "putting down the brothers," of "contributing to racial polari-
zations in which our country is being broken from within." I am
warned that I have invited the censure of the larger black
community.

But I believe I will dispel in this book these unfair and hurtful
charges. I am aware that suspicions of my racial attitudes lie in
the minds of responsible black citizens and even of my own black
friends. I realize this is perhaps inevitable in view of the loss of
life among blacks at Attica. I ask now for understanding, for an
honest, open-minded appraisal of all the facts.

First, I must say that I have never viewed a black man as any
less nor any more than a white man. I would not have changed
my decisions at Attica by one iota if the rebel inmates had been
predominantly white rather than black. As a matter of fact, the
percentage of blacks in the Attica population, so often stated by
the press as 80 per cent or 85 per cent, was actually 54.9 per cent.
The percentage of blacks among the rebels in D Yard, as far as it
could be determined, was somewhat higher. There were 1,232
blacks out of 2,243 prisoners at Attica at the time of the rebellion.
There were also 154 Puerto Ricans, or 6.9 per cent. There were
845 other whites, or 37.7 per cent, and twelve prisoners of miscellaneous ethnic background, or 0.5 per cent.

Neither is it true that the Attica Correctional Facility at the

time of the rebellion was a "black concentration camp," into
which blacks were herded from everywhere in New York State.
Blacks in the prison population statewide were 55.7 per cent as
compared to Attica's percentage of 54.9 per cent. Attica therefore
was approximately as black as the over-all state system—which
reflects the larger economic, educational, and social challenges
all of us must face.

In no way—to put it even more bluntly—was Attica a white
massacre of blacks. Yet, to read some contemporary literature on
Attica, this is what we are asked to believe.

Although the following might seem a particularly unkind way
to cite statistics, it *is* necessary if we are to develop our sense of
perspective and historical significance.

Among the thirty-two prisoner fatalities at Attica, twenty were
blacks and twelve were white including four Puerto Ricans. The
three prisoners murdered by their fellow inmates were white, one
of them a Puerto Rican. Although, to put it even more callously,
the prisoners did not die in exact proportion to the racial percentage of the population, it is very clear there was no open war
on blacks at Attica, no "black concentration camp," as some have
charged.

In the day-to-day leadership of the rebel prisoners, two black,
one white, and one Puerto Rican organization, along with lesser
groups, formed a loose, uneasy, and remarkably workable coalition
of the left. These were the extremist Black Panthers and the
moderate Black Muslims, the extremist Puerto Rican Young Lords,
and the extremist white Weathermen (a faction of the Students
for a Democratic Society). The over-all title the rebel leaders used
was "Attica Liberation Faction," or ALF. It has often been remarked that there was no "racism" in D Yard and there was not.
They were in it together. Similarly, it was noted how meticulously they were organized. They had been rehearsing together.

Our responsible black citizens everywhere in the country should
accept the fact that this was, indeed, no "Black Power" revolt.
This was an interracial, skilled, revolutionary skirmish against the
society in which most white and black Americans live and work
together—and must constantly strive together to improve.

According to some of the rescued hostages, the black and
white rebel leaders in D Yard really believed they would win because the Establishment would be "too soft" to risk the lives of

our own people. We would give way rather than hurt, or so they believed. They had only to hang on to the hostages, hold out for the demands that would make the structural break in society, and wait. If we reacted, so went the talk in D Yard, then black and white crowds, especially youth, would riot in the cities and tie down the National Guard; the prisons might even be broken into from the outside, as was the Bastille in the days of the French Revolution; and the blacks in the regular United States Army would be tested in their loyalties. In any event, in a limited or larger confrontation, so it was thought, the Establishment would find the game so difficult that we would come to terms.

But none of these things happened and they were not about to happen. The reason is that the overwhelming majority of the black community, as well as of the white community, has set its face to the future. Whatever the difficulties, we shall work out our problems together, because we must.

It is true that black people are convicted of a disproportionate share of crimes and it is equally true that black people comprise a majority of the poor and the ill-educated. Less well understood, and almost more to the point, black people are overwhelmingly the *victims* of the crime wave in the United States. They are robbed and mugged much more often than whites. They suffer far more than whites in neighborhoods where violence is not contained. It is black men and women, rather than whites, who feel the pain of the crime wave most intimately: it is their personal struggle, often prideful, often heartbreaking, to keep their young people on the straight and narrow amid all the appalling disadvantages.

During Attica I must say I did not believe for an instant that the larger black community would spring out into the streets to support the rebel demands. I was sure that the larger black community would follow *no* lead, for *no* purpose, set by that caliber of murderers, manslaughterers, felonious assaulters, robbers, and burglars in prison. After all, these had been the desperate men who, before their incarceration, had made life in the black neighborhoods all the more miserable. If *they* were proposing a revolution, then who needed it?

So when I ordered the police to rescue the hostages at Attica, I felt I was representing all of America—blacks as well as whites. Admittedly, we were under such pressure, and we were so dog-

tired—and the hostages were there with the knives at their throats
—that we were not preoccupied with such statesmanlike concerns.
Nevertheless, it *is* true: I was at Attica in everybody's name. I
spoke black words as well as white when I said, only a few minutes
after the action:

"Armed rebellion of this type we have faced threatens the
destruction of our free society. We cannot permit that destruction
to happen."

Out of the thousands of letters we have received since Attica,
I take the warmest comfort in the endorsement of black citizens.
One of them put it into two sentences:

> Dear Mr. Oswald:
> As a Negro, a resident of Harlem, and one who fights
> crime, I commend you on the action you took at Attica on
> September 13th and on your efforts before and since to se-
> cure prison reform.
> The loudmouths among my people are not the majority.
>
> Respectfully yours.

So what *really* happened at Attica was that they sounded a call
for a revolution—and nobody came.

Will we now sound a call after Attica for a new unity between
whites and blacks, for a new campaign for justice and the rule of
law, for new dignity for all in the spirit of the American Dream?
In the name of those who died at Attica, hostages and inmates
alike, these things must come to pass.

CHAPTER 2

The Rise of the Militants

Richard L. Clark was twenty-five years old when he became "Brother Richard," one of the seven leaders of the Attica revolution and one of the five leaders who survived. According to press reports nationwide during the Attica crisis, his parents abandoned him before he was two years old. He grew up in foster homes in New York City, made the track team in high school, joined the United States Navy after his senior year, put in three years service, and won an honorable discharge.

According to law enforcement officers, he began taking drugs soon after he left the Navy and in March 1969 he was accused along with two other men of holding up a store. He was released on bail. Within four months, he stole three shirts from another store in the Bronx, pleaded guilty to charges of petty larceny, and was sentenced to a maximum of four years imprisonment. He was released from Attica as scheduled on February 8, 1972, after serving slightly more than half of his sentence.

According to neighbors in New York City, Mr. Clark was an amiable man who liked to show off his twin sons. At least one relative could not believe he would have risked becoming a leader of a riot. "Would it have made sense for him to be violent?" the relative asked. But in the New York State Correctional Facility at Auburn, Mr. Clark became a Black Muslim and put his quiet style of leadership to work, advocating the violent overthrow of the institution, according to the authorities there.

Violent or not—and the Black Muslims say they are non-violent —Mr. Clark was one of the leaders of the radicals in a riot which took place at Auburn in November, 1970. Afterwards, he was transferred to Attica. We had to transfer some of the troublemakers in order to return to seminormalcy at Auburn.

In Attica, Mr. Clark became an authentic leader—Brother Richard. Once, he said, eloquently, "Feed the animals, feed the animals. That's what they treat us like here—animals." Throughout the uprising, this was to be the most effective theme of the rebels.

Bald, bespectacled, tall, and athletic, Brother Richard was a tough, resilient, devious adversary. As the principal Black Muslim among the leaders, he was a moderate on the rebel committee. He had leverage because no fewer than 200 Black Muslims were helping keep "security guard" on the helpless hostages. He was also the only leader who seemed free enough to talk substantively with us on his own, and yet he would always take a point back to "the people" for consideration. In my opinion, he was the ablest of the leaders of the rebellion.

Samuel J. Melville, formerly named Grossman, chose his new name after Herman Melville, the author of *Moby Dick*, the story of the hunt for the great white whale. But Sam Melville, an articulate white Marxist-Leninist of the Che Guevara persuasion, was best known in and out of Attica as "the Mad Bomber." He was one of the two rebel leaders who were killed during the police mission to rescue hostages on September 13. He was shot as he ran toward a fifty-gallon tank of gasoline with four Molotov cocktails in his arms, according to the State Police. Several of the inmates claim he was brought down by sniper fire.

Sam Melville, thirty-five years old, was more than six feet tall, broad-chested and muscular, his right eye a clear blue, his left eye brown-green, sightless, and expressionless. A skillful engineering technician, he had graduated from commune living in New York City. He also graduated from demonstrations and mass marches and, at a peace rally in support of Fort Dix GIs in 1969, he took along a hand grenade.

Sam Melville was the man who caused explosions at the United Fruit Company, Marine Midland Bank, Federal Building, and other locations in New York City. He was caught almost in the act and was sentenced in New York State Supreme Court in June 1970 for arson, first degree, six to eighteen years; reckless endangerment, first degree, two years four months to seven years; and assault, second degree, two years four months to seven years. He admitted the bombings and he had the reputation of being one of the most violent revolutionaries in the whole country.

A recent parolee from Attica, William R. Coons, who had served time before the uprising for drug possession (LSD), described in the New York *Times* Magazine how he first saw Mr. Melville:

" 'Who's that,' I said.

" 'The Mad Bomber,' said the . . . curly-haired white kid wearing thick glasses, up on an assault rap, doing a pound [five years] as a result of a motorcycle engagement.

" 'What's his name?'

" 'I don't know. They call him the Mad Bomber, is all.' He gave me a sidelong look, 'See those things on his knuckles?'

" 'Yeah, what are they?'

" 'Karate, I think.'

"The guy with the calloused knuckles turned out to be Sam Melville . . . It was curious that he'd been pointed out to me by my friend, the biker. There's no one more ultraright than the average biker . . . Here he was, pointing out Sam Melville, an ultraleftist, professed Weatherman, dynamite and demolitions expert."

Mr. Melville subsequently impressed Mr. Coons as a "dude," a warm and romantic fellow, and Mr. Coons wrote on:

"Sam was really the exception in the extremity of his doctrine, but his type was being heeded more and more by those who were daily seeing the hopelessness of their own efforts to attract attention to their plight."

As for me, I never met Mr. Melville, even though he once wrote me about the number of times he was being "keep-locked" in his cell for infractions of prison rules. We now know from his posthumous book, *Letters from Attica*, that his fascination with violence per se was matching his revolutionary ardor. He wrote: "More hard reality going down for the left—Mao backs Bandaranaike against the rebels [in Ceylon]; Mao backs West Pakistan in another bloodbath . . . Mao has to send planes and tanks to Yahya Khan. To any impartial observer, the primary contradiction today is not between the workers and the bourgeoisie, it's not between the neocolonialist and the Third World, [it is] between the armed and unarmed."

Sam Melville was the rebel field commander although he was apparently displaced from the top committee after he opposed taking me hostage. He was the man who ordered the forging of hundreds of weapons, the construction of barricades and trenches and the refining of explosives from paint thinner, fertilizer, and fire extinguisher compounds. He was even manufacturing what appeared to be an amateur rocket-launcher for use against low-flying helicopters. The last man from the outside to see him was William Kunstler, who asked on the Sunday afternoon to be taken to him. Sam Melville told the attorney, "Whatever happens, tell everyone that people here are as together as I once hoped they could be on the outside." One of his letters tells his epitaph and measures the commitment of our formidable opponent at Attica:

"The violent and irrespressible winds of change are swirling round us throughout a world that will no longer pay the bill of our government's rapine appetite. And . . . soon the tremors of the last couple of years will be as a sleeping lion lazily swatting a fly with his tail."

Elliott J. Barclay, twenty-one years old, was nicknamed "L.D." He was the coldest, most extreme of the rebel leaders and he convinced many of the hostages that he was the rebel leader who most wanted them dead.

Six feet tall, wearing granny glasses, L.D. was also the leader who had perhaps the sharpest impact on the negotiations. He was the one above all who stressed black nationalism. He was the most persistent advocate of the demand to release and transport the leaders to "non-imperialistic" countries.

L.D. was no major criminal amid the Attica complement of murderers, rapists, robbers, and burglars. He was, in fact, a violator of parole. According to law enforcement officers, his offense had been the forging of a check for $124 in his home town of Rochester, New York. He had also been using drugs and people told us they were fearful of him on the streets. But L.D. was in a maximum security institution because he was adjudged to be an instant militant and troublemaker. In fact, he appeared to be an effective instrument of the movement in its infiltration and indoctrination of a prisoner class.

On September 13, he was last seen by an inmate in the middle of the fight in D Yard, knife in hand. According to subsequent autopsy reports, he was killed by a single .270-caliber bullet from

a range in excess of fifteen to twenty feet. The evidence indicates
he was shot by a sniper as he attempted to stab a hostage.

But L.D. continued to serve the movement in death. No
fewer than 1,000 people attended his funeral in Rochester in a
scene fit for the Marxist-Leninist pantheon. The legend was
added to when two men claimed to have seen L.D. alive after we
had regained control of the prison. The implication was that L.D.
had not been killed in the fight, but had been assassinated later
on by a person or persons unknown. One who made the claim
was Assemblyman Eve of the Citizens Observer Committee—the
man who paid the air fare to Attica for Bobby Seale and the
Young Lords. The other was Frank Lott, a man serving fifty years
to life imprisonment for murder—he had been convicted of killing
a policeman—who had himself been one of the lesser rebel leaders.

To make sure that the L.D. legend did not claim another victim, we have seen to it that the man who saw L.D. in his last fight
has been transferred safely to another prison.

Herbert X. Blyden, thirty-four years old, was the rebel leader
along with Brother Richard whom I met most often face to face.
Brother Herbert was a Black Muslim, broad-shouldered and
gregarious, and he wore large dark glasses in one negotiating
session.

Mr. Blyden was born in the Virgin Islands and he came to New
York City when he was sixteen years old. Four years later he was
convicted of robbing a gas station—the stolen money was said to
have been less than $200—and he spent the next five years in the
Elmira Reformatory. After that Mr. Blyden avoided any brushes
with the law for four years. Then he was convicted of participation in a robbery of a car-rental firm in the Bronx. He was convicted on the word of one witness, who said that Mr. Blyden was
waiting in the getaway car. This time, he was sentenced to fifteen
to twenty years imprisonment. He promptly lodged his appeal. In
October 1970, while he was waiting for an appeal hearing, a prison
riot erupted at the Tombs in New York City. Mr. Blyden was
indicted on seventy-five counts in connection with this uprising.

If Brother Herbert had an inordinately hard early life, it could
not be doubted that he was later an outspoken militant. But after
our third meeting in D Yard at Attica, it was he who took the

lead and got me out alive when many of the rebels were shouting that I should be kept hostage.

"Brother Flip" at Attica was Charles H. Crowley, forty-one years old, a former narcotics addict serving a fifteen-year sentence for robbery. Although paroled once, he had been returned to prison in 1969 for possession of a weapon. Brother Flip was the Attica leader who made the unforgettable phrases. One was "If we have to live like animals, then at least we can die like men." That one impressed the journalists on the scene and it was quoted worldwide. It also won Brother Flip a public embrace by William Kunstler. Another was "Power! Power! Power! If we can't live together, we've got to die together."

Brother Flip was among the survivors. In fact, he got himself let out of D Yard, ostensibly for medical treatment, on the Saturday afternoon—later explaining that he feared the inmates were becoming uncontrollable. Thus he was safely away from the battle scene Monday morning. And one of the still unanswered questions about Attica is why I was not told that this rebel VIP was out. The members of the governor's staff were not told. It appears that corrections officers processed Brother Flip and saw fit not to let us know—which, to put it charitably, was an astonishing oversight.

That sharp observer Mr. Coons etched in Mr. Crowley unforgettably. Brother Flip "had seen New York State prisons most of his adult life . . . He had a grin and a rap and an ability to act that provided the grease for many an otherwise tense situation . . . I didn't always like Flip, personally . . . But he really knew how to sing 'Oh Happy Day' in the choir at Sunday services."

Jerry Rosenberg, thirty-four years old, had been sentenced to death in the electric chair for the murder of two detectives in Brooklyn in 1962. His sentence was commuted to life imprisonment after the passage of a new law on capital punishment, and he began to work on correspondence courses in prison for a law degree.

"Jerry the Jew," as he was called, was a principal "jailhouse lawyer" at Attica, and he frequently advised the rebel committee on legal technicalities. For example, he recommended the rejection of a federal court order that offered no administrative reprisals against the prisoners, because it did not bear the judge's seal. The committee sent the court order back to us and we obtained the judge's seal and sent the document back into D Yard. There and then, Mr. Rosenberg tore up the court order in front of the whole committee. He decided it was meaningless with or without the seal.

Roger Champen, thirty-nine years old, another Black Muslim and nicknamed "Champ," was the one of the seven leaders at Attica about whose role the least was known. He had already served fourteen years of a twenty to thirty year sentence for robbery and he was well known and liked by many of the inmates.

Early in the rebellion, on Thursday evening, Champ met personally with me and with Walter Dunbar in our office in the Administration Building. Champ, incidentally, was the only one of the rebel leaders to enter and leave our territory during the uprising. There had been rumors that some of the 962 prisoners retaken on the first day were being mistreated. We took Champ on a tour to convince him it was not so. We offered him a cup of coffee, which he turned down.

In our office, he talked easily and naturally about his prominent position, and he claimed that most of the men looked up to him. Mr. Dunbar and I commented on this, and I asked whether it was because of his athletic ability. I asked Champ whether he had been an athlete, but he broke off the conversation and went back to D Yard.

In my third visit to D Yard, when I was in real danger, I had expected help from Champ. He was right there—across the table from me. When the shouts went up, "Let's keep Oswald here," Champ stood up to speak. I thought he would be the one to say that I must be returned safely to our territory. But Champ did not: he talked about more grievances while the shouts against me went on. It seemed as though I could have lived or died so far as he was concerned. It was Herbert Blyden, and Brother Richard, as well as Champen who actually got me out.

Among the lesser leaders were: Peter Butler, a white member of the "Peoples Party" serving a life term for first-degree murder; Thomas Hicks, a Black Muslim associate of Brother Richard, killed at the end of the rebellion; Carl Jones-El, a Black Panther serving twelve years for first-degree robbery and assault; and two Young Lords, Juan Soto and Mariano Gonzalez, both of whom survived.

These improbable leaders of the Attica rebellion were featured against the background of a new kind of movement that originated in the California State Prison at San Quentin in the late 1960s and rapidly spread nationwide. The basic thesis of the new movement, as expounded by the late George Jackson, the most famous of the Soledad Brothers, was that nobody had a greater stake in revolution than men in prison, especially men serving long prison terms. What did they have to lose? And second, men in prison had a personal hardness that qualified them for a revolutionary struggle.

Although the thrust of the movement was interracial, the special rage of Black Panthers was useful in the militant leadership in the prisons. Of thirty Panthers who once invaded the California State Legislature, a black *Life* magazine reporter, Gilbert Moore, commented in a book he wrote: "They were not the one nigger in 100 that goes to Princeton . . . These were not slick cocktail niggers shooting down slick white chicks at parties [or] country club niggers with African goatskin rugs and bull-dashikis to hide the ashy skins. These were the cats that hang out at pool halls where mean m—— ——s kick ass just to stay in shape. These were niggers that get their heads slammed up against the wall at three o'clock in the morning by the police looking for niggers to slam up against the wall."

San Quentin was the first, the logical target. Located within fifteen miles of the University of California at Berkeley, San Francisco State College, the Oakland Induction Center, and the Haight-Ashbury district, San Quentin was an archetype, a traditional bastille. Here was an appropriate testing ground for new tactics (1) to generate disturbances against the repressive conditions sure to be found within a prison of this type; (2) to build up public sympathy; and (3) to extend the protest into a broader put-down of the Establishment.

On two occasions in 1968 an informal coalition of prisoners, former prisoners, academic penologists, and New Left organizers succeeded in disrupting operations at San Quentin. First, there was a traditional work stoppage inside the prison. Then there was a more sophisticated affair: many prisoners simply decided to stay in their cells during the weekend so that only their "voluntary activities" were limited. Outside the gates, demonstrators marched and were shown on national and local television, protesting inhumane prison conditions, and hailing "convict unity."

"These two experiments demonstrated, perhaps for the first time in American penal history, that outsiders could conspire with prisoners to cripple the normal operation of a prison," James W. L. Park, associate warden at San Quentin, wrote to me and to several other penologists.

"The age-old dissatisfactions of the convict were translated into a well-planned and sophisticated attack on state laws and policies, the operations of the paroling agency, the limitation on legal rights of parolees, the indeterminate prison sentence and other issues far removed from the usual minor food grievances."

The traditional prison outbreak used to occur, James Cagney style, whenever prisoners could stand no more their grim monotony of confinement, crowding, poor food and sanitation, with no incentive for rehabilitation. But from San Quentin onward, conditions were exploited by the new revolutionaries as a political weapon. They cast the prison in the public mind as the final citadel of the system, as a positive evil in itself. They urged all men to unite against this institution in order to destroy it.

After all, this was what had happened in the French Revolution. The Bastille in Paris was so atrocious that moderates joined the radicals to destroy the prison—and, soon, the whole system of monarchical France. But then the radicals went on to subvert the democratic regime, and they put moderates along with aristocrats to the guillotine.

The new tactics of the prison revolution typified specific planning toward specific objectives. No more the Cagney mutterings —"We gotta go *now*, I tell ya. *Now*." From San Quentin onward, demands had to be carefully prepared and objectives set before the uprising. The riot itself would be a carefully co-ordinated confrontation at a set time—prearranged so that external demonstrations could be synchronized and news media invited to the scene.

The theme of the in-prison disturbance would have to be related to an external issue with which outside groups might identify and support. Racism was a good theme, and steps were taken inside San Quentin in 1968 to make sure that white and black revolutionaries were working together in fact so they could cry "racism" in unison. An earlier riot in San Quentin had bogged down when white and black inmates began fighting one another.

The new techniques were similarly different and interesting. There had to be "people's" leadership of prison uprisings, but the control of the selected committees had to be as total and brutal as anything in Moscow during the October Revolution. There had to be planned assignments: who was to handle food, medical supplies, the procurement of weapons, and so on. There had to be well-managed time schedules so that an atmosphere of order and efficiency would impress outside observers. There ought to be good press relations. At San Quentin, for example, the demonstrators used colored balloons, specifically chosen to make a good color image on TV, and they brought in rock bands to fire up youthful crowds at prison gates.

The use of violence, and of non-violence, was calculated just as coolly. Violence was to be used, suddenly and overwhelmingly, in order to secure the essential, strategic points of the prison. Then non-violence was to become the order of the day, once again to impress gullible outside observers with the essential moderation of the revolution. This latter stress was also useful within movement politics: the assistance of non-violent Black Muslims could be obtained thus, and the Black Muslims were powerful in the San Quentin and other prison communities.

The most ingenious element of the new prison revolution was also totally new. The Establishment, as seen by the revolutionaries, was a web, and ways should be found to weaken the connecting strands. For example, prison authorities are simply not able, constitutionally, to handle demands for changes in parole. Payment for work in prison does not depend on prison authorities but upon the several state legislatures. Even the decisions of a governor are subject, as often as not, to review by the courts. Once the courts are brought into a situation, then the whole issue can be obfuscated, not so much because of the judges' liberality, or conservatism, but simply because the courts are so overworked and pressured it is hard to obtain rulings at all.

The new prison revolutionaries therefore set demands that would have to be passed upon by *several* elements of the Establishment and, democratic politics being what they are, there was sure to be debate and dissension. Thus there would be convict unity—but the Establishment would be fragmented from within.

Finally, the new revolutionaries in the prisons wanted no improvement in living conditions. They wanted—and sought to provoke—the kind of repression that would put the clock back and serve their purposes. For example, inmates would casually abuse corrections officers in order to provoke a reaction, and then they would shout they were being brutalized. This would horrify moderates inside the prison and outside. The last thing the radicals wanted was meaningful prison reform. Instead, they wanted to polarize the people of the United States against—and for—the prisons as the *paramount*, oppressive instruments of the power structure.

There remained the provision of in-prison leadership—and this was to be found in the bubbling brew of old-line roughnecks, with nowhere to go, and trained militants, youthful and street-wise, in prison for minor crimes and for violations of parole.

The rank and file? Nothing could be simpler than to convince convicts, psychologically, that they were not really criminals, but victims of the oppression of society. Tell the men they were political prisoners. Then the leaders had the cannon fodder for the revolution.

Through the late 1960s and early 1970s the traditional convicts and the new revolutionaries interacted. In March 1968 some 700 rebellious prisoners set fires that caused $2 million worth of damage at Oregon State Penitentiary. The following month, 400 prisoners erupted in a riot in Raleigh, North Carolina, and six were killed, seventy-seven injured. In August 1968 some 350 prisoners took nine corrections officers hostage in the Ohio State Penitentiary at Columbus, and National Guardsmen and police had to blast a hole in the prison wall in the counterattack. Five prisoners were shot to death and the hostages were saved.

There was a continuing series of blowups and near blowups at San Quentin. One prisoner was killed and forty-six injured in rioting at the state reformatory at Pendleton, Indiana. Twenty-six prisoners were injured in a situation at the Florida State Prison at Raiford, when fire was opened on a crowd of inmates who refused to work. Needless to say, this incident made headlines everywhere in the country.

"There's a feeling of constant crisis," said Sheriff William Lucas, in charge of the Wayne County jail in Detroit, to Steven V. Roberts of the New York *Times*. "You have to handle it each day as it comes in, and hope you have the right thread of strength going in the right direction."

Gus Harrison, Director of Corrections in Michigan for nineteen years, said, "The prisoners saw the welfare groups organize, the students, then the blacks organize for their rights. Prisons are like a microcosm of society. There's much more awareness that to organize is the way to go."

Said John O. Boone, warden of the Lorton Correctional Complex serving Washington, D.C., with a population 98 per cent black: "They're just like the black kids I saw in Gulfport, Mississippi, and Sandersville, Georgia. They're not going to tolerate the oppression their parents tolerated. They aren't taking it any more in the community—the prison community or the free community."

Mrs. Fay Stender, the founder of the Prison Law Project at Oakland, California, told the New York *Times* reporter that the concept of a convicted class, the role of victim, had considerable psychological appeal to prisoners: "They no longer think of themselves as pathetic, or evil, or sick."

"Our prisoners are consumed with bitterness and resentment, and are ideal recruits for the more sophisticated radicals on the outside who cloak their real intentions with talk of humanitarian reforms," added Warden Walter Craven of Folsom Prison in California.

A Black Panther party member named Wendell Wade, interviewed by *Newsweek* magazine in his cell at Tehachapi, California, said, "The prisons are now filling up with political prisoners—those brothers who were active in opposing the occupation of the black community by the Fascist police force and its domination by the exploitive businessmen and tyrannical politicians."

Meanwhile, however, the surface reaction of the public to the new prison revolution appeared to increase the polarization. "The hard core, the militants have in many ways destroyed much of the gains we have made in the last ten years," according to one veteran prison reformer in the federal system. "They have discredited progressive administrators who, right or wrong, were bringing the system around to new things, and they have given new credibility to the barbarians, the guys who want to chain everybody to the floor."

It was in the old bastille of the state correctional facility at Auburn, New York, built in 1816, that we faced our own first serious test in the new prison revolution. There was a planned uprising on November 4, 1970, in which several corrections officers were brutally beaten. After its conclusion, achieved by negotiations, our officers conducted systematic interviews with many of the inmates involved. From these interviews, we learned the new style:

"There is no place in this system where an officer or inmate is safe. There is no security from the militants. The officer who comes in for eight hours knows it. The inmate who is here for twenty-four hours every day knows it."

"The militants can use any incident to precipitate a disturbance. A bad call in a basketball game can start it."

"Militants march, train, wrestle, kick the wall, kick each other. The guards are afraid to break up the fights."

"Karate and judo practice by inmates is the rule."

"Agitators know how to brainwash the inmates who won't go along. If the leaders say, 'Cut throats,' they'll cut throats."

"Radical magazines such as *Panther E* and *Mohammed Speaks* ought to be banned. They won't let *Mein Kampf* in here."

"Militant literature is smuggled into the institution by visitors and some staff members."

"The school facility, established for inmate education, is being used by the militants to propagandize inmates."

"Militants own some officers and bribe others."

"Several shop foremen will bring in anything for a few bucks. Some guys bring in stuff, trying to be O.K."

"Militants get all their support from the streets, from lawyers and other supporters. They correspond with unauthorized individuals through the new sealed-letter procedure. All the writer does is indicate he is writing to an attorney. The letter is not opened."

"One of the best hiding places for contraband is the prison kitchen."

"One prison paint shop has thousands of gallons of paint."

"Fertilizer compound contains nitrates and mercury."

"The militants don't want prison reform. If you gave them the whole country, it wouldn't satisfy them."

Was it here at Auburn that the crunch in prison reform would finally come? Was the United States prison system to complete the circle?

Auburn Penitentiary was the first place in which our nation experimented with "the congregate system" of corrections. The rows of cells were built tier upon tier, facing on to galleries and corridors. The prisoners were kept locked up in individual cells at night but they were "congregated" at work by day, in cavernous halls, in silence. The men were marched to work and back, each with his hand on the shoulder of the man in front. Their eyes had to be turned in the direction of the guards. The first warden of Auburn was the notorious Captain Elam Lynds, an advocate of repeated flogging of the inmates. He reputedly would have them flogged for speaking in the halls or even for looking up from their work.

Auburn was regarded in those days as a considerable advance upon the Quaker system of solitary confinement and penitence, in which men would be left in their cells to live, to work, and to rot until their sentences expired. Charles Dickens wrote after a later visit to the Cherry Hill Prison near Philadelphia:

"I am persuaded that those who devised this system do not know what it is they are doing, that there is a depth of terrible endurance in it which none but the sufferers can fathom, and which no man has the right to inflict on his fellow-creatures.

"I solemnly declare that with no rewards and honors would I walk a happy man 'neath the open sky or lie me down upon my bed at night with the consciousness that one human creature, for any length of time, lay suffering this unknown punishment in his silent cell and I the cause, or I consenting to it, in the least degree."

The Auburn congregate system was opened to the view of the New York State population, and not merely for deterrent reasons. Thousands were invited to visit, on the payment of small admission fees, and in the year 1830 alone the prison made a profit of $1,500 on the conducted tours. The floggings at least were conducted in private, which showed we had advanced a little from the eighteenth century, but the visitors to Auburn were allowed to gaze down through tiny windows at the men working silently in the great halls.

San Quentin, in particular, was an early American horror. Naked prisoners were tied to ladders and whipped till they lost consciousness. They were stood up and jets of water were sprayed into their faces until blood dripped from their ears. The really intractable men at San Quentin were put into "the tombs," sheet-iron cells or coffins measuring six feet by four feet.

New York State was the scene in the late nineteenth century of our first real prison reforms. Our first prominent reformer was Zebulon Brockway, a practical administrator who had been warden of the House of Corrections in Detroit. There he had demonstrated how prison industries could be made profitable, and he encouraged the men to work and learn skills for their rehabilitation. The New York State Legislature invested what was then the astonishing sum of $1,500,000 for a model reformatory at Elmira with Mr. Brockway as the first warden. Soon he made a real prison revolution by organizing the prisoners there into three classes. New inmates went into the middle class and were promoted or demoted according to their behavior. After six months in the first class, prisoners were considered eligible for parole.

Zebulon Brockway worked wonders with academic and vocational training, a library of several thousand books, the abolition of striped prison clothing, and his "creative recreation" program of athletic fields, gymnasium, and a glee club. After the men learned their skills, they worked in the prison industries so enthusiastically that their products were considered competitive by the nascent trade union movement. He also lobbied so effectively that the state enacted the indeterminate sentence—the setting of a minimum and maximum term of imprisonment—and the men now had an additional incentive to work for their rehabilitation.

At Auburn in 1913 Thomas Mott Osborne, chairman of a New York State Commission for Prison Reform, served a week as a prisoner with the pseudonym of "Tom Brown." He wanted to find out for himself whether the men's grievances were justified. "The big majority in here will be square if you give them the chance," one of the inmates told him.

Afterward, "Tom Brown" came back to Auburn and, at Sunday morning chapel, he identified himself as the prison reform commission chairman. There was a gasp—a roar of approval—and Mr. Osborne steamed full speed ahead on his reforms.

In recent years we have become familiar with the growth of probation and parole and the reduction of prison populations. Brutality within the prisons is now illegal, except in Mississippi and Arkansas, where corporal punishment is still on the statute books. In the early 1930s, when I began my career in Wisconsin, corporal punishment was still permitted in California, Colorado, Delaware, Missouri, Indiana, Kentucky, Tennessee, Texas, and Virginia, in addition to the states of the Deep South.

In the 1950s and 1960s there was a strong surge of prison reform, in which I was privileged to play my part. My experience and my innovations as Commissioner of Corrections in Wisconsin and Massachusetts, and as chairman of the New York State Board of Parole, will be described in Part II. These years offer us many lessons for today and tomorrow.

The decisive change of the postwar years was the development of prisons without bars, the so-called "open institutions." Then came the first, faltering steps toward "work-release," in which selected prisoners were permitted to work in the community and return to the prison at night. This led to "study-release," for the combination of academic work and incarceration, and to "home-furlough," in which selected men could spend weekends at home. This last helped the men maintain their family ties and helped us solve the pervasive problem of sex in prison. Prerelease guidance centers, known as "half-way houses," enabled us to test men on limited ventures into the community before the grant of parole.

The success of these prison reform programs was spectacular, and toward the 1970s we were making such headway we were even cutting into the concept of "the criminal class." Then, as now, I defined my own, personal prison revolution like this:

—We want to provide the best possible opportunity for criminal offenders to take a place in normal society and provide society with the safety and security it desires while this adjustment takes place.

—We will provide a staff better trained to the wants and needs of the individuals, yet firm in the control of those who defy the rules.

—We will provide a total program geared to meet the individual's needs, strengthen him where he is weak, develop his potential and foster responsibility, motivation, and character.

—We will provide a humane approach to treatment, conditions and discipline with the dignity of the individual as a human being the prime consideration.

—We will hope those remanded to our custody and care will exhibit a responsive attitude that will enable us to return a better man to society than the one society sends to us.

On January 1, 1971, when I became Commissioner of Correctional Services for the State of New York, I announced my intention to press at once for the reforms I had long planned. In Governor Rockefeller, we had an unusual combination of a humane and progressive individual and a resourceful, decisive leader. I felt he would be very helpful to us in corrections. In sum, I believed we were going to make a *reality* of prison reform. And I think this is why the new prison revolutionaries moved so rapidly against us, perhaps even ahead of their own schedule.

The practical and psychological contest in the months between the Auburn and the Attica uprisings was tense and dramatic.

We said the best way to rehabilitate was not simply to lock up criminals—but to bring them into the normal life of the community. We also wanted to bring representatives of the community to do volunteer work in the prisons. But the radicals rewrote the message. They wanted to go into the community—but to spread the word about "prison brutality" so they could strike a blow at the system. The radicals also wanted people from the community to visit the prisons—not social workers and civic leaders, but militant attorneys and organizers from the movement.

We said we wanted to retrain criminal offenders in community values, such as good homes, regular work habits, and a creative use of leisure time. The radicals countered that these were precisely the community values they wanted to turn off.

We said we wanted more academic training programs in the prisons—and we were told we should hold more courses on Lenin, Mao, Che Guevara, and Régis Debray.

When we relaxed censorship, we were inundated with incoming publications such as *The Anarchist Cookbook*, which showed people how to make bombs.

We espoused the virtues of a stable Constitution, due process, and legal redress—and we were plagued by movement attorneys showing the inmates how to strangle the system with interminable writs, demands, and appeals.

We argued that robbery, burglary, all kinds of stealing were wrong—but how could we expect to rehabilitate men who were taught by the radicals that stolen money was a form of reparation for slavery, class discrimination, immigrant sweatshops, and other inequities of the past?

Even our athletic training programs ran into radical redefinitions of the wildest kind. Workouts on the athletic fields and in the yard became drill and discipline sessions, along with instruction in karate and judo for use against us.

We also learned in the months between Auburn and Attica that it took time to communicate our ideals, our beliefs in the real merits of the community, our insistence on humane treatment, to the corrections officers closest to the men. Tom Wicker of the Citizens Observer Committee at Attica asked how this was even feasible when most of the "guards" had a low level of general education, with 16 per cent not completing high school and 79 per cent earning less than $9,000 per year. He added a stinging comment: "We get from our guards, that is, just about what we pay for."

A wife of one of the corrections officers who survived Attica said, "I am sick and tired of hearing all about the demands of the inmates. What about the guards? Why don't we read about them? The place is too lax. The commissioner is giving and giving. And the more he gives, the more they want.

"The inmates say they want religious freedom. Well, why did they burn the chapel? They say they want to learn. Well, why did they burn the school and the shops?

"Some people think it's easy. It isn't. The guards have to put up with inadequate conditions. Their hands are tied. Their nerves are shot."

What of the silent majority of the prison population itself in the months between Auburn and Attica? Afterwards, a touching, revealing letter I received from a prisoner told one story of the struggle to win over the middle:

"Fact is, the militants are [organized] by ranks and I was approached to join them.

"Right after the Parole Board meeting is the right time set to enlist people that have been heavily hit and won't take long to be convinced and urged to hate.

"If I wasn't transferred to another prison then, God knows of today (where I'd be now).

"I'm not a member of any militant group, for all I preach is that there is a 'divine Power, God's,' and only He will punish us when the time comes.

"He cried, for September 13th was a rainy day."

During the late summer of 1971 the focus of our anxieties moved from Auburn to Attica. It was from Attica in July that I received a list of twenty-seven demands from the inmates. It was entitled "The Attica Liberation Faction Manifesto of Demands and Anti-Depression Platform." It was signed by five men: Donald Noble, Peter Butler, Frank Lott, Carl Jones-El, and Herbert X. Blyden. Of the leaders of the faction in July, only one, Herbert Blyden, would hold a dominant position in the September outbreak. All these signers of the manifesto survived. (It later turned out that Mr. Butler was in communication with a woman secretary to the attorney William M. Kunstler. She and Mr. Butler later asked for visitation privileges at the prison and for permission to marry.)

The manifesto was a statement of leadership. It said, "The inmates of this prison have vested the power of negotiation regarding the settlement of the stipulated demands within the judgment and control of these men."

The manifesto was actually a rewording of the goals of the leaders of the recent rebellion in the Tombs in New York City, in which Brother Herbert Blyden was alleged to have been involved. In fact, I communicated to Governor Rockefeller about that time my concern that the prison unrest had national implications. I pointed out that the pattern of demands, almost unvarying from coast to coast, even used identical wording in the several manifestoes of complaint.

The Attica July manifesto was a shopping list of demands for prison reform. I could have written a lot of it myself. The men wanted better food, the end of censorship, the right to join labor unions, and more imaginative rehabilitation programs. They also demanded to be paid the New York State minimum wage of $1.85 per hour for work performed in prison industries, but they

did not offer to pay any share of the kind of expenses the free
worker on the outside would have to pay out of his minimum
wage. In any event, the minimum wage grant would have to be
approved by the New York State Legislature, and this was to become one of the twenty-eight points we would offer in return for
the lives of the hostages.

Interestingly, the manifesto commented on the need for religious concessions, and so I knew the Black Muslims were involved.
This was one of the little-known intricacies of prison management
in relation to religious freedom. Muslims may not eat pork products. But ham, frankfurters, bacon, and sausages are staples of any
prison diet. One reason is that live pigs are neither costly nor difficult animals to raise, and they are popular with managers of
prison farms. In the last fiscal year, the farm at Attica produced
1,559 pounds of chicken, for example, and approximately 15,500
pounds of beef. But the farm produced almost 50,000 pounds of
pork.

So there we were. The prison system was so fiscally starved, so
we reasoned, that we had to feed the men some pork products.
Also, the white prisoners liked pork—or maybe they said they did
in order to needle the Muslim blacks. But the Muslims would not
eat pork products for religious reasons.

One day in August, Black Muslims lined up along one side of
D Yard at Attica, and Panthers, Young Lords, and Weathermen
formed on the opposite side. For some time past the more militant
groups had been trying to persuade the Black Muslims to join
them in whatever they had in mind. The Muslims had been reluctant. One of the Black Muslim leaders told the militants in
the yard that they would end up spilling their own blood.

The corrections officer who overheard this remark reported it
to one of his superiors who had surveyed the scene. The superintendent's staff had meanwhile found out, from their own sources,
that there was a "contract" out to have this moderate Black
Muslim leader killed.

Although this man said the next day he did not need protection, it was decided he had to be transferred to another institution
for his own safety. He was so transferred—and he left saying the
Black Muslims were not out to cause trouble. Then a new leader
of the Black Muslims at Attica emerged in the person of Brother
Richard Clark, and the groups formed their uneasy coalition.

We were constantly receiving warnings from almost everywhere in the prison system that serious trouble was at hand. We were told by an inmate at Attica that the riot would occur no sooner than the end of August and would break out sometime in September. We were told by an inmate at another of our institutions that the date was November 2—and he spelled out enough of the details of the plan to be highly convincing. We were told that the whole thing was to be tied in somehow to California, where Angela Davis was then being held on murder charges.

Two of the superintendents of institutions in New York State telephoned me personally in August. They had learned that "outside groups" supporting the revolutionaries would move to "take over" one of our institutions intact, by coming in from the outside, killing the corrections officers in the towers, and bringing in firearms and explosives.

These projected moves, all of them vouched for but none of them pinned down, were keyed to kidnapings of prominent people, who would then be exchanged for prominent militant leaders. These last invariably included Angela Davis. One such plot brought to our attention after its reported failure was an alleged plan to attempt to kidnap Caroline Kennedy, the late President's daughter, at her school in New York City. This was given up because she was "too well guarded."

Another of our sources said that David Rockefeller, chairman of the board of the Chase Manhattan Bank and the governor's youngest brother, was a likely target. We were told that militants had seized upon a recent, critical book about Mr. Rockefeller, entitled *David*, as a basis for focusing animosity against him.

After Attica we learned there was to have been a simultaneous plot to kidnap all nine members of the Adult Authority of California while they were touring the Chino Institute for Men near Pomona, California. They were there to consider the grant of paroles. The kidnap plot envisaged taking the nine men to a boat offshore, there to be held for the exchange of Miss Davis and a Soledad Brother, Ruchell Magee. Nothing happened because security was too tight.

Of course, we planned counteractions with the appropriate law enforcement agencies for every plot we were told about, and, of course, we realized that some of our inmates were making up plots just to relieve the tedium of prison life. One said, "I'll tell you when the next uprising will be if you give me $200." Of course, we did not make any such payment.

The situation went critical in August 1971, in my opinion, after the attempted escape of George Jackson in California, in the course of which he was shot dead. In the affray, three corrections officers and two other inmates lost their lives—a sobering fact generally overlooked in all the radical rhetoric over the "Soledad Brother's martyrdom." The media has etched the name of George Jackson on the minds of most Americans, but who can remember the names of the deceased corrections officers? Who can recall the name of the judge who was killed in the shoot-out in Marin County?

Late in August there was a kind of memorial demonstration at Attica on behalf of the late Mr. Jackson. At breakfast one morning the men formed up as usual, and they walked through the serving area, but nobody picked up any eating utensils and trays and nobody touched any food. They sat down and stared straight ahead. They were all wearing something black—an armband, or a shoelace, or scraps of black paper, or cloth pinned on their shirts.

A week or so later three times more than the anticipated number of men arrived on sick call at A Block—300 instead of the usual 80 to 100. The men asked only for aspirin or a laxative, and then they went on to their usual routine.

Confronted with this impressive evidence of "convict unity," not to mention effective planning, I told the governor in my monthly report for August that the situation was very dangerous. I wrote that:

"While it is not characteristic of me to 'cry wolf,' the recent tragedy at San Quentin has made it all too apparent that anything can happen in dealing with the kind of idealists and fanatics housed in our facilities . . .

"These ingredients of apprehension, militancy, revolutionary idealism, and race reaction are, individually, matters of serious concern. The combination of all these ingredients is dangerously explosive."

Early in September, just before the uprising, I spent two days at Attica reviewing the situation with Superintendent Mancusi and the corrections officers. I also saw Frank Lott, one of the signers of the original manifesto of the previous July, the one serving fifty years to life imprisonment on murder charges. At Attica I reviewed security plans, including projected liaison with the State Police. I came away convinced that there were many troublesome prisoners there and that changes in operations were indicated. But that was also true about several of our other institutions. We needed time.

I planned to circulate in the prison at Attica and to talk with groups of inmates. Unfortunately, I ran out of time to carry out this plan because my wife was in the hospital and I learned that she was suffering increased pain. I then tape-recorded a message which was played for the prisoners the next day, in which I discussed some of the changes I had made and others I intended to make. It was played for the inmates three times. I said I hoped we all could work on these reforms together.

After the events of the next two weeks, I would receive a personal letter from a prisoner at Attica that showed I had wasted that trip. It read, in part:

> Knowing many of the leaders of this riot, and knowing that at the most only 10 per cent of the population was actually for the riot, I can honestly state this riot was not really against prison conditions.
>
> Prison conditions were the excuse.
>
> The riot was 100 per cent politically motivated. The leaders and their followers were mostly Black Panthers, Young Lords, and Sam Melville's group of white activists . . . I did know L. D. Barclay, Flip Crowley and Champ personally and I can honestly state that they were avid, militant revolutionaries who would not have given up without killing the hostages.
>
> These people never talked about prison conditions.
>
> They constantly talked about the violent overthrow of the oppressive, capitalistic, imperialistic establishment, and, brother, that is a fact.
>
> You cannot rehabilitate that type of person. They are convinced they have done only what the system has forced them to do. They brainwash each other.
>
> Rehabilitation is when a man decides he has been a damned fool to lead the life he has led and sincerely makes

up his mind to do better. It must come from within the person, and his will.

All the education, all the vocational training, all the removal of walls will do no good unless you can motivate a man to want to change for the better."

CHAPTER 3

How to Take a Maximum-Security Prison
in Thirty Minutes

It was 6:00 A.M. on Wednesday, September 8, 1971. The shattering jangle of three bells rang down the corridors and galleries of the Attica Correctional Facility. This was not to be a day of rebellion, and most of the men lay awake on their cots for a while longer, staring, perhaps, at the fifteen bars on the cell doors, the locks, the rivets, the gray-green steel, the open-topped toilets in the corners. In Attica, as in every prison, everywhere in the world, sleep was the merciful refuge, the ironic equalizer between the controllers and the controlled. The moments of awakening to reality and monotony were not to be rushed, not at all.

The next two bells, at 6:30 A.M., were the savage sounds, because this was time to get up. Most of the men in the cells, forty-two individuals to each of the galleries, began to shuffle about the living space in which they spent thirteen hours and forty minutes locked up every day. They made their beds, washed up, and pulled themselves together, swept the cells, fixed themselves instant coffee from semicold water left over in the thermos, or smoked a "tailor-made," or a self-rolled cigarette made from a monthly ration of tobacco.

The next bell dinned and echoed and was followed by the metal clank of the cell doors opening for the new day. It was now 7:00 A.M. on Wednesday, September 8, and the laggards who had slept until the last minute stumbled and lurched out into the galleries along with the rest. There—through the arched windows of the galleries of the main cell blocks, through another set of bars—was the view that would soon become famous throughout the world: the low, flat skyline of the other blocks across the quadrangle, the tall chimney of the powerhouse, the hulks of the industrial building and the main mess hall, the four yards, the four tunnel-corridors, and the intersection known as Times Square. Out of sight of most of the men was the high perimeter wall, set back, thirty inches thick, its towers manned by armed corrections officers.

Yet not even the Attica Correctional Facility was impregnable. The first escape in the prison's history had occurred the previous spring, on Good Friday. It could have happened in one of two ways. Theory No. 1: While some inmates attracted the attention of a supply-truck driver with an impromptu guitar concert, some other inmates loaded a flour sack on the truck. Inside the sack was Joseph Sullivan, thirty-three years old, who had been serving a long sentence for a robbery in which a man had been killed. When the concert was over, the driver got into the seat, and drove off. Theory No. 2: Joe Sullivan simply smuggled himself out in a laundry truck.

Not until four weeks later was Mr. Sullivan found. He was arrested as he walked down East Eleventh Street toward University Place in Manhattan, wearing a sports jacket and carrying an unloaded sawed-off .22-caliber rifle. Our Bureau of Special Services, headed by John J. McCarthy, made the arrest. Joe Sullivan was sentenced to seven years for the escape—and he still has not said how he got out.

In August 1971 two prisoners on work detail outside Attica walked off their jobs and disappeared. This was always a risk to be run in selecting honor prisoners, and they scarcely ever betrayed our trust. The two men were arrested the next day in faraway Arkansas, but the situation became really embarrassing when it turned out they had been driven down there by the chauffeur of Superintendent Mancusi. This man, needless to say, was subsequently prosecuted—and he was convicted of aiding an escape.

The 2,243 prisoners in Attica on Wednesday, September 8, went to breakfast in the main mess hall in two shifts, according to routine. There were 1,536 men in two groups of 768 in the first shift, sitting down at 7:10 A.M. The rest ate later, some time between 7:40 and 8:20 A.M., whenever the place was cleared and ready for them. The meal was prescribed: a packet of dry cereal, eight ounces of milk, a cup of coffee with the milk premixed, a teaspoon of sugar, bread, and water. Three times a week, some prepared dry fruit would be added to the rest of the meal.

The head counts taken, the mess hall cleared, the first brief exercise in the yards completed, the men moved out for their work assignments of the day. The prisoners allotted to the garage were first on the job, beginning at 7:45 A.M. At 8:00 A.M., the work details reported to the barber shop, the carpenter shop, the commissary, the tailor shop, the powerhouse, the paint shop, the laundry, the hospital, the bathhouse. This last was where the men were able to take their ration of at least one shower every week.

At 8:00 A.M. the staff of the prison school reported for duty, followed, fifty minutes later, by the students on the academic training program at Attica. There was also a "D.V.R. project," a vocational rehabilitation training program financed by the federal and state governments. And there was "cell study," another program in which the prisoners were sent lessons to be read and papers to be completed in their cells. The observer of the future rebel leaders at Attica, William R. Coons, had been a cell-study inmate instructor before he was released on parole. He said, "Occasionally, you saw one of your students pass a Regents' [examination]. A good feeling. It meant you had helped somehow . . . you were still competent."

The last men on the job, at 9:30 A.M., were the workers in the shoeshop and the gangs assigned to the chapel and the coal yard.

Meanwhile, the honor gangs at work beyond the walls had reported to the prison farm, to five utility maintenance projects, to sanitation and tree-cutting details, and to special assignments for Superintendent Mancusi.

By 11:30 A.M. on Wednesday, September 8, all the men were back from their gang details, shopwork, and training programs, and a soup and sandwich luncheon was served. Between 12:25 P.M. and 3:30 P.M. they labored on for the afternoon shift, as they had the day before, and the day before that, and every day of the week before that. Then back to the yards for rest and recreation, supervised by corrections officers armed with nothing more than batons. Mr. Coons described a typical scene:

"As far as militant groups go, their activities were as obvious as the color of a hack's nose after a rough trip at the Legion Hall downtown. You could find three or four such groups in every yard. They were into rigorous discipline, physical exercises, speechmaking and all the rest; they made no pretense about it and eyed with something like equanimity the hacks half dozing in their high chairs."

Mr. Coons continued:

"It was [Brother] Flip who toe-to-toed me one day in cell study, saying 'Where will you be when the crunch comes?' All I could do was stare back at him. I honestly didn't know. I was there to do my job, which was teaching English, and I was doing it, and he knew it, and he was willing to let it go at that.

"As luck would have it, I was three months out [on parole] when the crunch came."

It came at approximately 3:45 P.M., Wednesday, September 8, in one of those unforeseeable and unplanned incidents that can throw even the choicest revolutionary schedule out of kilter. It happened in A Yard, the section of the quadrangle in the corner formed by D Block and A Block (*see chart of prison layout on p. 8*). A Block is close to the Administration Building, where Superintendent Mancusi was at that moment presiding over a labor-management meeting. The superintendent hoped to get away for a trip for a few days beginning September 10, and he was busy clearing his desk.

The details of exactly what happened are still being debated, but my own appraisal of staff and inmate testimony as to the events which occurred before my arrival at Attica are as follows:

A sparring match, then a punch-up began in A Yard. Involved initially were two black inmates, Leroy Dewer and another man still not identified for certain who slipped away in the crowd. It was a friendly affair in the beginning, but many who saw the fight thought it was rough enough to be stopped. Sparring in the yard was a violation of the rules, and the two men were no longer sparring but fighting, in the opinion of corrections officers on the scene.

Lieutenant Richard Maroney, an experienced corrections officer, attempted to put a stop to the disturbance. He put his hand on Leroy Dewer's arm, told him to break it up and to return to his cell to be "keep-locked." This was a mild disciplinary measure in which prisoners were taken out of the population and put back in their cells to keep them in line.

But Leroy Dewer refused to obey the order. Instead, he pushed Lieutenant Maroney away from him, squared off in a fighting

stance, and said, "Come on, old man, you're going to get it."
When Lieutenant Maroney made no move, Mr. Dewer struck him
a light blow on the chest—an unheard-of thing for an inmate to
do to a corrections officer. And when Lieutenant Maroney repeated
his order, Leroy Dewer struck him again on the chest. Inmates
crowded around the two men, shouting encouragement to Dewer
to stand fast.

An officer in an observation tower witnessed the incident and
reported to the guard captain. A group of civilian employees of
the prison watched from the tunnel near Times Square.

Lieutenant Robert T. Curtiss, another seasoned and highly regarded corrections officer, was walking along this tunnel when he
looked out on to A Yard and decided that Lieutenant Maroney
needed assistance. A circle of inmates, mostly blacks, was preventing the officer from going after Leroy Dewer, and a crowd of more
than 200 men was moving over to the scene. A white inmate
named Raymond LaMorie was among those angrily shouting that
Mr. Dewer had done nothing wrong. When another corrections
officer asked him to lower his voice, Mr. LaMorie shouted, "Get
your hands off me."

Lieutenant Curtiss now walked into the middle of the crowd
and joined Lieutenant Maroney. The prisoners began to
harangue them. One of the militants among the prisoners then
turned the mood of the inmates much more hostile. The man
pointed to Lieutenant Curtiss and shouted, "This lieutenant
hates all blacks."

Lieutenant Curtiss turned to Lieutenant Maroney and said,
"Let up. Let it lay. We're not getting anywhere out here. Let's
take care of it later." He motioned to several other corrections officers coming to the yard to return to their posts. As the two lieutenants left A Yard, one of the militants shouted after them, "If
you take those guys out tonight, we'll take this prison off you."

Almost at once a group of prisoners who seemed more reasonable came to the edge of the yard and asked for a word with Lieutenant Curtiss. The crowd behind them was breaking into smaller
units, and the tension was lessening a little. This new group was
composed wholly of black inmates and they said that Mr. Dewer
was afraid to come in from the yard for fear he would be beaten.

The corrections officer replied he had worked at Attica for more
than twenty years and had never seen a prisoner beaten. But

Leroy Dewer would have to go before the prison adjustment committee. This was a "prison court" made up of two officers—one of lieutenant grade or higher—and a civilian guidance supervisor, which presided over more serious lapses of discipline at Attica. Long since gone were the days when the old wardens were judges and juries who ordered men "to the hole."

Late in the afternoon Lieutenant Maroney delivered his report on the incident to Deputy Superintendent Leon Vincent, who was attending the superintendent's labor-management meeting. A little later, Lieutenant Curtiss delivered a verbal report with the comment that, in his judgment, the unrest among the inmates at Attica had now deteriorated to the point of crisis.

At 6:00 P.M. Superintendent Mancusi declared there was an acute emergency that required the attention of the whole staff. After all, an inmate had disobeyed and struck a corrections lieutenant twice, and the prison officers present had retreated when inmates turned a small argument into a major incident. All of this was unprecedented—and virtually incredible—to the professionals on the scene. But nothing more happened during the evening meal in the mess hall and there were hopes the whole thing might tide over, that the breach of discipline could be handled through normal channels.

Accordingly, Deputy Superintendent Vincent ordered that the inmates involved in the incident be removed from their cells after lockup and be quartered in Housing Block Z—the segregation unit—pending hearings the next day. Lieutenant Maroney and three other officers moved Mr. Dewer after an altercation in his cell and a struggling passage down the corridor amid derisive shouts and a hail of debris hurled from cells as they passed. And when three corrections officers began to move Raymond LaMorie from his cell in A Block to HBZ, again there were hostile shouts along the gallery. Many of the inmates began to hurl bits of furniture and personal effects through the bars at the corrections officers. After the man was moved, the uproar continued, and several more corrections officers poured into the gallery. One of them, Tom Boyle, was hit by an unopened can of soup. He suffered a contusion of his nose, a laceration on the temple, and his face was streaming with blood.

The corrections officers quickly identified the prisoner who had thrown the heavy soup can missile, William Ortiz, and he was ordered to be keep-locked in Cell No. 17 in the morning pending disciplinary action. The prisoners kept on yelling obscenities from their cells. One said to a corrections officer, "We'll get you in the morning, m—— ——."

Meanwhile, Mr. Boyle was helped to the prison hospital, where emergency first aid was administered. Later he was taken to the office in Attica village of one of the prison physicians, Dr. Selden Williams, where his cut was sutured. Tom Boyle was the first casualty of the rebellion that would see forty-three men killed and 130 men injured before it was all over.

Superintendent Mancusi held a meeting of all the supervisors and checked readiness for the next morning. Deputy Superintendent Vincent and Assistant Deputy Superintendent Karl Pfeil said they would be on duty by 7:00 A.M., and so did Captain Franklin "Pappy" Wald, a white-haired man in his sixties who was to become the most senior of the hostages, and one of the bravest.

Lieutenant Curtiss requested that two of the most troublesome of the companies of prisoners on A Block be kept in their cells during breakfast on the following morning. Mr. Mancusi and Mr. Vincent decided, instead, to monitor the first session of breakfast; if things were quiet, Company 5 would be permitted to go to the mess hall for the second session. If things were unstable, then the men of Company 5 would be kept in their cells.

Later that evening the prisoners in A Block shouted that Leroy Dewer and Raymond LaMorie were being beaten in HBZ. Even if true, there was no way the prisoners could have obtained such instant knowledge. And it was not true. There was always a supposition among inmates that corrections officers beat prisoners on their way to HBZ, in an elevator where there were no witnesses, but the supposition had yet to be proven. In this instance, the corrections officers on night duty even took a couple of the protesting inmates over to HBZ and showed them Mr. Dewer and Mr. LaMorie, unbeaten. But the mood in A Block was menacing. There remained a general opinion in Company 5 that LaMorie was being punished unfairly. After lights-out, a single voice taunted down the gallery:

"Get a good night's sleep, Whitey. Sleep tight—tomorrow's the day."

It was 6:00 A.M. on Thursday, September 9, 1971. Once again, as on every day through endless years, three bells jangled down the corridors of the Attica Correctional Facility. Another two bells were rung at 6:30 A.M., and the final bell at 7:00 A.M. But this day was to be different. The several hundred militants of the Black Panthers, the Black Muslims, the Young Lords, and the Weathermen—to judge from what was to happen—had prepared their weapons and they knew where they were going to go. How to take the strategic points of the prison as rapidly as possible—and how to take as many hostages as possible—and how to translate this into a larger revolutionary theme?

Well before 7:00 A.M., Assistant Deputy Superintendent Pfeil, Lieutenant Curtiss, Sergeant Jack English, and Sergeant Gerald Reger were on duty in the Administration Building. Sergeant English, the population count, or chart, officer of the day, went out to take 7:00 A.M. roll call. Lieutenant Curtiss warned the corrections officers going on duty to avoid confrontations and be ready to "button up", or lock the gates to the cell blocks, at the first sign of trouble.

Beginning at 7:10 A.M., right on schedule, first breakfast was served to the 1,536 first-shift inmates. Mr. Pfeil attended the breakfast in person to assess inmate attitudes. Lieutenant Curtiss and Sergeant Reger were also on hand for the tense meal. But there were no problems on the first shift, and the mess hall was cleaned up for the second shift. Lieutenant Curtiss returned to the Administration Building to begin to write his report on the previous day's disturbances.

Superintendent Mancusi arrived at this point, and he asked the lieutenant, "How does it look? How did breakfast go?" At that moment, Sergeant English brought word of new trouble. He had just received a report from Corrections Officer Elmer Huehn, the hall captain on A Block, that the prisoner William Ortiz was no longer keep-locked in Cell No. 17. Superintendent Mancusi instructed Lieutenant Curtiss to proceed at once to Cell No. 17 and find out what had happened. The superintendent was told that William Ortiz had been released by another prisoner. This man had tripped a lever in the lock box which a corrections officer had inadvertently left open, and the door of Cell No. 17 sprang open. This, too, had never happened before at Attica.

Superintendent Mancusi, although perturbed by this sign of

lax security, tried to keep cool and head off further incident. He directed that the troublesome companies of A Block be taken to breakfast in the mess hall on schedule in the second shift. But after breakfast they were not to be allowed to relax in the yard for a while, as was usual; instead, they were to be taken right back to their cells. Later, they would be released, except for Mr. Ortiz. Assistant Deputy Superintendent Pfeil said, "Look, we can't let the company into the yard with that Ortiz. We can't have another situation there like we did yesterday."

Afterward, one of the prisoners recalled, "We were supposed to start as soon as we were out of the cells, but the guys decided we should go to the mess hall . . . Some of us had sledge hammers and hatchets, besides the blades."

It was 8:50 A.M., September 9, 1971. On duty were 116 corrections officers, 78 male and 23 female civilian employees. There were 2,243 inmates.

The rebellion now began. It unfolded in violent, shocking paroxysms, not altogether according to plan. These were the principal phases of the fighting:

THE STORMING OF A BLOCK

At 8:40 A.M. Company 5 of the A Block prisoners trooped out of the mess hall after second-shift breakfast. This was one of two "grading" companies comprising "problem" inmates. Its membership included Brother Richard Clark, L. D. Barclay, Thomas Hicks, and Sam Melville, the Mad Bomber. Under the escort of a single corrections officer, Gordon Kelsey, the men of Company 5 marched back along the corridor-tunnels for their expected rest and relaxation period in A Yard.

Urgently, Lieutenant Curtiss grabbed Assistant Deputy Superintendent Pfeil's telephone. He called Corrections Officer Huehn in A Block and passed on Superintendent Mancusi's orders: The men were not to go to the yard but must be brought back to their cells. He told Elmer Huehn to have the door leading into A Yard securely locked and fastened.

Company 5 turned the corner in the corridor-tunnel around Times Square. Usually, the gates at Times Square were locked, but they were opened to let the men pass along from their cell blocks to and from the mess hall.

Lieutenant Curtiss next telephoned Corrections Officer William Quinn, on duty at Times Square, to close the gates the moment Company 5 had passed by. Then he went down to take over Company 5 from Corrections Officer Kelsey. He wanted to escort the company back to the A Block cells in person and "hash over the problems."

With considerable courage, Lieutenant Curtiss walked to his right along the company as the men faced him, heading for a point one third of the way along the ranks. There he intended to stop and make a few introductory statements before proceeding with them back to the cells. But he did not get past even the first four men.

"You're a no good m—— ——," somebody said. The Lieutenant was hit hard on his left temple and thrown off balance.

Then the whole crowd of Company 5 inmates was on to Lieutenant Curtiss, clubbing, pounding, and kicking. He was knocked to his knees. The men were so enraged they were even hitting one another. This was elemental violence and, as he covered his head and his face, he suffered a rain of kicks on his spine.

"Cut that out—leave that man alone," Corrections Officer Huehn shouted. Although he could have saved himself by retreating behind locked doors, Elmer Huehn, a veteran of fourteen years' service, plunged into the melee to rescue the stricken lieutenant. Another corrections officer, Raymond Bogard, charged in alongside.

This gallant rush—two men against forty or more—was so unexpected it threw the inmates into some disorder. Officers Huehn and Bogard reached Lieutenant Curtiss and unquestionably saved his life. They grabbed him by his armpits and fought their way out of the crush. Mr. Bogard was badly clubbed on the skull and Mr. Huehn was cut and hit repeatedly on the face and shoulders.

The three corrections officers staggered into A Block. The inmates did not follow them. Elmer Huehn later reported: "We backed away from about fifty of them, all of us bleeding. It was just a miracle that we looked so bloody, so horrid to them, with our eyes bulging out of our heads, that they feared us, they stayed off us."

But the rebels soon came storming into the cell block, brandishing clubs and four-foot staves. The officers made it from the hall to one of the north-end galleries. Inmates were shouting military-style orders—"Squads to your areas . . . Squad One go here—Squad Two go there . . ." Mr. Huehn desperately struggled to close the gallery door against the press of shouting prisoners. Officer Bogard and Lieutenant Curtiss rallied and added just enough strength to heave the door to and lock it.

Now Company 5 was joined by scores of inmates from all over this section of the correctional facility. Leaving the three officers locked in the gallery for a while, they swept through the rest of the cell block. They were shouting wild war cries and smashing up furniture but they were very much under control. When they broke windows, as we now know, they were giving the prearranged signal for the rebellion to get under way in other strategic sections of the prison.

The three corrections officers in the sealed-off gallery retreated to a single cell, closed the gate and began to throw up a barricade. Lieutenant Curtiss was bleeding from face wounds. Officer Huehn had face wounds, a torn mouth, and other lacerations. Officer Bogard had lost a lot of blood and was in a bad way with his head injury.

Next, the three officers heard a chunking and thumping as the rebels began to hammer at the cell block lock box with sledges and lengths of pipe. Then they heard what must have been a hundred or more inmates scurrying along the other galleries and along the utility corridors behind the cells. The rebels had obtained the keys and the whole of A Block had fallen.

It was only 8:55 A.M.—five minutes after Company 5 left the mess hall and the action started.

The rebel offensive now shifted its emphasis elsewhere. Such was the control exercised by the rebel leaders that they wasted no time at all on the three sealed-up corrections officers. A Block was quiet for a moment, and the three officers were astonished when an inmate popped his head into their cell, looked over the barricade, and said he had hidden in his own cell to wait out the riot. Then the man took up a mop and began to clean up the blood on the floor.

During the next half hour or so, and it might have been longer, the three corrections officers listened to the screaming of alarms and police whistles and heard somebody's voice, probably the superintendent's, booming through a bullhorn, "Who's in charge in there? I want to talk to him." The helpful prisoner, mopping up the blood, kept them informed on the new rebel successes: "They're in the shops. They've got B Block. They've burned the chapel, the school building." Then the inmate warned the officers, "They're heading back this way." Lieutenant Curtiss gave his wallet to the man, who said, "Don't worry about it. It will be safe with me." The man later gave the wallet to a prison chaplain, who in turn gave it to Lieutenant Curtiss' wife.

The prisoner was Barry Schwartz, a man serving time in Attica for manslaughter and one of the hidden heroes of our side. He was later to be one of the three inmates the rebels cut to pieces.

Now the rebels were thundering at the gallery door and it could only be a matter of time. Lieutenant Curtiss filled four or five trash buckets full of water so they could extinguish a fire, but it was hopeless. The inmates broke into the gallery, looked into the cell and one said, "Well, lookie here. Look who we got here."

One of the inmates said, "Come on out." Lieutenant Curtiss said, "I like it in here." But one of the inmates was carrying a gas gun and two were carrying gallon jugs of gasoline, so the three officers surrendered. One of these inmates said to Officer Huehn, "Come out. You've been a good hall captain. I will guarantee no one will hurt you." Another man said to Elmer Huehn, "You're a hostage. We don't want to hurt you."

They were out of the fight. Raymond Bogard had to be carried out; he was so far gone that the inmates let him go the same day.

THE OVERRUNNING OF TIMES SQUARE

Corrections Officer William Quinn was the man in charge of the intersection at Times Square as the rebel onslaught headed down the corridor-tunnel from A Block in his direction. He was twenty-eight years old, a graduate of Attica Central School, class of '61. He had first worked at the J. N. Adam School at Perrysburg, New York and later had helped open the West Seneca School for the Mentally Retarded. After a few years with the Iroquois Gas Corporation, Mr. Quinn joined the New York State Department of Corrections in March 1970, at the Green Haven State Prison. After attending Officers School at Beacon, New York, he joined the staff at Attica in May 1970.

William Quinn was a member of St. Vincent de Paul Church and of the Attica Fire Department, a supporter of Cub Scout

Pack 60 of Attica, and a one-time Eagle Scout himself. He was married to the former Nancy Ann Willard, and they had two children, Deanne Margaret, aged five, and Christine Renee, aged four.

Corrections Officer Quinn's father, Albert F. Quinn, was also on the staff at the Attica Correctional Facility, as a meatcutter. His mother was the Attica correspondent of the Batavia *Daily News*. When the rebellion began at Attica, Mr. Quinn, Senior, and two other employees barricaded themselves in a storeroom and were finally rescued by New York State Police.

But William Quinn was a man alone against hundreds at Times Square. He never had a chance. A Block gate at Times Square, with a hidden structural defect, broke open at the impact of the charging mob.

Some of the inmates have since said Mr. Quinn ran up a steep stairway to a trap door leading to the roof of Times Square, where he was caught, clubbed, and hurled down to the floor. Others say he was overwhelmed where he stood. He was the first corrections officer to be fatally injured in the rebellion.

Corrections Officer Donald Melvin was in the corridor leading from C Block to Times Square when he saw Mr. Quinn attacked by the rebels, one of whom slugged Officer Quinn with a board or a club. Then Officer Melvin was himself overrun, and was knocked unconscious with a blow to the head.

Corrections Officer Gordon Kelsey, the man who had escorted Company 5 back from the fateful breakfast less than ten minutes before, was still in the vicinity of Times Square. He was smashed on the head and struck on the nose with a sharp object. He heard the gates of Times Square crashed in before he was attacked again, knocked unconscious, and put out of the fight.

Corrections Officer Paul Rosecrans, a portly man, was captured in the vicinity, ordered to strip, and then hit over the head with an oak desk leg as he was undressing. One of the prisoners told him, "We're going to kill us some pigs." He thought to himself he would be a fat pig for them. He saw William Quinn lying inert in a pool of blood.

Once again the rebels had overrun a key point of the prison in the staggeringly brief period of two or three minutes. They now controlled the intersection between the four main cell blocks, a point from which they could command all four of the sections of the quadrangle. They had captured at Times Square a couple of tear gas guns and many tear gas projectiles, their heaviest armament to date. Their blows were so sudden that there could scarcely be a defense. They had also fractured Mr. Quinn's skull in two places and at 4:30 P.M. on the following Saturday he would die of his wounds.

After ninety minutes or so, Corrections Officers Melvin, Kelsey, and Rosecrans, along with a fourth man, were taken to rebel-held A Block and were locked up in cells there. But a Black Muslim inmate appeared and said, "I'm going to try and get you out." The prisoner left, but he returned—and he escorted the corrections officers out through the front of A Block to freedom.

THE CAPTURE OF THE QUADRANGLE

It was still not yet 9:00 A.M. and the rebellion was not ten minutes old. The rebel forces from A Block and from Times Square now swarmed out across the whole quadrangle and climbed on the roofs of the corridor-tunnels. They were armed with knives, hatchets, hammers, lead and steel pipes, clubs, boards, and hunks of iron and porcelain.

Corrections Officer Philip Watkins was savagely attacked front and rear. A black, bald-headed man came at him from the front with a broomstick, just as he was hit by a shovel across the back. He threw his right arm behind him to stave off the second blow, and the shovel broke his arm. He was helpless. But a third prisoner warned the other two, "That's enough," and possibly saved Mr. Watkins' life.

Corrections Officer John Stockholm was slugged on the back of the head and knocked unconscious in D tunnel as inmates from A Block ran into D Block.

In this group was L. D. Barclay—and he quickly established the nature of his leadership in the rebellion. He savagely attacked Corrections Officer "Red" Whalen with a broomstick, beating his head bloody and knocking him to the floor. Several friendly inmates rescued Mr. Whalen from L.D., sheltering him in a nearby washroom. Not long afterward, L.D. tried to break down the locked door of the washroom in order to resume the attack on Mr. Whalen—but other inmates led the badly injured officer away to D Yard.

Corrections Officer Dean Wright had just returned from sick-call duty to custodial work in B Yard. This yard was obviously not a planned target, as there was only one man there instead of the usual hundred or more. But the rebels broke the door into B Yard, and Mr. Wright, along with Corrections Officers John d'Arcangelo and Walter Zymowski, retreated to the roof of one of the corridor-tunnels. There the rebels let them be. But for one of them, it was a temporary reprieve. John d'Arcangelo, only twenty-three years old, a graduate of Liverpool Senior High School in Liverpool, New York, a graduate of Auburn Community College, Auburn, New York, a corrections officer at Attica only since June 24, would be killed on September 13.

The corrections officers in the quadrangle battle had improbable experiences afterwards, as the rebels moved on rapidly to the next objectives. Corrections Officers Wright, Zymowski, and D'Arcangelo locked themselves in an inmate toilet and were not discovered until the afternoon. They only gave themselves up when the rebels threatened to fire-bomb the toilet and burn them alive.

Corrections Officer Watkins, in severe pain from his broken arm, wandered into D Yard later in the morning, just at the time the rebels were organizing their command center there. He sat down on a bench near another corrections officer, Arthur Smith, who was lying on a sidewalk. Then two friendly black inmates came up and said they wanted to smuggle Mr. Watkins out of D Yard. He took off his shirt, put on an inmate shirt, and was ready to attempt the escape. But then the other hostages were brought into the yard and he was forced to join them.

Corrections Officer Stockholm, who had been knocked unconscious, was not made hostage until the morning of the following day. He hid out so successfully that he threw off the rebel and our own head count of hostages; each side suspected the other of keeping Mr. Stockholm concealed.

What happened was that two black prisoners carried Mr. Stockholm while he was still unconscious to a cell in D Block. He was placed on the bunk until he regained consciousness. Then he was given a cold compress for his head by friendly inmates. He was told to climb under the bed and the prisoners hung towels down the sides of the bed to hide him from view. He stayed there the whole night.

On Friday morning two of the prisoners told John Stockholm they would now try to get him out of the area. But at that time, some other inmates said that the hysteria of Thursday had now died down, and they did not believe he would be harmed. After a discussion, it was decided by all of these prisoners that it would be best for him simply to join the hostages in D Yard. With Mr. Stockholm's friendly consent, they blindfolded him and said they had just captured him so the rebel leaders would not believe they had concealed him overnight in D Block.

All these individual adventures were the aftermath, however, of the rebel capture of the quadrangle. This was the rebels' third sudden success.

THE DEFENSE OF THE HOSPITAL AND THE COAL YARD

Between 8:55 A.M. and 9:00 A.M. Sergeant Jack English, the chart head-count officer of the institution, did his utmost to co-ordinate a makeshift defense. He was told at once there was serious trouble in A Block, and he called all the other cell blocks, all the workshops, and asked for all available help to be sent to A Block. But there was no reply from B Block and D Block. It was too late. He succeeded in contacting Captain Pappy Wald, who was in charge of the men in C Block. He told Captain Wald to button up C Block and this locking procedure was completed with moments to spare.

Then our corrections officers scored their first success of the day, a small one but a limiting one. They drove back a handful of rebels from the coal yard behind B Block. This was their first move outward from the main cell blocks—and it was particularly fortunate that we stopped them, because the powerhouse was not far from the coal yard and was an obvious objective.

Corrections Officer Roger Dawson was assigned to the power-house that morning. He was outside, supervising the burning of some papers. When a truck pulled up with more paper to be burned, he unlocked the coal yard gate. Without warning, three prisoners surrounded him and told him to put down his baton. He did.

Then Corrections Officer Donald Head came out of the coal yard shack and the prisoners, startled by his arrival, ran over to

Mr. Head and smashed him on the mouth, on the back of his head, on his back, and in his stomach with lengths of pipe and clubs. Roger Dawson leapt at the inmates, but they turned and struck him several times on the head. Mr. Head and Mr. Dawson were now down on the ground and the inmates continued to beat them. It had all happened in an instant.

Before any more prisoners could reach the scene, Corrections Officer B. "Joe" Conway, on duty in an armed post on the perimeter wall, leveled his AR-15 rifle and shouted, "Stop—I will shoot." The three inmates ran back to B Block. Afterward, Roger Dawson and Donald Head were rescued by corrections officers and were taken to the hospital for treatment of severe head wounds.

Corrections Officer Conway phoned a report of the incident to Jack English, the chart officer. It seemed that the prisoners were now threatening generally to move out beyond the main cell blocks and the quadrangle.

Sergeant English telephoned the powerhouse, although it was no longer directly threatened, and the hospital, which was located behind C Block but within striking range of the rebels who had captured A Block. The hospital was a natural target, for here the rebels could obtain the medical supplies they might need to sustain a long siege. He was just in time. The rebels who ran toward the hospital were confronted at an intervening gate by an officer who lobbed a tear gas bomb. This was the first shot we fired at Attica. The rebels sheered off to support a gathering concentration against C Block, where Captain Pappy Wald was preparing to make a stand.

Presumably the rebels did not make the short, sharp rush from A Block to the Administration Building because they expected that here we would make an armed defense. Superintendent Mancusi had already ordered the twenty-three women workers in the correctional facility to leave the area and the senior officers were ready to meet the rebels. But the rebels headed the other way.

Superintendent Mancusi telephoned Troop A of the New York State Police in Batavia, Major John W. Monahan commanding, and was told help would be on the way—fast. He telephoned Deputy Superintendent Vincent at home. He called for all off-duty corrections workers to come to the prison. He telephoned the Wyoming County sheriff and the Genesee County sheriff, each of whom could rush several score of armed deputies to the scene. He telephoned the head office of our Department of Correctional Services in Albany, whence the governor would be informed.

Meanwhile, at only a few minutes after 9:00 A.M., the whistle at the powerhouse sounded the general alarm. It dinned and keened over the village of Attica. Richard W. Miller, the corrections officer who was also the mayor, talked with several inmates who were not involved. "They told me the rebels were running right on a watch," he reported. "A fellow would say, 'You have a minute and a half.'"

BRUTALIZING FARGO AT THE COMMISSARY

Shortly after 9:00 A.M. Corrections Officer Richard Fargo, a man with more than twenty years' service, was in the commissary with fifteen inmates under his control. Two other officers were working behind the counter, passing out food and toilet supplies to the inmates. One of these men went outside and, as a din in the distance grew louder, he said quietly, "Boss, there is a riot. Can you get the door closed?" Mr. Fargo closed the door at once but he could not lock it. The other officer behind the counter had the key.

Richard Fargo asked for the key but the rebels were already pounding at the closed door. He held it closed. They smashed the glass windows in the door and struck at him. He tied the thong from his baton around the door handle but the rebels soon snapped the door open. The fifteen inmates under Mr. Fargo's control fell back against the wall and watched as the rebels began to attack the corrections officer.

With ball bats, shovels, and shovel handles, the rebels slammed him on the back of the head, and they hit him on the side of the head with a shovel. Mr. Fargo fell against a wall, propped his back up on it, and covered his head with his arms and his stomach with drawn-up knees. The beating continued.

When the rebels turned away from him, they tore down the partitions and screens and forced their way across the counter to get to the merchandise. The two other corrections officers went down. Richard Fargo slipped out, but one of the rebels spotted him, yelled for him to come back, and ran after him with a long-handled shovel. Another crowd of inmates now headed toward him from the other direction. He felt his time had come. He stepped into a doorway half way down a hall, with his back against the door, and faced up to the rebels. Some demanded that the beating continue. A tall, black prisoner placed himself in front of the officer and said the beating would be done by him, and the crowd moved on. This prisoner now tried to get Mr. Fargo out safely, but another inmate followed them and struck the officer a terrible blow on the back of the head with a shovel.

Somehow, Richard Fargo got to his feet, to be felled again with a blow above the ear from the flat head of a machinist's hammer. He blocked some of the force of the blow with his forearm. Another inmate spotted his watch and demanded it. He let the man snatch it from his wrist. Then he was herded along to join the growing number of hostages.

The rebels now had the supplies of the commissary and they had put down one of our best men. They were still operating within the first half hour of the rebellion.

STORMING THE METAL SHOPS

The main rebel force of more than 400 men swept in from the captured areas of the prison and began a concentrated, coordinated assault against the various sections of the industrial buildings. It was approximately 9:15 A.M. and the alarm had been sounded and the corrections officers were ready to do what they could. A little earlier a raiding party of inmates had taken the garage and disabled Albert Robbins, a civilian motor equipment repairman, with a pipe blow in the gut. When one of the inmates working in the garage went to help Al Robbins, this man's arm was broken with the pipe by the rebels.

In Metal Shops #1 and #1A, two civilian industrial foremen, Frederick Miller and Edward Miller, waited along with Corrections Officer Eugene Smith while the rebels raged around the door. They had had time to lock it. But then there was an awful crashing. The rebels were using a forklift truck, handling it like a tank, ramming in the door. Behind the forklift "tank," the rebels charged into the metal shops. They were under the control of their leaders. The orders were given that the two industrial foremen were not to be harmed. But the corrections officer was beaten because he was wearing his blue uniform.

Sergeant Edward Cunningham was in charge of Metal Shop #2. He was fifty-two years old, a hero of the Second World War. As a sergeant in the 43rd Infantry Division, he had won a Bronze Star with cluster, had been wounded and awarded a Purple Heart. Afterwards, as a corrections officer, he had taken special courses in human behavior, correctional group management, and fundamentals of supervision.

Sergeant Cunningham had been warned by the defense coordinator, Sergeant English, that the rebels were heading his way. He did not have time to return his metalwork crew of inmates to their cells and he said to two of his corrections officers, "They're right in through B Block. They're tearing everything up."

Gary Walker, a corrections officer whose normal post was the shop gate leading to the commissary and the powerhouse, had run ahead of the rebels, giving the alarm in the industrial buildings. He rushed into Metal Shop #2 ahead of the rebels and said to Sergeant Cunningham, "Give me the key, and I'll lock the middle gate." Mr. Walker managed to lock the corridor gate between Metal Shop #1 and Metal Shop #2.

Corrections Officer Dean Stenschorn surveyed the very large group of 328 prisoners in his metal shop. Normally, they worked on such jobs as the construction of metal office furniture in the prison industries program, and now they were calm amid the thunderous noise outside. Mr. Stenschorn asked one of these inmates if he could expect any help from them. He was told, "It's too late." Then the rebels came through the shop door as if it were butter. It went right down, and fifteen to eighteen rebels came through waving clubs and boards, bits of pipe, and the batons of corrections officers they had already captured. Leading the invaders was Sam Melville, the "Mad Bomber."

Anthony Sangiacomo, a corrections officer with fourteen years' service, was supervising the inmates in the grinder section. This officer estimated that twenty-five inmates now moved into his area and took him captive.

The rebels now had their biggest bag of hostages since the beginning of the rebellion. They formed a circle around Sergeant Cunningham and Corrections Officers Lynn Johnson and Don Almeter, in addition to Mr. Sangiacomo, Mr. Stenschorn, and Mr. Walker. Another corrections officer taken in the metal shops was Carl W. Valone, forty-four years old, a very respected man in the village of Attica and a member of the Genesee County Democratic Committee. He had attended Batavia High School from 1940 to 1945, then served in the United States Army from 1945 to 1947 before joining the state service. After temporary service at Attica in 1962, he had worked at Green Haven before taking what was to be his final position at Attica in September 1964.

Sam Melville ordered the hostages in the metal shops to strip. When Sergeant Cunningham kept his underwear on, he was told to strip completely. Then the rebels forced the naked corrections personnel and civilian employees to run a gantlet out to D Yard —hitting the hostages with baseball bats and other weapons.

The rebels had now won all the machinery they needed to make weapons for a siege, short of firearms.

THE BLOODLESS FALL OF THE INDUSTRIAL OFFICES

The rebels kept right on going after taking the metal shops and a raiding party wearing football helmets, armed with clubs and lengths of piping, rounded up the staff in the upstairs industrial building offices. A tragic number of these men was destined not to survive our final assault on the morning of September 13.

Industrial Superintendent Robert Van Buren, a man with nineteen years of work experience, was the senior civilian employee taken hostage. He was pushed out of the building with the others, fully dressed, and a friendly inmate said, "I'm going to take care of you, Mr. Van Buren." But this man was brushed aside and Robert Van Buren was hit across the arm with a bit of lumber, across the hand with a two-by-four, on the back of the head with something he did not see, and in the stomach by something with a handle, which broke off.

Gordon Knickerbocker, fifty-four years old, was hit heavily on the head and was bleeding badly as he was escorted with the other hostages down to the yard. Ronald Kozlowski, a senior account clerk, only seven months on the job, was taken out with the others, fully dressed, and he was also beaten around the head and shoulders in the central square.

Elon F. Werner, a civilian employee in the offices, the principal account clerk, was one week short of his sixty-fourth birthday.

A native of Attica, he had one year of high school there, and after many positions in life, he became an account clerk at Attica prison in February 1959. He was promoted through the 1960s to senior account clerk and then to provisional principal account clerk, which final promotion was made permanent in January 1971. Mr. Werner's nephew was Corrections Officer Ronald D. Werner, aged thirty-five, a graduate of Alexander Central High School, and a four-year Air Force veteran, who was being taken hostage in the commissary. Both of the Werners would die on September 13.

Elmer G. Hardie, fifty-eight years old, was a civilian industries foreman who was well loved over the years by the inmates he instructed in vocational rehabilitation programs. He had attended St. Mary's and Technical High Schools and the Bryant & Stratton Business School in Buffalo. He had worked in business for many years before coming to Attica in 1968.

Senior Account Clerk Herbert W. "Skip" Jones, twenty-six years old, married, with one daughter named Lynda, was also a native of Attica. He too had attended Bryant & Stratton Business School in Buffalo, as well as the Sam Houston State Teachers College and the University of Ottawa. He served as a sergeant in the Air Force from 1966 to 1970, and he had worked at the Attica Correctional Facility for six months. He was also a member of the Attica Police Department.

The dressed hostages from the industrial offices and the naked hostages from the metal shops saw two badly beaten men as they passed through B Block on their way to the yard. These two officers had been overwhelmed there in the first moments of the rebellion. They were Corrections Officers Richard J. Lewis, forty-two years old, and Kenneth Jennings, thirty-one years old. The rebel inmates fell upon Mr. Lewis with particular violence, but he was a hard man and he survived serious multiple injuries. He was, however, destined to be killed during our recapture of the institution on September 13.

Corrections Officer Jennings was struck by one of the inmates eight times with a weight-lifting bar. Another inmate watched, smiled, and said, "Now, Pig, we got you."

LAST STAND AT C BLOCK

No later than 9:15 A.M. the rebels began the attack on C Block. They had mopped up the central rectangle, set fire to the chapel and schoolhouse, and were engaged in the assault on the industrial buildings. They had also taken E Block almost by default. This was the block set behind C Block, where elderly and infirm prisoners were often housed. As one of the corrections officers at E Block later told the New York *Daily News*:

"It was the most unbelievable, frightening thing I've ever seen. They ripped off a couple of those cast-iron steam radiators from inside the tunnel, and they used them as battering rams, with fifteen to twenty men on each one. They just kept beating until the gate [of E Block] caved in."

In C Block, Captain Pappy Wald thought that both of his main gates would hold a tank. He locked them and stood guard, unarmed, along with Sergeant Gerald Reger and Corrections Officer Richard Delany. Even without the radiator battering rams, however, a group of rebels, shouldering the gates in unison, broke them open. "They just popped," Captain Wald thought.

Pappy Wald, Gerald Reger, and Richard Delany had just enough time to run back to the C Block office. They closed the door, found some wire, and wired the door handle to a piped conduit. Officer Delany held on to the handle with his hands.

The rebels smashed the windows of the office door, ran around behind the office, and yelled for our men to come out. The officers refused. Then the rebels tore up some mattresses outside the door and set fire to them. The rebels expected to smoke out Pappy Wald and the others but decided this would take too much time. Through the smoke, they turned three fire hoses and aimed them at the three officers. They turned a jet directly on to Richard Delany, who was still hanging on to the door handle.

Then the rebels found some long poles and jabbed them through the broken door windows. They hurled in lye soap. But Captain Wald, Sergeant Reger, and Mr. Delany did not surrender and were not about to.

Next, the rebel leaders ordered up the tear gas materials they had captured at Times Square. They threw a large gas grenade into the room and that should have been that. But, incredibly, the door had been locked during the attack *on the outside*. One of the inmates must have done this either to help our men defend the place or, alternatively, to imprison them amid the choking fumes of the gas.

Now the three officers were all down, lying in six to eight inches of water from the hoses, gasping for breath in the gas, taking vicious jabs from the long poles.

The rebel leaders finally sent for an acetylene torch and began to cut off the lock. But this took a little time. Pappy Wald used it to crawl to a barred iron grating at the back of the office and look outside for help.

Captain Wald called out to an inmate, and asked what could be done to help. The inmate said, "If you turn yourselves over to me, you will not be hurt." Captain Wald told the man to come round to the front of the office.

At last, the lock was cut off and the door burst open. There, holding back a furious crowd of rebels, was the inmate who had promised help, with five or six Black Muslims. Captain Wald, Sergeant Reger, and Mr. Delany were now taken without further injury to join the rest of the hostages.

But the last stand at C Block was not over.

On the third floor of the block, Corrections Officer Frank Kline was on duty. With the prison apparently blowing up all around him, he had plenty of warning. He had not only locked up the galleries, but he had also locked up all the cells, and his area of responsibility was secure. Frank Kline had been fifteen years at Attica and he knew all his inmates by name and number. He kept them quiet enough even while the rebels stormed the C Block office and took Captain Wald hostage. A few of the inmates tested the locks but found them too much trouble to force for the time being.

Not until 10:20 A.M., by Mr. Kline's reckoning, did the rebels attack his third-floor stronghold. The fighting had long since died down and this was kind of an aftermath. The rebels started smashing at the doors with a crowbar, ineffectually, and then they shouted they had an acetylene torch and were going to cut their way in. There was nothing more Frank Kline could do—one man against however many hundred the rebels cared to send against him—and so he opened up. One of the white prisoners, a reddish-haired man wearing a football helmet, wanted to beat him but was stopped by another inmate.

When he was taken down to the yard to join the other hostages, Officer Kline was smashed in the face with what he thought was the end of a fire hose. On September 13 he would be one of the hostages who had their throats cut by the inmates. Frank Kline had to have fifty-two stitches in his neck.

On the morning of Thursday, September 9, 1971, the rebels had fought the swiftest and most skillful revolutionary offensive since the 1968 Tet attack in South Vietnam. They did not use firearms and no firearms were used against them, by standing order. They had manufactured literally hundreds of weapons during what must have been weeks of supervised imprisonment. They had worked out an attack plan while in captivity under the eyes of our corrections personnel.

Within thirty minutes, certainly within forty minutes, they had seized control of most of a maximum-security correctional facility. They had won A Block, B Block, C Block, D Block, and E Block, the quadrangle, the industrial buildings, the commissary, the chapel-auditorium, and the school. We continued to hold the Administration Building, Housing Block Z, the hospital, the mess hall, the powerhouse, the vehicles, and the perimeter wall. There had been no attempt to break into the prison through the wall from the outside.

The rebels at Attica had taken the very large number of forty-nine hostages, including Captain Wald, Lieutenant Curtiss, Sergeants Reger and Cunningham, and Industrial Superintendent Van Buren. They now took these hostages to D Yard, threw blankets and bits of clothing to the men they had stripped, and attempted to impose some form of order. It was tenuous: one man, nicknamed "Psycho," strolled up to Pappy Wald, held a captured gas gun at his head and pulled the trigger twice. It was not loaded, and other inmates chased Psycho away. Other inmates walked up to corrections officers and hit them in the mouth, broke bits of wood over their heads, or kicked them in the stomach.

But the Black Muslim faction within the rebellion now formed a 200-man security guard and set up a cordon to protect the hostages. The plan was to hold our men for the ransom of major concessions.

The Black Muslims won a point in the rebel leadership when they said that Corrections Officers William Quinn and Kenneth Jennings were in too serious a condition to be held and must be let go. An inmate who Mr. Jennings said was a Black Panther threatened to kill him with a knife. But a Muslim security guard

said, "If you do, you're gonna have to stick me first, man." Mr.
Quinn and Mr. Jennings were carried out by the inmates. Kenneth
Jennings needed twenty-five stitches in his head. William Quinn
was taken to the hospital in critical condition.

Yet there were many thoughts afterward that the rebels had
won a flawed success. According to one theory, they had intended
to wait until approximately 10:00 A.M., when all of the inmates
would have been out on their work details, instead of merely most
of them. Again, according to this theory, it was the decision of
Superintendent Mancusi to return Company 5 to their cells,
and/or the decision of Lieutenant Curtiss to lock the yard doors
and talk to Company 5 about the problems, and/or even the unknown inmate who had sprung the lock of Cell No. 17 to release
the prisoner William Ortiz and so alerted the corrections staff—
that led the rebels to start at 8:50 A.M.

One corrections officer speculated, "If they'd waited until ten
o'clock, they'd have had everything including the women employees. At ten o'clock, we'd have been outnumbered at least ten to
one. We wouldn't have had a chance."

Even so, the rebels were off to an excellent start from their
point of view. Now we would make our countermoves.

In the brief interim there were shouts heard from the tailor's
shop. One of our corrections officers drove up a utility truck, threw
a chain to the man inside, and pulled out a window so he could set
himself free. It turned out to be Corrections Officer John Drier.
He had locked himself in when the rebellion began. The rebels had
set a minor fire and moved on. Now John Drier was free, back on
our side, and like every corrections officer, every sheriff's deputy,
every state policeman within minutes of Attica, he was ready for
a decisive, crushing counterattack.

CHAPTER 4

My Decision to Negotiate

At 5:30 A.M. on Thursday, September 9, 1971, I was awakened by the ringing of the alarm clock in my home in a suburb of Schenectady, New York. I showered, shaved, got dressed, and took our dog Jolly for a half hour's walk. Jolly is a pedigreed female Airedale terrier, called more formally Fuzzy-faced Joslyn. We strolled in the cool morning air, up and down the wooded lanes around the home where my wife and I had lived for more than a dozen years.

I was alone in the house this morning because my wife had already entered Albany Medical Center in Albany, ten or twelve miles away, for a myelogram and other tests.

After I got back to the house with Jolly, not much later than 6:00 A.M., I did what few dishes were left over from the previous night and prepared a light breakfast—tomato juice, black coffee, and a single soft-boiled egg. Then I got some things ready for the cleaners, a couple of suits, a few ties, and two pairs of trousers. I pulled together some papers I had been working on, and drove to the hospital to visit with Jane and then on to the Department of Correctional Services headquarters in downtown Albany. It is on the ninth floor of the modern Twin Towers office building, across the street from the old State Education Building, within a long stone's throw of the New York State Capitol.

Around the corner from the Capitol, on Eagle Street, overshadowed by the gleaming, white skyscraper tower of the South Mall project, was the old Executive Mansion in which Presidents Theodore Roosevelt and Franklin D. Roosevelt had lived during their previous service as governors of New York. The present occupant, Governor Nelson A. Rockefeller, was not there; he was in Washington for a meeting to be held that morning of President

Nixon's Foreign Intelligence Advisory Board, of which the governor is a member.

At 7:45 A.M., one hour and ten minutes before the Attica rebellion broke out, I looked out of my office window across a panoramic view of Albany, with its small streets and houses, the dip of the Hudson River Valley, and a distant sweep toward the Berkshire Hills in Massachusetts. Then I settled down behind the desk and prepared for what I expected to be an irksome day—there had been few that were not since I took on this assignment the preceding January.

Since I had visited the Attica Correctional Facility the previous week, things at least from my distance had seemed to be quieter there. My tape-recorded speech to the Attica inmates had apparently had no ill-effects, at least. Almost a week had gone by without incident.

The principal meeting of the morning was to be a conference with George McGrath, the corrections commissioner of New York City, and with several members of his staff. I had known George McGrath in the 1950s when I was corrections commissioner in Massachusetts. I had benefited from his advice based upon his experiences in prison work in that state. He is a top correctional administrator and followed me with distinction as Commissioner of Corrections in Massachusetts.

Now there was a problem between Mr. McGrath and me, because New York State had recently offered to accommodate 3,000 prisoners from the overcrowded jails of New York City, and a fair percentage of these men were militant radicals. The first streetwise arrivals had begun to proselytize the state prison population so rapidly that one of the governor's senior staff members commented, "The city has sent us the bottom of the barrel."

My secretary, Mrs. Helen T. David, brought me coffee, and we went over administrative matters together. There was correspondence from several of our twenty-two correctional institutions, but, taken as a whole, there seemed to be less tension in the system than there had been the week before.

At 9:16 A.M. the telephone rang in the office of Walter Dunbar. The call was from Superintendent Mancusi at Attica. Five minutes later, Walter strode into my office and gave me my first word of the rebellion. This was now about the time the rebel prisoners were conquering the industrial buildings and herding the hostages into the yard, about the time they were beating, hosing, and gassing Captain Wald and his men behind the C Block office door. Walter's summary of Superintendent Mancusi's report was terse:

"At about nine o'clock, bad trouble in all major blocks; one officer badly hurt; there are a number of hostages; the perimeter is secure; all women employees are out of the institution; outside work gangs of inmates are being brought into the institution; assistance has been requested from State Police and local law enforcement people; the district attorney has been informed; there was an incident in the yard the previous afternoon; he will endeavor to regain control, block by block; the general alarm whistle has been blown and corrections officer personnel are on their way in; location and activities of the majority of inmates uncertain; Mancusi will keep us advised."

"Mancusi reports it's a regular mess," he added.

I decided at once to go to Attica and inquired as to the fastest means of transportation possible. I decided to take Walter Dunbar with me as my executive officer. I told him to inform the superintendent we would be on our way as soon as possible. I also approved, with the single word "Fine," Vincent Mancusi's very important statement that he would "endeavor to regain control, block by block." Although this was standard operating procedure, the size of the uprising made such formal approval on my part desirable if not mandatory.

I then telephoned Governor Rockefeller's office and made contact with his first assistant counsel, Howard Shapiro, who was later to serve on our informal staff at Attica. I reported the situation and asked that the governor be informed as soon as possible. Mr. Shapiro informed Michael Whiteman, the governor's counsel, who in turn contacted Mrs. Ann C. Whitman, the governor's personal secretary, who had accompanied the governor to Washington. Mrs. Whitman reached Governor Rockefeller at the Foreign Intelligence Advisory Board meeting in the old State Department Building next to the White House—and this call plunged him into five days of crisis.

Superintendent Mancusi called for the second time at 10:15 A.M. He reported that the rebels had control of A, B, C, D, and E Blocks and the Times Square area and that we still held the Administration Building, the mess hall, the powerhouse, the hospital, and the perimeter wall. Walter Dunbar and I now knew that the rebel inmates had won most of the maximum-security correctional facility in an amazingly brief period of time.

An official New York State plane had now been made available to us, but the two State Police officials who were to accompany us had to go home to collect some clothes and this meant delay.

At 10:32 A.M. the word of the rebellion was running on the Associated Press wire, although there was no indication of its severity. One of the earliest bulletins of a story that would transfix the world and eventually draw more than 500 national and foreign correspondents to Attica read like this:

ATTICA N.Y. A DISTURBANCE WAS REPORTED TO HAVE BROKEN OUT TODAY IN ATTICA STATE PRISON.

A SWITCHBOARD OPERATOR AT THE MAXIMUM SECURITY FACILITY DECLINED TO GIVE ANY INFORMATION OR PUT THROUGH CALLS TO SUPERINTENDENT VINCENT MANCUSI.

IN NEARBY BATAVIA, STATE POLICE SAID THEY HAD NOT SENT A RIOT DETAIL TO THE PRISON. SEVERAL TROOPERS WENT TO THE PRISON TO CHECK ON WHAT WAS HAPPENING, A TROOPER SAID.

That was all.

Somewhere around 11:00 A.M. Commissioner McGrath and his men came into my office for the scheduled meeting. They had come especially from New York City to see me, but I could only spend five minutes or so with them, performing the civilities; I explained that we had a problem at Attica and I accepted expressions of regret and concern.

Superintendent Mancusi phoned in his third report, which Walter Dunbar relayed at once. "Mancusi says it is a real bad situation. He tried to talk to the inmate leaders; they will only talk to the governor or the commissioner. State Police and local law enforcement people are now on hand, helping in various ways. Three employees who were hostages have been released. They were in bad shape."

At 11:35 A.M. the superintendent's fourth report: "The inmates are foraging. The staff is trying to mop up bit by bit."

At 11:40 A.M. we left the office, and it took a while to get the car out of the crowded garage. Then there was a lot of traffic on the roads to the Albany County airport. There our team assembled. In addition to Walter Dunbar, I was bringing two senior officials of our Department of Correctional Services. They were Francis "Bump" Daley, our Director of Budget and Finance, and Gerald T. Houlihan, our Director of Public Information. The New York State Police officers to travel with us were Chief Inspector John C. Miller and Deputy Chief Inspector Robert D. Quick.

We left Deputy Commissioner Wim van Eekeren in charge at Albany with instructions to have a command post manned twenty-four hours a day, to maintain liaison with the state government, and to keep a sharp watch for trouble at the other correctional facilities.

I thought this was a good command line-up. Walter Dunbar was a combination of stylish leader and detail man, an excellent exec. Dr. van Eekeren was thorough, tough, and a brain. "Bump" Daley was a marvel at obtaining the emergency supplies and money we might need at Attica. Jerry Houlihan was a fine community relations man, a friend in whom I had great confidence, a man with a deep feeling for people.

At 12:40 P.M. we took off in a twin-engined Beechcraft King-Air and flew to the south of the Thruway and across the Finger Lakes to Batavia. The air was calm and the flight was smooth. There was not much conversation and I leafed through some of the letters I had received from prisoners at Attica and other institutions, full of approval for my announced new reforms in the prisons. I could not help wondering whether things really would be as bad as Superintendent Mancusi had indicated. Could this possibly be a brief if turbulent flurry of discontent, I thought hopefully? Would the inmates return to their cells after stating their grievances and setting the hostages free? But I was only too aware of the infiltration of our prisons by militant revolutionaries.

In retrospect, I am grateful for the single hour of the flight from Albany to Batavia, because I had a little time to think, to contemplate, to go over again what we were really trying to accomplish in the prisons. It was on this flight, I believe, that the genesis of an important decision formed in my mind.

I had to balance emotion and reason. I had to live with myself and with my conscience in whatever I was about to do. The harsh choice would be to put down the rebellion on the spot at whatever cost in lives and anguish or to negotiate with the inmate leaders at the risk of demoralizing my own men. In any event, the priority for me was clear—and it would remain clear during the days that followed our landing at Batavia airport.

Our first responsibility as public officials and as human beings was to save as many lives as possible. The burning question—how best to accomplish this—could not be decided until we were on the scene and could carefully weigh the alternatives.

Superintendent Mancusi moved fast and hard through the rest of the morning to retake as much of the correctional facility as possible. He had limited means at his disposal but, as they say, he had a lot of heart. He was the traditional type of prison administrator, and for all our previous differences of emphasis, he was a good team player in the clutch. He remained the superintendent of Attica while commissioners, a governor, a President, and millions of his countrymen focused on his bailiwick.

Vincent Mancusi, fifty-seven years old, was the son of a detective on the police force of New Rochelle, New York. He won his bachelor's degree from the State Teachers College at New Paltz, New York, and taught grammar school for three years before entering the correctional field as a guard. In his climb through the ranks, Mr. Mancusi worked in three major New York State institutions, Elmira Reformatory, Clinton State Prison at Dannemora, and at Auburn of historic fame.

He obtained a master's degree in correctional administration from St. Lawrence University, and his attention to the new directions in penology countered the criticism that he was too much of a bureaucrat. As superintendent of Attica for the previous six years, he signed most of the checks in person. One of the inmates confided that the men disliked "all the petty things he do," but he was never a brutal disciplinarian.

The superintendent's first call for reinforcements was received by Major Monahan of Troop A of the New York State Police when the rebels were still in the midst of storming C Block and the industrial buildings. Major Monahan informed his division headquarters and put his troop on the road to Attica. At 9:45 A.M. the first detail of approximately fifty troopers arrived at Attica, under the command of Lieutenant J. C. Moochler. Fifteen minutes later, Major Monahan himself arrived at the correctional facility, accompanied by Captain A. T. Malovich, and he took over the operational command of the State Police that he would exercise for the duration of the crisis.

Superintendent Mancusi drew Major Monahan's attention to the fact that a fire was in progress in E Block. He believed many people were in the building. There was also a fire in the laundry. To regain the facility block by block, Vincent Mancusi now determined to extinguish the fire in E Block and rescue anyone still in there. This meant recapturing E Block—the first territory to regain.

Lieutenant Moochler led thirty State Police troopers to E Block with fire-fighting equipment, ready to confront the rebels. He had a backup detail of an additional fifteen men. But the rebels withdrew to C Block and B Block without a fight. Our men put out the E Block fire and took charge of the inmates still there. Then they put out a smaller fire in the laundry.

Superintendent Mancusi had also warned the office of Wyoming County Sheriff Dalton Carney in the first half hour of the uprising. Heavily armed deputies soon came pouring into the correctional facility with rifles, shotguns, and revolvers. These men were held in readiness.

The Wyoming County sheriff's office next called the Division of Military and Naval Affairs in Albany. The caller said the riot at Attica was a big one, and it appeared to be beyond the control of prison and law enforcement personnel. He asked how to obtain National Guard assistance. He was referred to the governor's office.

Now the caller said the sheriff had declared an emergency and he requested advice as to whether deputies from the surrounding counties should be summoned. One of the assistant counsels to the governor told the caller to follow the directions of the New York State Police, who were in charge of law enforcement at Attica.

This was a very important point. The plan to use the State Police in the first line became even more important when Sheriff Carney called in deputies from the surrounding counties and the influx of heavily armed men into the community increased.

At 11:15 A.M. senior officers of the Army National Guard met at Albany to develop plans for any National Guard assistance that might be needed at Attica.

At 11:45 A.M. Mike Whiteman instructed the New York State Police not to take any action to recover the cell blocks by force without first clearing the decision with the governor's office. Approximately one hour later he was informed that the Legal Aid Society was sending three lawyers to Attica, presumably on the prisoners' behalf. He said they were not to be admitted, at least not until I arrived to take charge.

At 12:30 P.M., although the action was completed much earlier, Superintendent Mancusi reported to Deputy Commissioner van Eekeren at Albany that E Block had been recaptured. This was his fifth formal report of the day. Dr. van Eekeren, in charge of the Albany command post, reported the retaking of E Block to Mr. Whiteman.

Superintendent Mancusi and Major Monahan, heartened by the unexpectedly easy recapture of E Block, now decided upon major countermeasures. They were also under intense pressure from the crowds of off-duty corrections officers and sheriff's deputies to go in and do something.

By 12:20 P.M. Major Monahan had 200 state troopers at Attica under command and another 100 on the way. Soon afterward, he committed 100 troopers to recapture A Block, where the rebellion had originated, only a few yards from our headquarters in the Administration Building. This force was also ordered to retake C Block, where many inmates were staying in their cells, declaring they wanted no part of the rebellion.

The rebels pulled back rapidly and in good order before the rifle- and shotgun-equipped state troopers. They covered their retreat with tear gas from their captured supplies and by welding shut a few strategic doors. The rebels formed a perimeter around D Yard, with the hostages visible in the middle of it. They continued to hold D Block and B Block, whose corner formed D Yard, and they were ready to contest possession of the other three yards of the quadrangle, as well as Times Square. They continued to hold almost all the industrial area and all the shops.

This force of 100 state troopers was ready to go on against the more than 1,200 prisoners around D Yard, but if they did, they would most likely have to use firearms if they were not to lose a hand-to-hand battle. The troopers had tear gas, but they did not have a viable supply of CS gas, the disabling agent effective against large numbers of men. This gas forces men to double up, and it disables them for several minutes without permanent injury. If used skillfully, CS gas can be a decisive and humane antiriot weapon. Superintendent Mancusi and Major Monahan now faced another crunch—and it was up to them, because we were still airborne, somewhere between Albany and Batavia.

The State Police officers recognized the tactical deficiencies. These were:

1. With no CS gas on hand, the state troopers *would* be opposed by hundreds of men heavily armed with less than firearms but capable of effective and bloody hand-to-hand fighting.

2. There were still fewer than 300 state troopers at Attica.

3. They would *have* to open fire.

4. There would be no way to protect the hostages, not only from gunfire but also from inmates who were still enraged after the first morning's battle and were still trying to get through the Black Muslim security guard to get at our men.

5. The hostages in D Yard might well be executed by the rebels if we stormed the rest of the prison.

The balance of the decision was clear to Superintendent Mancusi and Major Monahan. They held further action "in abeyance" until my arrival, but continued their build-up of State Police forces from all over the state. They posted armed men on the roofs of recaptured A Block and C Block against any attempt by the rebels to come back. And they drafted contingency plans for the recapture of the whole prison later that day.

They had won a very satisfactory victory with the recapture of A Block and C Block and there was a lot of mopping up to do. Out from under beds, out from every conceivable kind of hiding place known to men who had been incarcerated in the place for years poured literally hundreds of inmates. Some were scared to death, others were overcome by emotion. They swarmed around our forces and shouted that they wanted no part of the rebellion. These were blacks, whites, Puerto Ricans—murderers, robbers, parole violators—a cross section of the prison population. They said the militants were "wild men," "crazy radicals," who had been planning the thing for weeks, threatening to kill any inmate who informed on them. They also warned that the rebels were not kidding in their threats against the hostages.

So—without firing a single shot from rifle or shotgun, we had recaptured A Block, C Block, and E Block and restored control over 962 of the inmates. This was a creditable performance, and it said much for the skill and leadership of the State Police we had placed in the front line. And the comeback was even more remarkable in view of the fact that we had been caught so badly off balance in the morning and had suffered such a serious setback.

Who could blame the people who awaited my arrival at Attica for word to put an end to the whole thing by sundown?

At 1:40 P.M. our plane made a smooth touchdown at Batavia airport. There were several State Police cars there to meet us and we clambered in for the brief drive down to Attica. One reporter was at the airport; how he knew we were there was beyond me. But we could reward him with little for his initiative. "I've nothing I can talk about with you, because I don't know any more about it than you do," I told him.

Our small convoy rolled fast through rich green fields and rolling hills and plantings of sweet corn, past red barns and silver silos, and white clapboard farmhouses set amid zinnias and newly mowed lawns.

At Attica the scene was different. Already the place looked as if there was a small war on. Police cars patrolled with sirens screaming and lights rotating. Heavily armed sentries were posted outside the prison. Huddles of townsfolk, some of whom were relatives and friends of the men unaccounted for, were beginning a four-day vigil. There were other huddles of friends of the prisoners, upon whom the State Police appeared to be keeping a close eye.

Above all, as always in a calamity, there was the omnipresence of the mass media, scores of newspaper reporters, radio cars and TV trucks, cables littering the ground, discarded coffee cups and cigarette butts tossed in all directions. As I got out of the State Police car and hurried to the Administration Building I was surrounded by reporters. One asked, "Do they want to meet with you, sir?" I replied, "I haven't—I don't know. They say that they only want to speak with the governor or me."

Then the reporters asked a series of questions that led me into a damaging slip. One said, "Have you made any—have the inmates made any demands that you know of?" I said, "Not recently," immediately aware of the fact that the radicals of the "Attica Liberation Faction" had sent me that manifesto in July. The next question was beginning "When you say . . ." when I threw in "A couple of weeks ago, they did." The next question: "Could you talk about some of them?" and I replied:

"They're all kinds of demands, you know—for the—change in the whole world. I was out here last week and talked with many of the prisoners. I've been . . ."

"Are you willing to give in to any demands?"

And I said quickly, "Not to demands."

Here at the outset I was confronted with a barrage of questions from the prisoners' point of view. I was not asked what I knew about the welfare and safety of the hostages.

But the mistake I made was to characterize the manifesto as asking for a "change in the whole world." Whatever I thought of the manifesto, if I intended to meet with the rebel leaders, if I meant to negotiate for the release of the hostages, I would clearly have to discuss it. I ought not to have allowed myself to be forced into a derogation of anything at that preliminary point in the game.

Very much in evidence at the gate when I arrived was the massive form of New York State Police Captain Hank Williams, one of Major Monahan's most effective officers. Captain Williams was now picked up for national television, giving instructions to some of his men. He said:

"Your instructions are that your weapon is not to be taken, nor are you to be taken. You will be sent in in groups of five-man teams, and you'll operate as a five-man unit. You're to meet force with force. There have been some of the prison personnel severely injured here this morning, and we certainly don't want to see any of our people hurt. But just remember—no indiscriminate fire.

"However, you're not to be taken—nor is your weapon to be taken away from you. So you'll use whatever force is necessary to maintain your own security."

A sergeant's voice was picked up, "Draw your—how about your nightsticks. For the first clash—right around—helmets. All right, you're going to go first class. When you get back, fall into the same squad."

And another voice chimed in, "Okay, Sarge."

These strictly routine instructions must have sounded terrifying in isolation to a national television audience. They could not help but sound provocative.

In retrospect, however, I was very pleased we had a formal

record, and not from a friendly source, that we had issued our governing instructions on the very first day:

"But just remember—no indiscriminate fire."

Into the Administration Building I went, followed by Mr. Dunbar, Mr. Daley, and Mr. Houlihan of my staff, and by Chief Inspector Miller and Deputy Chief Inspector Quick of the State Police. In the corridors there seemed to be scores of corrections officers who were only waiting for me to say something like "Let's drop the atom bomb." These men had seen Corrections Officers Quinn and Jennings carried out of the prison in terrible condition. They had talked with the officers the prisoners had brutalized but released. They were discussing a frantic rumor that one of the hostages had been castrated.

I greeted Superintendent Mancusi and we all conferred in the warden's large office on the second floor of the Administration Building. Mr. Mancusi filled us in on the situation, much of which was a repetition of his telephoned reports to Albany. He brought us up to date on the territory the rebels held, the territory we held, and he enumerated the head count of the hostages. He stressed that the prisoners would talk only with the governor or with me.

Because time was so short, and because the decisions we had to make were so urgent, I did not then get into the serious questions of what had gone wrong in the first phases of the battle.

Why had our security been so lax? How had all those weapons been manufactured and hidden? Why had the warnings not been heeded? Why were so many corrections people so vulnerable? Why were the gates, locks, bars, and flanges so breakable? How had the rebels been able to take over almost all the maximum-security prison in a half hour?

I found later that the many reasons for our lapses, in essence, boiled down to one: We were ready to meet a riot—but not a rebellion. To have had the defensive force on hand to meet an attack of this size, at this prison—and at the other maximum-security prisons in the state—would have required something like a semipermanent mobilization of major security forces. And, of course, the rebels must have known this.

There was not enough manpower at Attica: How could a single corrections officer control a company of forty men if they were determined to jump him? There was no way. Also, there was not enough protective, defensive gas immediately available, obviously. There was insufficient telephonic communication: The switchboards were jammed in the first minutes of the rebellion and our men were even short of the simple two-way radios carried by the police of almost every city in the United States.

There were depressions of morale among many corrections officers, who felt hamstrung by recent court orders on behalf of prisoners' rights. The corrections officers felt they were dealing with dangerous men, and they had wanted to use firmer disciplinary methods.

Many of the officers were also disenchanted with the new direction of prison reform I had set since becoming Commissioner of Correctional Services. They felt I was exercising far too much control over day-to-day matters that had previously been left to the corrections officers on the galleries. Some of them unquestionably let their resentment of "Albany" downgrade their interest in their work.

The only thing that might conceivably have nipped the rebellion in the bud would have been the arming of corrections officers on duty with instructions to fire at the first sign of trouble. Even if this had been considered wise in itself, however, it would have begged the question of how to keep the officers' firearms secure. It would have been asking for trouble to let the handfuls of guards carry rifles and shotguns in among the hundreds and thousands of prisoners.

Now, from the warden's office, I went down with Superintendent Mancusi through three barred gates and through A Block to the entrance that led to the corridor-tunnel to Times Square. This was the frontier we would later call the "DMZ"—the demilitarized zone.

I stared down the tunnel and could scarcely believe what I saw. There was a rebel patrol, four men, all of them wearing towels over their heads and sheets over their bodies, with bizarre face markings, carrying spears.

I had a sudden wry thought: *This* is prison reform?

Assuming I was confronting an organization, I asked one of our corrections lieutenants, who seemed to have a rapport with the inmates, whether I might talk with the leaders. At his call, the rebel patrol strolled up to the gate. All of our institutional entourage fell back, leaving Walter Dunbar and me alone with the corrections lieutenant as we talked with the prisoners. I said, "What do you want? Why don't you release the hostages?" The four men said there were bad conditions at Attica and they had demands they wanted to make. I said, "Well, why don't we talk about them?" One of the rebels said, "All right, do you want to talk about them?" I said, "Yes, I do."

Another of the rebels said, "Well, we'll go back and you can come in and talk with us." I replied, "Well, why don't you appoint a committee and we can—I can talk with the committee out here in this passageway, or we can meet in a neutral yard or meet on neutral ground somewhere where we can talk." The men said, "No. We can't have a committee. There are no leaders. Everyone is the same. All the people have to decide this. You will have to come in on this ground and talk with the people."

Returning to the Administration Building, I was counseled by Vincent Mancusi, by Walter Dunbar, and by the others not to go into the yard. I recognized that the rebels were only a few hours out of their violent spasms of brutality and terrorization. I was also aware of the fact that the rebels were clearly out to take hostages and that I would make a very valuable one from their viewpoint. To go into the yard might be not only personally foolhardy, but also strategically unwise.

At this point, a visiting card was brought in to me. It was that of Professor Herman Schwartz of the University of Buffalo, who had been active on the inmates' behalf after the riot at Auburn Prison. He had scrawled a handwritten note on his card: "Mr. Commissioner: I'm out here on the grass in front, if I can help." For all our former disagreements, I liked Professor Schwartz personally and recognized him as a man of warmth and convictions. I accepted his offer to help and also that of a New York State assemblyman, Arthur O. Eve; Mr. Eve's constituency was in Buffalo, and it had not taken him long to get to Attica.

At 3:25 P.M. Professor Schwartz and Assemblyman Eve went in alone to meet the rebel leaders. They felt they had friends there and I had to agree that if it was safe for anybody from the outside to go into that yard, it would be safe for them.

The professor and the assemblyman were frisked for weapons and escorted to a negotiating table in D Yard—where they were promptly presented with five "immediate demands." These called on Governor Rockefeller and President Nixon for complete amnesty, transportation to a "non-imperialistic" country, placing the inmates under federal jurisdiction, reconstruction of the prison by the inmates, and immediate negotiations through friends of the inmates for settlement of the rebellion. These first demands—formally presented—were the very first statement of the goals of the Attica revolt.

In other words, the revolutionaries were in charge from the outset, with revolutionary demands that plainly could not be met. This was clear evidence to any fair-minded man, it seemed to me, that Attica was certainly something very much more than a spontaneous riot against poor prison conditions.

At 3:58 P.M. Messrs. Schwartz and Eve came back out again through the DMZ and said the rebel leaders wanted to meet me and that, in their opinion, it was safe for me to proceed.

Once again, Walter Dunbar and Vincent Mancusi sought to dissuade me. "It is ridiculous for you to do this," they said. "It just isn't wise for you to go in there. Insist that they meet with you on a neutral spot where you can have some protection. Do *not* go in there alone."

Now I had a battlefield decision to make. I had expected to meet with the rebel leaders when I came to Attica, but I had expected to meet them on neutral ground. I had wanted to conduct a reasoned discussion without an atmosphere of force, of pressure, of implied compulsion. But I felt I had no choice. I could not live with myself in the future if I did not walk down that tunnel to try to save the lives of the hostages.

In any event, the State Police had not by then completed their build-up and we were not really ready to countermove.

I approved one last attempt, to be made by Professor Schwartz and Assemblyman Eve, to set up a meeting on neutral ground—but they found out the rebel leaders would not do it.

At 4:25 P.M., accompanied by Herman Schwartz and Arthur Eve, I walked down the tunnel. The rebel security guard met us, and they must have reviewed many times in the past how they would organize such a situation. They made signals to somebody farther down the tunnel and said, "Our security people will see you are well protected." Our group turned the corner around Times Square and then we were out into D Yard. There, three of the security people formed on each side of us, and they took hold of each of my arms and shouted, "Don't let anyone near him."

D Yard was a tangle of violence still, festooned with fallen wire and charred bits of furniture, saturated with water, mud all over the place, with an occasional whiff of smoke or uncleared tear gas hanging amid the incredible throng of more than one thousand.

Through the shouting crowd, I was almost dragged, ahead of the professor and the assemblyman, toward a negotiating table set up on the other side of the yard. I could see some of the hostages sitting behind a circle of inmates who seemed to be protecting them. One man shouted, "Let's throw this pig out in the middle and get rid of him." The man meant me. There was a thunderous roar of approval from the rebels. But another man shouted back that they had promised safe conduct and they were going to keep their word.

There they were, behind the table, the rebel leaders who had stood Attica on its end. They were ranged in line before me, some standing, some sitting, and there were brief introductions. There was Brother Richard, Richard L. Clark; Brother Herbert, Herbert X. Blyden; and a white People's Party leader, Peter Butler. Another white face was that of the rebel "lawyer," Jerry Rosenberg, the murderer of the two detectives in Brooklyn. I looked for Sam Melville, the Mad Bomber—but he was off somewhere else. Already, the State Police had told me, he was probably the insurgents' chief military man.

Down toward the end of the table was Frank Lott, the murderer who had signed the Attica Liberation Faction manifesto, the prisoner I had seen the previous week. He was down the table some distance, and he did not seem to be the key man he had indicated to me that he was.

Gazing across the table at me with ill-disguised malevolence was the young one in the granny glasses, L. D. Barclay, the pure revolutionary. Standing in the background was the mystery man, Roger Champen, Champ.

The security guards let my arms drop, and I sat down on our side of the table with Professor Schwartz and Assemblyman Eve. The crowd closed up behind my back, with more of the inmates hanging on to the wall of D Block behind the rebel leaders and at windows to one side.

Led at this point by Richard Clark and Herbert Blyden, they started off by saying they were not treated as men at Attica, that it was a racist institution. One man yelled into my ear from behind: "You've no interest in humanity. You've no interest in me as a human being." There was another roar. I replied that we knew there were many things wrong at Attica. I had indicated in my earlier tape recorded statement that I was pressing for reforms, and I stood on that statement now. But the leaders said there were many things that needed to be done in terms of changing attitudes before any of these reforms could be accomplished.

Then the rebel leaders, speaking in no set order, said they had a list of demands, and they asked me what I thought of the manifesto I had received the previous July. I had told them long since that I would consider it. Now I commented in the yard that these were demands that "prisoners all over" were making and did not specifically fit Attica. I said, then, and I wonder how I had the nerve, that these demands were identical to those made at Folsom Prison in California:

"All you did was change the name of the institution on them and send them on in to us."

I added that we were working on these and other demands and that we were working on our own programs, but the demands from Folsom were so carefully drawn and so radical in nature they were something that would take a lot of study.

One of the rebel leaders said, "Don't talk about the Folsom demands." Another said, "We're talking about *our* demands." A third leader said, "Why did you say to that reporter that we wanted the world?" Of course, the rebel leaders had transistor radios and a prison TV set was still working. They had picked up my slip at the prison gates.

I strongly urged the prisoners to release the hostages. They told me in reply to study their demands. I made three procedural concessions that turned out to be more than that. In response to their requests, and to improve the atmosphere for the next round of negotiations, I agreed to admit news media for the next meeting, to order state police sharpshooters off the roofs of A and C Blocks, and to give the men a pledge of no administrative reprisals. This was not an offer of amnesty, which no member of the executive branch of our government is empowered to grant. It was simply a promise not to take administrative reprisals against inmates after and if they surrendered.

At 5:00 P.M. Professor Schwartz left D Yard and reported to my anxiously waiting staff that there were no results in the talk, but that our safety was being maintained. Then he came back to join us.

At 5:15 P.M. the three of us were escorted out of D Yard by the security men through the mass of inmates and we cleared Times Square and the DMZ and returned to base. One of the rebel guards at the gateway said as we walked through, "You see, we kept our promise." "Yes," I said, "I acknowledge that."

After I left D Yard, as I have since learned from our hostages, pandemonium broke out. Militants among the rank and file screamed at the leaders that I should have been kept in the yard, I should be "Hostage No. 1," "the fattest pig of all." The leaders kept control of their coalition of factions—but the argument lasted almost half an hour.

At 4:55 P.M., twenty minutes before we left D Yard, Major Monahan said that "sufficient force is now marshaled to regain control of the facility." In addition to more than 500 State Police, 250 sheriff's deputies were on hand from all the surrounding counties and more than 250 corrections officers also were ready to go in and reinforcements of officers were available from Auburn prison. But there was still no viable quantity of the CS disabling gas.

When I came out of D Yard, however, I ordered that all of our forces, with the State Police in the front line, must still be held "in abeyance" pending the outcome of the negotiations. I was now quite sure that we should negotiate to try to obtain the peaceful release of the hostages. I believed the rebels would fight a furious hand-to-hand battle, even with the 1,000 or so men we now had at our disposal. I knew this meant we would probably have to use firearms to prevail. In this situation, I felt the hostages would not survive any new engagement on September 9. As it happened, the terms of the battle would have been much more equal, to the prisoners' advantage, than they turned out to be on September 13, when we had plenty of CS gas. Moreover, I felt that a September 9 battle might be closely fought and long drawn out—and that the hostages would be exposed and in danger for a longer period of conflict.

I had also sensed the mood of the rebels for myself by now. I had felt the scarcely controlled fury almost breathing down my neck. Those men *were* capable of murdering the hostages.

It is important to stress that I had no illusions about the rapid success of any negotiations, although I hoped that forthright talk and a sensible attitude might lead eventually to an accommodation. I was sure, on the other hand, that if we opened fire on D Yard, the rebels would tear the hostages to pieces with their spears and clubs, their bare hands, and "the blades."

At 5:45 P.M. I went down to the DMZ for the second meeting. Once again, members of my staff attempted to dissuade me from going in. They were more certain than ever that the rebels meant to take me hostage and use me as their trump bargaining card.

Once again, I passed through the Black Muslim security guard, along the tunnel, around Times Square, into the ankle-deep mud and shards of glass in D Yard. Still there was the whiff of dying fires and tear gas. I was accompanied as before by Professor Schwartz and Mr. Eve and this time, also, by New York State Assemblyman James Emery of Genesee County. On hand too, were five courageous journalists who had volunteered to cover the meeting at the risk of being taken hostage.

The five journalists were Fred Ferretti of the New York *Times*, Bob Buyer of the Buffalo *Evening News*, Myron Yancy of WOFD-Radio Buffalo, and a television team, Stewart Dan, commentator, and Terry Johnson, cameraman, of WGR-TV Buffalo.

The rebel escorts told the television men what they could and could not photograph, and they produced a couple of hostages who said they had been well treated to date. Almost all the rest, with their bloodied faces, broken bones, and bruises, were kept off the yard, out of sight. One of our hostages, Lieutenant Curtiss, was thrown a towel and told to clean the blood off his face for the TV camera. He turned his back and stuffed the towel under his shirt.

In front of the cameras and the national television audience the rebel leaders had fought so hard to get, there rose an authentic revolutionary leader, L. D. Barclay, twenty-one years old. Here is what L.D. told the people of the United States:

"We have composed this declaration to the people of America

to let them know exactly how we feel and what it is that they must do, and what we want, primarily, and now what we—what someone else wants for us. We's talking about what we want.

"The entire incident began—it seems to be a little misunderstanding about why this incident developed here at Attica, and this declaration here will explain the reasons.

"The entire incident that has erupted here at Attica is not a result of the dastardly bushwhacking of the two prisoners September 8 of 1971, but of the unmitigated oppression wrought by the racist administrative network of this prison throughout the year. We are *men!* We are not beasts and we do not intend to be beaten or driven as such.

"The entire prison populace—that means each and every one of us here—has set forth to change forever the ruthless brutalization and disregard for the lives of the prisoners here and throughout the United States. What has happened here is but the sound before the fury of those who are oppressed.

"We will not compromise on any terms except those terms which are agreeable to us. We call upon all the conscientious citizens of America to assist us in putting an end to this situation that threatens the lives of not only us, but of each and every one of you as well.

"We have set forth demands that will bring us closer to the reality.

"We want complete amnesty, meaning freedom from all and any physical, mental, and legal reprisals.

"We want, now, speedy and safe transportation out of confinement to a non-imperialistic country.

"We demand that the federal government intervene so that we will be under direct federal jurisdiction. We want the governor and the judiciary, namely Constance B. Motley, to guarantee that there will be no reprisals, and we want all facets of the media to articulate this.

"We urgently demand negotiations through William M. Kunstler, attorney at law, 588 Ninth Avenue, New York, New York; Assemblyman Arthur O. Eve of Buffalo; the Prison Solidarity Committee of New York; Minister [Louis] Farrahkan from the Muslims.

"We want Huey P. Newton from the Black Panther party, and we want the chairman of the Young Lords party. We want Clarence B. Jones of the *Amsterdam News;* we want Tom Wicker of the New York *Times;* we want Richard Roth from the Buffalo *Courier-Express;* we want the Fortune Society, Dave Anderson of the Urban League of Rochester, and we want Jim Ingraham of the *Michigan Chronicle* of Detroit, Michigan."

There was applause for Mr. Barclay's oration, amid which another leader said, "Good. Good."

Then I replied, less formally: "I've complied with the several things I said I would do as my part. I've brought the press and other media in here to listen as we talk. I earlier promised you there would be no reprisals other than what any law enforcement district attorney might take in terms of any crimes that might have been committed.

"I also asked that the man with the rifle put it down, on the outside, and now, my question is, I asked earlier, when will you release the hostages? And isn't now the time for us to talk about that?"

One of the rebel leaders down the table, whom I did not recognize, interjected: "In view of the fact now that the sheriff's department, the various counties, and the state troopers has taken over because it has been declared now a state of emergency, you couldn't guarantee no reprisal anyway. This is now out of your hands, isn't it, Commissioner?"

I replied, flatly, "No, it is not."

"You still control the state troopers?"

"Absolutely."

Then Mr. Blyden, I think it was, said, "All right, now, you want to put your no-reprisals in writing? Would you start doing that?"

I began to write: "This is to warrant that there will be no administrative reprisals for any actions taken by prisoners on September 8 and September 9, 1971," and I read it aloud while I was writing. Then a rebel interrupted, "Check, check, check. September 8 and 9?" I asked, "Isn't today the ninth?" A rebel said, "Well, what do you mean, September eighth and ninth?" I replied, "Why, anything that might have happened last night or yesterday." The rebel said, "Nothing happened." And another rebel said, "Write eight . . ." I said "All right," and I did.

The rebel leaders then gave me a typewritten, single-page list of fifteen "practical proposals," which had been dreamed up by Jerry Rosenberg. These were by now completely overshadowed by

L. D. Barclay's demands, made direct to the nation, especially by the demands for "complete amnesty" and "now, speedy and safe transportation out of confinement to a non-imperialistic country." For the record, I list the fifteen "practical proposals," as they were handed to me that incredible late afternoon in D Yard. They were:

PRACTICAL PROPOSALS

1. Apply the New York State minimum wage law to all state institutions. STOP SLAVE LABOR.

2. Allow all New York State prisoners to be politically active, without intimidation of reprisals.

3. Give us true religious freedom.

4. End all censorship of newspapers, magazines, letters, and other publications coming from the publisher.

5. Allow all inmates, at their own expense, to communicate with anyone they please.

6. When an inmate reaches conditional release date, give him a full release without parole.

7. Cease administrative resentencing of inmates returned for parole violations.

8. Institute realistic rehabilitation programs for all inmates according to their offense and personal needs.

9. Educate all correctional officers to the needs of the inmates, i.e., understanding rather than punishment.

10. Give us a healthy diet, stop feeding us so much pork, and give us some fresh fruit daily.

11. Modernize the inmate education system.

12. Give us a doctor that will examine and treat all inmates that request treatment.

13. Have an institutional delegation comprised of one inmate from each company authorized to speak to the institution administration concerning grievances (QUARTERLY).

14. Give us less cell time and more recreation with better recreational equipment and facilities.

15. Remove inside walls, making one open yard, and no more segregation or punishment.

Mixed in with political demands, an unacceptable amendment of parole, and a call for the removal of disciplinary measures, was what I considered to be a traditional statement of prison reform. I could have written many of the "practical proposals" myself. I had in fact been working toward their implementation before Attica and not, as was afterward charged, in response to Attica.

But the second meeting in D Yard left me deeply depressed. Any concession to demands for complete amnesty and for transshipment to "non-imperialistic" countries would mean an impossible infringement on the rule of law and an immense stimulus for crime and militancy. This was, indeed, as we had begun to see ever since San Quentin, a call not for prison reform but for revolution and anarchy beginning in the prisons.

At 5:55 P.M., only seven minutes after I had gone into D Yard, Deputy Commissioner van Eekeren received an urgent telephone call from Superintendent J. Edwin LaVallee at Dannemora. The superintendent had "buttoned up" the institution for the night, locking the men in that early because they were in an ugly, explosive mood. The news of Attica was all over Dannemora by television and transistor radio. There were rumors that the industrial buildings would be set on fire in the morning. A white, Italian-American group of prisoners was particularly active.

Superintendent LaVallee said he was holding overnight more than fifty corrections officers from the day shift. There were fifty State Police troopers on the alert at nearby Malone, New York, and there were two State Police officers remaining in the institution to co-ordinate any action that might be needed. Superintendent LaVallee said he would take no chances, but he thought that everything was safe till the next morning.

At 6:00 P.M. Governor Rockefeller told his staff he was concerned about any flow of outside people into the Attica vicinity and he inquired about emergency powers to cordon off the entire area.

At Attica at 6:44 P.M. our despondent delegation came trooping tiredly out of D Yard. We had no alternative, I felt, but to continue the negotiations.

Shortly before 7:00 P.M. I spoke with Mr. Whiteman in Albany and briefed him on the situation at Attica. Major Monahan joined the conversation and, in response to Michael Whiteman's question, ventured his private opinion that I was pursuing the proper course of action.

At 7:00 P.M. Governor Rockefeller was informed there was no need to cordon off the Attica area, because the access routes were adequately controlled. He was also informed of my decision to continue negotiations. He inquired about relief for the State Police troopers who would have to stay on at the correctional facility during the night. He was told there would be 500 to 600 troopers, working in shifts. Finally, the governor expressed concern that delay might attract numerous people and extensive discussion that could prove to be counterproductive. He expressed the hope that any appearance of vacillation and indecision could be avoided, whatever the course of action.

Not long afterward, I spoke with the governor on the telephone and told him why we were going to continue the negotiations. I said we would hold further police action "in abeyance" until we found out whether we could obtain the peaceful release of the hostages. Governor Rockefeller was affirmative on my decision.

Deputy Commissioner William Baker, one of my closest associates and friends, visited my wife in the hospital at Albany at eight o'clock that night. He told her I had been into D Yard not once, but twice, and that I was safe and busy with the negotiations. "I knew he would go in," she said. "I was very proud that he did. He's that kind of person. He always feels he should reason with people and try to get them to see the other side of the story, not be hasty and rash about things, about a decision.

"But, I just keep wondering, how long can he keep his composure?"

It had been a long day since I awakened at 5:30 that morning at my home in Schenectady.

CHAPTER 5

Out of Chaos Came the Twenty-eight Points

Now Governor Rockefeller sent two of his senior advisers to the scene. I conferred with them in the superintendent's office between midnight and 1:00 A.M. on Friday, September 10. Also on hand for the meeting were Walter Dunbar, Vincent Mancusi, and Chief Inspector John Miller of the New York State Police.

One of the gubernatorial advisers was Dr. T. Norman Hurd, with whom I had enjoyed close personal and working relationships for the previous twelve years. Dr. Hurd, sixty-one years old, is a native of Cedar River, Michigan, a graduate of Michigan State College in the class of 1931, with a Ph.D. in business management from the New York State College of Agriculture at Cornell University. By appointment of Governor Thomas E. Dewey, Dr. Hurd was state farm manpower director during the Second World War and, after the war, secretary of the New York State Food Commission.

Norm Hurd served both Governor Dewey and Governor Rockefeller as Director of the Budget. I considered him to be one of the most influential friends of our parole concepts and programs in the state government. He had recently been promoted to the over-all responsibility of Director of State Operations.

Major General Almerin C. "Buzz" O'Hara was another old friend of my thirteen years' service with the state government. Sixty years old, he had begun his military career as a private in the 10th Infantry of the New York Army National Guard in 1934 and six years later he entered federal service as a first lieutenant with the 27th Infantry (New York) Division. During the Second World War he served in the Pacific campaigns as a company commander, regimental S-2 and S-3 and as battalion commander of the 2nd Battalion, 106th Infantry Regiment of the 27th Division.

After combat service on Majuro and Saipan, Buzz O'Hara planned and led the first night attack of the Okinawa campaign, spearheading the drive through the Shuri Line at a crucial point in the battle. He won the Silver Star for gallantry on Saipan and the Bronze Star with oak leaf cluster for valor on Okinawa.

With steady postwar promotion through the National Guard, he became commanding general and chief of staff to the governor. His new assignment was commissioner of the Office of General Services, in charge of much of the logistics of the state government.

In our meeting in the small hours of Friday, September 10, the discussion concerned my decision—endorsed by the governor—to hold further action against the rebel prisoners in abeyance. Our emphasis was now to be focused on negotiations for the peaceful release of the thirty-eight remaining hostages.

Since my second meeting with the rebel leaders in D Yard, we had conducted what might for simplicity's sake be termed a three-point approach to the problem. We were seeking a federal court order in which would be embodied our assurance that there would be no administrative reprisals against the prisoners. We agreed to form a committee of outside observers including nominees of the rebel leaders. We were also considering the fifteen "practical proposals" given me by the rebel leaders. Their fifteen proposals, unlike their five "immediate demands," included several very reasonable prison reforms.

Earlier in the evening of September 9 we had made some progress on two of these points, or so it seemed to us. Walter Dunbar revisited D Yard on two occasions, accompanied by Professor Schwartz and Assemblymen Eve and Emery, to refine the fifteen "practical proposals" with the rebel leaders. In the course of these discussions, he heard that one of the hostages, Corrections Officer James Clute, was in considerable pain from injuries. Mr. Dunbar advised the rebel leaders they should release Mr. Clute "for your own good," and the officer was brought out on a stretcher and taken to the hospital. On the following Saturday afternoon Corrections Officer Anthony Sangiacomo, suffering from a high blood pressure condition, would also be released by the rebels.

Mr. Dunbar and the rebel leaders agreed that an outside doctor and a chaplain would be permitted to visit the hostages. Dr. Warren Hanson of Warsaw, New York, treated the hostages and some of the inmates and reported that most of the hostages had been blindfolded since Thursday midday. But they were otherwise in as good a condition as might be expected. An Episcopal priest made a round of the hostages and said he would contact their families.

Later, the three chaplains of the facility, Father Eugene Marcinkiewicz, the Reverend Eligius Rainer, and Rabbi Daniel Kerman visited the hostages. Their services were exemplary. We also took three prisoners' representatives, including the leader, Roger Champen—Champ—on a tour of C Block. Together, they verified that the inmates there had been neither beaten nor gassed and had been given their evening meal.

Mr. Dunbar sent two of the inmate representatives back to their territory and brought Champ to the superintendent's office for a talk with me. He went over some of our ideas on the wording of the proposed court order and then returned to D Yard.

None of this amounted to a single, specific concession from the rebel leaders, but the atmosphere was more positive and promising than anything we had yet experienced at Attica.

At the midnight meeting with Dr. Hurd and General O'Hara, we now took stock of the somewhat more stabilized situation. The rebels were tense and hostile, but would probably take no further action against the hostages in the current phase of the negotiations. The rebels seemed genuinely concerned about the federal court order and about the formation of the group of outside observers. So we decided to proceed at full speed.

At 1:00 A.M. Professor Schwartz and I telephoned Judge John T. Curtin, of the U. S. District Court in Buffalo, who was attending a judicial conference at Manchester, Vermont. Judge Curtin, protégé of former Attorney General Robert F. Kennedy, had once defined his philosophy: "The court should be a place where anybody can come—whatever they have in their pocket— and be able to file a complaint in simple fashion and at least have somebody give consideration to it and give them opportunity to be heard."

Judge Curtin agreed to sign a federal court injunction forbidding us to take administrative reprisals against the prisoners and I agreed to sign my consent to it. I was grateful to the judge for his attention to our problem in the middle of the night. I was also quite optimistic that the injunction would lead to release of the hostages.

Professor Schwartz shared my hope. He volunteered to make what we called the "night ride to Vermont." He took with him Ernest Montanye, the Director of Correctional Camps of our department, whom I had now brought to Attica as an additional executive officer. I was watching Mr. Montanye's performance carefully, and months later I would designate him to be the new superintendent at Attica upon the retirement of Vincent Mancusi.

Professor Schwartz and Mr. Montanye headed out of Attica in a State Police car to the Buffalo airport, where a state plane was waiting for them. They attempted to fly to Glens Falls, New York, not far from Manchester, but the weather was too thick for them to make the landing. So they came down at the Albany County airport and drove on through the night to Manchester. At 3:30 A.M., in this most picturesque of Vermont communities, Judge Curtin signed the federal court order. Herman Schwartz and Ernest Montanye were driven at high speed back to Albany. They caught the plane for Buffalo and soon were brought to Attica.

At 7:00 A.M. Friday, September 10, Professor Schwartz reported to the superintendent's office at Attica with federal court order in hand. It looked good to me. I had been waiting up all night for it.

Here it is:

United States: District Court
Western District: New York

INMATES OF ATTICA CORRECTIONAL FACILITY
Plaintiffs

VS   ORDER

NELSON ROCKERFELLER, GOVERNOR: COMMISSIONER OF CORRECTION OSWALD VINCENT MANCUSI, WARDEN

Defendants.

Upon the consent of defendants, it is hereby ORDERED that:

Defendants, their agents and employers, are enjoined from taking any physical or other administrative reprisals against any inmates participating in the disturbance at the Attica Correctional Facility on September 9, 1971.

John T. Curtin
U.S.D.J.

U.S.D.J.

September 10, 1971

Consented to:
  Russell G. Oswald
  Russell G. Oswald
  Commissioner of Correctional Services

I intended to use the court order as a dramatic demonstration of my good faith. I hoped it might be a useful lever in the next round of talks on the rebel leaders' demand for complete criminal amnesty. I also intended to honor it to the full in the event that the rebels accepted it, released the hostages, and returned to their cells.

But the rebel leaders turned out to be not as impressed with the federal order as they had been the night before—and this was the first indication of a hardening attitude, rather than vice versa. They were especially concerned that Judge Motley had not signed the court order, as they had hoped.

Our first indication came when Thomas Soto, a representative of the Prisoners' Solidarity League, affiliated with Youth Against War and Fascism, was shown a copy of the federal court order by Professor Schwartz. Mr. Soto was one of the rebel nominees for the outside observer group, and he had already arrived at Attica. Thomas Soto had not been inside the prison, but he said the court order would not be acceptable to his group at least, presumably meaning the radical Prisoners' Solidarity League. He said the order could be appealed and therefore meant nothing. Professor Schwartz explained that the order was not subject to appeal, because it was an order by consent. But Mr. Soto then said protection from administrative reprisals was meaningless and the prisoners ought to be freed because their crimes were only crimes of "survival."

At 8:30 A.M. Professor Schwartz went to the DMZ and showed the court order to the rebel leader Brother Richard. According to one account of this meeting, Brother Richard said, "What are you doing, playing games with us? This paper's no good. There's no seal on it." Here showed the influence of the jailhouse lawyer, Jerry Rosenberg, but, in fact, the court order did not have a seal on it. The reason was that Judge Curtin did not have his sealing machine with him in Manchester, Vermont. So we had a "morning ride to Buffalo," and, in Judge Curtin's office, the judge's staff affixed the seal.

When the federal court order was taken into D Yard for consideration by the rebel leaders as we began our next scheduled meeting, Jerry Rosenberg took it in hand and tore it down the middle. He said the federal court order was meaningless. The crowd of inmates in D Yard roared their consent.

During the morning of Friday, September 10, Dr. Hurd and General O'Hara now moved to the forefront. Dr. Hurd coordinated our efforts to form the outside observer group. General O'Hara concentrated on improving our capability to recapture the rest of the prison as humanely as possible if the negotiations broke down. At all times they stressed that I was in charge at Attica and they did nothing that morning or at any other time without consulting with me and, when necessary, obtaining my approval. They maintained just as effective liaison with Walter Dunbar, Vincent Mancusi, Chief Inspector Miller, and Major Monahan.

This cordiality of operations was a testament in itself to the experience of Dr. Hurd and General O'Hara. The arrival in the midst of a crisis of men as senior but not as talented as Dr. Hurd and General O'Hara might have precipitated a command problem. But I was always glad to have these two friends on board.

Dr. Hurd telephoned Michael Whiteman, the governor's counsel, at 8:00 A.M. He said the radical nominees of the prisoners for the proposed outside observer group were doubtless on their way, but that it ought to be possible to bring more moderate community leaders to Attica to achieve a balance. He put up one idea of mine for a panel of ombudsmen to consist of Assemblyman Eve, a black, plus a white minister from Buffalo, and a designee of

United States Congressman Herman Badillo, a prominent Puerto
Rican politician in New York City.

At approximately 10:00 A.M. Norm Hurd and Michael Whiteman conferred again, and Mr. Whiteman was asked to look
into the possibility of inviting Minister Louis Farrahkan, a prominent Black Muslim in New York City. Minister Farrahkan had
proven extremely helpful in listening to prisoners' grievances during an earlier disturbance at the Men's House of Detention in
New York City. Dr. Hurd also asked Mr. Whiteman to follow up
my suggestion about Congressman Badillo. Within the half hour,
Robert R. Douglass, the governor's secretary, spoke to Congressman Badillo, who said he was willing to go to Attica himself, and
to take a young Puerto Rican with him if that would be helpful.
Mr. Douglass spoke with the Reverend Wyatt Tee Walker, a
special assistant to the governor for Urban Affairs, who told him
that Minister Farrahkan was so important he was deemed to be a
possible successor to the mantle of Malcolm X. But Minister Farrahkan could not be located, and this would turn out to be another of the disappointments of Attica, since the Muslims were
the most moderate group in the rebel coalition.

Mr. Douglass invited Mr. Walker himself to go to Attica with
Clarence B. Jones, the publisher of the *Amsterdam News* in Harlem. Both were veterans of the civil rights struggles in the
Deep South, as aides to the late Reverend Martin Luther King,
Jr. Mr. Badillo asked State Senator Robert Garcia of the Bronx
to accompany him. The governor's staff arranged for air transportation for these community leaders, who would be joined by Alfredo Matthew, Jr., principal of Community School District No.
3 in New York City.

Norm Hurd reported these fast-moving and encouraging developments. I was delighted that we were achieving a much more
balanced observer group than would have otherwise been the case.

I also thought it would be advisable, and so did Dr. Hurd, if
several responsible state legislators were invited for the discussions. Assemblymen Eve and Emery were already on hand. They
would soon be joined by State Senator John R. Dunne, forty-one
years old, of Garden City, Long Island, chairman of the Joint
Legislative Committee on Crime and Corrections; and by State
Senator Thomas F. McGowan, who had served ten years on the
Buffalo police force before he became assistant district attorney

for Erie County. Two other assemblymen, both Republicans, more
or less dropped by to do what they could to help. They were Frank
Walkley, representing Allegany and Wyoming Counties and part
of Erie County, and Clark C. Wemple, of Schenectady, who is
much interested in prison reform.*

It is important in retrospect to remember how the moderates
strove to make the outside observer group work—especially since
the group was often considered by the corrections officers and
others to be little more than a radical front.

One of my associates commented to me, "You've gone completely out of your mind permitting these radical people to come
into a prison. Some of them have been kicking the daylights out
of the Establishment from all vantage points and for years. They
will contribute nothing to you in settling these issues."

On the other hand, even as far as the radicals were concerned,
I had had a great deal of dialogue over the years with black and
Puerto Rican inmates as well as whites, and I felt the radicals
might be helpful. I knew how many of the prisoners at Attica
found it difficult to relate to "straight" people and regular personnel. If we could talk to the rebel inmates through the radicals
in the outside group, balance the judgments within the committee,
and refine the rebel terms for the release of the hostages, then I
was for that.

Meanwhile, General O'Hara was working effectively in his own
sphere. His major move, and I approved and applauded it, was
to bring to Attica, through the co-operation of Major General
John C. Baker, two National Guard helicopters with the capability
of dropping CS gas. A helicopter drop of CS gas had never been
used in a prison riot anywhere in the world, but General O'Hara
was confident it would be effective. However, the helicopters
would not be available until late that afternoon, and an additional
period of ten hours or more would be needed to prepare gas canisters and prime mechanisms.

General O'Hara and the New York State Police also monitored
the military standoff closely. At 8:00 A.M. Friday we were told by
one of our sources inside the prison that the rebel leaders were
going to try to take back C Block and the hundreds of inmates
inside. Our State Police troopers on guard at C Block were given

---

* New York State Correction Law, Section 146, expressly permits any state
legislator to visit, at pleasure, all correctional facilities.

orders to open fire if and when any rebels broke the locks on the now-securely fastened C Block doors. General O'Hara passed instructions to the New York National Guard to send a liaison team to Attica—in civilian clothes and equipped with a two-way radio.

Governor Rockefeller was briefed on this potentially explosive new situation. At 10:45 A.M. some rebels made a move across their occupied yards toward C Block. They viewed our defenses there and apparently concluded C Block was a tougher nut to crack than when Pappy Wald, Sergeant Reger, and Officer Delany held the block office on their own, for no attack came.

Then there were rumors in midmorning that the rebels intended to try to break out across the wall, using hostages as shields. I reiterated my orders to prevent any attempt at a breakout, using gunfire if necessary. But nothing happened.

It had been a difficult morning.

Our success in obtaining the federal court order from Judge Curtin had come to nothing. Our truce looked extremely shaky. The formation of an outside observer group was going well—but would there be any rapport with the rebels?

Everything was now pointing to my third meeting with the rebel leaders. At 10:06 A.M. we sent a message through the rebels in the DMZ, requesting that their leaders meet with me, with three outside observers, and with news media coverage in the DMZ, with security guaranteed for both sides. The message came back with the handwritten notes across it: "No good. . . . We will meet only in D Block."

At 11:00 A.M. a handwritten message from the rebels was passed to us through A Gate in the DMZ. It read: "This is a people issue, not a group. Therefore you must bring your observers, etc. to the people. What happened to the people who were on our list of demands? Also, what has happened to the food, water, etc.?" (See reproduction of notes on following page.)

The climate for the third meeting was chill.

At one point that morning, Governor Rockefeller was on the telephone with Mr. Whiteman about a water problem at Attica: "Why was the water cut off?" he asked. It turned out the rebels had broken a standpipe in the first battle and, as a consequence, the water reserve had drained away. It was another crisis within a crisis. But we had ordered water trucks to Attica. We also ordered up 1,400 fried egg sandwiches, 1,400 sliced American

This is a people issue not a group therefore you must bring your observers, etc to the people.

What happened to the people who were on our list of demands???

Also what has happened to the food Water, etc?

9/10
Rec'd 11AM

WE will MEET only
in D-Block

9-10-'71
10:06 A.M.

Pt. #1 —
Meeting effected within one half hour with Commissioner Oswald and 3 outside observers and representatives of news media, and your Committee.

Pt #2 —
Meeting to be held in A Block corridor between the square and A Block, with guaranteed security for both sides.

Pt #3 —
Double checked — No Shooting D Block area.

NO GOOD

cheese sandwiches, and coffee with milk and sugar in fifteen-gallon pots along with Styrofoam cups.

At 11:24 A.M. on Friday I went down to the DMZ for the "ritual-and-routine" procedure before entry into rebel territory at Attica. This was to be my third meeting with the rebel leaders and I had with me, once again, Professor Schwartz, Assemblymen Eve and Emery, and five representatives of the news media. I also took into D Yard four newly arrived members of the forming outside observer group. They were State Senator Thomas McGowan; Lewis Steel of the movement-oriented National Lawyers Guild; and the Reverend Marion Chandler and the Reverend B. T. Scott, both associated with FIGHT, the principal black anti-poverty and community improvement organization in Rochester.

This time, the members of my staff seemed ready to restrain me physically from entering rebel territory. Buzz O'Hara joined Walter Dunbar at A Gate and they counseled me emphatically to meet the rebels only on neutral ground. Walter seemed quite sure, this time, that I would be taken as the principal hostage. He gripped my arm and said, "Commissioner, I've never given you an order before, but I'm ordering you not to go back to that yard." I said, "I'm going in," and I shook my friend to one side.

Now for the ritual-and-routine we had established with the Black Muslim patrol at the gate: Whenever one of our side wanted to go into rebel territory, the Muslims would get the word of the rebel leaders that the outsiders would not be harmed and would be permitted to come out safely. Then a time period would be established. A deadline would be set for the exit of our people. If it turned out they needed more time in D Yard, then a member of the group would come back to the DMZ to set a new time deadline.

Often it was Assemblyman Emery who volunteered for new deadline duty, and this was a more dangerous mission because it meant that he had to spend more time than the rest of us passing through the mercurial crowds. Forty years old, a graduate of Livonia Central School and the University of Cincinnati College of Business Administration, Mr. Emery had served as an Air Force officer in the Korean War and was a major in the United States Air Force Reserve. He had been elected to the Assembly in 1964 from the 136th Assembly District of Genesee and Livingston Counties, and he had been re-elected ever since. In my opinion, Assemblyman Emery was one of the outstanding members of the outside group.

There, once again in front of us, on the other side of the negotiating table in D Yard, was the rebel leadership, once again less Sam Melville, who was off somewhere probably working on the defenses. Brother Richard was seated in the center of the table, shaven-headed, bespectacled, incisive as ever, with Jerry Rosenberg at his right. Brother Herbert was standing behind and to the left of Brother Richard, wearing a T-shirt, cloth skullcap and a pair of enormous black sunglasses. L.D., with the granny glasses, wore a light sports shirt over his prison issue trousers. He looked young enough to be the son of many of the other men behind the table. L.D. remained standing; his tall, thin body seemed almost like a spear held by the rest.

At once there was an uproar from the hundreds of men, and I was no longer a negotiator—only a target for the crowd. A young man standing right behind me started to shout in my ear. Soon others screamed that I had given incorrect information to a newspaperman, that I was not to be trusted, that no corrections people were to be believed, that "Oswald's a liar," "Oswald's a racist pig," and all the usual unprintables.

I tried to reason with some of the men closest to me, but it was useless. Now they were on the subject of reprisals—no mention of the federal court order. A man shouted there had been reprisals after the riot at Auburn in November. "How can you tell us that there won't be reprisals?" I said, "Because I'm telling you there won't be reprisals." "How can you say that?" "Did I ever tell you before that I would do something and not do it?" I said, "It just so happens that if I say there will be no reprisals, there will be no reprisals, and let's let that stand."

One man in the crowd started yelling, "Let's keep Oswald." The shouts went up, "We ought to keep Oswald." "We better keep Oswald here."

Now there were men over on my left, over beyond the end of the negotiating table, who were yelling, "We better keep Oswald here. He doesn't believe we mean business," and they added more obscenities.

One man's voice broke through the tumult: "We'll tell you this, that if any armed force is used here, we'll kill every one of these hostages, and maybe we ought to show him we mean business by hanging one of them right now."

Shouts of "Right on!" and more cheering, and then another voice spoke lucidly from the crowd:

"We want you to remember this, that if you come in with force, you may take over, take back this facility, but you won't be able to keep us locked up forever. And the first time we're unlocked again, we'll take the institution again, and if we're locked up again, we'll be unlocked, and we'll take it again, and we'll take it again." There were more shouts of "Right on!"

It was incredible to me that the leaders behind the table were sitting there silently amid this appalling noise. Eventually I realized why: It was movement doctrine to let "all the people" speak and it must have been prearranged, presumably with a view to intimidating me.

So I sat across the table from them as calmly as possible, and I asked them all, staring at them one by one, whether they were men of their word. I said, "I came in here in good faith. I presumed you were men of your word. You promised me safe passage back to the institution and I'm expecting you to deliver." I reminded them that we had returned Champ back to rebel territory after his tour of C Block and his visit in our office the previous evening.

But then Champ came from a huddle at one end of the table and stood up to make a speech. I expected him to try to bring some sense into the crowd and to demand that I be let go, but Champ talked about some of the grievances and sat down.

So I addressed myself to Brother Richard and Brother Herbert. "What goes on here? Can't you control this group?" I asked. Brother Herbert looked at me and he shook his head and said, "You think you've got troubles. How would you like to be us? How would you like these troubles? How would you like to try and control this?"

I said, "Well, you know I've got my own troubles, and I see you've got troubles, but that's your job to control them now. I'm in here and I'm expecting you to get me out. And please keep in mind that I'm worth a lot more out there to you than I am in here."

And I added, "Sooner or later there is someone you are going to have to trust—you are going to have to trust me."

I reminded them, "If I weren't out there, do you think that you would be here on this Friday afternoon? There would have been an armed force in here for you, before you hardly even got here.

"I'm the one who's trying now to talk with you and reason and hopefully the two of us can be sufficiently mature to work out of this and improve conditions at the same time."

Brother Herbert replied, "Well, you just relax now. Don't get uptight about it. We'll get you out of here. Don't worry about that. We'll see that it happens."

There was some discussion with the leaders; they confirmed they had rejected Judge Curtin's federal court order as a guarantee of no administrative reprisals and they repeated their demand that the leaders be released and transshipped to other countries. The rebel leaders intensified their demand for an outside observer group and were told this was being formed.

Then came time for Brother Herbert to deliver on his promise to get me out—which had neither been approved nor opposed by any of the other leaders. This was done when enough members of the Black Muslim security force surrounded me, lined up with linked arms along the route back to the DMZ, and rushed me out through an insanely screaming mob.

At 12:45 P.M., one minute after our set deadline, we emerged from rebel territory. There could be no question of my going back in there again. Of course, Walter Dunbar and the others were right: I would be *the* logical hostage to hold for ransom. In retrospect, I was lucky to get out.

All through Friday we kept watch not only on the Attica rebellion but on the tense situation at all of the six other maximum-security institutions statewide. All of our efforts had to be concentrated on maintaining routines and schedules elsewhere in the system, not for bureaucratic reasons but simply to keep things cool. To lock the men in their cells, for example, would be to bottle up and increase tensions to the detonation point. On the other hand, the men had to be kept under a greater degree of security during Attica, if only because they were jumpy and excited. At all costs, Attica must not become a flashfire spreading across the state.

During the day a stream of reports arrived in Albany from Superintendent LaVallee at Dannemora indicating continued tension. However, by 4:20 P.M. Superintendent LaVallee reported all quiet under a reinforced staff, with the State Police standing by at nearby Malone. If the calm was maintained, he said, there would be normal routine the next day, including movies. This was the best news we were to hear all Friday.

Meanwhile Allen F. Mills, director of the Division of Industry, arranged for emergency shipments of food, clothing, and bedding to be trucked to Attica, often under State Police escort.

At 4:30 P.M., however, Deputy Commissioner van Eekeren received a call from Deputy Commissioner Baker that the corrections officers at Elmira were now extremely concerned about the whole situation. The Elmira branch of the principal corrections officers' union—Council 82, American Federation of State, County and Municipal Employees, AFL-CIO—was meeting to decide whether or not to keep the men locked up in their cells on Saturday morning.

Bill Baker told Dr. van Eekeren that the superintendent of Elmira, Daniel E. Damon, Jr., seemed to be willing to go along with the union local if the men decided not to unlock the cells.

Dr. van Eekeren instructed Mr. Baker to alert one of our ablest superintendents and trouble-shooters for possible emergency assignment to Elmira. This was Harold Butler, superintendent of the Wallkill medium-security institution. Meanwhile, John Van De Car, our Director of Manpower and Employee Relations, maintained constant communication with the union leaders.

That evening Harold Butler went to Elmira as an acting deputy commissioner in over-all charge. The superintendent co-operated and the union did not lock in. I approved the decisions taken.

This confrontation at Elmira was very important and had it not occurred in the midst of Attica, it would have been sensational in itself.

Later on Friday evening, the Albany command post heard from our public information director, Gerald Houlihan, at Attica, suggesting that they check out a rumor that the situation was tense at Auburn. That might have been the real blowup. But at 10:10 P.M. Assistant Commissioner Robert Fosen talked to Corrections Lieutenant Issensmith at Auburn and was told it had been a normal day.

During Friday afternoon and evening, a total of thirty-four outside observers arrived at Attica to serve on what would now be formally called the Citizens Observer Committee. At 3:30 P.M. I made public our invitations to Congressman Badillo, Senator Garcia, the Reverend Wyatt Walker, Alfredo Matthew, and Clarence Jones, to sit with me during the negotiations. They arrived in an official New York State plane. Other observers were arriving, some with prepaid tickets from Assemblyman Eve and his office in Buffalo.

Assemblyman Eve, a prime mover in assembling the Citizens Observer Committee, was a VIP at Attica. Since his election to the Assembly in 1966, Mr. Eve, a Democrat, had been responsible for the development of Project SEEK in Buffalo and upstate New York. This project was funded at $7 million in 1969 and $10 million in 1970. He had served as temporary chairman of the first national attempt to organize black elected officials. Although he was later to reflect and inflame the radical mood of the inmates—and seemingly to lose all perspective in his vicious attacks on the governor and myself—I shall not forget how he stood by me through my three meetings with the rebel leaders in D Yard.

The assemblyman brought to Attica almost at once the key nominees of the rebel leaders. These included two members of the Young Lords, Juan Ortiz and José "G.I." Paris, and the man who would become the principal celebrity and television performer of the Citizens Observer Committee, Attorney William Kunstler. Thomas Soto of the Prisoners' Solidarity League had been waiting for some time outside the prison gates.

Assemblyman Eve also brought in another celebrity whose attendance the inmates had requested. This was Tom Wicker, a columnist for the New York *Times*. Mr. Wicker is one of the practitioners of the so-called "new journalism." In this style, the journalist becomes something more than an objective witness and reporter of events to the public. He becomes personally involved in his story, in the people he is writing about, and he writes to communicate feelings and emotion to the public as well as interpretation and fact.

The "New Journalist" pays for this, of course, in reduced credibility among readers more interested in facts about an event than in a reporter's emotions.

Mr. Wicker had once written movingly about how he watched a parade of demonstrators go by at the Democratic National Convention at Chicago in 1968, and how he had longed to join it but felt he should not. But now Mr. Wicker was a columnist, rather than a reporter, and he was entitled to express his emotions and opinions as he chose.

Tom Wicker was shocked by the fact of imprisonment itself— and he was to identify with the imprisoned as a part of "what's wrong with America." Mr. Wicker, a North Carolinian, was intensely sympathetic with oppressed blacks anywhere. But Tom Wicker went utterly overboard, in my opinion, in a subsequent column that said the state had no heart for the "animals" caged at Attica. This was writing that was simply not true.

The Citizens Observer Committee was joined that day by several other "involved" newsmen. These were Richard Roth of the Buffalo *Courier-Express,* who had only recently interviewed inmates at Attica and understood the problems; James Ingraham, of the *Michigan Chronicle* of Detroit, requested by the inmates; and two TV reporters, Roland Barnes and Jay Lamarche of WGR-TV Buffalo, who stayed most of the time in D Yard and defied our instructions to come out.

David Anderson, former executive director of the Rochester Urban League, served on the committee along with his fellow townsmen the Reverend Marion Chandler and the Reverend B. T. Scott of FIGHT, who had attended my third meeting with the rebel leaders. William Gaiter was the director of BUILD in Buffalo, one of the leading anti-poverty organizations in the state, and he served on the committee along with another man from BUILD, Domingo Rodriquez. Alberto O. Cappas joined us from the State University of New York at Albany. The Reverend Franklin Florence was also of FIGHT in Rochester.

Daniel Skoler of the American Bar Association in Washington called and asked me if he could be of assistance, and I said something like "Come right on up if you choose." Two other volunteers came from Washington at the same time: Julian Tepper and W. O. Fitch of the National Law Office. Lewis Steel was already on hand from the National Lawyers Guild.

Into this improbable blend of talents swept the Reverend Jaybarr Ali Kenyatta of a Sunni Muslim sect in Los Angeles, swathed in cloaks and robes, topped by a blue turban. He latched onto reporter James Ingraham at the Buffalo airport and was later vouched for by Assemblyman Eve, after he had literally gatecrashed the committee at Attica. Many thought he was the

Black Muslim member of the committee. I must admit I let him in because I thought he was the highly regarded black nationalist leader Charles 37X Kenyatta of New York City.

Jaybarr Ali Kenyatta was one of Attica's disasters. Instead of a moderate Black Muslim voice on the committee, we soon had rabble-rousing dialectics. He also said he had been a prisoner at Attica and this made him "relevant." Once accepted on the committee, he was kept on till the end.

All afternoon and all evening I briefed the newly arriving members of the committee on the fifteen "practical proposals" submitted to me by the rebel leaders. I was still convinced there was a potential prison reform program mixed in with the unacceptable demands and so, to my surprise, was William Kunstler.

Mr. Kunstler had arrived at Attica in the evening with a shocking initial statement. "If they were my clients," he said, the issue would be complete amnesty. He would later do incalculable damage, in my judgment, with his persistent advocacy of the amnesty demand that we could not and would not grant. But Mr. Kunstler performed yeoman service with his lawyer's pencil as he went over the fifteen proposals and helped me fashion them into an acceptable program.

While I was updating the latecomers, usually with Walter Dunbar's assistance, some of the members of the new Citizens Observer Committee went in small groups into D Yard. I thought it interesting, and perhaps significant, that one of the loudest rounds of applause went up not for the radicals but for State Senator John Dunne. He was well known and apparently admired by the inmates for his stands for prison reform. If the opportunity for us was now to negotiate the real demands of prison reform—while splitting off the revolutionary demands—then Senator Dunne would be a real help.

Almost at midnight the last three members of the committee arrived at Attica. They were Mel Rivers, Ken Jackson, and David Rothenberg, executives of the Fortune Society, an organization devoted to helping former convicts. Their reaction was that the committee was far too unwieldy to be effective. They suggested forming a five-man subcommittee. Later, we would indeed form a nine-man subcommittee, with all the other committee members free to join in the discussions. The three Fortune Society men

thought the whole thing was going down, so they went back to
New York City and played no role at Attica.

Just before midnight—it was almost the start of the third day—
the first army of twenty-nine of the observers passed through the
DMZ to meet with the rebel leaders in D Yard. Not long before,
Julian Tepper and W. O. Fitch of the National Law Office and a
few others had met to try to define their mission. "In a hurried
but careful manner," they wrote later for the Washington *Post*,
"we decided that we must remain neutral intermediaries if we are
to have any chance of preventing the loss of the hostages' lives."
But at least one observer, Thomas Soto, said he was for the inmates all the way. Mr. Eve had felt Mr. Soto should not be
admitted but, at William Kunstler's urgent request, we let him in.

Mr. Tepper and Mr. Fitch described the scene in D Yard: "We
enter a different world, as if crossing through the looking glass into
a scene which is more awesome and forceful than that of the
walled prison. The sky is cloudless tonight. The half moon and
numerous bonfires illuminate the courtyard. The inmates are
standing arm in arm on both sides of a path leading to the negotiating tables which are at one end of the yard. Behind one line, in
the yard, are numerous makeshift tents. Sporadic greeting and
feelings of appreciation are voiced from inmates whom we pass."

All night the twenty-nine observers, joined by the three men
from the Fortune Society, with the two TV reporters from Buffalo
hovering somewhere in the yard, made contact with hundreds of
rebel prisoners. The first two hours or so were devoted to what
Mr. Tepper called "a controlled, efficient discussion of the issues."
All the rebel leaders were there, even Sam Melville, who slipped
out a handwritten message through one of the citizen observers:

Agincourt. Evening around the campfire.
Power People! We are strong. We are together. We are
growing. We love you all.
Ho Ho Ho Chi Minh. Please inform our next of kin.

At 1:15 A.M. there was a scare in D Yard that National Guardsmen were crawling in for a night attack. Not true, but the rebels
were able to demonstrate some of their organization and efficiency. The Citizens Observer Committee was moved behind the

tables and a solid wall of security men stood on and in front of the tables arm in arm, presumably to protect our members from the intransigent gunfire of the Guard. Senator Dunne said later he thought it was a deliberate false alarm.

The third phase of the all-night sessions was a kind of town meeting on prison reform, as one of the observers put it, in which Brother Herbert Blyden acted as a moderator of sorts. He asked the inmates to state their grievances and one by one many did. Mr. Kunstler wrote the grievances down so he could later add them to the fifteen "practical proposals."

In fact, the whole meeting encouraged the inmates. Here were the representatives of the outside world, brought there in the third day of the revolution, writing down everything the inmates had to say. There had never been anything like this in their prison before—and the prestige of the leaders was augmented.

Then the all-night affair moved into an impassioned bout of revolutionary oratory. Brother Flip Crowley was in his element. In one of several speeches, he said, "We do not want to rule, we only want to live. But if any of you gentlemen own dogs, you are treating them better than we are treated here." Elliott Barclay, the formidable L.D., tried to inspire the inmates with their world-wide role, and he demanded again and again that the political prisoners be released and transshipped to "non-imperialistic" countries. At that point, Mr. Kunstler did not think the inmates were serious about that particular demand, but L.D. was. Tom Wicker noted a remark by an inmate that later was revealed in the *Village Voice*. Mr. Wicker's inmate said, "I stand on my own. If amnesty can be had for all of us, and it's guaranteed that we get it, I'm ready to do what we've got to do to get behind that. But the silent majority ain't saying s——. I'm not concerned about Algiers, Africa, or anywhere else." But L.D. was.

At 4:30 A.M. twenty-eight members of the Citizens Observer Committee left D Yard and passed through the DMZ. They were welcomed back by Walter Dunbar, who had kept watch at A Gate all night. But four members of the committee stayed behind in D Yard to take down messages and notes to be smuggled out of the prison. They encouraged the men to stand fast. These four were the Reverend Jaybarr Ali Kenyatta, the two Young Lords, Juan Ortiz and José Paris, and Tom Soto. I was still up in my office, listening to the distant cheers and "Right ons," when I angrily sent for the four men to come out of D Yard at once. Also, the two TV men from Buffalo were somewhere in the yard and could not be located.

Between 4:30 A.M. and 7:15 A.M. the Observer Committee met in the steward's small office on the second floor of the Administration Building. Mr. Wicker described this meeting as "an encounter group." But Assemblyman Eve put an end to the shouting matches when he put down one of the radicals: "You're talking about all these other places, and you're going on with your rhetoric b—— when we're concerned about the lives of the men right here in this prison. You're wasting our time. So just shut up."

At 7:15 A.M. the meeting adjourned, but not without an imaginative, helpful decision. A delegation consisting of Julian Tepper, Tom Wicker, and Clarence Jones was selected to explore the limits of the amnesty situation with the district attorney of Wyoming County, Louis R. James. Julian Tepper telephoned to make the appointment, and the district attorney served a mammoth breakfast of pancakes to the exhausted committeemen at his home in nearby Warsaw. After hearing how sensitive the question of amnesty had become in the Attica situation, with the lives of the hostages at stake, the D.A. agreed to sign a letter that, according to Clarence Jones, "Mr. Frank Hogan, the most powerful district attorney in the state, would never have signed." Here is the letter:

LOUIS R. JAMES

WYOMING COUNTY DISTRICT ATTORNEY

WARSAW, NEW YORK 14569

September 11, 1971

I have been asked by Mssrs. Clarence Jones, Tom Wicker and Julian Tepper, representing the Committee of Observers at Attica Correctional Facility, to express my views as to the possible prosecutions that might arise from recent events at the Facility.

First, I deem it to be my duty as a prosecuting attorney to prosecute without fear or favor ALL substantial crimes committed or apparently committed within this county, if sufficient evidence exists to warrant prosecution.

Second, in prosecuting any crime, I do and would endeavor

to prosecute fairly and impartially and for the sole purpose of attempting to see that justice is done.

Third, under the circumstances of the present situation at Attica, I deem it to be my obligation to prosecute only when in my judgment there is substantial evidence to link a specific individual with the commission of a specific crime.

Fourth, in this particular instance at Attica, I am unalterably opposed to the commencement of indiscriminate mass prosecutions of any and all persons who may have been present, and to prosecutions brought solely for the sake of vindictive reprisals.

Fifth, in the prosecution of any crime, in this as in every other situation, I would endeavor to prosecute honorably, fairly and impartially, with full regard for the rights of the defendants.

Finally, as a prosecuting attorney, I regard it as my paramount duty to attempt to assure justice, both in the trial itself, the outcome of the trial, and in the possible sentence.

Louis R. James
Louis R. James
Wyoming County District Attorney

So yet another amazing day at Attica had come to an end with a bizarre episode. It had begun with the night ride to Vermont. It ended with the pancake breakfast. Already Attica was taking on the shape of a legend even while we lived it.

At any rate, I drove out of the embattled correctional facility for the first time since I had arrived, for two hours sleep and a shower in the Treadway Inn Motel at Batavia. For security reasons, I checked in under an assumed name, as "Mr. George Russell." Nevertheless, a state police plainclothesman kept watch outside my door.

At 10:30 A.M. on Saturday I returned with Walter Dunbar to Attica, refreshed and ready for another day. General O'Hara now had the helicopters on hand with the CS gas drop capability. Governor Rockefeller had telephoned to stress that the State Police must be in the front line of any move to retake the rebel-held territory. The governor would not let this point get away from us in the blur of the crisis.

Already, I found that Norm Hurd had been on the telephone to Michael Whiteman to say that three members of the Citizens Observer Committee were doing more harm than good—Jaybarr Ali Kenyatta, Tom Soto, and William Kunstler. Dr. Hurd stressed that the committee had been formally briefed and shown that the grant of complete criminal amnesty was out of the question, and he thought it was extremely misleading and highly dangerous to continue to talk about amnesty as if it were attainable.

Mr. Whiteman telephoned the governor and re-emphasized that no member of the executive branch could offer complete criminal amnesty since this was outside our constitutional limit. He suggested the most we could agree to was that I would not be a complainant. He stressed to the governor the fact that the governor could not bind a district attorney, a grand jury, or any individual complainants, such as individual corrections officers who might have suffered injury. The governor expressed his agreement on these points.

Around this time, Messrs. Tepper, Wicker, and Jones returned from their breakfast with the district attorney, reasonably pleased with the letter they had brought back. But William Kunstler did not think the letter should even be shown to the inmates because it was, in his view, nothing more than a commitment to uphold the law. He felt the committee might appear to be sanctioning *any kind* of Attica prosecution—and to pass on the letter might seem to be an endorsement of it. Mr. Kunstler was not upheld by the committee, but the decision made was to present the letter to the inmates without comment.

All Saturday afternoon I conferred with the Citizens Observer Committee on the specifics of what now seemed to be our best if not our only mechanism for reaching agreement with the rebel leaders. These were the fifteen "practical proposals" of prison reform, expanded during the all-night meeting in D Yard to almost twice their number. But I made it plain to the committee that the "immediate demands" for complete amnesty, transshipment to other countries, and removal of the superintendent were not negotiable.

Then, together, we sat down as professionals, and we wrote, together, the twenty-eight points of prison reform at Attica. It was the high tide of unity in the crisis. Assemblyman Emery was calling Mr. Kunstler "Bill," and Mr. Kunstler was calling Mr. Emery

"Jim." I felt a tinge of optimism. If the rebel leaders were really interested in prison reform, then they might well accept the twenty-eight points.

The twenty-eight-point proposal was the most a modern prison administration had ever offered rebellious prisoners. On one of the points, our offer to pay prisoners the New York State minimum wage of $1.85 an hour for work in prison industries, I was concerned we might not be able to deliver. I thought the men ought to contribute to their living costs out of their minimum wage, much as all men in the "free world" had to do. I was also aware that it would be extremely difficult to win the needed assent of the New York State Legislature for a minimum wage for convicts. I was also unenthusiastic about one or two of the other twenty-eight points.

I would accept the twenty-eight points, however, and I believed we might be able to obtain approval for all of them if the rebels released the hostages and honored their side of the agreement. When Governor Rockefeller telephoned his approval of the twenty-eight points, I was jubilant.

Here are the twenty-eight points as we wrote them at Attica with my subsequent comment in italics:

PROPOSALS ACCEPTABLE TO COMMISSIONER OSWALD AT THIS TIME

1. Provide adequate food, water, and shelter for all inmates.

2. Inmates shall be permitted to return to their cells or to other suitable accommodations or shelter under their own power. The Observer Committee shall monitor the implementation of this operation.

3. Grant complete administrative amnesty to all persons associated with this matter. By administrative amnesty, the State agrees:

   a. Not to take any adverse parole actions, administrative proceedings, physical punishment, or other type of harassment such as holding inmates incommunicado, segregating any inmates, or keeping them in isolation or in twenty-four-hour lock-up.

b. The State will grant legal amnesty in regard to all civil actions which could arise from this matter.

c. It is agreed that the State of New York and all its departments, divisions, and subdivisions, including the State Department of Corrections and the Attica Correctional Facility, and its employees and agents shall not file or initiate any criminal complaint or act as complainant in any criminal action of any kind or nature relating to property, (or) property-related crimes arising out of the incidents at the Attica Correctional Facility during September 9, 10, 11, 1971.

d. The District Attorney of Wyoming County, New York, has issued and signed the attached letter as of this date.

This was the critical section.

4. Recommend the application of the New York State minimum wage law standards to all work done by inmates. Every effort will be made to make the records of payments available to inmates.

This was the point on which I believed we would have trouble.

5. Establish by October 1, 1971, a permanent ombudsman service for the facility staffed by appropriate persons from the neighboring communities.

I thought this was a splendid point. I was also working on an electronic ombudsman, a closed-circuit TV videotape running day and night in disciplinary quarters so that superintendents could see—and courts rule on—whether guards were beating inmates or vice versa.

6. Allow all New York State prisoners to be politically active, without intimidation or reprisal.

This was a major concession to the radicals.

7. Allow true religious freedom.

8. End all censorship of newspapers, magazines, and other publications from publishers, unless there is determined by qualified authority which includes the ombudsman that the

literature in question presents a clear and present danger to the safety and security of the institution. Institution spot-censoring only of letters.

I wrote in the qualification so we could continue to control such incoming publications as The Anarchist Cookbook.

9. Allow all inmates, at their own expense, to communicate with anyone they please.

This would have to include political contacts within the movement.

10. Institute realistic, effective rehabilitation programs for all inmates according to their offense and personal needs.

This was the whole objective of my administration.

11. Modernize the inmate education system, including the establishment of a Latin library.

This meant Spanish and other modern Latin languages, not traditional Latin.

12. Provide an effective narcotics treatment program for all prisoners requesting such treatment.

13. Provide or allow adequate legal assistance to all inmates requesting it or permit them to use inmate legal assistants of their choice—in any proceeding whatsoever. In all such proceedings, inmates shall be entitled to appropriate due process of law.

This one would be very difficult to manage.

14. Reduce cell time, increase recreation time, and provide better recreation facilities and equipment, hopefully by November 1, 1971.

15. Provide a healthy diet; reduce the number of pork dishes; increase fresh fruit daily.

This met a major, justified grievance of the Black Muslims.

16. Provide adequate medical treatment for every inmate; engage either a Spanish-speaking doctor or inmate interpreters who will accompany Spanish-speaking inmates to medical interviews.

Budget shortages limited our ability to hire Spanish-speaking doctors at twenty-two prisons, unfortunately.

17. Institute a program for the recruitment and employment of a significant number of black and Spanish-speaking officers.

This was another key objective of my administration.

18. Establish an inmate grievance commission, comprised of one elected inmate from each company, which is authorized to speak to the Administration concerning grievances and develop other procedures for inmate participation in the operation and decision-making processes of the institution.

This was one of the key demands of the original fifteen "practical proposals."

19. Investigate the alleged expropriation of inmate funds and the use of profits from the metal and other shops.

20. The State Commissioner of Correctional Services will recommend that the penal law be changed to cease administrative resentencing of inmates returned for parole violation.

This would require legislation.

21. Recommend that Menenchino hearings be held promptly and fairly.

The complex Menenchino parole decisions, which I describe in Chapter 10, hold in general that parolees are entitled to counsel in violation hearings. These hearings now threaten to overload parole officers and caseworkers.

22. Recommend necessary legislation and more adequate funds to expand work-release programs.

23. End approved lists for correspondence and visitors.

24. Remove visitation screens as soon as possible.

25. Institute a thirty-day maximum for segregation arising out of any one offense. Every effort should be geared toward restoring the individual to regular housing as soon as possible, consistent with safety regulations.

26. Paroled inmates shall not be charged with parole violations for moving-traffic violations or driving without a license, unconnected with any other crime.

27. Permit access to outside dentists and doctors at the inmates' own expense within the institution, where possible and consistent with scheduling problems; medical diagnosis; and health needs.

28. It is expressly understood that members of the Observer Committee will be permitted into the Institution on a reasonable basis to determine whether all of the above provisions are being effectively carried out. If questions of adequacy are raised, the matter will be brought to the attention of the Commissioner of Correctional Services for clearance.

> 9/11/71
> *Approved*
> *Russell G. Oswald*
> *Commissioner of Correctional Services*
> *State of New York*

There they were.

Out of chaos, we had brought twenty-eight points. I had accepted them and the governor had accepted them. All the inmates had to do was to say yes—and there would not have been any deaths at Attica other than that caused by the injuries the rebels inflicted on Corrections Officer Quinn in the takeover. Had the rebels said yes, prison reform would have moved ahead at a greatly accelerated pace—instead of being inhibited by polarization and diversion of staff energies in multiple investigations.

I felt most of the twenty-eight points were reasonable—and the rest were part of the price we would have to pay to save thirty-eight precious lives. If the rebel inmates cared about prison reform, they would accept the twenty-eight points. If not, we would soon know. In any event, our overriding purpose was to secure the peaceful release of the hostages, to save lives.

But was there a chance that, out of the turmoil of Attica, there would be a new opportunity for us to advance toward more productive treatment of criminal offenders? Was there a chance we could thus protect society more efficiently from the pervasive problem of repeat offenders? Was there a chance for us to deter the onward rush of crime?

After all, these were the stars I had looked to, the goals I had set for myself during my life as a professional prison reformer.

James Madison had written, and it inspired me:

"To live and let live is not enough; to live and help live is not too much."

And what a stormy, boisterous life it had been.

PART II

"Many honest and sensible judgments express an intuition of experience which outruns analysis and sums up many tangled and unnamed impressions. . . ."

JUSTICE OLIVER WENDELL HOLMES

CHAPTER 6

Wisconsin—Years of Struggle

Racine, Wisconsin, is a place of fond memories, wonderful companions, loyal friends. Mention of Racine conjures up recollections of a marvelous boyhood—years of fierce competition on the tennis courts, the softball diamonds, the basketball courts, and in boxing rings, of joyful participation as a member of the glee club, of heavy involvement in interscholastic sports while in junior and senior high school.

Well, there was little time during Attica for sentimental memories of these halcyon days, but I did think of Attica as part of a personal continuum. I realized that my decisions at Attica would affect history, for good or ill, and I could only base these decisions upon my own professional and personal experience.

In retrospect, therefore, among the answers to the questions of why and how these decisions were made must be included the answers to other questions:

What kind of background did I come from?

What kind of history did I live through?

Why did I choose to go into the field of correction?

What kind of training did I have?

What had I accomplished in my corrections career?

Had anything like Attica ever happened to me before—and how did I handle it and what did I learn from it?

Was I really up to the responsibility?

At Attica these were battlefield decisions, really, with no time for detailed examination of all the factors pro and con. The information upon which I was acting was often fragmentary and unclear.

I was aware that grave issues were at stake at Attica—life, justice, anarchy, law, order, chaos, progress. I hoped that somehow, something of our prison reform program might be salvaged. I was honored by the support—"One thousand per cent endorsement" was the way he put it—of the governor, who could have removed me in a minute. I knew this was not emotional but reasoned support from a fellow professional with a stout heart. I was strengthened—and yet I *was* alone.

In the final analysis, I would make what I profoundly hoped would be "honest and sensible" judgments. History must determine the degree of their success or failure. However, in the spirit of Justice Holmes' observation, I do believe that my "many tangled and unnamed impressions" of my life are relevant. For what I did at Attica was in great measure due to how I had come to Attica.

I was born in Racine, on August 4, 1908. Mother was an attractive, dark-haired woman, Irish and outgoing. Her mother and father were born in Ireland and she was proud of her Irish background. Her own mother's name was Susan Dolan, and her father's name was Michael Cullen. She loved people and loved life.

My father, George Oswald, owned a small grocery store. He was of German extraction and had moved from Syracuse, New York, to the Middle West sometime in the 1890s. His mother and father had left him behind temporarily with a grandmother while they relocated. At the age of twelve my father was working as a messenger boy in Syracuse and he had to deliver messages to the Onondaga County Penitentiary. Often, he used to tell me about the penitentiary—and I was both frightened and fascinated. He thought it was a foreboding place, the kind of place no one should ever get sent to.

My father and mother were Roman Catholics and extremely religious. They were God-fearing people and they never had anything bad to say about anyone. They went to church a great deal and they made sure I attended with them, which I think now was of tremendous importance. Unfortunately, we do too little of that today. All too often, the youngsters go out by themselves, and family church-going has diminished. As I look back on it, it seems so important. My parents believed in prayer, and I do today. In fact, I prayed before every one of my major decisions at Attica.

My boyhood and young manhood in Racine were quite wonderful, at least until the onset of the Great Depression. Our home
was headquarters for the kids in the neighborhood. Mother was
an excellent cook and baker and always had goodies around for all
comers. Both she and Dad loved all of them. Dad was about the
most generous man I have ever known. He was always passing
out money to us, making his car available as we became older,
and just generally being a part of the young group. He always
saw to it that athletic equipment was available—basketball hoops,
baseballs, footballs, boxing gloves, and a pool table. He saw to it
that I received boxing lessons "just so that you can handle yourself."

I loved athletics and was captain of the championship team in
the city midget basketball league, made up of players twelve years
of age and younger. At high school I enjoyed my studies and I also
won ten letters in athletics, four as a basketball guard, three as
a football guard, and three as right fielder on the baseball team.
In fact, I won the American Legion award as the best all-around
high school scholar and athlete in Racine. I suppose it was at high
school that I developed what my friends, and enemies, later
called a "fierce, competitive spirit." But I think I learned much
more about fair play and hard work.

For two summers while at high school, I worked with a friend,
Howard Large, as a gandy dancer on the old interurban railroad
tracks between Racine and Milwaukee. We tapped ties and carried rail, and it was the hardest I ever worked in my life. My friend
and I and the foreman were the only members of the section
crew who spoke English. The others all spoke Italian or Spanish.
Some days I got home at 6:30 P.M. so tired I went up to bed right
after supper, to get up again at 5:30 A.M. the next day.

Another time, Howard Large, Ken Bergan, Dick Baggott and I
borrowed money from our parents, bought a Model T Ford truck,
and went into the waste disposal business. In those days, the city
did not pick up ashes—many places were heated by coal those
days—from many private homes and commercial establishments.
So we began hauling trash after school in the evenings and on
Saturdays and soon, we were able to underbid the professional
sanitation men around Racine. We began to do extremely well.
It was a popular thing to joke around school about the money
we were taking home—some twelve to fifteen dollars apiece after

a hard day, which was not at all bad for high school boys in the 1920s. I must admit we spent a great deal of it at the haberdashery.

Later I worked as a summer social director at various youth centers in Racine. We trained younger boys in track, softball, and touch football and my social center won two city championships in a row. There were underprivileged boys, mostly black, all the way from nine and ten years to fifteen and sixteen years old. I also worked with the little girls at the centers—once I had the assignment of helping them decorate their doll buggies for the doll buggy parade in Racine.

In February 1926 I got my high school diploma and went to work within the week at the Seaman Body Company plant in Milwaukee. I worked on the assembly line the first day from 6 A.M. to 9 P.M. and earned nineteen dollars. In this year my father sold his grocery store after several business reverses and he also worked at the Seaman plant. I felt great riding to work with my father and two other men, leaving home in Racine soon after five in the morning. Seaman was an affiliate of the Nash Corporation, and I also worked along with my father at the Nash plant at Kenosha.

In fact, I worked more than three years in factories after graduation from high school. I had not made up my mind what I really wanted to do, although I was increasingly interested in social work. But then a dreadful event in our national history crushed down on all of us, and we no longer had the luxury of choice.

The Depression hurt the industrial Middle West more severely than almost anywhere else and Racine was demoralized by unemployment. My father and I both lost our jobs. He had invested rather heavily on margin in the Seaman Body Company and in the Nash Corporation. He found it impossible to cover all the margins, and he lost a considerable sum of money.

How well I remember those days when everybody was looking for work—and few if any were able to find it. I remember with pain my poor father, who could not find a job, walking thirteen miles to Kenosha on one occasion without getting any rides. He sold clotheslines from door to door—anything to pick up a little money. My mother went back to work as a checker and cashier in the grocery store we once had owned. Since I was also out of a job, I decided to try my luck at the University of Wisconsin. It may seem unreal today, but lots of unemployed men con-

sidered college in the Depression because they could not get jobs.
But how to pay for it?

We needed money so badly that I sat down and wrote letters to
several outstanding people, all over the United States. I told them
how much I needed money to stay in school and I asked if they
would help me. I was amazed when several of these people replied
to my letter, and even more surprised when one industrial leader
sent his male secretary, an Englishman, to look me over to see if
I "had what it takes."

The industrialist was William J. Horlick, chairman of the board
of the Horlick Malted Milk Company. He ultimately decided to
lend me sufficient money to attend the University of Wisconsin.
I also received a loan from William R. Wadewitz, vice president
of the Western Printing and Lithographic Corporation in Racine.
These two loans totaled several thousands of dollars, which they
let me repay at the rate of twenty-five or thirty dollars a month.
I did not complete the repayment until after my marriage in 1935.
They did not charge me a single cent of interest. I paid every
penny back. I was intensely grateful.

Thus was it made possible for me to take liberal arts courses
for two years. In the summer of 1932, I moved on from the University
of Wisconsin, with high grades but without a degree, to
enter the Marquette University Law School in Milwaukee. My
objective was to obtain a law degree and enter into the Wisconsin
State Bar. In the following spring I also got a job—as a caseworker
in the Racine County Welfare Department in my home town.

Every day I was up around 5:30 A.M., caught the 7 A.M. train
to Milwaukee, and attended classes at Marquette all morning.
From 2 P.M. until 10 P.M. I worked at my caseworker's chores in
Racine. From 10 P.M. until midnight or later I worked in the offices
of several lawyer friends to prepare my papers for Marquette.
The lawyers even gave me the keys—and somehow the whole
thing, as they say today, began to come together.

To explain how I decided to go into social work, I would have
to credit several people and one in particular, Howard G. Large,
who is now chief probation officer in Wichita Falls, Texas. We
had grown up together from the age of nine, played football,
basketball, and baseball together. He had been one of my fellow
workers on the ash-and-trash pickup venture, and I admired him
tremendously. When he decided to go into welfare work, his in-

fluence upon me was very strong, and his advice to me was very clear—to do it.

My first weeks as a welfare caseworker in Racine County were also extremely important. I had a strong impression that disadvantaged people needed help from government and that clichés about individual enterprise would not do. The Depression was bleak indeed. I found myself working with fine people who found it very difficult to ask for help of any kind. One of the groups I worked with was Italian by extraction and they were incredibly proud. From my own experience, I knew how they felt. Subsequently, I was given an area which was populated almost entirely by Armenians. I had a very pleasant time getting to know them, reading their (to me) unfamiliar history, and helping to solve their problems. One of my warmest memories of my caseworking days concerns a block in Racine in which all the families were Armenians, welfare recipients, and clients of mine. I would get out in the street and play ball or skip rope with the children and then go in and talk with the parents. They gave me presents in return— nothing of great intrinsic value, but often the gifts were spectacular. Sometimes they gave me huge rubber tree plants, which they would grow in their homes. I kept two of the rubber tree plants in the living room of my parents' home until they grew to the ceiling.

By now, it seemed I was set for a law degree and a career in social work. But there were two important interruptions. One year, out of sheer idealism, I decided to run for public office, the only election I have contested anywhere to this day. I ran for the Racine City Council against the incumbent chairman of the Finance Committee. My campaign consisted entirely of going around and ringing doorbells myself, but I came within a hair of winning it. My campaign theme was that corporations ought to be more socially responsible to their employees in these hard times. It was a popular message.

Meanwhile, in addition to my studies at Marquette and my casework in Racine, I had taken a Saturday job as a clerk in the sporting goods department of the Sears, Roebuck & Company store in Racine. I worked until 9 P.M. to help finance my education and I began to enjoy it. After a while, I was promoted to the appliance departments of two or three Sears stores, and I became pretty good at selling washing machines.

I enjoyed this in a sense, because I could remember my mother doing her washing, rubbing with her knuckles, and I wanted to help make women's chores easier. Soon I was selling twenty or twenty-five of the things every Saturday as the women caught my enthusiasm. I used to tell them how my mother worked so very hard, and how I wanted them to have things a lot better. I guess I was a good salesman. At one point, in fact, I was the No. 1 washing machine salesman for Sears in Racine.

In the summer of 1935 I obtained a law degree from Marquette and was admitted to the Wisconsin State Bar. I considered opening a legal practice in the small town of Waterford, Wisconsin, simply because I liked the place. Also I considered an offer from Sears, Roebuck to become the assistant manager of one of their stores. Instead I accepted an offer to become the director of the Washington County Public Welfare Department in West Bend, Wisconsin. At the age of twenty-seven my vocation in life was thus determined.

On September 7, 1935, I was married to Miss Jane Hurlbut of Racine. We had met when we were seventeen, in front of the high school where we were practicing for a school play, and we had gone together ever since. We were married in the rectory of St. Rose's Church. Then we had dinner at the Racine Hotel and left for a two-day honeymoon in Chicago. When we got home, we were flat broke. But we survived until the next payday when I took my cut-steel cameo ring down to the pawnbroker and pawned it for twenty-five dollars.

My wife encouraged me more than all others to become a full-time social worker. She said she knew I loved people and liked "doing for people," and therefore was a natural. She told me she knew I was not going to be wealthy and that was not important. She said she knew this was what I really wanted to do, and she pushed me.

So we went to West Bend—sixty miles from Racine—and I worked for three years as director of the Washington County Public Welfare Department. I sometimes wonder today if people realize just how long the Depression went on. It was not just a single catastrophe in the fall of 1929. The Depression was with us every day, every week, every year we spent in West Bend. I was paid $150 a month and was glad to have it. I also had to have a car for getting around the county and I bought a new, maroon

Plymouth for $900 on which I had to pay forty-seven dollars a month. Our apartment rental was fifty dollars a month.

In comparison with our clients on welfare, Jane and I felt we were living well, as long as we budgeted everything meticulously. Jane took one dollar a day for food and we got along nicely. We were very happy together. We did not have much of a social life, but every now and then, on Saturday evenings, we got together with our neighbors and played poker—a one-dollar limit. No one could win or lose any more than that. We called it "poverty poker."

It was too bad, because I usually did reasonably well at poker.

After three years (1935–38) in Washington County, I took a state-wide civil service examination to qualify for promotion and was astonished when I placed first, for I had no formal academic preparation for social work. But those who scored my paper said they were impressed by the feeling it showed for human needs.

Almost at once, I was appointed district supervisor in the Milwaukee office of the State Public Welfare Department. The Depression was still wearing us down, and the work was more of the same. Not until United States industry was geared up to aid the Allies in the Second World War did the national economy turn around. Then we were attacked by the Japanese at Pearl Harbor and we were fighting for survival.

I wanted to join the Navy, but I ran into one of the more vexing problems of my life. I stood 5 feet 9½ inches and weighed 225 pounds, so when I applied for a Navy commission, an officer told me, "Unfortunately, you're too heavy. We can't accept you although, with your background, we would like to have you." So I started to go to a gymnasium in Milwaukee. Every lunch hour, from 12 P.M. until 1:15 P.M. or so, I worked out to get my weight down for the Navy. I went on a soup and juice diet for thirty-nine days and this did produce results. It really is the only way to diet, in my opinion—simply do not eat.

In the end, I took off thirty-nine pounds, which seems incredible to me today. I went through the Navy physical examination and was sent home to await what I trusted would be my orders to Navy duty. But nothing happened. Days went by, then weeks. Finally the Army ordered me to report for a physical, found me in excellent shape, and ordered me to report for duty.

For thirteen weeks at Camp Lee, Virginia, I underwent Army basic training. I was thirty-five years old; in fact, I was about the oldest man at Camp Lee. I found the course extremely fatiguing— and I lost another fifteen pounds. Then one day, after I had finished crawling about beneath the barbed wire, feeling frustrated and disgusted, I met one of the training officers. He was a second lieutenant and, to my astonishment, he threw me a salute. I saluted back without comment, and he said, "Didn't you know I saluted you rather than wait for your salute?" I said, "No, I'm sorry, I didn't notice." And he said, "You outrank me now."

It turned out that the Navy had finally sent through my commission the day before my Army training was due to begin. Incredibly, the Army had insisted that I was not to be notified until I had finished basic. I therefore was still wearing my new Army private's uniform when I was sworn in as a Navy lieutenant junior grade. A picture of the commissioning was printed in a Virginia newspaper with appropriately cutting captions.

My war service was also one for the books. I went through naval officers' training and gunnery school for what seemed like forever—while Western Europe and the Central Pacific were being won back. Finally, I was assigned as a gunnery officer on merchant ships. It was the end of 1944 before I made my first voyage in this capacity, aboard the S.S. *Alan-a-Dale*, named after a member of Robin Hood's band. Unlike other merchant vessels of this type, which were then being used to deliver ammunition for the Battle of the Bulge, our ship was loaded with Christmas mail.

This was my first mission of the war, and it did not seem very warlike. But late on the afternoon of December 23, about ten miles off the coast of Holland, we were struck by a midget torpedo. All hands were saved, but our good ship was torn asunder and went down. After an hour or so in the lifeboats in the choppy waters of the Scheldt estuary, we were picked up and taken first to Terneuzen and then on to Antwerp, Belgium.

At Antwerp, the main target of the German *Wehrmacht* in the Battle of the Bulge, we were placed in underground shelters, where we would be safe from V-1 and V-2 explosions. There we remained for something like ten days or two weeks. My principal remembrance is of a Christmas Eve party in which a Royal Navy commander, with the usual British reserve, proposed a toast "to our American friends—whom we like not a little." I had resisted going to the party but was ordered there by the commanding officer in Antwerp. He even lent me a uniform to wear.

We shipped out of Antwerp in January and ran through an air attack by German Messerschmitts as we left the estuary and headed into the channel. But we came through the attack and made it to London where we remained for another week before returning to the United States. Upon arrival in New York, we were permitted to call home. I telephoned Jane at once and told her I was back in the States. She said she could not understand why I was back so rapidly. I said I was on survivors' leave. That was almost too much for her! Anyhow, that was the Second World War as I knew it.

There was another mission. In New York City, at the conclusion of my survivors' leave with Jane, I was assigned to command a troop train, of all things, taking 900 other Navy survivors to a rest camp at De Land, Florida. The trip was memorable because I decided to take Jane with me. She would be the only woman on board.

Jane told me she thought the whole idea was "very interesting" and she enjoyed being with these men. We had no door or curtain on our compartment of the troop train, but the 900 men respected our privacy. And when we went along to eat in the dining car, I would go first to make sure the men were all dressed before Jane passed through.

When the train arrived at De Land, the 900 men checked into their camps and a hotel, and Jane and I into another hotel. Soon some other wives and families arrived and we began to visit back and forth. It turned out to be quite a mission and we are still corresponding with some of the wonderful people we met on this adventure. I figured the Navy owed us something—and this was my favorite episode of the Second World War.

But good things do end—and upon our return to New York I was directed at eleven o'clock one night to board an ammunition ship at Gravesend Bay in Brooklyn which was leaving for the Pacific. Jane went out there with me by subway and went back alone. I wrote each day and went ashore and mailed the letters from Kwajalein. But they never were received.

When the war in the Pacific ended on August 15, 1945, Jane was visiting in West Bend with friends. There was a national celebration. Along with the rest of our countrymen, the West Bend contingent was ecstatically happy. Suddenly one of our dear friends, Mrs. Pearl Gehl, interrupted to say that the war still was not over for Jane—she had not heard from me for many weeks.

I arrived in Mukilteo, Washington, on our anniversary on September 7, 1945, and immediately telephoned Jane who was living with my parents. After I had talked with her and with Mother and Dad, Jane told my parents that I must have been drinking. Surely there was no place named Mukilteo.

After the war I went back to the district directorship of the State Public Welfare Department. I had long since decided that this was to be my field in life, but I felt I could do a better job if I had some specialized training. So I enrolled in the graduate school of Loyola University School of Social Work and took the psychiatric sequence. I was able to take the courses at the Loyola Center in Milwaukee the first year, working in the Welfare Department days and attending classes in the evenings. Consequently it took me a year and a half to finish the year's course.

For the second year, I had to go into residence at Loyola in Chicago, and so I took an educational leave from my job. I still could not pay for this without working, and at the advanced age of thirty-nine I began once more to work my way through college.

I now had many more responsibilities. Our son, Kurt, was born in August 1947. Our monthly bills were also much larger because Jane and I had decided to invest in an insurance program. I was able to get a scholarship to Loyola that paid something like $125 a month, and Jane obtained a Saturday job at Gimbel's department store in Milwaukee. But these earnings were quite limited, and so I answered an advertisement in the Milwaukee *Journal* to get a job as night-shift foreman at the Omar Baking Company in Milwaukee. It was a three-nights-a-week job, on which I had to push pie carts and help load trucks from 11 P.M. until 7 A.M.

This was another schedule to remember. Every working day I used to commute 180 miles. In the morning, I would ride the rapid transit line from Milwaukee to Chicago for classes at Loyola, and I would get back to Milwaukee at about 9 P.M. After working all night on the pie carts, I would catch one or two hours rest, and then back down the railroad to Loyola. Even this pressure grew greater when I was given academic field work. I put in several additional hours every week in the Child Guidance Clinic in Milwaukee County, where I worked under the direction of psychiatrists and psychiatric social workers.

This was all too much for a man of my age, but life at the Omar Baking Company was not without compensations. It was a large place in downtown Milwaukee. The ovens were all on an upper floor, and the hundreds of carts were on the floors below. It was friendly there and I found many men with whom I got along very well. One of my fellow foremen was an epileptic. He had all the fears of the epileptic and he talked with me, on and on, asking if it would be all right for him to marry, even to drive a car. In talking with him about his problems, I thought I had better do more reading about epilepsy in the libraries at Loyola, and soon I felt more qualified to give advice. In general, I told my friend he should lead as normal a life as possible, and I referred him to a Dr. Gibbs, a specialist in Chicago. In time, he did get married and he lived much more happily within himself.

In February of 1949 I obtained my master's degree in social work at Loyola and, because I had won straight A grades through the years there, I was selected for membership in Alpha Sigma Nu, the national honorary society. This award was supposed to recognize scholarship and personal contribution to the life of the school.

I had learned at this point in my life that I could stay on my feet despite heavy pounding, and my self-confidence was firmly rooted. I do not believe I experienced such pressure again until the crisis at Attica. In fact, I sometimes wonder whether I could have survived the strain upon stamina, emotions, and judgment at Attica if I had not lived through early experiences like these.

Academically speaking, I now had a lot of momentum, and I took almost every competitive examination in sight. I also wanted to move ahead to larger responsibilities. So I took the national examination for director of the Cook County Public Welfare Department in Chicago and finished second in the country. I ranked first in another examination for the superintendency of a "colony," as it was then called, for mentally retarded children. But the big one upon which I set my sights was for the directorship of the Wisconsin State Bureau of Probation and Parole. It seems strange nowadays that such a senior position was to be filled by competitive examination, but in Wisconsin the civil service tradition was extremely strong.

It happened that four of my friends from my years in the Wisconsin Public Welfare Department were parole officers, and they knew the probation and parole field intimately. At first, I was hesitant to move into this more specialized field of welfare—for in Wisconsin, probation, parole, and the whole penal field of corrections were regarded as functions of the public welfare system.

I said to my friends, "I have no real experience in probation and parole. How in the world will I ever qualify for the directorship?" It was a fair question. But one of my friends answered, "Well, the examination is coming up, and you have to get this job. We need you as head of our programs in this state." Another said, "You're great with people—you're a natural." Another said, "That's what parole is all about." I said, "I don't have the most time in the world." My friends replied, "Well, let's work it out."

So my friends, the parole officers, decided to help me prepare for the competitive examination. They collated the best information and the newest literature, and they marked the most useful passages for me. Every evening I would find a stack of books and papers waiting for me, all tidily and efficiently earmarked at the most important places. These four parole officers prepared me so well for the examination that I came out No. 1 in the results. I was to get the directorship of Probation and Parole for the whole state! Out of my four friends, one is now dead, one is retired, and the other two are still doing parole work in Wisconsin, one of them as a member of the State Board of Parole.

Thus ended what might be termed my early years.

I was now used to going without money, without food, without sleep, without any kind of vacation. I had developed drive and direction of almost obsessive intensity, while preserving a family life I cherished. According to newspaper accounts of this time, my personal style was "rotund, tough, and monosyllabic." That was probably true, as I did not say too much. As Gary Cooper used to say about one of his movie roles during the Depression, "One nice thing about silence is that it can't be repeated."

CHAPTER 7

"With Our Imperfect Knowledge
of Twisted Minds"

It was a world in which living had become almost too complex, in which nerves were keyed to a higher pitch, in which spiritual values had been ignored, in which religion had been displaced by a pseudoscientific conglomeration of half-baked superficialities which some people called a philosophy of life.

It was a world in which there were no ethics other than not to get caught, where there were no set principles of right and wrong, where children were brought into the world and let grow up to express their personalities without inhibition.

It was a world in which self-discipline and self-restraint and consideration for the rights and tastes of others were neglected as old-fashioned or too difficult to take seriously. It was a world in which the really governing philosophy was "I'll try anything."

On December 1, 1948, I became state supervisor of the Bureau of Probation and Parole of the Division of Corrections in Wisconsin, and, according to my own notes, that was how I viewed the scene at that time.

It is in fact all too easy to be agitated about the "permissive society" of the 1970s while forgetting that we had our own permissive society in the aftermath of the Second World War. If there is a generation gap, it is caused perhaps by differences in time, rather than by differences in attitudes. What is really needed is a sense of proportion and perspective.

In Wisconsin at the end of 1948, I moved into new responsibilities amid an atmosphere of doubt and suspicion. Almost everybody appeared to have high hopes for me, which was encouraging, but it also meant I was subjected to considerable scrutiny. The problem was that my predecessor had run into serious troubles for which, in my opinion, he ought not to have been blamed. In any event, the situation showed me how sensitive the public was to questions of law and order and to the reputation of probation and parole in particular.

It was a classic tragedy. A parolee had gone on a rampage that culminated in the murder of two schoolteachers. One of our most respected newspapers did a first-class investigative job and uncovered a great deal of information about this man's background and activities that the parole officials had not known. Small wonder, when the parole officers were carrying personal caseloads of between eighty and ninety parolees apiece—but the public was infuriated and clearly wanted much more stringent limitations on parole.

I wanted precisely the opposite—a much more open concept of parole—and I had to introduce people quite gradually and carefully to my viewpoint. I believe then, as I do now, that most probationers, prisoners, and parolees reach their unhappy state because of their own unresolved emotional conflicts. This specifically includes radicals, the self-styled political prisoners, who would find most of their problems within themselves if they really looked.

People then as now said they were ready to accept the reality of psychological illness, but the sick were often despaired of by their families, employers, and friends and by the community as a whole. The parolees who fell into this category tended even more to be rejected after their release from confinement. Their friends had to be the parole officers, the men and women from the Salvation Army, from Alcoholics Anonymous and the Wisconsin Service Association, and others with great hearts, undying faith, and small budgets.

I felt we needed to accept parolees as people everywhere in the state. We had to make it clear they were within the community, even while we made it equally clear we did not condone their original offenses. We needed to inculcate a sense of security in the insecure. We needed to permit freedom even while we required a sense of responsibility for their own good behavior from the parolees themselves. After all, they were being released before the formal expiration of their sentences.

In the late 1940s, as a result of the incident I mentioned, parole itself was on probation even in Wisconsin, the progressive land of the La Follettes. Government ought never to move too far ahead of or lag too far behind public opinion, as I sometimes cautioned myself, for a democratic system must rely on the understanding and support of the public in order to function. On the other hand, I felt we were too long on public supervision and too short on public understanding at that time—and the same is perhaps true today. Does the majority of our people really believe that convicted criminals ought to be released before the expiration of their sentences and turned loose into the no man's land of parole? Even in 1972 I wonder.

So I progressed with extreme care. First, I recruited six additional caseworkers in token of my intention to share our caseloads among more professionals and so provide better service to the parolees and to the public. Then I hired sixteen more and another twelve after that. Soon I was able to seek a requirement of master's degrees in social work, and this increased the quality of our personnel as it upgraded the significance of parole officers in the mind of the community.

Next I formed four clinical teams, each consisting of a psychiatrist, a psychologist, and a psychiatric social worker, to travel statewide for the diagnosis and treatment of disturbed parolees. These clinical teams also worked effectively with the courts in providing estimates of the usefulness of probation. They were able to keep the courts informed on how well the probationers actually were doing.

I thought it advisable in these early days to set a visible personal example. So I risked charges of cornball showmanship and began to come to work at 4:00 A.M. I was pleased when the newspapers picked this up, because the public seemed to be intrigued, and parole took on more of a positive image in Wisconsin.

Soon we had things rolling. There were no more parole scandals. There was a reduction in the numbers of parolees who had to be returned to their institutions. We created a momentum of change. This attracted the attention of able and compassionate state administrators and legislators, and I was earmarked for larger responsibilities.

In the early summer of 1950, at the age of forty-one, I was promoted suddenly to serve as Director of Corrections for the State of Wisconsin. I expected great things from my superior, the recently appointed State Director of Public Welfare, a well-known humanitarian named John Tramburg.

Tall, handsome, and extremely intelligent, John Tramburg had been a farm boy in rural Wisconsin. He distinguished himself at Whitewater Teachers College, then went to Washington, D.C., where he served as a probation officer in juvenile court. In his early thirties he was Director of Welfare in the nation's capital, where he showed outstanding leadership qualities, in particular the ability to inspire his staff to accomplish things they might otherwise have deemed impossible.

Under John Tramburg's leadership in Wisconsin I began to press rapidly for a series of reforms. Specifically, I advocated two major and basic changes in the state laws regarding the handling of criminal offenders. First, I recommended making presentence examinations mandatory in all criminal cases. I wanted to reduce the incidence of those disastrous episodes in which judges passed sentence upon people after conviction with scant knowledge of their character, personality, background, and interests, with little more to go on than the nature of the crimes. These occurrences were disastrous because many offenders, though recognizing their guilt, bitterly resented the magnitude of their sentences. These men were almost paranoid about the ignorance of "the old man on the bench." They were often the most difficult of all to rehabilitate because their hostility was not only profound, but well founded.

The new presentence examination procedure I proposed would be introduced everywhere in Wisconsin. I wanted our caseworkers to compile a dossier on the convicted offenders for study by the judges *before* passage of sentence. I felt this would be a very useful extension of the casework techniques we were already using for probationers and parolees. It would improve the quality of justice immeasurably.

Then I recommended the development of a "conditional release" barrier for prisoners who had served their minimum time but who had been consistently denied parole. It seemed to me they must have been denied parole for good reasons and perhaps they ought not to be released at all. Specifically, I felt we should deny release to sex offenders we deemed to be psychopathic and dangerous to the community. In what was described as a "hard-line proposal," I recommended that we keep such people in custody—with a lesser level of supervision—until medical authority adjudged them to be no longer dangerous if released to society under supervision.

In my first, formal speech on corrections, I pleaded:

"With our imperfect knowledge of ways of dealing effectively with twisted minds, can we permit their return to society when they are judged dangerous by competent medical authorities?

"Can we in good conscience release them after paying fines or serving prison sentences merely because we know so little about effecting a cure for their abnormal behavior?

"Is it not time for us to insist that a law be passed, permitting the state, after proper medical review, to retain in custody those found incurable, that is, until the doctors feel they are no longer dangerous?"

Both of these major proposals were soon enacted in Wisconsin.

Next, I drafted a memorandum to John Tramburg calling for changes in the state prison system. I asked, first, for the establishment of a fifty-cell maximum-security unit in the Wisconsin State Prison at Waupun. In what was to become one of the principal elements of my penological doctrine, I wanted to remove the malcontents so I could proceed more rapidly with the rehabilitation of the majority.

Second, I called for the completion of a medium-security prison that had already been authorized, in order to relieve overcrowding at Waupun. It seemed a waste of time to me to set up costly rehabilitation programs for men who did not feel like trying too hard because they were herded and degraded in overcrowded prison conditions.

Third, I asked for the installation of a central food storage and processing plant at Waupun. I wanted this to be used to serve all the state institutions, to reduce costs, simplify operations, and, I hoped, to improve the quality of the food. I was often amused by the way in which the more theoretical of our prison reformers often overlooked such obvious items as the provision of a more nutritious diet and more appetizing menus. This was not coddling convicts; it was giving us practical assistance in the changing of men.

Fourth, I asked Mr. Tramburg for a $750,000 vocational school to be constructed at the state reformatory at Green Bay. I argued that, if we were to rehabilitate in terms of character and aspiration, then we ought to augment our instructions in skills.

We began to receive extremely helpful assistance from the newspapers. The Milwaukee *Journal*, then and now one of the great newspapers in the country, gave us consistent editorial support. Two of their editorial writers, Perry Olds and John Baker, themselves became experts in the correctional field and were quoted as authorities nationwide.

Appearing on the Milwaukee *Journal's* television station, WTMJ-TV, I declared, "The public must realize that prisoners are not mad dogs and maniacal killers." On the same program, John C. Burke, warden of the state prison at Waupun, said it would be technically possible to lock prisoners in their separate cells, keep them fed, and never let them out for any reason—that we could throw away the key. "But these people would come out inhuman and looking for revenge on society," he warned. "All prisoners come out sometime, and most of them within a few years. Once, punishment used to be the sole objective. Now, we're trying to do other things."

John Burke then told the viewers that, as an example of how far we had to travel even in Wisconsin, there were only three guidance officers and one psychiatrist working full time at Waupun—among 1,200 prisoners. At that point, I added indignantly, "We're saddled with what was good in the 1850s, but it is entirely inadequate for us right now."

During the next few years we translated our hopes and our programs into progress that could be measured. Mr. Tramburg and I each benefited by the leadership of the celebrated Governor Walter Kohler, a progressive Republican and a suitable heir to the tradition of the La Follettes. For one such measurement of progress, out of 6,345 criminal offenders, only 2,738 of them were in traditional institutions, in prison farms, work camps, and other minimum-security facilities. The other 3,607 were on probation or on parole, living at home for the most part, working, supporting families perhaps, paying taxes, and supervised by thoroughly trained professional field agents. Wisconsin at this point in its history was locking up a smaller percentage of its criminal offenders than any other state in the nation. And its crime rate, reflecting as well an orderly population, was also among the lowest. The Milwaukee *Journal* wrote:

"Probably the biggest factor in Wisconsin's success in holding down the prisons' population is the almost missionary zeal of everyone connected with the probation and parole program from Oswald on down."

It was because of the breadth of our basic concept, viewing probation, prison, and parole as part of the same welfare process, that we were able to recruit outstanding professionals over the country. Soon we had sixty-one male and thirteen female field agents working out of Milwaukee, Madison, Green Bay, Rhinelander, and Eau Claire. Most of these agents had a minimum of six years college training and held master's degrees in social work. We were paying them between $4,344 and $5,124 a year plus expenses, so they were clearly motivated by factors other than money. Supervising agents worked for $5,434 to $6,504, and this did not amount to much during the years of the Eisenhower boom.

I told the Milwaukee *Journal*: "Beside the academic training, we require our people to be dedicated to the work, to think with their hearts as well as their minds. We insist that the men be manly and the women feminine. Many of our agents were veterans of World War II who developed a social conscience during their years in service."

During the early 1950s the weekly time reports of our agents told me they were working sixty hours or more every week, even though they did not receive overtime pay. They were looked up to everywhere in the state. Their dedication to the service idea was recognized and applauded by their neighbors. They gave their time freely to speaking engagements and they often worked with private and public welfare boards in local communities. Above all, our field agents and other workers were judged by results. Their success was assured when people saw how the men and women on probation and parole were making good much more often than not.

As so often happens, the tactical gains achieved by the men and women in the field affected strategic planning. As far as probation was concerned, the Wisconsin judges began to rely on the presentence reports and on the case studies in general, and they would refer to the field agents as "our" probation officers. The judges almost without exception went all the way with our programs and put their own prestige behind our reform movement. As for parole, Wisconsin was unique in these years in important respects. A prisoner would become eligible for parole, at the minimum, at the half of his maximum term or at the end of two years, whichever was less. An exception was that a first-degree murderer would have to serve a minimum of eleven years and three months before he was considered for parole.

But we made it a practice to assign every prisoner, as soon as he arrived in an institution at the start of his term, to the individual parole officer who would handle his case when he was released. This was an innovative prison reform whereby the parole officers would consult with the prisoners at least once every three months while they were serving their time. The field parole officers would help maintain liaison between prisoners and their families, their friends, and their present or potential employers. They would thus help to prepare the men's return to their communities in advance.

The effect of this innovation was dynamic. One of the main reasons that prisoners would sometimes not respond to rehabilitation in the institutions was because they felt cut off, dehumanized, and isolated from the real world. At the same time, one of the main reasons for the failures of parole was an inadequate preparation of home and employment for the men coming out of the trauma of physical confinement. By bringing our skilled parole officers *into* the prisons, and at the start of sentences, we struck vitally at both of these reasons for failure. We increased the odds for successful rehabilitation, and we increased the odds for successful parole.

The "Wisconsin Way" became known throughout the nation. We believed in using the combined forces of religion and behavioral science as well as working for mental and physical health, full employment, recreation, education, and the stimulus of the family and the community. On a foundation such as this, plus a reliance on the intelligent application of social case work principles and techniques, we *hoped* that men and women could be restored to society as effective citizens.

I took a lead myself in this process, by serving on the three-man Wisconsin Board of Parole. We met for five days each month at the state prison at Waupun, among other places, and we heard about one hundred men on each visit. We paroled an average of approximately forty out of every 100 men, at their first times of asking, and when one of the newspapers scolded us for being too lenient, we invited two of the editors to sit in on the next hearings. Afterward, one of the editors told me, "I think we understand your problems better. I think we would have granted more paroles today than you did."

We had the typical budget problems for probation and parole with the state legislature but John Tramburg was an able advocate, and we were able to demonstrate specific savings. After one budget hearing, one of the senior Republican assemblymen, a financial expert, said to me, "If we didn't have that probation and parole program of yours, we would have to build a couple more prisons." That would have cost the state of Wisconsin, even in the 1950s, between $14,000 and $20,000 per cell. So the humane way was also the thrifty way, and we all felt good about that, too.

Within the prisons progress often seemed glacial, but the results were very encouraging. There was not a single riot in any one of our institutions in the five years I was Director of Corrections in Wisconsin.

"There's hope for every man in prison," I told the men in our institutions. "I couldn't do this job if there wasn't. If you put a man in a cage, he'll act like an animal. If you take away his hope of some day being freed, he'll stop at nothing to hurt you." I was believed—and I was trusted because the men knew I was making a reality out of parole programs that in other states were mere gestures.

We were also able to win some physical improvements, among them the new vocational school at the Green Bay Reformatory. A smaller but symbolically important gain here was the reactivation of the swimming pool, built in 1898 but used for thirty years for the storage of potatoes and grain. We won a new reformatory forestry camp, helped clean up some of the county and city jails, and increased the use of foster homes for delinquent youngsters.

In terms of prison life, we doubled the number of social service units in all of our institutions and provided higher pay for work in prison industries and maintenance. In each of these instances, our advances were minimal—but we were moving far ahead of almost all other states in the nation. Prison menus were examined every week by a dietician—and one of the chefs in each of the prisons had to walk around the dining halls during meals to receive complaints and, we hoped, a few bouquets.

By the time I moved on to my next assignment, more than 350 of the 1,200 inmates of the state prison at Waupun were taking grade school, high school, or University of Wisconsin extension courses. About 140 out of 725 at the Green Bay Reformatory were also enrolled. All 150 of the women residents of the Home for Women at Taycheedah were taking academic and vocational training that would help them upon their release.

I paid special attention to the Home for Women at Taycheedah and now, as I look back over my career in corrections, it seems this was the finest institution in which I ever had the privilege of working. It is well known that women commit fewer crimes than men, are arrested less frequently than men, receive more lenient sentences than men, and make more tractable prisoners than men. Because they do not tend to commit the crimes of violence most feared by society, they are paroled with the best wishes of the public. If prisons are in time to be done away with by our society, it is probable that women's prisons will be torn down first.

Taycheedah was designed to reflect the concept that female offenders need and benefit from personalized treatment far more than men. It had much less security and it was run by matrons with far better than average education and motivation.

As is so often the case in penology, Taycheedah reflected the special quality of its director. Mrs. Marcia Simpson was a home economics major, and she and her staff taught the residents how to prepare for their return to the community with a skill, insight, and intensity I have never seen equaled in prison work. She would even teach the women by actual demonstration to take old pieces of furniture and fix them up, to make them attractive and usable. She taught them how to blend colors in room decoration. Everybody on the staff seemed ready all the time to run classes in sewing, cooking, and household management. Mrs. Simpson taught the residents how to make themselves more attractive, gave them courses in beauty treatment, and also in conduct and deportment in office work.

Although the women residents at Taycheedah had IQs no higher than male prisoners anywhere else, Mrs. Simpson and her staff did not hesitate to work in their spare time to set up "great books" reading and discussion courses. There would also be art ap-

preciation classes and dramatics, and the residents would produce
and act in their own plays. I would often take down some interesting new book to Mrs. Simpson, perhaps several copies of it, and
she would pass them around to the residents. Two or three days
later, I would go back to join a group of eight or ten of the women
and Mrs. Simpson in what we hoped was a thoughtful literary
discussion.

In another corrections field, there were the forestry camps, for
which I have been given more credit than I am due. Wisconsin
was the first state in the nation to introduce forestry camps for
adult offenders and the first three were opened in 1931, long before I appeared on the scene. Michigan introduced forestry camps
for adult offenders in 1947, the year in which California introduced
an integrated forestry program for youthful offenders in large numbers. Massachusetts and Ohio were among the next states to bring
in forestry camps, but Wisconsin was sixteen years ahead of anybody else.

Today, forestry camps appear to be even more significant. They
contribute not only to criminal rehabilitation but also to environmental protection, and these are two of the most positive trends
of our times. My predecessors had indeed been farsighted, and I
took every opportunity to expand the camps. The prisoners were
pleased to move to a more healthful atmosphere in which there
was harder physical work but infinitely less confinement and regi-
mentation. The public was quickly convinced that the men sent
to forestry camps had been so thoroughly screened that they were
not dangerous. The courts soon came to like forestry camps too
much—and they had to be persuaded not to use them as a substitute for probation in the treatment of marginal offenders.

Finally, the camps provided an efficient and extremely economi-
cal labor service for the state on such chores as land clearance,
road and firebreak construction, the installation of telephone lines,
and the maintenance of tree-cutting equipment.

I liked to visit the forestry camps around the state and I often
would take my young son along with me. Once, while I was talking
with the corrections officers, I asked one of the young inmates to
take Kurt off fishing somewhere and have a good time. They cast
their lines and did not catch anything, but they had a wonderful
conversation. When they got back to the forestry camp, Kurt told

me I should release the young man there and then. "He's such a nice man," Kurt said.

In November 1954, at a convention of the American Federation of State, County and Municipal Employees (AFSCME), I struck a blow at what I often thought to be the basic problem of prison reform. This controversial statement was on the quality of correctional personnel—or the lack of it.

In Wisconsin we had managed to accomplish much for corrections officers. We had won salary increases, fringe benefits, the introduction of work-study courses, and cross-training sessions between groups of custodial and caseworker employees. We had made a tentative start on the recruitment and promotion of members of minority groups. We had also devoted considerable attention to the senior people in our probation, prison, and parole programs. Almost all of our superintendents were now college graduates, and many had graduate training in law and social work. We had, in fact, a completely cohesive unit, with strong mutual loyalties, and I believe we had talented as well as humane men in charge.

But in almost all the other states, it seemed to me we were in serious trouble. So I laid it on the line to the correctional workers in a speech I think I could deliver again today:

"In the opinion of progressive penologists as well as that of many leading thinkers and humanitarians, the American prison scene presents no pretty picture. In the judgment of such people, our antiquated prison system is a blight on the public conscience. They regard it as a blasphemy against the rights and dignity and potential for worth-while citizenship of those committed to its towering walls and its monotonous existence. They see it as a fraud upon the public since, in their opinion, it neither protects our citizens against crime and criminality, nor does it rehabilitate the offender.

"If so, it is up to us to change things around a bit. And institutions do not change overnight, but people can. Institutions do not vanish into thin air merely because they have become obsolete and people have lost faith in them. Our prisons will be with us a long time and none of us are in danger of losing our jobs.

"We do, however, have the obligation of removing one by one the weaknesses in our institutions and we must improve our *serv-*

ices. We must realize that success or failure rests not on stone walls and iron bars but on the men and women the institutions can attract to work in them, train, promote within the ranks, and hold.

"We must be ever mindful that the custodial worker has rights which must not be denied him. He is not just a screw. He is a man. He is entitled to respect on and off the job.

"But I would utter a word of warning. We must be able to demonstrate to the taxpaying public that the modern correctional worker is a far cry from the old prison guard who was chosen on the basis of his brawn rather than his brain, and his political connections rather than his fitness for the job.

"I have long advocated the disintegration of our present prison system in which bigness, security, and the destruction of human values through fear, force, and violence were the altars on which we have worshipped too long. But compounding the difficulty is the struggle that too often exists between the custodial and the treatment staff. Each wants to dominate the other. In the end, no one wins.

"The custodial group in the maximum-security institutions says that treatment, euphemistically used, is most effective when it is given under lock and key. The social workers and classification committees see much of their work made ineffective by the custodial group's indifference. Who prevails? Normally, it is the security group.

"Teamwork is what is called for, and nowhere is it more important. A good custodial worker is of supreme importance to every prison administrator.

"We can do a routine, day-to-day job of only watching prisoners closely.

"Or we can do an inspired, self-sacrificing job that calls for not only being our brother's keeper, but our brother's brother as well. It seems to me as simple as that."

In Wisconsin, I proposed these measures designed to increase even further the incentives of our custodial officers:

1. Raise correctional personnel standards by requiring high school diplomas from all new applicants;
2. Encourage, through grants-in-aid, the attendance of correctional workers at graduate schools in social work and allied fields;

3. Blanket all correctional workers into civil service status and award professional status through civil service procedures;

4. Provide advancement opportunities through graduated promotions and transfers of qualified personnel between institutions;

5. Make salaries of correctional workers equal to that of their fellow peace officers in the police force;

6. Limit the work week and pay overtime;

7. Provide pensions after twenty-five years of successful service;

8. Provide in-service training possibilities and credits through the state university for promotion within the civil service;

9. Assure that job continuity will not be affected by anybody's political whim.

Most of these reforms have since been put into effect in Wisconsin. Even today they are rare in most other states. This is one reason why we have a custodial problem in most regions of the United States.

Austin H. MacCormick, one of the founders of the Federal Bureau of Prisons in Washington and one of our foremost reformers, once said he could run the best prison in the country in an old red barn if he had the right kind of people to help him.

He is so right.

On November 1, 1955, I resigned as Director of Corrections in Wisconsin to take up a similar position in Massachusetts. Meanwhile, I had a little time to take stock of myself in the personal sense. I was now making $12,000 a year. It seems hard to believe, but I had taken over the directorship in Wisconsin at a salary of $7,500 a year. I was worn out from overwork, but I suspected this was compulsive. I was used to life without vacations. I had a hobby now, golf, and I enjoyed broiling two-inch-thick steaks on the charcoal grill in the backyard. I liked martinis but preferred beer, and this did not make it easy for me to hold down my weight. I was back up from my Navy weight to 210 pounds. I often smoked ten cigars a day.

In case it appears I was some kind of Middle American stereotype, I must admit I was of little use as a handyman. One evening

I was driving from Milwaukee to Madison with a few of my corrections staff members and we had a flat tire. None of us could operate the jack, so we flagged down a truck driver. He changed the wheel for us and remarked to me, "I suppose you're a college graduate. I never finished high school but I know how to change a tire."

I was very happy with my wonderful wife, Jane, and with our son, Kurt. I recall one evening, not long before we left Wisconsin, when many of our corrections people gave us all a farewell party. They invited my parents, too, and we were all together at the head table. We had come a long way from the Depression, or so it seemed.

Then the toastmaster asked Kurt if there was anything he would like to say to the group. I thought he was joking, but Kurt, only eight years old, said, "Yes." He walked up to the microphone and told the 500 people in the room he hoped they would continue to help people the way his father had.

The Milwaukee *Journal* bade me good-by: "Oswald will be sorely missed, but the offer he has accepted reflects credit on Wisconsin's program, the board which has guided it, the legislature, the Governor, and the State, but it is especially a tribute to Mr. Oswald's leadership and accomplishments. He has built well."

In Wisconsin we had boosted the corrections program to No. 1 in the nation. In Massachusetts, for the next eighteen months, there would be almost nothing but trouble.

CHAPTER 8

Massachusetts: One Damned Crisis
After Another

The walls of the cells were of raw granite, unplastered, unpainted, unclean. There were no windows, no views of any part of the outside world—only the prison corridors seen between bars. The cells were eight feet in length, six feet in width, enough to encase and entomb a man. The furniture consisted of a bunk and small tables and carts for leftover food. Light bulbs hung down from overhead wires.

There were no toilets. The prison cells had been built in 1805 and no provision had been made for them. None had been put in since then. Instead, the men in the cells used buckets, each imprinted with the number of his cell. Every day, the men in the cells took their personal buckets to a disposal station in the yard where they would be emptied and washed out by fatigue details. Later, the buckets would be trundled back to the cells on a trolley known as the "honey wagon."

This was the state prison at Charlestown, Massachusetts, a section of Boston not far from Lexington and Concord, Harvard and MIT, a filthy hole made all the more offensive by its proximity to the cradle of American liberty and knowledge. This nauseating place, built in the year that Napoleon defeated the Austrians and Russians at Austerlitz, had been in use almost continuously ever since. The good men and women of Boston held their noses and passed by.

In January of 1955, while I was still in Wisconsin, the maximum-security section of the Charlestown Prison, known as Cherry Hill, exploded into a savage riot. It was a miracle that it had not happened before. The ringleader was Teddy Green, who had had his first brush with the law as a youngster in the 1930s when he went to see the Edward G. Robinson movie *Little Caesar*. At the end of it, Teddy Green stood up and shouted "Rat-tat-tat-tat-tat-tat-tat" like a submachinegun. The audience was terrified into a near stampede and he was booked on juvenile charges. He subsequently graduated from reformatories to pass through a series of state and federal jails on more serious charges.

In the riot, Teddy Green and four others seized five corrections officers and held them hostage pending a promise by the state to investigate conditions. The authorities mobilized an impressive display of firepower but decided the request for an investigation was reasonable. The hostages were released. Teddy Green later went all the way to the federal maximum-security prison at Alcatraz and he came all the way back to rehabilitation and release. Recently, he was a salesman in Boston.

The state set up a new committee to investigate Charlestown and the whole Massachusetts prison system. The chairman was President Nils Y. Wessell of Tufts University, and the committee included such luminaries as Joseph Ragen, warden at the Illinois State Penitentiary, Will C. Turnbladh, executive director of the National Probation and Parole Association, and Robert J. Wright, assistant general secretary of the American Correctional Association. A committee of state legislators and a special legislative advisory group supported most of the Wessell recommendations. These included the codification of penal laws, which, in Massachusetts, had not been done.

The Wessell Committee recommended the creation of a training school and program for corrections officers, the establishment of a reception center for the classification of new prisoners by character and abilities and the modernization of prison industries. The men were to be paid for their work. The committee also recommended a grant of power to the corrections commissioner to move lesser offenders around minimum-security institutions and camps, while retaining felons in three maximum-security prisons.

Finally, the Wessell Committee recommended the abolition of solitary confinement in dark cells on a diet of bread and water. Things in Massachusetts had been as bad as that.

Governor Christian A. Herter of Massachusetts brought me from Wisconsin to serve as the new Commissioner of Corrections. I accepted the mission with alacrity and enthusiasm. Here was an opportunity to take one of the worst prison systems in the country and to turn it into one of the best. Here was a chance to translate the admirable concepts of the Wessell Committee into correctional reality.

I hated to leave Wisconsin, but how could I refuse?

Governor Herter assured me I could set up my own personal organization and bring in my own men. My salary had been set by the legislature at $15,000, and I would have three deputy commissioners at $10,000 each, in addition to an advisory committee to be named by the governor.

A DAWN OF HOPE the Boston *Globe* headlined its front-page story of my appointment. The *Berkshire Eagle* of Pittsfield, Massachusetts, wrote, "Oswald is admirably fitted for the job. He's a reformer and has progressive ideas without the fanaticism to which reformers are prone, and with a practical point of view." The Boston *Traveler* said, "Oswald is short, stout, and an inveterate cigar smoker. He looks more like a politician than a leading exponent of prison reform, but no one can be misled when he talks about his work. He believes there is no such thing as a hopeless convict."

The Worcester *Gazette* said (and it is important that I quote these editorials at some length because of what happened later), "Governor Herter is to be commended for keeping the corrections commissionership out of politics. He has not hesitated to go beyond the boundaries of the state to find a qualified man for the job." The *Gazette* added its touch of security, "Russ Oswald, who is only forty-six years old, has been head of the Wisconsin penal system during a period in which there have been no riots or uprisings."

In all my professional career, I had never felt so wanted, and by a whole state, from the governor on down. Caught up in this spirit, I wrote an article for all the newspapers in the state that I intended as thanks for the welcome. I declared:

"Prisons involve people—inmates and the taxpaying public who foot the bill.

"Prisons also help persons change and, let's face it, there is a school of thought which considers some prison reforms mollycoddling. Its proponents are often strident but seldom helpful. Resistive to change, they cling to the old pattern of prison management and, at the same time, they proclaim prisons generally a failure.

"Treating prisoners like human beings is not soft-heartedness.

It is hard-headedness. It has a chance of paying off in better prisoners and better ex-prisoners. The old system has no chance of paying off in anything but bitterness, despair—and repeat offenders coming back to the jails."

This opening statement of intent was prominently featured everywhere in the state. The reformers acclaimed me tumultuously; the rest were uneasily quiet. Reporters camped on my doorstep for the next few days, asking me to name names and to express my opinion on related issues such as capital punishment. When I said that "I feel there are other ways just as effective to handle first degree murderers," there were more bannerlines state-wide. Wisconsin had long since done away with capital punishment. Massachusetts retained the electric chair, but had not used it since 1947.

This time I modified my statement: "I shall not be crusading for my point of view on capital punishment since the people of the Commonwealth of Massachusetts have given considerable thought to it, and have kept it on the statute books. I will definitely work within the framework of the law established for me, and follow the mandate of the people."

The storm warnings were there for me to see, but I had come from Wisconsin to reform a shocking prison system, and I was ready to fight for the privilege.

For the next eighteen months I was locked in an unending, up-again, down-again battle. It was one damned crisis after another. There was drama, color, and bitterness—and a kaleidoscopic insight into the real problems of prison reform.

THE HUNGER STRIKE CRISIS

Before I left Wisconsin, I received a letter of welcome signed by almost all the prisoners at Charlestown. The men wrote that they had heard of my reputation as a reformer and that they wanted to see me as soon as I was in Massachusetts.

It turned out they meant that literally. I was invited on my arrival to address the 477 members of the prison population and I was told the time was right now. It appeared that the men were feeling somewhat heady after the riot and the concessions by the Wessell Committee. I thought I needed to make it clear that I was in charge, not the prisoners. So I did not immediately accept the invitation.

When I did not appear instantly in the yard at Charlestown, several things happened. Sixteen of the prisoners turned down their breakfast of biscuits and coffee and said they would not eat until I showed up to hear their grievances. Three of them also missed lunch. When I went to the prison on routine business that day, I sent word that I was too busy to listen to unreasonable demands. All sixteen prisoners now declared a hunger strike and the newspapers talked about the perils of another Charlestown riot.

The hunger strike went into its second day and the whole prison was on edge. I went there again, and passed the word, "They want to find out who is boss. Well, I'm the boss, and I will not see any of them as long as they are behaving so irresponsibly. They are not going to intimidate me. They have no priority." I got a letter by hand from one of the prisoners in apparent reply. It said perhaps there was a misunderstanding—and that there was no intention to embarrass me, especially when I clearly had such great plans for reform.

Lunch that day was more than usually appetizing by prison standards. We served shoulder of lamb, cabbage, boiled potatoes, bread, tapioca pudding, and coffee. One of the hunger strikers ate everything on his plate, and I sent him a message: "I am happy to learn that you have decided to act responsibly." Later that day, the hunger strike was called off. Then I said I would talk with the prisoners at the earliest free moment on my schedule.

There were bannerlines across Massachusetts and in faraway Wisconsin, the *State Journal* in Madison commented, OSWALD WINS FIRST SKIRMISH.

THE MEETING WITH 477 PRISONERS

Several days later I made arrangements to address the prison population of Charlestown and promptly ran into resistance from the prison staffs. I insisted that I go in alone to talk to the men and listen to their grievances without having corrections officers staring at them over my shoulder. I was warned this was totally unsafe so soon after the Charlestown riot and I was warned I might be taken hostage. I was also aware the prison staff was at-

tempting to make points with me. In the end, I agreed to be accompanied by one token guard.

In Charlestown I told the men about some of the programs my
associates and I had succeeded in developing in Wisconsin. I said
it was now my intention to introduce some of these programs in
Massachusetts, and I was received with scattered applause. I assured the men of my concern for their welfare. I said I hoped they
would co-operate with me in the months to come. I pledged that
I would work closely with the parole board in Massachusetts, that
I would do all I could to make sure we were preparing men properly for their appearances before the parole board and for their
return to their communities.

At the conclusion of these brief remarks I was bombarded by
questions. Some were very pointed: "How do you think *you're*
going to change all this?" and "Where do you think *you're* going
to get the money?" This angry and suspicious atmosphere was new
to me—nothing at all like Wisconsin. There was a lot of tension
and I did not know what might happen. But the large majority
treated me with respect and asked intelligent questions, some of
which I answered and some of which I said I would answer by
mail. In the end, I was glad to get out of there, and I decided to
expedite the evacuation of this monstrous prison. To bottle men
up in a place like that was only to invite more rioting, bloodshed,
and disaster.

THE MEETING WITH THE RINGLEADERS

My wife had been understandably anxious during this initial
confrontation, but it was Jane who urged me to take a greater
risk on Christmas Eve.

Four of the leaders of the January riot, not including Teddy
Green, were still in segregation at Charlestown. They had also
asked to meet with me, but it was difficult for me to find the time.
On the other hand, they had been isolated for almost a year and
I wanted to hear their story. The day before Christmas I called
home about something or other, and Jane asked me when I was
ever going to see the leaders of the riot. I said, "I want to as soon
as I can," and she said, "Well, you must do it today."

That afternoon, about 4:00 or 4:30 P.M., I went down to
Charlestown, shook aside the usual pressure for escorts, and went

to a room deep in the ancient institution. There I talked alone with the leaders of the revolt. "Commissioner," said one man, "if you will put us back in the general prison population, you will never have a minute's worth of trouble from any of us." I said, "Well, that's my goal. That is what I hope to do at the very earliest point."

Then the prisoner said, "Only one thing I want to add, and that is, don't leave the gates open." I thought I understood what the proposal was: they would be trying to escape, but, within the institution, they would behave.

I took them at their word, brought the men back into the prison population, and had no more trouble with them. I told Jane it was a Christmas present. But my attitude sent a shock wave through the Massachusetts prison Establishment.

THE GUARD ASLEEP

Three reformatory officers at our institution at Concord testified at a departmental hearing that they had found a guard asleep on duty. An assistant deputy superintendent said the man had been fast asleep in the security section at 4:00 A.M., stretched out on a table with his shoes off, covered with a blanket. His keys had been left in a table drawer twenty feet away.

The guard said he often made his rounds in stockinged feet so the prisoners would not hear him, and he had just lain down for a minute to rest stomach cramps. He said he had not meant to go to sleep.

I ordered him suspended the next day, declaring we intended "to insure the safe custody of those confined for the protection of the officers and the public."

No sooner were the hearings over than I was bombarded with angry appeals to reinstate the man. The correctional officers' union intervened. I held my ground and was upheld in the end by the Civil Service Commission, but I had made many more enemies. "You can't do that," some politicians told me.

THE DEPUTY COMMISSIONERS FROM OUT OF STATE

In response to Governor Herter's mandate to bring in the best men, wherever I could find them, I engaged Raymond Davidson and Dr. Asher R. Pacht, both of Wisconsin, as two of my three deputy commissioners. The Springfield *News* said, "We can expect criticism from some quarters that the new prisons chief is skipping over Massachusetts men but he should be given a free hand to bring order out of chaos." I appointed a Massachusetts man, Edwin Powers, an official of the United Prisons Association, a statewide group of private citizens interested in prison reform, as the third deputy commissioner. I also brought in Walter R. Achuff, a dynamic leader from California, to be the warden of our new $9 million Massachusetts Correctional Institution at Walpole.

But the Massachusetts Executive Council which, in this state, has to approve the governor's major appointments, gave Dr. Pacht a hard time. Two of the Democrats voted against him and a third, the celebrated Endicott "Chub" Peabody, conspicuously abstained. One of the Democrats said, "We are stripping Wisconsin of its top officials. I wonder who's minding the store back there." The Republicans on the council pushed the Pacht nomination through, but I was distressed to find we had so much politics in what Governor Herter had assured me would be a non-political endeavor.

The politics continued. Early in 1956, in a speech before 250 people at a United Community Fund meeting, I blew up. I said I found the Massachusetts penal system "loaded with political interference and pressure groups." I said there were more people seeking jobs whose only qualification was friendship "with people in high places." I charged that the guards in some prisons were holding concessions "such as selling submarine sandwiches." I complained of "a shortage of psychiatrists and an absence of educational programs" and of the fact that there were mentally ill prisoners "who had only one examination in three years." Then I raised the ante:

"What you should remember in Massachusetts is that the people in the other states will not judge you solely because of the grand job that is being done in the field of electronics and nuclear research by the finest educational and cultural institutions. They will judge you in the end by the way we take care of our lesser citizens—by the degree to which we elevate human relationships, expressing our concern for human rights and human needs."

Riding in the train the next day from Wellesley, where I lived, to Boston, I was surprised and delighted to hear favorable comments from citizens reading the newspaper stories under the headline OSWALD'S BLAST. But it was not long before I got as good as I gave. *La Gazzetta del Massachusetts*, the largest circulation Italian-language newspaper in the state, paid its respects:

"Massachusetts has a new regime which appears to have far too much of a Wisconsin flavor, where the making of cheese is one of the principal industries. A Catholic prelate with many years of contact with prisons and criminals ridicules the contention that criminals can be rehabilitated. He maintains that criminals are nothing else but that, and they would always be enemies of society."

I never found out who "the prelate" was, but I wondered, and I suspected he was real enough. Nor was I able to find out why *La Gazzetta* was interested in keeping the prisons the way they were.

Governor Herter and I now moved to evacuate the hideous Charlestown prison as rapidly as possible. I transported the men out in groups of ten or so every day to the brand-new correctional institution at Walpole, giving priority to prison industry workers so we could get Walpole operational as rapidly as possible. It may seem strange at this historic moment in prison reform, but one of our concerns was to maintain a steady production of the 1957 automobile registration plates for the state.

After I had completed the evacuation, I thought I would shock the public into some realization of what was involved in prison reform. So I showed newspapermen around Charlestown for the first time in its history. I pointed out the tiny cells and the honey buckets, the chains hanging from the granite walls to which men had long ago been tied while they were whipped. I tried to summon some of the twenty-two cats whose job it had been to hold off rats almost as large, but they would not come. Later, I persuaded the Animal Rescue League to take care of the Charlestown cats.

There were two principal points of interest on the tour. The first was the "cell-within-a-cell" in which a prisoner had been held in solitary confinement for thirty-eight years. His name was Jesse Pomeroy, and he had been convicted in the late nineteenth century of murdering a four-year-old boy and of torturing and murdering an eleven-year-old girl. Because he was only fourteen, he was spared the death penalty. But he spent the first sixteen years of his life sentence in a cell as small as a coke oven. After several escape attempts, the prison staff invented and designed a horrifying thing for prisoner Pomeroy—a contraption of steel bars set up inside his regulation, granite-walled quarters. He ultimately had to be transferred to a hospital for the criminally insane and died there in 1932.

The second item of attention was a memorandum sent to the prison staff by the former warden, John J. O'Brien, not long before the 1955 riot. It is especially interesting in the light of the Attica parallel: "If at any time, day or night, any inmate or inmates are successful in seizing, holding, and using an official, guards or any other persons, including the undersigned, for the purpose of using them as hostages to attempt to escape, the official or officer on duty will disobey any order which said hostage or hostages might issue, including the undersigned, even though it might mean the life of such hostage or hostages, including the undersigned."

My objective was to awaken a civilized state to the uncivilized practices that were conducted in its name. At Charlestown, I said, "Some people think that prisons like this should be intended only to punish. And for a long, long time, society had only one solution to the ever-present problem of the law violator—lock him up behind stout bars and high walls, keep him under constant watch by strong-armed guards, depress, degrade, even mistreat him into penitence.

"Human nature being what it is, men and women come out of such prisons no better, subdued, possibly, but unrepentant and unchanged, in many cases bitter and vengeful at the treatment to which they have been subjected. Such prisons never have, never can do more than keep people locked up and afford society short-term protection, and finally release people likely to offend again."

With sensational picture spreads of the horrors of Charlestown in all the newspapers state-wide, for once I was not contradicted. Only the Worcester *Gazette* warned, "Mr. Oswald's attitude will not sit well . . . Massachusetts unfortunately still has some in public office who consider rehabilitation efforts a waste of time."

Governor Herter and I wanted to make sure that Charlestown

would never again be reoccupied by prisoners of the state. So I recommended, and the governor ordered, that the place be torn down. In the end I was to remain only eighteen months in Massachusetts—but Charlestown *was* torn down.

Into our new Massachusetts Correctional Institution at Walpole we brought virtually instant reforms. One of my principles was to remove the troublemakers, as in Wisconsin, so that the rehabilitation of the majority might proceed without hindrance. So we created a small, maximum-security unit for the more difficult prisoners at Walpole, some thirty or forty out of 600 or 700 men confined. The more difficult prisoners were not political radicals, but practitioners of aimless violence. They would harass the corrections officers or attack other prisoners just to express their general resentment of everything. Perhaps today's self-described political radicals are not all that different.

In any event, I felt that prisoners had a right to be protected from the violent in their midst. I would not tolerate gangs, cliques, and bullies at Walpole. I was determined to make it possible for men to serve out their sentences in peace and to work for their rehabilitation in preparation for parole.

In this spirit, the state legislature advanced $400,000 for the new maximum-security unit and $150,000 for three additional camps and minimum-security installations I wanted elsewhere in the state. The legislature also authorized the expenditure of $60,000 for lighting the dark segregation cells that the Wessell Committee had recommended abolished.

Warden Achuff of Walpole was the man who sparked the new Massachusetts prison reform program. He was a fearless individual, an innovative thinker who had served as director of training at Folsom Prison in California. His first move at Walpole, and one of his most controversial, was to set up a new disciplinary system. He created a board including a social worker, a work assignment officer, a senior corrections officer, a deputy, and a chief clerk to pass on disciplinary problems. Previously, the deputy warden at Charlestown had been the judge and jury of everybody he beheld.

Walter Achuff required that the disciplinary board grant hearings to every inmate charged with violations of the rules at Walpole before it passed sentence. The board was also required to consider the prisoner's case history and to weigh the impact that the form of punishment might have upon the man's incentives for rehabilitation. There was a strong, implied pressure here toward leniency. The old-line prison personnel resented this intrusion upon their traditional dominance, but the results were excellent. There were markedly fewer violations of the rules.

Warden Achuff placed a new emphasis on academic and vocational training in the correctional institution. Only ten of the 500 men at Charlestown had been taking courses. But 329 of the 600 or more men at Walpole wanted to take courses. This was real change—the kind of trend prison reformers work for and dream about. He and I had only enough money to pay teachers for classes for the first fifty men, so I went to the Harvard Graduate School of Education and asked for volunteer teachers. This was the beginning of one of our most promising new programs, in which groups of graduate students taught classes at Walpole without pay.

Then I went to the man who was to become president of the American Psychiatric Association, Dr. Harry Solomon, and to Dr. Jack Ewalt, who was head of the State Division of Mental Health. I told them the mental health situation in our prisons was lamentable and beyond our control. For example, we had one psychiatric worker serving the whole population of 385 men in the correctional institution at Bridgewater.

Dr. Solomon and Dr. Ewalt said they would do all they could to help, and it was not long before forty or fifty psychiatrists and psychologists were working in our prisons as volunteers. These men gave us their evenings and their weekends and told us they found the work fascinating, for they did not come into contact with such socioeconomic patterns in their private practices. They were particularly helpful in bringing back the less tractable prisoners toward a state of mind suitable for parole.

The Division of Legal Medicine in Massachusetts also gave us valuable help, and in this category at least we were moving ahead well. The medical schools of Harvard and Tufts, also Massachusetts General Hospital conducted research projects, and soon we were building casework components into every one of our institutions.

Warden Achuff made many "routine" improvements I considered to be of great importance. He prescribed a nutritious diet, and he insisted on eating the same menus as the prisoners at mealtime. He had the inside of the buildings painted a lighter, more cheerful color than the miserable prison gray. He brought in landscape experts to plant and seed the spacious grounds, and he assigned vegetable and flower plots to several of the prisoners who were interested. He offered free X-rays to prisoners and prison personnel—and he was astonished that this had not been done before.

There was a little more attention paid to prison industries after Governor Herter and I persuaded the legislature to pay the men from $54.75 to $109.50 per year—also something new, at least in Massachusetts. Walter Achuff instituted a safety program at Walpole and he asked General Electric Company and Pittsburgh Plate Glass Company to send voluntary consultants to suggest improvements.

I was also an advocate of sports programs in the prisons as a tool of rehabilitation and to help the time pass by. One day I was walking around our institution at Norfolk with the advisory committee on corrections and I went down to the ball field, took off my coat, and asked some of the prisoners there if I could have a turn at bat. They all whistled and cheered. The pitcher threw the first one much too close to me, and they all began yelling that he had lost his chance for parole. But he grooved a couple, and I hit one of them practically to the wall.

On July 4, 1956, Warden Achuff and I thought we would relax the routine at Walpole and have the first prison holiday in the history of the state. The day began as usual with early call, breakfast was served, and the rooms tidied, but after that the prisoners were on their own. They had the full run of the grounds for the day.

At 1:00 P.M., after a turkey luncheon, all the visitors poured into the correctional institution—wives, sweethearts, relatives, and friends—and stayed for three or four hours. There was also a baseball game between the Walpole All Stars and the Johnson Bombers, a black outfit from the neighborhood. They asked me to throw out the opening ball, but there were a lot of newspapermen there and I thought it would look too contrived. I said "No," and wished I had not, but there it was. In any event, the day was a smash hit, and we received a very favorable public reaction. The

Boston *Traveler* summed up what was probably the high point of my brief stay in Massachusetts:

"A move such as the Fourth of July affair can have good influence beyond measure. It can be the ray of hope in an otherwise drab life. It can smooth a convict's philosophy and make him more palatable to the changes he must undergo if he hopes to regain a place in society.

"Oswald's innovation undoubtedly helped to smooth out some mental kinks and make life a bit more pleasant."

Tragically, hardly two weeks later, Mrs. Darlene Achuff, the warden's wife, was killed in a grade crossing accident. Without any kind of encouragement, the prisoners at Walpole raised a fund of more than $1,000 for a memorial fund for Mrs. Achuff. The warden would accept only a dollar or less per man, and he spent the money on prisoner benefits and more books for the prison library.

At the end of September 1956 *La Gazzetta* wrapped up a dreadful period with one of its spiciest editorials. WHEN WILL HERTER MOVE? ran the headline, and what followed was a demand that Governor Herter remove me from office. The editorial declared:

"Conditions in the prisons are becoming progressively worse. The new policy of rehabilitating hardened criminals with belly dancers, theatrical shows, and other innovations may be liked by the 'long-haired men' and the 'short-haired women,' but men whose lives have been devoted to prison work, who know and understand criminals, are fearful of what they say is sure to happen. Correctional Commissioner Oswald and his protégés imported from the west have very limited experience in prison management."

Once again, it was crisis after crisis in Massachusetts.

THE "MISTER ROBERTS" CRISIS

In September, eighty-four of the prisoners at the correctional institution at Walpole presented their own production of the play *Mister Roberts*. Three of the former ringleaders of the Charlestown riot, who had lived up to their promise and given me no trouble, worked as production manager, associate production manager, and stage manager. We invited members of the outside community to come in and see *Mister Roberts*—a businessmen's club helped with the organization and one of the women's clubs helped hang the curtains—and we took the risk of letting prisoners act as ushers.

At once came an uproar from the corrections officers. They said there would be kidnapings and captures of hostages, or prisoners would disguise themselves in civilian clothes and make their escape when the people left after the show. Doubtless these were valid fears, but the bitterness of the corrections officers persisted even after *Mister Roberts* went off without trouble. I realized these were risks, but I felt it was worth while to involve the community more in what we were trying to accomplish at Walpole.

THE STRIPTEASE CRISIS

Through the American Guild of Variety Artists, we began to bring in volunteer entertainers to make life a little brighter at Walpole. The AGVA would send over touring artists who were working in Boston and we never dreamed there would be trouble. Not all the entertainers were Metropolitan Opera singers, nicely dressed baritones, and so on, and lots of the girls wore the usual, abbreviated costumes.

One evening the performer was Flo Morris, a ballet dancer who noted with some pride that she was one of the very few authorized by the local police to dance on Sundays. Her manager, Smiley Hart, said, "It is true she uses fans, but there is absolutely no removal of clothing and her costumes are not scanty by any means."

In fact, Miss Morris did not do a striptease in our correctional institution, but several of the corrections officers told the newspapers that she had. "It brought back memories of the Old Howard," one of them remarked. Warden Achuff was at the show, and he said, "I've seen burlesque and it was not burlesque." Miss Morris bristled: "My costume and my dance were neither suggestive nor vulgar. I have never been rebuked by any official anywhere for my performance, and this has upset me very much, to find that I have been compared to a burlesque actress."

Nothing we could learn or say made any difference. The Boston *American* made this the lead story of the day: FAN DANCER

PERFORMS IN PRISON. The AGVA demanded a retraction. We just had to wait for *l'affaire Flo Morris* to fade into history.

THE MILDEWED-BOLOGNA STRIKE

Our reputation for preserving an almost miraculous peace in our new prisons blew up with a sit-down strike at Walpole. No fewer than 150 of our men refused to work at their jobs in the metal shop and the newspapers were told about it almost at once.

Not until the damage to us had been done did we learn that several of the men were ill. They protested they had been served frozen bologna which had mildewed. This was the reason for the sit-down strike. Unfortunately, this was the kind of thing which could happen even in a prison run by Mr. Achuff, but, coming at that time, it was a disaster for us. The mildewed-bologna strike made headlines as if it had been another Charlestown riot.

THE FOSTER FURCOLO AFFAIR

Early in 1957 incoming Governor Foster Furcolo said he wanted to address the whole prison population at Walpole. I was devoted to the outgoing governor, Christian Herter. He had even been thoughtful enough to send a letter to my parents on their golden anniversary, "We in Massachusetts are thankful we have your son working for us." He was like that. On the other hand, I felt that Governor Furcolo was an advocate of prison reform who might be able to spread our message more widely in less friendly segments of the Massachusetts community. In any event, I was in favor of Governor Furcolo speaking at Walpole. Unfortunately, Warden Achuff was not.

Walter Achuff felt his worst fears confirmed when the prisoners began asking the usual, pointed questions, and the new governor said nothing to keep their expectations within bounds. One of the aides was standing beside the governor, saying, "We'll advise you . . . We'll get back to you," and so on, and taking things down.

Mr. Achuff felt the men were expecting results we might not be able to deliver and that they might lash back at us. He also felt it was the beginning of a new politicization of the prisons. In fact, Governor Furcolo did a good job. But Mr. Achuff was almost ready to resign.

In February 1957, Warden Achuff did resign amid widespread reports that he was at catastrophic odds with his staff. There had been protest meetings of corrections officers in which the warden's policies were damned for "going too far," and in which I was criticized for making critical remarks about corrections officers. There was probably some jealousy because Walter Achuff's widely publicized reforms had led to an unusual situation in prison staff recruitment. There were actually more men who wanted to work in our prisons than we could handle, even though the starting salary was only $3,490 per year.

Actually, we had done much to upgrade the status of the corrections officers and to improve conditions of work. One of our clear successes was to run training courses not only for new workers, but also for groups of our existing correctional staffs. The first group of sixty out of our 800 correctional workers went off to the first course in October 1956 and took refreshers in psychology, law, social work, and techniques of prison administration. "It's the best two weeks of my twenty-two years in the department," one of our officers said. But it is entirely possible some of the others might not have agreed.

It was certain that Warden Achuff's old-line staff members were dragging their feet—and that many considered him to be a do-gooder and a dreamer. It is possible there was minor sabotage of his programs. This can be done when corrections officers harass prisoners, not by beating them, but by making minor charges and cranking up the disciplinary mechanisms, thereby reducing the men's desire to co-operate with the rehabilitation programs. It is also true that Walter Achuff, in creating inmate advisory councils through which the prisoners themselves participated in non-strategic areas of prison administration, moved too far ahead of his times and invited the reaction.

I could not dissuade Mr. Achuff from resigning, from returning to California, where he is now serving with distinction as an associate warden. I brought in a career man rather than a political appointee to replace him—John A. Gavin, who had done much to make new forestry camps in Massachusetts a success.

Reading back over the speeches I made and the statements I issued at this time, it is clear I was being run ragged—and that I was a long way from home in Wisconsin.

Not long before we lost Mr. Achuff, I commented we were in a "rudderless, drifting society," that the prisoners were "products of a neurotic society," and yet "a naïve public deludes itself that they should behave like gentlemen as soon as they are behind bars." I added that a society that burns billions of cigarettes a year, drinks a million cases of liquor, and believes people are naïve to pay parking tickets has no right "to expect prisoners to be paragons of virtue. Society itself must be to blame when 45 to 50 per cent of our prisoners in Massachusetts are repeaters."

And so when a splendid offer came my way, to move to New York State to become a commissioner of parole, I was ready to go. It had been one thing after another in Massachusetts, none sufficient to make me move, really, but when the next opportunity came, Jane and I were sure that we had better move on to New York, even though we hated to leave our home in Wellesley.

On May 15, 1957, I resigned, putting an end to a very bumpy period of my life. I was pleased when almost all the newspapers praised me for the reforms I had been able to introduce and I was amused that the Boston *Traveler* noted in its headline, OSWALD TAKES HIGH-PAID NEW YORK POST. But the Boston *Globe* reported my resignation like this:

"During his eighteen months, it has been common knowledge that many of his ideas for modernizing and streamlining the penal system have been met with open hostility by the old guard. In some instances, prison personnel have even encouraged inmates to balk introduction of new procedures.

"These men, some of whom are veteran employees in the Corrections Department, have openly demonstrated they disagree with the basic philosophy of modern penology for which Oswald stands, and they had battled him all the way."

Governor Furcolo paid me the compliment of saying he would have appointed me Commissioner of Corrections himself if Governor Herter had not spotted me first. There were so many good people in Massachusetts that I could not help feeling sorry to leave.

But my favorite good-by came from the prisoners, from *The Mentor*, their newspaper at Walpole. It read: "We're grateful to you not only for what you were able to accomplish, but for what you would have liked to accomplish. It might be some consolation for all those headaches to know you succeeded in getting through to a lot of us, which was something past prison administrators never seemed able to accomplish."

CHAPTER 9

The Cliff-Hangers, the Heartbreaks,
the Humane Victories of Parole

John Baker was six feet tall, and he weighed 174 pounds. He was twenty-four years old, white, dark-haired, brown-eyed, and his complexion had the sallow pallor of an inmate of a New York State correctional institution. He had been in trouble since he was fourteen years old, and was serving a five-to-ten year sentence for robbery with violence. After completing more than three years of his sentence, he was now seated before a three-member panel of the New York State Board of Parole. He was silent, tense, well-scrubbed, and ready to make a good impression.

I had accepted the invitation to serve on the New York State Board of Parole in 1957—at the insistence of Governor Averell Harriman. I had served as a parole worker and director before serving as Commissioner of Corrections in Wisconsin and in Massachusetts. In September 1958 I was elected chairman of the New York State Board of Parole and now I was about to participate in interviewing one of approximately 4,000 men I would see in an average year.

Mr. Baker was married and he had two children. His parents had been separated since he was ten, and he had not seen his father since he was twelve. His first offense had been vandalism, and he had been a truant, a dropout from school. By the time he was sixteen, he had also become a fairly serious drinker.

John Baker's first formal arrest was at sixteen, for automobile theft. He was convicted and placed on probation. He tried to make a go of this, working at a car wash, marrying a seventeen-year-old girl he had made pregnant, and co-operating with the probation officers. But then he joined an interstate automobile theft ring and was apprehended in another state. He served a full three-year sentence there before returning to New York.

Once again, he attempted to work—but he also began to drink

more heavily. He tried to make a living for his wife and child, and a second child was on the way. He decided to run some risks and committed a series of robberies. He was arrested as he fled from a store in which the owner had been badly beaten with a lead pipe. This was much more serious; hence, the five-to-ten year sentence for such a young man.

After he had identified himself for the record, I took the lead in questioning him. I tried to put him at some ease by asking how he was, how he was getting along. The two other members of the parole board meanwhile examined the mass of data our caseworkers had compiled in his community and in the correctional institution. Persuasive though this material was, we would lean very heavily on the interview.

Since 1930, when the New York State Board of Parole was created, prospective parolees had been required by law to appear in person, to tell their own side of the story, to supply their own corrective to the personal, medical, psychiatric, behavioral, and prison disciplinary material in our files.

I zeroed in on Mr. Baker's crime of record. "Did you do it?" I asked. "Was the conviction just? Why did you do it? How did you feel about the crime then? How now?" I was pleased when he readily admitted to the robbery and also to some others that had not previously come to light. All too often in these interviews, we had to sit through phony claims that the men had been framed. John Baker's candor was a promising start.

"How about your record in the institution?" I asked. "What have you been doing there? Do you have a prison job? Are you learning any trade? Are you trying to get your high school equivalency? Have you been talking to any of the correctional people or the psychiatrists about your drinking problem?"

John Baker said he had a useful job as a porter, but he had signed on for none of the academic or vocational training courses. He was simply serving his time. He had seen the psychiatrist on several occasions, but he did not regard his drinking as a serious problem. These were negative answers but they verified the information we had in hand from the prison. The man was not attempting to mislead us.

"What about parole?" I asked. "Where would you live? What kind of job would you get? What about your family? Who would help you get a job? How do you think you would react to parole supervision? Would you obey the orders of your parole officer, for example, if your drinking problem reappears? Most important, what makes you different now from when you were admitted to the institution? What changes have you made, or have been made in you, which would cause us to grant parole?"

He said he believed he had changed greatly during his three years in prison, that he had matured and had a different outlook on life. He wished to rejoin his family and, although there was no visible job opportunity, he would of course co-operate with the parole officer. He maintained that his drinking was not a problem, since he had merely been young and foolish before.

When the interview was over, my two fellow members of the parole board and I tried to reconcile the conflict. He had been admirably honest with us. But the three of us doubted he was really being honest with himself. His good intentions notwithstanding, the fact was that he was merely "doing his time." And our career caseworkers had learned from the state in which he had previously been imprisoned that he had just done his time there, too.

Mr. Baker showed what seemed to us to be a lack of any real evidence that he would work for his rehabilitation. But his good intentions, his acceptance of rehabilitation as a desirable goal, were extremely important. His behavior in prison had been good. He had abided by the rules and caused no trouble. In some states this would have been regarded as more than ample reason for release. But we now measured as best we could whether he was really any better equipped to handle society now than he had been when he robbed the store. Also, what were the prospects for improvement, if any, after his release? Although John Baker's family and friends were ready to help him, was he really ready to help himself?

This was really a cliff-hanger for us. And it was interesting that, for all the brilliant documentation our people had compiled on John Baker and despite an unusually honest interview, we found ourselves leaning against him. We realized this would come as a shock to him after his sincere effort before us. And the gut reason was the gut nature of the crime for which he had been sentenced. Robbery with *violence* was many steps more serious than robbery—and Mr. Baker had escalated to this level of criminality *because* his personal problems had deepened.

We had to be sure that he would work on parole, straightforwardly and systematically, to sustain himself and his family. We had to be absolutely sure there would be no drinking. And we had to be sure, because if things did not work out right for him, and even though he had the best intentions, he might be desperate enough to consider committing another violent crime. His initial break into violence had already been made.

With many regrets, we therefore decided to keep Mr. Baker in prison and to call him up for another hearing after a relatively long eighteen-month period. We felt he had to demonstrate much more of a track record in the prison rehabilitation programs, while maintaining his good behavior. We felt he should also show much more drive toward a specific acquisition of skills that would help provide a livelihood. We felt he needed more of a program in his own mind about how he intended to live in the future. We felt finally that, considering the violence of Mr. Baker's crime, all these factors were valid concerns of society.

We praised Mr. Baker's deportment, however, and we said that if he showed these new motivations during the next eighteen months, then we might be justified in releasing even a violent offender. We also felt that our insistence on these motivations would be of profound help to Mr. Baker. If he wanted to get out of prison, he would have to face up to himself.

The John Baker decision was one of 12,000 or so decisions the Board of Parole makes every year in New York State. We reached these decisions in New York as we had in Wisconsin—with an awesome awareness of our responsibility for the freedom and welfare of individuals as well as of our responsibility for the safety and welfare of the community to which parolees would inevitably return. If we held the prisoners too long or denied them parole unreasonably, even capriciously, then we ran additional risks. The men might become embittered and vindictive, more rather than less of a danger to their neighbors. On the other hand, if we let them go before they were able to handle their problems in "the free world," then we would be giving them something less than a fair chance, and we would be inviting them back to imprisonment.

Section 213 of the New York State Corrections Law specifies the nature of the godlike responsibility we sometimes felt we were laboring under:

"No prisoner shall be released on parole merely as a reward for good conduct or efficient performance of duties assigned in prison, but only if the Board of Parole *is of the opinion* that there is a reasonable probability that, if such prisoner is released, he will live and remain at liberty without violating the law, and that his release is not incompatible with the welfare of society."

This phrase "is of the opinion" of the parole board was a scant mandate for our control over several thousand individual freedoms—almost four times as many as in Wisconsin. But we did attempt to administer this responsibility in the belief that all men were capable of change. And it was a source of incredible personal satisfaction to be helping people change. We watched our success-to-failure ratios with an intensity that only those men and women in the "parole business" could even begin to fathom.

In the year in which I moved from Massachusetts to New York, for example, there was a parole scandal concerning Joseph "Socks" Lanza, a lawbreaker of some repute. It was alleged that he had received favored treatment from a member of the Parole Board, a man who had almost certainly done no wrong, but nonetheless resigned under pressure. I was the man's successor—and I was soon seething under the ill-informed public criticism of our parole men and motives.

To many, it seemed that parole was simply another extension of the "coddling of criminals." But even in those years, the record of the New York Board of Parole was excellent. In the year 1956, for example, there were 3,502 prisoners released on parole in the state. During a subsequent five-year measurement period, only 177 of these men and women were recommitted to New York State correctional institutions for new felony convictions for offenses committed on parole. This was a recommitment recidivism rate of only 5 per cent.

Even in these early years we were achieving a 60 per cent record of success. This was even more remarkable when it was considered that, in our *first* interviews with prisoners, and in our first readings of their case studies, we were making value judgments much as we did in the John Baker case.

In one typical year we conducted 4,690 first interviews with people imprisoned for offenses ranging from vagrancy to murder. Eight out of ten had previous convictions. Four out of ten had a history of alcoholism, narcotics use, abnormal sexual proclivities, or a combination. Yet we paroled 53 per cent of them and obtained the results we found so encouraging.

There was also the very important statistical measurement not only of parolees released in a single year, but of *all* people living under parole supervision in a single year. In 1959, for example, there was a total of 14,660 men and women out on parole in New York State. Only 14.8 per cent of these people were involved in that year in even technical violations of parole, such as taking a drink, having a dubious love affair, or driving an automobile without notifying the parole officer. The comparative percentages for 1957 and 1958 were 15.2 per cent and 14.4 per cent, so there was a steady record of success.

So where did our society's high percentage of recidivism come from? This is the rate at which people are returned to prison for repeat offenses. It came primarily from the men who were not accepted for parole, who served out their allotted sentences and were then released to perpetrate new crimes. The tragically high percentage of repeat offenders therefore was really not a charge against parole at all.

How many parolees actually absconded, then? Was the record that astonishing? Well, in my first year as a member of the parole board, only 646 men and women absconded out of almost 15,-000 who were on parole. This was less than 5 per cent. In the years to come we would be able to reduce even this percentage as we tightened our procedures, increased staffs, reduced caseloads, refined our professional judgments, and investigated more deeply into the prisoners' personal and community backgrounds.

Parole *is* a crime-fighting tool that works. Even in the defensive sense, it is hard to argue against parole. It costs New York State $908 per year to supervise a parolee as against an average of $5,080 per year to care for an inmate in a correctional institution. And parolees become working members of the labor force, paying federal, state, and local taxes. In one of these early years of my parole experience, they earned $20 million in the state and paid taxes on it.

In fact, then as now, it was good business to hire parolees. Parolees have skills certified by our personnel specialists on the Parole Board. They have parole officers who see to it that they get to work on time and stay on the job in general. They have employers, more often than not, with a streak of altruism, who are aware of the parolees' problems and who travel more than the extra mile to help the men get on top of their jobs. Parolees, in fact, have so much more incentive than most of us to make good that they make outstanding employment prospects.

Despite criticism from members of the public who feel that our parole rules are too harsh, we find our pettifogging niceties to be useful. The layman might have argued, "Well, what's so bad about a fellow driving a car, even buying a car, without the parole officer knowing about it?" But the purchase and the driving of automobiles, after confinement in prison, can sometimes be a heady experience. And in order to get money for cars, or for payments on cars, there might be a temptation to steal.

The layman might have argued again, "Well, why should a parole officer have to know who the poor guy is sleeping with?" The answer is that we are concerned far more about renewals of criminal associations than in holding to unrealistic moral standards.

Until recently, the rules of parole forbade any and all consumption of alcohol—but, in effect, we did not prohibit every parolee who came out on the street after months of imprisonment from walking into a bar and buying a beer. We do view very seriously any instance of parolees with previous alcoholic histories attempting to do the same thing. We do not want them to head back down the old road to new convictions, to do violence to their own futures, or to undermine public confidence in the parole program.

It is tremendously important that parolees confide in their parole officers—and these confidences often govern the attitude of the authorities even in narcotics cases. Whenever parolees tell their officers they are slipping back and need help, we are inclined to treat the new addiction in outside clinics and watch what transpires before sending the men back to the institutions. We also, of course, watch with redoubled care before letting them back out on the street. So even though the parole rules might seem to define an unreal social conduct, they really reflect professional common sense.

Theoretically, in the late 1950s and 1960s, many supposed that otherwise blameless parolees could be returned to prison for such "dreadful" deeds as drinking too many beers or having girls they were not married to stay overnight, but it did not happen quite like that. It might not have been proper for me to say it, but often we made some parolees lead a better life than many free citizens lead. And it worked.

To put it another way, parolees, far from being a menace to society, were often the most law-abiding members of the community. They had reasons that went far deeper than a fear of being returned to prison. They were doing something for themselves. They had learned lessons that hardly any of us could have even imagined. And—as we liked to think as we went about our rounds —the parolees were succeeding a little for us.

In a personal sense, these early days on the Board of Parole in New York were among the happiest of my life. In place of the spectacular progress in Wisconsin or the constant controversy in Massachusetts, we were winning quiet, humane victories in tens of thousands of peoples' lives. Furthermore, I was not being called upon to handle any crises—for a change.

In fact, the New York parole program was already very good indeed and, along with Wisconsin's, was far and away the best in the United States. As former New York Governor Herbert H. Lehman once put it, "Parole should be judged by the gold it refines, not by the dross it inherits." Our problem was merely to make a good system better and to apply its lessons more extensively.

In this unaccustomed atmosphere of peaceful routine, I had excellent relationships with my new superiors. I accepted Governor Harriman's offer to serve as a Parole Board member after a personal conference in his town house in Manhattan that I thoroughly enjoyed. But in New York State, the chairman of the Board of Parole is elected by the members, rather than appointed by the governor. My elevation to the chairmanship in September 1958 was to replace Lee B. Mailler, who resigned because of ill health.

As chairman, I was strongly supported by Governor Harriman, and when Governor Rockefeller took office as his successor in 1959, he made this flat statement to me: "I'm happy that you are here and I know you will do a progressive job in the parole program." I knew at once from this greeting that my job was to be kept out of politics—and for me this was of critical importance.

I knew there had been correspondence between the incoming governor's staff and Republican officials in Massachusetts. It was known that I was an admirer of former Governor Harriman and there had been questions as to whether I was in fact a Democrat, too political for the parole job. The Republican state chairman in Massachusetts wrote back that I was completely non-political and that this was one of my great strengths in penology. The state chairman even sent me a copy of the letter.

Governor Rockefeller had also done his own homework about me. As Undersecretary of Health, Education, and Welfare in the Eisenhower administration, he had met my former superior in Wisconsin, John Tramburg. Now Governor Rockefeller had sought out Mr. Tramburg's judgment on my capabilities and had heard good things. Long afterward, Governor Rockefeller told me John Tramburg had said I was outstanding in the whole correctional field in the United States. This perhaps helped explain the strength of our initial relationship—a friendship that would grow through twelve years of ever-closer confidence and philosophical kinship. On this, perhaps, was based the governor's decision to leave to my professional judgment the handling of the Attica crisis in the gravest moment of his own political life.

Not long after Governor Rockefeller was elected, I heard that he was going to appoint a man named T. Norman Hurd as Director of the Budget. This was the Dr. Hurd who would later play a notable role at Attica. My secretary happened to mention to me, "Dr. Hurd is a tremendous person who was budget director under Governor Dewey. I think you will get the kind of help you need from him in parole."

So before Dr. Hurd took office I wrote him a letter in my capacity as chairman of the Board of Parole. I spelled out for him the concepts and problems of parole as I saw them—it was a long letter—and I asked for his sympathetic help when he took over the Division of the Budget. Dr. Hurd called me as soon as he arrived in Albany, and we had a lengthy talk. This began a marvelous relationship of twelve years that would serve us well at Attica.

Right from the start, in our discussions in the Executive Mansion at Albany and elsewhere, Governor Rockefeller pressed me to probe new frontiers in parole. He is a very warm individual with a deep personal feeling for people in need of help. He particularly enjoyed it when I told him about unusual cases we had heard on the Parole Board, about how we had weighed our judgments, and what the results were. It was an elixir to him when he heard of parolees who really turned around and did something worth while. He wanted to hear about people succeeding.

One evening, for example, I was having dinner with the governor and I happened to mention an idea of mine that we should have a special unit for handling parolees with unusual gifts. I had been interviewing some youthful offenders at one of the reformatories when I came across a boy who had not attended high school. But in the reformatory, he had whizzed through his high school equivalency and university mathematics courses and his professor had written me that the boy was a near genius. I began thinking that, if I was a parole officer, I would love to have some raw material like this. I could go to a top-level employer and say, "Let's really see about this—here is a boy who perhaps is not emotionally acting up to capacity but has tremendous intellectual ability." I wanted to help him and similar young offenders and also I felt a few success stories of this type would upgrade the public concept of parole.

As often happens when dealing with Governor Rockefeller, if you offer a good idea and he happens to like it, you have a full-grown program growling and biting at you in the office the next morning. "Why don't you get going on this right away?" the governor's voice came over the telephone. "How much would it cost to institute the . . . the . . . gifted parolee program?" Now the thing even had a title. I quickly got it going and set up in the Division of Parole a Gifted Parolee Unit. Now I had a new element of the state government to growl back at Governor Rockefeller, and he was delighted.

So what actually happened? We took an initial, limited survey of sixty potential candidates in four of our institutions. They were mostly thirty years old or less, with IQs of 111 and above and with special aptitudes and success potentials. From our study of these young people, we determined that the gifted parolee program would work provided we could limit the caseload of each gifted program parole officer to no more than twenty-five people.

We classified the gifted parolees at the outset into three categories—academic, artistic, and vocational—and we found upwards of 130 young men and women qualified for immediate entry into the new unit. We found to meet their needs more than thirty different colleges, schools, and institutes who accepted gifted parolees and frequently offered financial assistance and formal scholarships. We had to keep potential employers away, the demand for gifted parolees was so great.

For our own part, we set up an emergency fund within the unit to help the gifted parolees buy books, music, art supplies, and also to pay emergency rent, food, and carfare whenever they needed it. Our traditional allies in the service fields, women's clubs and voluntary organizations, gave us 1,000 per cent support and, even in these limited numbers, we had a hit on our hands.

How, then, did we limit the numbers, and were we just skimming the cream of the parole crop? Governor Rockefeller was impressed when I told him that of one group of 139 gifted parolees, 82 per cent were felony offenders whose crimes had included robbery, burglary, assault, manslaughter, and even sex offenses. The remaining 18 per cent were misdemeanants, youthful offenders and girls term respondent cases.

Governor Rockefeller was also very interested when I told him that during the first twenty-two months of operation of the Gifted Parolee Unit only eight young men had been returned to their institutions even for technical violations of parole. "How many had committed new crimes?" he asked. I told him, "Three." He said this was really fantastic.

One of the graduates of the Gifted Parolee Unit obtained his high school Regents' diploma with exceptional grades before leaving the institution, entered college immediately upon his release, and did so well there he was accepted for law school. Another parolee wrote what seemed to us to be excellent short stories, and his parole officer obtained a job for him in a leading newspaper. He became a reporter and was soon promoted to the editorial desk. A third gifted parolee was enrolled by his officer in the Visual Arts School of the New York State Division of Rehabilitation, and from there he was signed on as an assistant art director by a national magazine. He has since received several promotions and is now earning a high salary. A fourth gifted parolee put most of his effort into business management studies but found himself becoming more interested in art. So while his brother promoted him upward in a family business, his parole officer put him into night arts courses in New York City, and he was soon earning a substantial side-income on freelance assignments.

We soon learned we had barely scratched the surface—and we did not have the answers to the needs of those who nearly, but not quite, qualified as gifted parolees. We learned that, in the development of an individual's level of achievement, we had to recognize that some men had to be very carefully and skillfully handled. They could not be pushed too far, too soon, past their own determination of their own potential.

Gradually the near-gifted began to realize they could attain only temporary satisfaction until their ambitions expanded. Then we were ready. Until then, we learned, they must not be pushed or there would be a risk of breakage under mental strain.

It went without saying that participation in this type of program—even the knowledge that such a program existed—was a powerful incentive in our recruitment of the right type of parole personnel. I have never seen parole officers happier than when one of their parolees excelled.

This complete success of, admittedly, one of our smallest programs encouraged us to continue our other special units for special needs. We expanded special units for narcotics offenders, for retarded youngsters, and for parolees with need for psychiatric assistance. Soon our special programs were no longer small.

In 1962 and again in 1968 I was re-elected chairman of the New York State Board of Parole and as such, executive officer of our parole supervision program. I found myself presiding to an increasing extent over our mainstream of care. Essentially, we now had more men and women coming out on parole than ever before in the history of the state—and a smaller percentage than ever before were being returned even for technical violations.

We started out from one of the most effective measures we had taken in the closing years of the Harriman administration. Previously, men had to have guaranteed employment before they could be released. This meant we often had 2,000 or more men qualified for parole but backed up in the prisons waiting for jobs. Now we were able to substitute what we termed "reasonable assurance" of employment for parole and we interpreted this broadly. This was, as always, controversial.

In the Rockefeller years we were soon releasing more than a

thousand additional parolees per year than we had during the Harriman administration with "reasonable assurance" of work and without serious danger to the public. Our first study, conducted in 1960, showed that out of a sample of 241 men released on parole with no employment in view, no fewer than 221 lived up to our interpretation of reasonable assurance and found work within sixteen days.

These results made us wonder why there had ever been a controversy in the first place. That is how things often are in the parole business.

To handle the larger volume of parolees, we employed larger numbers of parole officers. We were able to obtain adequate funds for this purpose from the New York State Legislature, whether controlled by Republicans or Democrats. Sometimes I think one reason for these good relations might have been that I always presented my budgets in person, speaking only from notes and from my own experience of what was and what was not necessary. We were also able to fill our ranks by creating the function of parole officer trainees, young men and women who had completed four years of college and were now working for higher degrees.

As I had done myself when I was in my late thirties, many of our social workers went back to graduate schools and we helped them with a variety of grants and scholarships. Our idea was to grow our own masters of social work, so to speak, and they emerged with new degrees and skills that qualified them for substantial promotions.

As our parole force thus increased, we were able to make the fundamental improvement in our services that I had always envisaged—the reduction of the caseload of each parole officer. When I became chairman, the caseload was, on the average, approximately seventy-five parolees per parole officer. By the end of the 1960s we had reduced the caseload drastically to an average of forty-one parolees per officer, although, because of enduring recruitment problems there, our average was still a caseload of fifty in New York City.

The membership of our own Board of Parole was increased from five to twelve, in part because it was manifestly impossible for us to handle our own caseload adequately. We maintained our system of three-man panels, however; we simply mustered more panels. But soon we were running to catch up with ourselves once again.

In a typical week I would leave my home at Schenectady at 8:00 A.M. on Monday and drive to a central point where we would pick up the other two commissioners on my panel. We would also have with us a hearing reporter. Then we would drive to the appointed institution and commence hearings in the afternoon, work until 7:00 or 8:00 P.M., and, after we had finished the interviews, would compare our findings often into the small hours. On Tuesday there would be more interviews, more consultations, more decisions that would change people's lives.

Late Tuesday afternoons we would drive the hundred miles or so to the next appointed institution, have dinner there at approximately 11:00 P.M. and call it a day. All Wednesday and all Thursday it was the same procedure, and we would not drive home until late Friday afternoon. Weekends, inevitably, we spent completing our reports.

It was probably this intense, personal pressure—and his own conscientious involvement in the lives of the potential parolees —that brought about the tragic death of one of the ablest members of the board, Edmund Fitzgerald, formerly chief of probation in Kings County in New York City. He died of a heart attack.

It is interesting that two of Mr. Fitzgerald's daughters have been doing summer work for our office in New York City. They are very attractive, with fantastic IQs, and one is a Ph.D. candidate at Princeton. Sometimes I have noticed them filing things in the office and reading over their father's old decisions. He was a wonderful man.

My wife and I had only one full two-week vacation in my twelve years on the Parole Board. This was a trip to the west coast of Florida. And in May 1964 we did win first prize in a strange competition; Jane and I came closest to judging the weight of a new house that had just been constructed in Schenectady. We estimated that it weighed 289,363 pounds. It weighed 290,382 pounds. Ours was the closest of more than 19,000 entries—and so we won a two-day trip to the New York World's Fair. I must be honest—Jane made the estimate!

Swamped though we all were by the volume of our interview caseload, we now planned major moves in keeping with the Rockefeller Administration's progressive mandate. Our next proposal sprang from research findings that only an infinitesimal number of parolees committed violations after they had been under parole supervision for five years. So the Board of Parole proposed to the governor that we draw up new laws that would permit us to discharge parolees after five years.

So we could document our case for the legislation, every member of the board read the histories of *every* individual who had been on parole for five years or more at that moment. We found that people who had committed absolutely heinous crimes had been restored to normal and useful lives and this tended to reduce our previous emphasis on the nature of the original offenses.

We moved on directly to propose the granting of access to parole to those convicted of murder in the first degree—"murder one," as it is called. We also proposed to extend the existing parole provisions for murderers in the second degree. We said, "Let's make all the murder twos eligible after thirty years minus good time, which makes them eligible after twenty years." Then we took a deep breath and added, "For murder one, let's make them eligible in forty years—twenty-six years and eight months after credit for good time." Once again we had enough case histories on hand to support our proposals and we obtained the necessary legislation.

Our first measurements of paroled first- and second-degree murderers over a five-year period showed a much better rate of non-return to our institutions than for other categories of offenders. We felt we had been justified in suggesting the new legislation. We thus gave a new hope to long-term prisoners, who had previously done little toward their own rehabilitation because they had no reason to, and we had accomplished this at little increased risk to society.

Meanwhile, in the mainstream of the parole program our percentages were quite satisfactory. At the end of the 1960s, only two out of ten parolees over a five-year period were committing even technical violations. Only 1.7 per cent in the average year were committing new offenses that brought them back to our institutions with new convictions.

Governor Rockefeller increasingly mentioned us in parole and featured us as a success story in his over-all campaign to improve the quality of law enforcement agencies and the administration of justice. In time, this campaign would draw closer together the police, the courts, and our associates in "the probation business," as well as most other departments of the state government, especially education and labor. In this regard, we assumed responsibility for the administration of parole of all eligible inmates of all local correctional institutions in the state. We were able to enlist the help of the Department of Labor in increasing the employment of parolees and in training them for better jobs. Governor Rockefeller intervened personally to ask all state departments to hire qualified parolees.

All the while, the governor was inspiring and driving us as he insisted that crime was increasing at a rate almost beyond our capacity to react to it, let alone control it. He set for us all his controlling policy on crime and rehabilitation:

"I am in total accord with those who insist that the way to fight crime is to cure the social ills in which desperation breeds.

"But I also want to put criminals under control, under care, on the road to rehabilitation, rather than let them continue to roam the streets and parks, to rob, to assault, and sometimes to kill.

"I want to make our streets safe again.

"I want to check the rising tide of crime.

"I want to return thousands of our young men to happy and useful lives.

"I yield to no man in my determination to eradicate the slums.

"But crime is something else."

During all these years our sharpest setback was administered not by organized opponents but by an improbable, grizzled parolee in his late forties named Frederick C. Wood. This was the most dramatic episode of my chairmanship of the Board of Parole and it was another tragic sequence of my life.

Mr. Wood was released from Clinton State Prison at Dannemora, New York, after serving seventeen years of a twenty-year sentence for murder in the first degree. He had been convicted of beating a man to death with a beer bottle in Elmira, New York. There was also some evidence that he had previously clubbed a woman to death, after which he had allegedly stabbed the body 150 times. And there were additional reports, with less confirmation, that Frederick Wood, as a young teen-ager, had murdered a sixteen-year old girl by putting arsenic in her cream puffs.

After his conviction and before sentencing in 1943 Frederick Wood, in some horrendous oversight, was not given a psychiatric evaluation. Shortly after he was received in prison, he was found to be psychotic and he was transferred for seven years to the mental hospital at Dannemora. He recovered, rejoined the prison population, and compiled a perfect record of prison behavior. Twice he was turned down for parole, but on the third occasion one of our panels, on which I was not seated, recommended that he be released under parole supervision.

At the time of the original conviction at Elmira, the judge and prosecuting attorney said that Frederick Wood was a highly dangerous individual who probably should never be set free. Now, seventeen years later, we heard again from these men. Appellate Division Justice Walter B. Reynolds, the original prosecutor, and former County Judge Bernard Newman, the original judge, now formally and openly opposed the grant of parole. They were joined in this unusual protest by the police chief of Elmira, Eugene Golden, and by the Chemung County district attorney, Paul McCabe.

At this difficult juncture, I ordered another parole hearing for the prisoner, but the new panel upheld the judgment of the other. So I called a special meeting of all the commissioners of parole to discuss this one case alone. On balance, we decided to grant parole subject to the condition that he never go back to Elmira unless accompanied by a parole officer. His aged mother lived there. I talked with the law enforcement people in Elmira, detailed the man's exemplary record in prison, and I attempted to calm their fears. I had no success.

On the day of Frederick Wood's release on parole, in June 1960, I waited late in my office at Albany to make sure he made the trip safely from the state prison and reported in. We had located a place in Albany where he was to live under parole supervision, with a landlady in whom we had confidence, and we had also arranged for his mother to come and visit. The board had advised him and our parole staff that drinking *any* alcoholic beverage would be considered a parole violation because of his past behavior when he drank. Even though Frederick Wood had not touched a drop as far as I knew for seventeen years, drinking had played a part in his crime.

In the days that followed I made sure the parole officer was calling at Wood's lodgings at odd hours of the day and night and searching the place when he was out. Increasingly, I felt that we had made the correct decision in paroling the murderer with the perfect seventeen-year record. But one month after release he disappeared. When the parole officer searched everything he had left behind, the man found two bottles of wine hidden in a slit in his mattress. We called out a maximum search operation by the police and by our own Bureau of Special Services, a force of special investigators to whom we assign our most serious problems. A busy clerk in the bus office told us she remembered selling a ticket to New York City to somebody who looked like the fugitive, even though she could not be sure.

Not seventy-two hours later, in the Bowery, our own investigators picked up Wood and arrested him. His hand was cut and he said he had been in a fight in some bar, in some inconsequential scuffle. He said a man had been demeaning the late Senator Joseph R. McCarthy of Wisconsin, and he had gone after the man. Wood said he was a great admirer of Senator McCarthy and was a strong anti-Communist. Our officers booked him for violation of parole and held him in New York City. We checked with the police; he was not wanted.

Next day the bodies of two elderly men were discovered in a basement apartment in Queens. I had a chilling presentiment that Frederick Wood had been involved. One of the men had been battered with a bottle. This was precisely the nature of the crime for which Wood had been convicted seventeen years before. I wondered how such a pattern could conceivably survive for almost two decades. My worst fears were confirmed when he refused to talk with the police, but would talk with our own John McCarthy, head of our Bureau of Special Services.

Wood said he had been panhandling on Times Square when he was approached by one of the elderly men, who had apparently bought him a bottle of wine and invited him to the apartment in Queens. The story soon came pouring out to the police as well as to us, and a detective summarized it brutally:

"Wood planned to rob the old man. When they reached the apartment, they drank some beer and the man made an indecent proposal, according to the killer, and sealed his fate.

"Wood said he hit his host over the head with a quart beer

bottle, smashing the bottle. Then he slashed the man's throat with the jagged edge, beat him repeatedly with the bottle and a chair, took two dollars and some change off the corpse.

"Peering in the next room, Wood saw the man's roommate asleep in his bed. Wood picked up a small shovel from a coal stove in the kitchen and crushed the man's skull with the shovel and a chair."

After Wood had been returned to confinement to await trial for the double murders, I attempted to explain to our state government, to the Elmira law enforcement officers, to the press, and to the public what had gone wrong. I stressed that all of us had felt this was a proper parole and that seventeen years of good behavior simply could not be disregarded. After surgery, I said, complications of an unforeseen nature sometimes set in, and death results. In this case, the complication in New York City had been drinking, but this did not explain his leaving parole supervision in Albany nor the violent nature of the attack.

This was the first serious incident of its kind in our years on the parole board, and it was to be our last. But the Wood case was so explosive it threatened to destroy everything we were working for. The New York *Journal-American* wrote this editorial:

"We think Chairman Oswald should resign and be replaced by someone whose 'honest mistakes' would not let a maniac loose to murder people. The freeing of Wood raises serious implications as to the parole board's competence.

"The board was aware that Elmira officials were strenuously opposed to freeing Wood, yet it went ahead with the parole . . . The supervision placed over Wood in Albany could not have been too strict because the convicted killer managed to elude his parole officers and slip into New York . . .

"The parole board, it seems to us, cannot fall back to the excuse that the paroling of Wood was merely an 'honest mistake' since the board had been forewarned of the risks by all of the prosecuting authorities."

The Albany *Knickerbocker News* came to my defense. It said that "the parole board can never be absolutely certain in any instance in which a prisoner is released. It has to weigh a number of imponderables." But the New York *World-Telegram and Sun* was preparing a series that would run beneath headlines that read: PAROLE IS DYNAMITE: UNDER LAX SUPERVI-

SION. CAN TEN THOUSAND RELEASED CONVICTS
WITHOUT PROPER CONTROL STAY OUT OF TROU-
BLE?

When I refused to resign under fire, when I refused to resign,
period, the New York *Journal-American* then took a step the like
of which I have not seen in public life, before or since. For four
or five nights, they ran editorials calling for my resignation and,
at the bottom of each editorial, there was a coupon for readers to
clip and mail to Governor Rockefeller. The coupon said, OSWALD
SHOULD BE FORCED TO RESIGN.

Then a New York newspaper quoted me out of context. The
paper claimed that I said Frederick Wood's prison record was
outstanding—"But I guess we made a mistake. After seventeen
years in jail, he did not commit a single infraction of the rules."
All the other newspapers picked up the statement and ran major
stories that the parole board chairman had now confessed a mistake in the handling of the Wood case. I did not think we had
made a mistake, and I do not to this day. Oddly enough, some of
the upstate newspapers picked up the statement and praised me
for my "midwestern candor."

Governor Rockefeller, when he asked to talk to me about the
whole affair, said he admired the way I had handled the situation and, particularly, how I had stood up under the pressure of
a very genuine ordeal. I did not tender my resignation at this
time, as was reported, and I continued to believe our decisions
had been justified on their merits. Obviously, the results had been
tragic.

Governor Rockefeller and I subsequently worked out a new
executive order designed to minimize the risks of paroling men
such as Frederick Wood. This provided for a panel of psychiatrists to review on a preparole basis the case of any individual
who during his time of confinement had been admitted to a mental hospital. The panel of psychiatrists was also to review any individuals who had been convicted of murder or of violent sex
offenses. This meant that a minimum of two psychiatrists would
have to examine and file a detailed report on all offenders in these
categories who were being considered for parole.

Although sections of the press held that the governor was now,
belatedly, "cracking down" on me and my "lax" parole program,
I believed the new executive order was a positive contribution. It

was a good idea. On the other hand, I did not believe that the psychiatric examinations would protect society absolutely and they might not have even singled out Frederick Wood.

What happened to Frederick Wood? At his new trial psychiatrists could not agree whether he was psychotic or not. A second panel said he was not, and he was convicted of murder in the first degree. When the court asked Mr. Wood if he had anything to say before sentence was passed, he came up with an atrocious, sick pun.

"Yes, sir," he said. "Please send me to the chair. I'm anxious to see what effect electricity has on wood."

The judge did.

CHAPTER 10

The Eve of the Storm

On January 1, 1971, Governor Rockefeller appointed me commissioner of a newly created Department of Correctional Services of the State of New York. The new department merged the former Department of Correction and our own former Division of Parole. I had recommended the creation of the new, unified department while serving in the late 1960s as co-chairman of Governor Rockefeller's Special Committee on Criminal Offenders. The other co-chairman was Paul D. McGinnis, then Commissioner for Corrections, an able administrator who was approaching retirement. The committee had grown out of the governor's concern about the increase in the crime rate and out of his intention to search for new solutions.

The Committee on Criminal Offenders did other useful work—in fact, it formulated seven bills that were enacted into law and it planned and established several projects of major potential significance. The Clinton Diagnostic and Treatment Center at Dannemora was established in 1966 under a plan and legislation drawn by the committee. The committee also drafted a new law in 1966 permitting the courts and the parole board to issue certificates to first offenders preserving or restoring the right to vote and to apply for or retain state licenses. During the first eighteen months of operation, 850 certificates were issued, and only three had to be revoked.

The committee was particularly effective, in my opinion, in the field of mentally defective offenders. A 1966 law established a new institution for these offenders, and a 1967 law eliminated the setting of indefinite, up-to-lifetime sentences for mental defectives; if these men had the capacity to stand trial, then they must be sentenced like other offenders. And reductions of sentence for good behavior were made available to mentally defective prisoners who were serving indeterminate sentences in special state institutions.

The big year for correctional services was 1970, in which the legislation was passed for the new Department of Correctional Services. We eliminated artificial distinctions between different types of state institutions—and all, thenceforward, ceased to be termed "prisons," "reformatories," and so on, and were officially renamed "correctional facilities," to be classified and graded administratively. Outside our own new department, an independent Division of Probation was created within the executive department of the State.

In 1970 new legislation gave the state's courts an additional option—to impose intermittent sentences for offenses punishable by up to one year in jail. These offenders would be able to hold a job or live with their families while serving their sentences in aggregate on weekends, evenings, or on specified days of the week. This was prison reform of an advanced order and ought, in itself, to deflect inaccurate and unfair charges that we only discovered prison reform after Attica. On the other hand, the intermittent sentence is the type of reform considered by many to be "going too far."

Another 1970 bill amended the correction law to enable the state to enter into agreements with counties or with New York City in essence to transfer prisoners. The state would be able to take custody at state expense of local prisoners who had been sentenced to more than ninety days. The state could also arrange for custody in local facilities of state prisoners who were ready for work-release programs in local communities. The state had previously authorized the establishment of work-release programs in state facilities. The new bill specifically provided for the transfer of locally sentenced prisoners to state institutions during times of civil disturbances and other emergencies. As it turned out, the shift of militant, street-wise New York City prisoners to state facilities, where they interacted with the long-term prison population, was counterproductive. But these men would have caused trouble wherever they were.

In a special message to the legislature in March 1970, Governor Rockefeller said the 1970 bills would "mark a watershed in the treatment of criminal offenders in this state. The changes in state law embodied in these measures will enable a comprehensive modernization of the state's program of correctional services, placing it in the forefront of national efforts to reduce criminal recidivism."

The cutting edge of the new programs would be our new Department of Correctional Services. And although my predecessor, Mr. McGinnis, was regarded by some of our law enforcement friends as a hard-liner, while I was tabbed as a soft-liner, the truth was that we were both dedicated advocates of rehabilitation as opposed to mindless punishment. The creation of the merged new department reflected our basic belief that:

1. The new department should provide a continuum of rehabilitative services for criminal offenders from the moment they entered our correctional facilities, through their release, to the moment they were discharged from parole; and

2. The new department should orient its new programs to the reduction of criminal recidivism and to provide more safety and security for the law-abiding community.

A brilliant, visionary, but practical lawyer, Peter Preiser, was the administrative director of the Special Committee. He helped us to forge the best of the old with the most promising of the new and ignited the department for new happenings insofar as our programs were concerned.

Governor Rockefeller announced my appointment as the first commissioner of the new department thus: "Russell G. Oswald is a specialist in parole and rehabilitation, who brings to this challenging new assignment an unmatched combination of professionalism, administrative experience, and human understanding." Several prisoners wrote me privately at this time; I quote one letter, from a man at Attica, who would later be killed by his fellow inmates during the uprising. This man wrote:

"To be brief, sir, prison life by its very nature is inherently oppressive. Therefore any true reform or liberalizing act is as a breath of fresh air. It is *now* common practice to fantasize with a 'measure of realism' on what good things the future will bring to us. Your name is spoken with esteem, and I only hope that your obvious belief in rehabilitation will not be dampened by the few who will abuse this new trend, or by critics of it."

On assumption of the office from which so many people expected so much, I defined a governing philosophy for the new department. I wrote that, "in keeping with the legislative intent and mandate, our philosophy is to *re-direct* our total effort of rehabilitative services toward the development of community-based and community-oriented programming. This will provide a greater perspective of normality in an institutional setting.

"It is incomprehensible to expect that an individual will adapt to a normal setting when he is placed for long periods of time in a totally abnormal setting.

"An atmosphere of community life-style, even though in a confining situation, holds greater promise for successful rehabilitation and for a more reliable reading of how an individual will react to the problems, pressures, and realities of society."

What I intended to move toward was nothing less than a marked reduction of men in the traditional prisons and toward the creation of community treatment facilities.

I envisaged the creation of community centers of one-story buildings, designed to handle peak loads of 400 men with living quarters for twenty men in each house. Under this program there would be dining rooms, a recreation room, and hobby centers with bathing facilities. In a separate area would be an administration building, a social service center, reception and terminal facilities, schools, library, hospital, gymnasium, chapel, athletic field, and a disciplinary security unit for the confinement of people who broke treatment center rules but were not dangerous enough to be returned to the maximum-security institutions.

The maximum-security institutions should be designed to hold 600 men each in humane but spartan conditions, in isolation from the community.

Unlike other prison reformers, I believed there should be some correctional facilities with walls or at least with double fencing—but these should be designed to blend with the landscape, not to jut out like constantly visible barriers to freedom.

Our parole centers around the state would be multipurpose houses, designed not only to provide working space for the officers and social work personnel, but living accommodations for parolees who needed it. A new feature of the parole centers would be temporary detention quarters. Our new idea would be to hold technical violators there for a while before or instead of returning them to prison.

Ranged about these basic facilities would be dozens of special

units, staffed by specialists, for people with special needs such as
narcotics addicts, alcoholics, the retarded, the gifted. This would
be a massive expansion of the small, special programs we had introduced with such success while I was on the Board of Parole.

Already, the former Department of Correction had set up a complex of multipurpose facilities in Dannemora, in upstate New
York. The guidance of Peter Preiser, now head of the Division of
Probation, was very valuable in this undertaking. There was the
traditional bastille of Clinton State Prison, now renamed a correctional facility, and there was also a modern hospital, an adja-
cent but separate hospital for those adjudged criminally insane,
and the new Clinton Diagnostic and Treatment Center for persistent offenders. I termed this newly integrated complex our "Intensive Correctional Care Unit," much like the intensive care
units of well-equipped hospitals.

Here I hoped to put together the diagnosis and pinpoint treatment of the more violent type of offender. I wanted to set an unprecedented example of special care for special needs. I planned to
use ever-increasing numbers of medical and psychiatric personnel
from McGill University in Montreal, Canada, from the University of Vermont at Burlington, and from thirty-two units of
the State University of New York, especially from the social work
and criminal justice units around Albany. In this endeavor, the
National Institute of Mental Health had already evidenced great
interest and so had the federal governments of the United States
and Canada.

Out of our experience at Clinton I hoped would emerge a corps
of splendidly skilled corrections officers, better trained than any
others in penal history, with perhaps the most important mission
of all.

Our whole concept of different types of facilities for different
types of offenders would stand or fall on our selection of who was
a troublemaker and who was not. To put it another way, we
needed corrections officers who would know as expertly as possible who was who and who ought to go where.

Ideally, I intended to move criminal offenders around all our
complexes, from place to place, virtually in a floating state, to
conform to our initial diagnosis and our continuing estimates of
progress or lack of it. We would move men in and out of
the maximum-security institutions, in and out of the community

treatment centers, in and out of the special needs units, toward the next-to-final destination of the parole centers.

Ideally, I intended to return to the community a new type of rehabilitated individual who would not only commit no further crimes but would set an example in community values to others.

If this kind of supervised behavioral control smacked of 1984, I believed that the seriousness of the crime situation in the United States justified our taking the risks. In fact, it seemed to me we had very little time and perhaps none at all.

It did not seem to me we were living in a sick society, but by 1971 we were getting there. Since 1960 the incidence of all forms of crime had risen by 120 per cent as against an increase in the population of 13 per cent. Violent crimes had increased by 130 per cent and property crimes by 151 per cent. Narcotics arrests were up over the decade by 600 per cent. The President's Commission on Law Enforcement and the Administration of Justice reported in 1967 that 15 per cent of all Americans wished to move to other neighborhoods because of the fact of crime and the fear of crime. The Federal Bureau of Investigation shocked the nation with its revelations that murders and rapes were taking place everywhere in the United States every few minutes.

What was wrong when juveniles between the ages of ten and seventeen, whites and blacks alike, committed one out of every three crimes in the United States, including 20 per cent of all robberies and 40 per cent of all burglaries?

What was wrong when the highest rate of increase of crime was taking place in our affluent suburbs?

What was wrong when one out of every three business failures could be ascribed to embezzlement, phony bookkeeping, and other forms of "white collar crime?"

Since 1960 the solution of serious crimes by our police forces had declined by 34 per cent. Often it seemed there was little effort made even to begin to apprehend "non-serious" criminals because of the work overload. In this kind of climate, the sneak thief who was not even tracked, let alone caught, would graduate to burglary and soon become a candidate for admission to our correctional systems.

Even in the federal criminal justice system, for all its high proportion of non-violent inmates and for all its humane reform programs of the 1930s and 1950s, there was a shocking rate of recidivism. Out of 18,567 offenders released by the federal prisons in 1963, 65 per cent had been rearrested by the end of 1969. Interestingly, of those persons acquitted in 1963 of federal charges or who had their cases dismissed, 92 per cent were rearrested for new offenses. This would appear to confirm that there was something seriously wrong with our federal criminal system.

The truth at the beginning of the 1970s, in my opinion, was that facts scarcely seemed any longer to be an issue in the courts. Trials hinged on technicalities, with whole rafts of pretrial motions and postconviction pleas. Deluges of writs were flooding the courts, along with requests for new trials and dismissals, and our whole system was swamped to the point of ineffectiveness. There was a serious trend away from justice for the law-abiding citizens, away from respect for legal forms.

I do believe that the United States Supreme Court under the leadership of Chief Justice Earl Warren did much to bring about the lessened respect which our citizens have for our courts today. Individual rights obscured society's rights. I know the theory is that when an individual's rights are protected, society is best protected. In practice I submit that it has not turned out that way.

By 1971 it was also a misconception that crime in the United States was being committed by mere handfuls of our people. Actually, more than 2,250,000 Americans were in prisons, reform schools, training schools, and other custodial institutions as the decade turned. One boy out of every six had the prospect of appearing in juvenile court in the early 1970s. Four out of every ten male children would be arrested in their lifetime for other than traffic offenses. A recent Harris Poll claimed that, of a large sample of people questioned, 91 per cent admitted they had committed a criminal act for which they might have been sent to jail or prison if they had been caught.

Whenever prisoners or parolees from our own correctional system in New York ever ventured to testify against organized crime syndicate people, they often had to be given a totally new identity —new names, new Social Security numbers, new jobs, new facial disguises, and sometimes new homes in new countries.

New York State took the lead in fighting the narcotics problem in the 1960s, and this one state did take 9,500 narcotics users off the streets and into treatment. By comparison, the federal government, with its much larger national responsibilities, had handled only 6,800 cases in the previous thirty years, and 90 per cent of these had left their treatment facilities before they were considered cured. But New York City was ever more the narcotics center of the nation.

As chairman of the Board of Parole, I was deeply troubled by the fact that 55 per cent of all our releases to the New York City area had, prior to sentence, been dependent on drugs. In the early 1970s, heroin users needed between $60 to $100 per day to maintain the habit, and they committed more than one half of violent crimes reported in the city to obtain these substantial funds.

The Gallup Poll reported that large majorities of Americans felt that our law enforcement system in general and the courts in particular were too lenient with criminal offenders. In 1965, 48 per cent told Gallup that the courts were not dealing "harshly enough" with criminals, but in 1968, 63 per cent held this view. The Gallup Poll did find that 72 per cent of Americans believed that rehabilitation should be the goal of incarceration. But only 33 per cent were ready, according to Gallup, to pay for the increased costs that would be needed for improved rehabilitation programs.

In another measurement of the crime climate into which our new Department of Correctional Services prepared to move in the State of New York, a group of teen-agers was given a list of thirteen types of employment they would like or least like to take up. A job as a correctional worker finished dead last. Apparently, the teen-agers rejected the job not so much because of the low pay and trying conditions, but because they felt they would be working with difficult cases in difficult circumstances. They doubted, as a matter of realism, whether they could really accomplish anything or provide any real help.

In the first six months of 1971, on the eve of the storm of Attica, I prepared to make major changes in corrections in New York State. Our Department of Correctional Services, working closely with the Division of Criminal Justice, analyzed our program needs. Nine programs totalling $3.4 million were approved by the Crime Control Planning Board. I was preoccupied by the increase in the crime rate and the decline in social morality that might make our programs irrelevant or too late. Increasingly, I set in motion small changes designed to create a larger momentum.

I began by revising the rules to permit prisoners to send and receive uncensored mail, in sealed envelopes, to and from the President of the United States, members of Congress, the governor of New York State, members of the New York State Legislature, the commissioner of the Department of Correctional Services, the chairman of the Board of Parole, judges, and attorneys of record and their assistants. I directed that first-class mail postage be supplied by the institution in limited amounts for this kind of mail. Outgoing mail would be sealed and sent out by the prisoners. Incoming mail would be opened in the presence of a corrections officer, so as to protect against the import of contraband material, but would not be read by him. Previously, all incoming and outgoing mail was read and censored.

Then I changed the rules to permit visitation and mail privileges between prisoners and common-law spouses. This had not been permitted before, incredibly enough.

We increased the availability of newspapers, books, and magazines, let newspaper reporters make visits to correctional facilities, and removed screens, barriers, and partitions in visiting rooms in several institutions so as to create a more convenient and comfortable atmosphere for family visits.

In these first six months of 1971 I suffered, along with the heads of other departments of the state government, from the budget cutbacks necessitated by our shortage of funds. These would result in the layoff of more than 400 employees and in the removal of funds for existing as well as future programs.

We had to send "pink slips" to 165 women employees at the Albion Training School for Women near Batavia, and we would have to close the facility. We had to lay off some 100 employees from the Matteawan State Hospital for the Criminally Insane because the State Narcotics Addiction Control Commission was moving its own program there as a result of its own budget cuts. An additional 160 employees would be laid off at two maximum-security prisons, Green Haven near Poughkeepsie and Great Meadows at Comstock, New York. We were able to maintain the staffs at the maximum-security correctional facilities of Auburn, Clinton, and Attica virtually intact—but when vacancies occurred they were not filled.

"Russell G. Oswald may have some justification in saying he

took over the job at the wrong time," the Albany *Times-Union* commented.

But I came out of the budget squeeze with a per annum figure of $94,022,900, which we would live with, even though we were conscious of the fact this was less than 5 per cent of total state expenditures. As Deputy Commissioner van Eekeren subsequently commented, "Prisons are not visible. There is no political gain in putting money into prisons when there are so many other more visible priorities."

These were tight money days, but all of us in the state government were in the same leaky boat. Governor Rockefeller devoted his energies in these months to propounding the concept of federal revenue-sharing, with more funds to come from the federal government to the states and localities; I was for the governor all the way, and we even got some federal money on our own. Specifically, our new Department of Correctional Services won a federal grant of $3.5 million through the Office of Crime Control Planning. This was the largest federal grant ever advanced to a correctional system through the federal government's law enforcement assistance program. The grant was to be used as seed money and as other financing for projects jointly approved for federal funding. The date on which the new projects would be approved was set at September 1, 1971.

I had high hopes for the first of the innovative ideas thus made feasible. We planned to set up legal assistance offices in Albany, Buffalo, Syracuse, and New York City to provide our prison and parole staffs with rapid and accurate legal advice in the correctional field. We also planned to set up legal reference libraries in six of our correctional facilities for use by the prisoners. These libraries would contain books relevant to the civil and criminal legal problems of the inmates. The material would emphasize recent statutes, case law, and treatises in criminal law.

Then we planned to establish four new experimental community treatment facilities in Albany, Buffalo, New York City, and Hempstead, Long Island. In these forerunners of the kind of new prisons I had in mind, we would start out by determining whether we could safely release selected people on parole from three to six months ahead of schedule. If the four new facilities were successful, we would create more of them, and we would consider paroling selected prisoners even earlier if they merited it.

We planned to set up a brand new planning and evaluation unit to provide systems analysis for all our institutional and parole operations. We would create a new support services bureau to assess our physical properties, monitor grants, and help staff funded projects. We would initiate a new model reception-classification project out of which would grow recommendations for statewide adoption.

In direct support of emphasis on academic and vocational training, we also planned to extend evening programs. In the past, classes had been conducted only by day in New York State institutions, and classes had lower priorities than the daily routine—prison jobs, provision of meals, and so on. We had also suffered from a shortage of daytime teaching staff and inadequate classroom space. All too often our educational programs were carried on the backs of inmate volunteers who wanted to help their fellows read or learn a trade. With our federal seed money we planned to start evening academic and vocational classes in two maximum-security institutions, in one reformatory, and at the correctional facility for women. We would also provide additional tuition support to corrections officers who wished to obtain higher education and in-service training in advanced correctional work.

Finally, we planned to introduce a volunteer services unit, with a director and a co-ordinator in each of four regional parole offices statewide. We thought this would be a useful way to expand the recruitment of civilian volunteer workers to help us within the institutions and with the parolees. There would also be a client and correspondence service operating out of our central offices in Albany. This would handle inquiries from potential volunteers, process their suggestions and comments, and steer them to where they could be most useful.

This was to be a trail-blazing mission. We wanted to plan and execute the minor moves so meticulously that we could obtain major federal investment in our correctional grand design. I also believe this statement of the facts should dispel the charges we have heard so loudly that our department was dead on its feet before Attica.

In July 1971 we prepared to attack the perennial problem of sex in prison. We announced a "furlough plan" to permit prisoners in New York State to visit in their own homes from time to time. This was part of an over-all program to introduce more "nor-

mality" into the corrections scene. If the state legislature approved
changes in the law that would be needed, we would let selected
prisoners out on furlough on their own promise to return to the
institutions before a set deadline. We guessed that approximately
8,000 to 10,000 prisoners might eventually meet the standards for
selection.

Immediately it was asked whether it would be safer to solve the
sex-in-prison problem by introducing the system of "conjugal
visits." These visits of wives to their husbands in prison had been
tried with success in the "red houses" of the Mississippi State
Penitentiary at Parchman, Mississippi; this supported the idea that
almost any way to reduce sexual isolation and tension in prison
was better than none. But I turned down conjugal visits with a
statement that made my last "traditional" news before Attica. I
said:

"To bring women—wives—to the institutions for sex purposes,
and mainly that is what it is, is debasing to women and to the
man himself, too. He and she are subject to jeers and whistles and
the like. And—how does this help the single man?"

As our time before the showdown was running out, I received
a second letter from Attica, from the prisoner who had written
me that letter of welcome and encouragement when I became
Commissioner of Correctional Services. This letter was delightful
and, written as it was on the eve of the storm, significant:

> I was totally animated by the receipt of your letter, Mr.
> Oswald, and find myself compelled (pleasantly so) to write
> you another. To be candid with you, sir, the type of letter
> that I had expected to receive from your office was that of a
> perfunctory nature. Therefore, when your correspondence
> did arrive, and it was sensitive, and caring, and not the usual
> form letter, I received a nice feeling that has been unfamiliar
> to me for a long time.
>
> I formally request that you consider me an adherent and
> a staunch supporter of your ideals. You probably can discern
> that I am a lonely person and that I exploit every opportu-
> nity for intelligent conversation. In addition to the above, I
> am a seeker, who is striving in a hostile environment to
> achieve goals that I know could be made more available if only

your concepts of penology could somehow be implemented.

It is such a pleasure to hear you speak of a progressive and humane system, and I truly admire your courage in espousing these hopes in view of the pragmatic obstacle that you face. It is known to all inmates here that your first reform (the removal of censorship of official and attorney mail) has met with bitter opposition and that pressure has been brought to bear upon you.

I am aware that to update institutions that dwell in the past and the staff of which long for the good old days, when unchecked discipline was the vogue, will be difficult to say the least. How you plan to re-orient their parochial minds is beyond me. But then again, I am only 25.

What I would like to know is how can I help. What more could I say without being verbose.

Respectfully yours.

My friend who signed the letter had not long to live.

The rise of radical violence in the prisons now imposed its calendar upon us.

March 5, 1971: I addressed the basic recruit graduating class of the New York State Police in the auditorium of their new academy on the State Campus at Albany. I spoke to the eighty-three graduates and their families and friends and stressed how greatly we needed the State Police and relied on them, not only in time of rising violence but at all times:

"I am sure that today is a proud day for each graduate, his family, and the staff here at this academy. It is the kind of pride you will carry with you throughout your careers, for the New York State Police have a proud heritage. I can think of no other that even approaches New York in levels of competency, training, professionalism, know-how, and education.

"Our Department of Correctional Services is not at all unrelated to your work. Our goals, basically, are the same: to provide safety and security to society from criminal offenders. Your job is to investigate, apprehend, and provide sufficient evidence for conviction. Our job is to provide meaningful services that will correct and rehabilitate . . .

"Tomorrow, do you realize, you'll be 'the fuzz'? But the names I am being called by hard-core, militant revolutionaries make terms like 'fuzz' and 'pig' seem like words of endearment. Thank God there are dedicated, selfless individuals such as you who are willing to provide protection—even to those who berate you!"

March 11, 1971: In Richmond, Virginia, I analyzed, for corrections officers from all over the nation, the lessons of the Auburn riot of the fall of 1970. Without any qualifying phrases, I said the riot had nothing whatever to do with prison reform. On the contrary, a mere 120 radical militants had brought rehabilitation programs for 1,800 to a complete standstill. I stressed that, months after the event, the ringleaders, placed in special housing, still provoked, harassed, harangued, and made life miserable for officers, doctors, nurses, and all prisoners within earshot. These militants were throwing food and excrement at corrections officers and were still destroying beds, urinals, any form of equipment given them to use. They still sometimes screamed "Pig!" and profanities in unison hour after hour.

March 19—June 1, 1971: At my direction, Walter Dunbar sent a memorandum to all superintendents of correctional facilities everywhere in the state. He requested that riot control plans be submitted for our review and approval no later than May 1, 1971.

After the responses to the riot control memorandum had been received from Superintendent Vincent R. Mancusi of the Attica Correctional Facility, among others, the meetings were held in which very important riot decisions were taken. The essential decision was that State Police, riot trained, would suppress an insurrection with minimal force, rather than our own corrections officers, who might become emotionally involved.

On June 1 Commissioner Dunbar and I, at my request, met with Superintendent William E. Kirwan of the State Police and Colonel Kennedy of the National Guard to review our mutual plan for our joint responsibilities in the event of a riot.

June 25, 1971: The Department of Correctional Services did not know at which of our institutions the first radical blow might fall. On this day a savage little outbreak occurred at Clinton State Correctional Facility at Dannemora. Some militants in the segregation unit broke up the plumbing and used jagged bits of steel and porcelain as weapons and projectiles. Corrections officers restored order with riot sticks and tear gas.

Donald Singleton, a conscientious reporter on the staff of the New York *Daily News,* toured this prison not long afterward and found primitive "strip cells" in use by the prison authorities. I was embarrassed because I had denied not long before that strip cells were in use. Then I had said, "I don't think that kind of punishment, which is inhumane, fits in with my humanistic view of treatment." In fact, the cells had been stripped by the inmates. They had wrecked the bedding and the plumbing themselves.

Mr. Singleton continued his report, "Most of the prisoners are steel-hard militant blacks and Puerto Ricans whose speech is filled with revolutionary rhetoric . . . One man . . . serving a seven-year term on a weapons charge is representative of many of the prisoners in segregation. He is in a cell without most amenities. His reading material includes books by Marx and Lenin. He told me, 'They are keeping me locked up in this procrustean den to try to force me to live by their racist, military rules in here.' "

Superintendent LaVallee said there were only sixteen men in segregation out of a total prison population of 1,958. But the militants in the population had the correctional facility on edge.

June 28, 1971: "Just what should we do with a criminal?" I asked my own associates in a pre-Attica memorandum. And I answered: "Treat him fairly!" In the belief that my associates might need more than this, I stressed that the courts would in any event require it. It had been the general feeling in correctional circles, as well as in the public mind for years, that prisoners had no rights other than for decent and humane care. But courts were now looking in and were holding that prisoners had most rights that the rest of us have.

I cited the Kritsky decision in the United States District Court in 1970. This held that men and women in prison must be advised of prison authorities' charges against them, must be informed of the nature of the evidence, must be heard, and must be judged on the weight of substantial evidence. I thought this ruling fair in general, even though it would add greatly to the pressure on our corrections personnel.

Then I discussed the Sostre decision, also in the United States District Court in 1970. This held that prisoners were entitled to written notice of charges against them, to cross-examine accusers and call witnesses, and also to retain counsel or counsel substitute. The Sostre decision, which also awarded damages to the aggrieved prisoner, was appealed and modified by the appellate courts, though the award of damages was upheld.

Meanwhile, the Menenchino decision was threatening to overload our parole system. This gave defendants the right to counsel at parole revocation hearings. And the Maggio decision made the Menenchino decision retroactive under certain circumstances. Somehow, our parole officers were proving able to cope with these new burdens and the system was still viable.

But I warned: "Interjection of the courts ultimately can lead to conditions whereby the courts will assume all control over correctional programs. Should this occur, the result would be to take the professionals out of the profession. If the courts substitute their judgment for that of parole boards, they will get what they deserve."

July 6, 1971: This was the day the Department of Correctional Services received the list of the twenty-seven demands signed by the negotiating committee of the "Attica Liberation Faction." I acknowledged receipt of the manifesto, stating I would respond after I had had the opportunity to study the demands.

This was also the day on which several prisoners who had been involved in new disturbances at Auburn were transferred to Attica. But I did not accept the recommendation of Superintendent Mancusi that five prisoners, those who signed the manifesto, be transferred away from Attica. I feared they would cause just as much trouble anywhere else.

August 31, 1971: Corrections officers representing each state facility conferred with me in a special emergency meeting which lasted for six uninterrupted hours. They expressed their concern that militants in their institutions would explode into riots and alleged that the situation was aggravated by shortages of security staff. This had been caused by the fiscal problems of the state, they said, but the situation was now urgent. Actually, at that time there was only a 3 per cent vacancy among corrections officers— 102 positions vacant out of 3,340—and at Attica there were only four posts vacant out of the authorized corrections officer force of

380. Another question was whether the authorization was adequate.

I was impressed enough by their concern to include an urgent warning to the governor in my monthly department report. The corrections officers did not learn about this until the crisis was past. I was not guilty of their charges of staff neglect. I wrote to the governor: "While I am fully aware of the gravity of current fiscal conditions, I feel strongly that no other state agency holds the potential for disaster in terms of dollars and—more importantly—lives, than this Department." The fiscal freeze on new hiring, I added, the shortages of all categories of staff, and a growing trend toward sick leaves by corrections officers was leaving us dangerously undermanned.

September 2, 1971: I visited Attica and was briefed exhaustively on the situation. As I have noted earlier, I had intended to address the men there personally, much as I had the population of the Charlestown State Prison in Massachusetts. Unfortunately, my wife had to be taken to the hospital and I returned to Albany to be with her—leaving the tape-recorded message to be heard by all the prisoners in Attica the next day.

My recorded voice reported the reforms we were making everywhere in the state and echoed through the eve of the storm. Almost lost, but not quite, were these final statements about what I was trying to do:

"Of course, the main impact of the new directions we envision for the department is the recognition of the individual as a human being and the need for basic fairness throughout our day to day relationships with each other.

"Many of you have voiced confidence in me, and in the directions I have talked about, and I appreciate this. I am certain you realize that change cannot be accomplished overnight, but I can assure you that changes will be made—just as changes have already taken place in the brief period of eight months.

"Some of your suggestions have been helpful to us in formulating new policy and direction, and Superintendent Mancusi and I welcome your constructive suggestions and views.

"Let me conclude by saying that I appreciate your patience and your expressed trust and confidence in what we are trying to do together."

PART III

"Our obligations are not cancelled by the crimes of the guilty . . . The links which bind the human family together must, under all circumstances, be preserved unbroken . . . There must be no criminal class."

THE PHILADELPHIA SOCIETY FOR ALLEVIATING THE MISERIES OF PUBLIC PRISONS, late Eighteenth Century

CHAPTER 11

"Let Them Give Their Agenda of Death"

At 4:30 P.M. on Saturday, September 11, Corrections Officer William E. Quinn, aged twenty-eight, died in Rochester General Hospital. Clubbed on the head by the rebel inmates when they swept through the Times Square intersection at the Attica Correctional Facility in the uprising of September 9, his skull had been fractured in two places. Now William Quinn was the first known fatality of the rebellion and his death put an end to the uneasy weekend lull.

"Not one of the prisoners is worth an eyelash on his face" said a man on the street whose sister had taught Mr. Quinn in high school. In small huddles, the people of Attica discussed the corrections officer's death in their old, tree-shaded, Victorian-style homes, in the small frame houses along the road from the New York Thruway, in the commercial section near the red-brick Citizens Bank, around the clapboard Timm's Hardware Store.

A hush fell across the Tipperary Restaurant, where there were angry complaints in particular about the allegedly pro-prisoner bias of the newsmen in town. Not far from the prison, a corrections officer told a reporter from the New York *Daily News* that almost everybody in Attica resented the press:

"They feel that all the reporters did their best to make the corrections officers look bad and the prisoners look good. People don't take into account that some of the men in that prison really are bad men. The way things are nowadays, people don't get sent to prison right away. To be sent to prison these days, you have to be bad, and some of these men are bad. Bad people."

Another townsman would say, "The prisoners are outlaws who are out to destroy our country and burn our cities and now want to destroy our prison."

Superintendent Mancusi said he did not see why the inmates were rioting and destroying property because, after all, Attica was "their home."

Reverend Charles F. Williman, pastor of St. Paul's United Church of Christ, one of seven well-attended churches in Attica, said, "These are just plain normal people in a typical, rural American town. They aren't people who hate minority groups. They're just people who live far away from the kinds of problems that are affecting the cities, and they haven't got a perspective on problems like race and welfare and things like that."

Between the small homes and the tall, gray walls of the prison, scores of men and women with reddened eyes and slept-in clothing kept the weekend vigil for their relatives who were being held hostage. One of the men said, "If I were one of the hostages in there, I'd be praying now for the guards to come in shooting." The women tended to shake their heads whenever they were asked for interviews, and said, "Please leave us alone."

At another side of the road, facing the prison gate, a group of about fifty people kept a parallel vigil. They were relatives and supporters of the prisoners and they too were reluctant to give interviews. There was always a question whether they would move from vigil to demonstration, in the style of the prison-gate demonstrations at San Quentin in California, but they remained silent.

Once, a busload of black people brought in from Buffalo was waved away by sheriff's deputies. Members of the New Age Labor Alliance and a group of University of Buffalo law students briefly displayed a banner in support of the inmates and then went home.

Between the prison wall and the inner Administration Building, scores of state police and sheriff's deputies were always on hand in a grassy area broken by four small, circular flower beds and a gray sidewalk. They were patrolling, changing shifts, waiting in line for a bite to eat or something to drink, or relaxing. "I'm no hero," said one of the sheriff's deputies who had been called in from Livingston, Genesee, and Erie Counties to reinforce the deputies from Attica's own Wyoming County. "But as long as I'm here, I want to do more than just sit around and wait." A corrections officer going on duty said many of the hostages were his friends, and he did not approve of our offer of no administrative reprisals. We had offered the assurance that inmates would not be mistreated in our endeavor to obtain the peaceful release of the hostages, but this corrections officer said, "Every tool should be used to get our guys out."

The troopers of the New York State Police were correct and outwardly unemotional—as if this were just another mission. They were very conscious of their professional reputation. Their officers explained that the men went through sixteen weeks of basic training. They spent two of these weeks on the firearms range where they became proficient in the use of the .38-caliber service revolvers and the 12-gauge shotguns they now had on hand at Attica. Although there had been cutbacks in the retraining program, in which all troopers have to requalify in three one-day sessions every year, "nobody's exempt from it if they carry a gun," according to one State Police official.

Pointing toward State Police sharpshooters who were out of sight in their vantage points overlooking the rebel cell blocks, an officer said there was additional training for the men who were chosen to bear .270-caliber rifles with telescopic sights. Major S. A. Chieco, director of training for the State Police, emphasized, "*Any* man assigned that weapon goes through special training."

Major Chieco said he was under orders not to discuss the attack plan, but he added, "The State Police train every trooper for every kind of situation, including that situation."

One young trooper was saying he would rather not be at Attica, but, when a call went out for four volunteers with shotguns to meet an emergency, he was one of fifteen or twenty men in his troop who leapt to their feet at once.

Every now and then during the weekend when I came out of our discussions with the Citizens Observer Committee, I liked nothing better than to brief the state troopers on our talks, to tell them how I thought we were getting along. I would simply walk up to them and chat. I felt a deep professional gratitude to these men who might have to risk their lives.

On a couple of evenings I visited in the grassy zone outside the Administration Building with one of the relatives of the hostages, the son of Elmer G. Hardie, the fifty-eight-year-old industrial foreman who had been seized when the rebels stormed the industrial buildings on September 9. Mr. Hardie was extremely popular among the inmates. The son struck me as being a fine young man, a member of the Lions Club in Attica, running his own business there, and he said he was praying for me in this situation. He made me feel that our long negotiating grind to try to obtain the release of the hostages was worth every drop of my energy and blood. It was with special horror that I would later learn that Elmer Hardie was one of the hostages who did not survive the September 13 assault.

From several corrections officers in the corridors of the Administration Building, who resented my decision to negotiate with the rebels, I received such treatment as I have never before experienced in my career. Often when I passed by, they would utter curses, epithets, and obscenities. These remarks would not be made in conversation with the intent that I overhear them. They were made to me, and at me, as I passed. I did not respond because I knew the pressures these men were responding to. Their friends were in trouble in the prison yard and they wanted to charge in and get them out, whatever the risk, whatever the cost.

In other prisons around the state at this time, many corrections officers worked up petitions calling for my resignation, and at least one of these was sent to Governor Rockefeller. A group of corrections officers at another prison even drafted a personal petition, to be signed by individual officers, asking the Federal Bureau of Investigation to come in and rescue them if ever they were taken hostage in a prison riot. In the petition was a requirement that neither I nor Walter Dunbar was to be permitted to intervene. The petition read on, "These two men, with their policies and programs, have left a sickening number of dead correctional personnel from coast to coast"—a gross falsehood.

There were more pleasant interludes at Attica. I remember particularly how the Attica Lions Club set up a refreshment stand at the expense of its seventy members, just inside the prison gate. This was a generous decision, and by Saturday the Lions Club had given away more than 3,000 pounds of hamburgers, 500 pounds of hot dogs, and 120 dozen doughnuts. One of the Lions volunteer workers, Greg Newell, said they were there "for the fellows here who are trying to help our buddies in there."

But there was one embarrassing incident at the Lions Club refreshment stand. This was fortunately not typical. When United States Congressman Herman Badillo and New York State Senator Robert Garcia, two of the members of the Citizens Observer Committee, came down to the refreshment stand, they were turned away. One of the volunteer workers told the legislators that the food was not meant for them, and Mr. Badillo and Mr. Garcia felt they were suffering a racial slur. But another volunteer worker ran after them with their order and the atmosphere by the gate was improved.

Actually, the black and Puerto Rican members of the committee were subjected to much more harassment away from the prison. In one diner, a group was kept waiting endlessly for service, while a waitress explained to somebody else who asked about it, "Why should we feed the enemy?" Another time, a woman came up to me with what must have been the best of intentions and said the likes of these committee members "are not for you, Commissioner."

New York State Assemblyman Eve, the influential black legislator from Buffalo, was startled one day when he walked along one of the corridors through the corrections officers there. One of them called him "Boy."

Omnipresent as ever were the media, and some 300 newspaper, radio, and television people were on hand by midday on Saturday. They had come from New York City, mostly, but there were newsmen from Great Britain and West Germany, from Sweden and Australia, along with whole contingents from Chicago and Los Angeles. This was the story of the year, or so it seemed, for black journalists, and I was pleased at one point when a black TV reporter approached me with a microphone. She was Juanita E. Young of WGR-TV (Channel 2) Buffalo, their community relations director, and we had talked on the telephone before when I had arranged for her to visit her fiancé who was then in prison. The man had since rehabilitated himself and was now doing well on the outside.

Afterwards, Miss Young was to write me about our unexpected meeting during the Attica crisis:

Dear Mr. Oswald:

I would like to take time out to thank you for all that you have done and all you are attempting to do in your department. Little did I know when I called you the first of this year that we would meet under circumstances so tragic.

I would like to thank you for being so kind and gracious to me and my fiancé. He is out and attempting to do his job that we all have, as human beings, trying to help his or her fellow men.

It is a thankless job and we all are and will be criticized a great deal because many people think that they have all the answers. Unfortunately, the answers are not as clear-cut as many think they should be. The situations across the nation are in traumatic condition and we need the wisdom of God and the strength of many to keep the goals we want to reach clearly in mind.

I pray sincerely that you will remain steadfast in your goals and keep the strength, wisdom, and intelligence you have shown to complete your task at this appointed hour. May God bless you, and keep you for many days and years, for you have been appointed not by man but I truly feel by God to do his bidding.

Thank you once again for all you are doing.

s/*Juanita E. Young,* Director of Community Relations WGR-TV

Late in the afternoon and early in the evening of Saturday, September 11, the news of the death of Corrections Officer Quinn filtered into rebel-held D Yard through the transistor radios. One of the inmates said, "Brothers, one of the pigs is dead. They killed their own pig, now they're going to blame us. Now it's a whole new ball game." Others who heard the bulletins doubtless remembered how Mr. Quinn had been felled at Times Square and how he had been carried out on a stretcher. But it *was* a whole new ball game. The rebel leaders had been holding out for complete criminal amnesty; now they would have to ask amnesty for murder.

In D Yard the lineaments of what would be called the "D Yard Nation" were coming clear. There was a virtual mimicry of an Establishment community, with residential and commercial districts, a security police headquarters, a food distribution center, and a first-aid station, all set up in sections of tents in the yard and in the built-up cell blocks.

Through the D Yard Nation most of the 1,281 rebel inmates worked and wandered, wearing any kind of outlandish dress they could put together to symbolize their new freedom. They fashioned dashikis out of sheets, and burnouses out of towels, and often they wore football helmets or makeshift bits of "armor." They carried their weapons almost everywhere they went—the knives, spears, and clubs, the lengths of lead piping, the wire bolos, the baseball bats studded with nails with which they had won control of most of the prison on the previous Thursday. They slept outside even when it was raining—and who could blame them? No more, for a brief moment, the clang of the cell doors locking, and the obliteration of the evening sky.

The hierarchy of D Yard Nation functioned downward from the informal oligarchy of rebel leaders, drawn from Black Panthers, Young Lords, and Weathermen (SDS) on the radical side, speaking for blacks, Puerto Ricans, and whites; and the numerous Black Muslims of a more moderate bent.

Strict rules of conduct were promulgated—no drugs, no fighting among the inmates, no harming of the hostages, and no homosexual relations, even by consent. And the penalty for violating any of these rules, it was announced on the D Yard bullhorn, was death. In practice, the penalties were less severe: Five men caught in illicit sex activity were compelled to pick up cigarette butts all over D Yard, and a group of white prisoners who wanted to surrender were put to work digging one of Sam Melville's defensive ditches.

The Black Muslims controlled the security force of approximately 200 men, keeping a remarkable degree of order over the hardened convicts and others in D Yard. Sam Melville himself headed an effort to recruit whites and Spanish-speaking men into the force when it became obvious that the group was almost entirely black. The security men governed and guarded the remaining hostages, escorted the outside observers and guaranteed their safety, and enforced a rough justice on the lawbreakers of D Yard Nation.

Then there was the slaying of three of the inmates of D Yard at a time as yet unknown, at the hand of fellow inmates as yet unknown, for reasons as yet unknown. The victims were Barry Schwartz, serving ten to twenty years for manslaughter; Kenneth Hess, serving four years for grand larceny, and Michael Privitera, serving twenty-five years to life imprisonment for murder in the first degree. Mr. Schwartz and Mr. Hess were white; Mr. Privitera was a Puerto Rican.

After our recapture of the prison, we found that the bodies of these men showed more than twenty stab wounds apiece, indicating these were collective killings. Our autopsy reports showed they had been dead at least twelve hours before we retook D Yard.

Surrounded in an enclave of D Yard and in several sleeping areas inside the cell blocks were the thirty-eight hostages. They were protected by circles of Black Muslim security guards from the rest of the prison population. The hostages were well enough treated after the first day's mayhem, but their lives were in constant danger. One typical incident occurred when an enraged prisoner succeeded in breaking through the guards to get at our men. One of the Muslim guards slugged the man in the stomach with a pickax.

The worst experience of the early days in D Yard was the blindfolding. Originally, the rebel leaders ordered the hostages blindfolded so that the leaders would not be recognized and later identified as participants in the rebellion. The blindfolds, made out of torn sheeting, were not tied tightly, but the lack of vision was terrifying when strange voices and choruses would din into the hostages' ears, "We're going to kill you," "You're next, Pig," and so on.

The rebel leaders ordered the blindfolds taken off on the Friday afternoon. In any event, the leaders had by now revealed themselves not only to our negotiating personnel but also to a national audience on network television. Furthermore, the visiting outside physician, Dr. Warren Hanson, warned the rebels that prolonged blindfolding was a danger to the hostages' eyesight.

Through Saturday the hostages rested on mattresses better than those of the inmates, shared the stolen food from the commissary and the sandwiches sent in from the outside, and had more than they needed of cigarettes and hot coffee. Their medical needs were taken care of by Walter "Tiny" Swift, an inmate medical assistant, who had been sentenced to life imprisonment in 1951 after he had killed a man in a robbery which netted him one dollar. Mr. Swift was a hero to most of the hostages throughout Attica as he tended them and succored them amid the constant rebel threat. Captain Pappy Wald, the most senior of the hostages, said Tiny Swift "definitely" risked his own life to help the hostages. Afterwards, many corrections officers and civilian employees urged us to recommend commutation of sentence for "the angel of Attica." Governor Rockefeller agreed—and Tiny Swift walked out of Attica early in 1972, under parole supervision.

Pappy Wald, in his sixties, the most senior of the hostages, had been captured after his desperate attempt to keep the rebels out of C Block on Thursday morning. He thought the most remarkable thing about the D Yard Nation was the discipline. The leaders would command and would be instantly obeyed. He was fascinated that the hostages had to pass through five "layers" of security guards whenever they wanted to walk from their enclave to the steel negotiating tables of the leaders.

The inmates who did not approve of the rebellion had no choice but to go along. L. D. Barclay was the rebel leader who, according to Captain Wald, was the most militant. He felt that L.D. wanted to kill all of the hostages. Corrections Officer Lynn Johnson said, "The Black Panthers were ready to kill us right from the beginning. But the Muslims never failed to protect us."

Corrections Officer Gary Walker said, "We didn't have much to eat the first day, but neither did they." He suffered from the blindfolding, however, and his hands were tied behind his back on the first day until he complained of numbness. Then they were tied in front of him for several hours longer.

Corrections Officer Frank Kline was also hurt from the blindfolding and the numbness and he listened to the threats and semithreats of death along with the rest. Once Mr. Kline heard an inmate say that he wanted to "give in to the administration." Then Mr. Kline saw twelve or fifteen other inmates come over to the man near the D Yard toilet and exchange loud words. Then things were quiet and there was no more trouble. He thought that all opposition in D Yard was beaten, killed, or silenced and that the D Yard Nation was the most brutal he had ever seen. How could they complain about "prison brutality," Frank Kline thought, when they ran a society of their own that was infinitely more brutal?

Corrections Officer Dean Wright suffered from a virus infection throughout his captivity and could not keep his food down. He was sick and feverish but received capsules and treatment from the visiting outside doctor and from Tiny Swift. He thought the inmates he saw in D Yard were acting irrationally, "like a bunch of nuts." Philip Watkins, another corrections officer, said the

Black Panthers threatened him, but were held off by the Black Muslims.

Corrections Officer Michael Smith brought an inmate over to Lieutenant Robert Curtiss at one point, and the man dictated supply needs for the hostages on a prescription pad. These were for more blankets, mattresses, clothing, and shoes. Lieutenant Curtiss noticed that the request was for nine pairs of inmate shoes, even though the requisition was for the hostages.

Gordon Knickerbocker, a senior stores clerk who had been captured in the industrial area, felt things grew quieter in D Yard after the blindfolds were removed from most of the men, and he believed the hostages' chances for survival were good. But then he was perturbed by the fact that groups of inmates kept trying to break in toward them through the cordon of Muslim guards. He thought the guards were remarkable: the hostages only had to raise their hands and they would be asked what they wanted, and they would be brought water, or cigarettes, or would be taken to the latrine.

Mr. Knickerbocker, along with some of the others, was much more disturbed by the evidence of the rebels' continuing military build-up. From the direction of the industrial shops he listened to the grinding, and he knew they were sharpening and forging hundreds of weapons for the resistance and, perhaps, for the final execution of the hostages. In the factories of D Yard Nation, the sparks flashed and flew without letup.

At 6:00 P.M. on Saturday, September 11, the members of the Citizens Observer Committee reviewed the twenty-eight points of traditional prison reform we would soon present to the rebel leaders. This was a high point of unity on the committee. Mr. Kunstler, as noted, had even helped me with the wording of the twenty-eight points. He said he was ready to urge the leaders to accept them and release the hostages.

At 6:15 P.M., the chairman of the Black Panther party, Bobby G. Seale, arrived with two bodyguards at the gate of the Attica Correctional Facility. The rebel leaders had asked for a Black Panther party representative to sit on the Citizens Observer Committee. William Kunstler had tried to arrange for Huey P. Newton, their Minister of Defense and perhaps the most powerful of the Panthers, to come to Attica. Assemblyman Eve, in bringing

Bobby Seale to Attica, was introducing into the situation one of the authentic revolutionaries in the United States.

At once, the governor's senior advisers on the scene recommended that Mr. Seale not be permitted to enter the prison. Their concern was sharp and valid. Surely, they argued, it would be unwise to bring an inflammatory militant onto the scene just at the time the committee was ready to present twenty-eight solid points to the rebel leaders. Bobby Seale himself refused to enter the prison unless he could keep his two bodyguards with him. I called the gate and approved the bodyguards if they were adequately frisked.

William Kunstler now took the lead in the committee in what would be an hour-long argument. He implored me to let Bobby Seale join in the negotiations; he said Mr. Seale was above all others *the* man the rebel leaders wanted to see, *the* man who might be able to persuade them to release the hostages.

He assured me, as I questioned him, that the Panther chairman would not make inflammatory speeches in D Yard and would be asked to support the twenty-eight points and further negotiations on neutral ground. I decided, with skepticism and concern, to go along with Mr. Kunstler's plea even though the governor's aides were advising strongly against it. I did this mainly because Bobby Seale was still an unknown quantity in the equation and, as I had from the beginning, I was trying almost everything to win back the hostages safe and well. I knew it would be risky to let Bobby Seale into D Yard. I took the risk. It was to be another hour before we located him because he had become tired of waiting and had left the prison. We sent a State Police car to find him on the highways, and we brought him back to the correctional facility.

Now it was 8:15 P.M. and here he was—the chairman of the Black Panthers, in leather jacket, sharply creased trousers, and highly shined shoes, his frisked bodyguards on either side, moving urbanely among the Citizens Observer Committee. After the niceties, Walter Dunbar stressed to Bobby Seale: "Now, what are you going in there for? What is your purpose in going in there? Not to inflame them. You are going in there—do you understand this?—to try to make them understand that they must release these hostages and that we will bring about prison reform, that we're headed in that direction and that we will make meaningful changes."

"Well, yes, I understand that," Mr. Seale replied.

Then he listened intently while Clarence Jones, the former counsel to Dr. Martin Luther King, Jr., explained the historic significance of the twenty-eight points. Here was not only an opportunity to obtain the release of the hostages, he said, but to move prison reform ahead by 100 years.

Bobby Seale read over the twenty-eight points and commented that he would not do anything nor recommend anything until he had consulted with the Black Panther leader Huey Newton. He also said he would not do anything until he had heard from "the brothers" in D Yard. This was an appalling disappointment to me. I realized with a sense of foreboding that Bobby Seale was not, in fact, going to support the twenty-eight points at the decisive moment.

There was some discussion, and it now seemed that Bobby Seale might not even go down to D Yard. "At least, go in and show them your face," said one member of the Citizens Observer Committee.

At 9:30 P.M. what we hoped would be the crucial meeting with the rebel leaders now began in D Yard. Most of the members of the committee went in, and with them went Bobby Seale. Before getting down to the twenty-eight points, the committee drew attention to Seale's presence and he was asked by the inmates to speak.

Bobby Seale kept his word to me; he said nothing in an inflammatory tone. Sitting on a table facing the inmates, he said quietly, "We can only achieve what we need by revolutionary means," adding that he would bring back the recommendations of the Black Panther party within the next four hours. He spoke for only five minutes or so, and he was greeted by listless "Right ons." But it was what Bobby Seale did *not* say that made the tragic difference. He did not say a word for the twenty-eight points.

The Panther chairman then got up and left D Yard, and several members of the committee moved to accompany him. One of the rebel leaders, observing what he thought was an exodus by the committee, said, "What's this mean? You're gonna drop a piece of paper on us and walk out?"

State Senator John Dunne left then, because the mood in the yard was so tense he could not predict what might happen. "When Seale left, I left," he said, "because frankly I saw him as my ticket to getting out of there." Senator Dunne was also exhausted and had not slept since his arrival at Attica thirty-six hours before. He commented on Bobby Seale's appearance and his nonendorsement of the twenty-eight points: "We tried to impress on Seale how important it was for him to propose to the prisoners that our recommendations be accepted. He left with the message that he would abide by their decision. That was useless."

Congressman Badillo also nervously left D Yard at this point. "Some other members of the committee stayed to talk further with the rebels. But I saw no point to it. Without Seale, there was nothing to talk about," he reported.

When Bobby Seale passed through the Administration Building on his way out, Walter Dunbar and I intercepted him. I asked, "Why are you out this quickly? Did you tell them to end the rebellion at this point?" He said, "No. I did not tell them that. I wasn't able to tell them anything they didn't want to do." I said, "That isn't the reason you went in there in the first place. We think you had an obligation to tell them that this rebellion should be ended and the hostages be returned."

Bobby Seale said, "Well, maybe I could say that, but I will have to clear that matter and these demands and what we are going to do about them with Mr. Newton."

I said, "Well, where do you want to telephone from?" He said, "No, I will have to go out of the institution. I will have to call Mr. Newton." I said, "Well, where are you going to call him from?" He said, "I'll have to go back to Buffalo or Detroit." He added, "I'll see you again either tomorrow or I'll call you," and he was off.

After Bobby Seale's exit from D Yard, Clarence Jones, with great personal courage, now began to address the inmates. He said it was his experience in life that politics was the art of the possible. So he said that he would now introduce the twenty-eight points we had hammered together and also that he would read out loud the letter promising no administrative reprisals and no wholesale prosecutions obtained earlier in the day from Wyoming County District Attorney Louis James.

Clarence Jones told the inmates he could neither recommend nor guarantee the package proposal, but he said—and this was the crucial point—"it is the best possible."

Then he began to read out to the inmates, word for word, the content of the twenty-eight points. He was heard in silence by the mass of men held back by the security guards. He read Point 1, then Point 2, and then Point 3, which offered civil amnesty. But Point 3 did *not* offer complete criminal amnesty—and this was what the inmates wanted to hear. From Point 3 onward the rebels laughed or jeered after each of the points, all the way to Point 28. This reading of the rest of the points was an emotional massacre for Mr. Jones and for all of us who had labored so long for a peaceful solution at Attica.

At the end, after Mr. Jones had not even mentioned the rebels' other non-negotiable demands—transshipment to "non-imperialistic" countries and the removal of the superintendent—there was a low roar of disapproval from the men. But amnesty was the sharpest edge of their discontent.

"You are now looking at a bunch of dead men," Brother Richard said. "What amnesty means to us is what insurance means to a family."

But Clarence Jones had not yet finished his courageous work. He now read out loud to the inmates, word for word, the letter from the district attorney. There was another angry roar from the inmates after he had finished.

At this point William Kunstler returned to the negotiating tables—he had left D Yard with Bobby Seale to see him off the premises. Although the attorney's insistence on holding out for amnesty was his most notable disservice, he now made his most helpful contribution. An inmate asked, "And what do *you* think, counselor?" William Kunstler replied unequivocally that the twenty-eight points were the best they could get. He said, "It's the best we could do. If you say it's not good enough, it's your life and your decision."

Then he added, "I realize the amnesty section is not acceptable to you, especially now that a guard has died."

There were gasps from the audience in the dark yard. Though transistor radios had been chattering into bits and pieces of rebel territory the word of Corrections Officer Quinn's death, this was still not generally known. The gasps came because the rebels knew that the murder of a corrections officer was an offense punishable by execution in the State of New York and that, conceivably, almost all of them could be charged as accessories.

The jailhouse lawyer, Jerry Rosenberg, said, "Now we're due for the electric chair and we've got to hold out for total amnesty."

The Reverend Mr. Kenyatta, a radical member of the committee, now got up to speak. He said he, Kenyatta, had nothing whatever to do with the drawing up of the twenty-eight points. Then another radical, Thomas Soto, of the Prisoners' Solidarity League and Youth Against War and Fascism, said he had nothing to do with the twenty-eight points either. There were roars of approval for Mr. Kenyatta and for Mr. Soto. Plainly, the mood of D Yard was militant.

In the early hours of Sunday, September 12, the Committee came out of D Yard. I was relieved to see them back in their safe quarters in the Administration Building. I was tremendously grateful to Clarence Jones, who had risked his life merely to read out the twenty-eight points on which we had all placed our most profound hopes.

Mr. Jones commented acerbically that some of the prisoners had shouted things like "Live like a man, or die like a man," and he had told them that if they did not accept the twenty-eight points "they might just be given that opportunity."

At 3:00 A.M. on Sunday, Bobby Seale telephoned William Kunstler and said he would return to Attica at approximately 7:00 A.M. The attorney omitted to have this word passed to the rebel leaders, who waited up all night for the Panther chairman. The rebels were becoming jumpier and more agitated all this while.

Through these small hours I too was waiting for Bobby Seale. That evening Mr. Kunstler had told General Buzz O'Hara that he and Bobby Seale might need transportation to the prison early in the morning. General O'Hara gave Mr. Kunstler his room number at the Holiday Inn at Batavia and said that if the attorney would call at 4:00 A.M., he would be happy to pick him up with Bobby Seale and bring them to the prison. But Buzz O'Hara received no telephone call and neither did I.

At some point between 7:00 A.M. and 8:00 A.M. on Sunday, Walter Dunbar received valuable but depressing intelligence from rebel territory. Our informant said that four of the most important leaders were holding out for complete criminal amnesty. These were Roger Champen and Jerry Rosenberg, from whom we had not expected concessions, but also Richard Clark—Brother Richard—and Herbert Blyden—Brother Herbert. We did not doubt that L. D. Barclay was even more extreme and would also hold out for transshipment to "non-imperialistic" countries.

At 8:30 A.M. Bobby Seale returned to Attica, unheralded and unannounced. He asked for permission to return to D Yard to speak with the inmates. Several members of the committee asked what he intended to say and were given no answer. Several members told him they did not want him to return to the yard unless they knew what he would say there. When permission to re-enter was denied, Bobby Seale left the prison, followed by William Kunstler.

Clarence Jones commented acidly: "If they're not ready to urge acceptance, then let them give their agenda of death."

In a drizzling rain outside the walls of the correctional facility, Bobby Seale read out the statement to reporters that he had intended to make to the rebels. He made it to the rebels anyway, because he spoke to their transistor radios, and he laid down the hardest line heard at Attica until then:

"This morning, the commissioner and his aides would not let me in, saying that if I was not going inside to encourage the prisoners to accept the so-called demands made by the committee, they did not want me. I'm not going to do that.

"In addition, the commissioner said that full amnesty was non-negotiable and the removal of the warden at Attica prison was not negotiable. The Black Panther party position is this: The prisoners have to make their own decision. I will not encourage them to compromise their position.

"The Black Panther party position is that all political prisoners who want to be released to go to non-imperialistic countries should be complied with by the New York State government."

Bobby Seale then said to Mr. Kunstler, in the rain, "Let's try not to compromise the demands," and he left for California—where he said the demand for the release of political prisoners specifically included the release of Angela Davis. On Sunday evening he telephoned me and said "Commissioner, I'm on my way back. I think maybe I can help you toward ending this thing. I have to talk with the Observer Committee about some other points we can get together."

Mr. Seale said nothing would be done to harm the hostages but neither would they be released until I had spoken with him after he got back to Attica.

How did he know that?

This was—and it still is—one of the most significant, one of the most important, of all the unanswered questions about Attica.

And how high was the rebel price for the hostages going to rise?

In faraway Algiers, Eldridge Cleaver, the former Black Panther leader, the author of *Soul on Ice*, said the rebels of Attica, if freed and transshipped, would be welcome in Algeria, Congo (Brazzaville), Cuba, mainland China, or North Vietnam.

All those who still maintain there was no collusion inside and outside Attica—all those who still think the rebels were pitiful, downtrodden, harmless men—should ponder all these points. How naïve can they get? Yet the whole thrust of subsequent investigations has been against the representatives of the state. When, O when, will the spotlight turn upon the rebels at Attica and on the other men in the shadows?

CHAPTER 12

"We Want the Governor Here, Now!"

At 11:00 A.M. on Sunday, Governor Rockefeller's secretary, Robert Douglass, met with the Citizens Observer Committee in the Administration Building. Among the members present were Congressman Badillo, State Senator Garcia, Assemblyman Eve, William Gaiter, Tom Wicker, and William Kunstler.

Mr. Douglass, who had advised against the entry of Bobby Seale into rebel territory, had watched with growing concern the decline of the negotiations with the rebel leaders.

Mr. Douglass was also an unknown quantity for the committee members, if only because media people on the scene were speculating upon his arrival that I was being downgraded by the governor. It was known there had been concern on the governor's staff about my decisions to admit radical leaders into our discussions with the rebel inmates. In any event, I continued to be responsible for the decisions at Attica, subject to the governor's approval, and Bob Douglass, Norm Hurd, Buzz O'Hara, and I worked closely together through the most agonizing experiences that almost anybody could imagine. We were then, and we are now, good friends.

Robert Douglass, about a month short of forty years old, was a native of Binghamton, New York, a graduate of Binghamton public schools and of Dartmouth College, class of 1953. After two years' Army service, he entered Cornell Law School, won his degree in 1959, and was president of the Cornell Law Student Association. He engaged in the private practice of law in his home town of Binghamton and later worked for Governor Rockefeller at the Rockefeller family office in New York City.

Mr. Douglass was appointed first assistant counsel to the governor in 1964 and was promoted to counsel in the following year.

He became expert in the field of crime and rehabilitation, working closely with the Special Committee on Criminal Offenders in drafting its major reforms of the state's system of criminal justice. He pioneered along with the governor in the modernization of the correction law and treatment of the narcotics problem. He became the governor's secretary, or principal deputy in the state government, in 1971.

In the Sunday morning meeting at Attica, Robert Douglass zeroed in on the prime fact: The rebel leaders had escalated their demands throughout the negotiations and they had not considered the twenty-eight points. The rebels were, in fact, holding out for revolutionary demands that had nothing to do with prison reform. It bears repeating that their demand for complete amnesty for a murder and manifold injuries was a total negation of the rule of law and a threat to the fundamental American system. Their demand for freeing the leaders and transshipping them to "non-imperialistic" countries, subsequently endorsed by the Black Panther party, was a demand of the worldwide revolutionary movement, not of prison reform. Their demand for the removal of the superintendent was a statement that convicts could demand real power in managing the prisons and in converting them into ideological citadels.

But Congressman Badillo, Mr. Wicker, who seemed to be shaking with fatigue and emotion, and other members of the committee now delivered an important new proposal to Mr. Douglass and me. They asked that Governor Rockefeller come to Attica in person to meet with members of the Citizens Observer Committee.

What could Governor Rockefeller specifically accomplish at Attica?

The members of the committee had nothing specific to suggest —nothing really new. Negotiations were stalled and there was an impasse. There was nothing more the committee seemed able to do. They wanted to "buy time" and avoid having to admit to their failure and to the reality that was becoming increasingly clear—namely, that the instransigence and the impossible demands of the prisoners were forcing the state toward undertaking a mission to rescue the hostages.

It seemed clear to me that members of the committee were

afraid that if the governor did not come, the responsibility for any impending loss of life might fall on them.

Mr. Kunstler took the floor with this extraordinary statement: "If the governor does not come, and if the prison is forcibly retaken, there will be uprisings all over the country."

Mr. Douglass, calm and correct, told the members of the committee he would convey their demand and the sense of the meeting to Governor Rockefeller at once.

I sat beside Mr. Douglass in the superintendent's office while he talked to Governor Rockefeller about the meeting just adjourned. He reported the views of the members completely and accurately. He did not insert his own interpretation, judgment, or opinion. He said the sense of the whole committee was that the governor's presence at Attica might result in the freeing of the hostages.

The governor, however, expressed his conviction that his presence would serve no useful purpose and directed preparation of a public statement to this effect.

Then I met with Mr. Douglass, Dr. Hurd, General O'Hara, Howard Shapiro, and with my own staff in the superintendent's office. We thrashed out the pros and cons of whether the governor's presence might or might not be helpful and useful. Almost all the individuals in the room felt it would be useless for the governor to come to Attica. Nobody had any specific suggestion as to what he might accomplish.

Then I took a decision I had been weighing with the utmost care. I recommended that the governor indeed come to Attica to meet with members of the committee. I believed Governor Rockefeller could achieve nothing at Attica, given the present impasse in the negotiations. But I was extremely concerned about the governor's great name as a humanitarian and I felt it might be damaging for him in this context if he seemed in the public mind to be disengaged. I felt I had to put to him my deep concern for his humane reputation, in the nation and the world.

As Governor Rockefeller described the situation later:

"The committee knew they had reached an impasse. They were grasping for straws. We now had passed the last possible vestige of hope that this uprising was going to be settled on the basis of a desire for prison reform.

"Russ had tried, this broadly representative group of citizens had tried. They had been turned down, and the group leading the rebellion had hardened. I just felt that, in the face of this, the time had come when Russ was going to have to take this back in his own hands, making his own presentations to the prisoners by whatever means he felt was right. He was the man who was responsible, the man in charge.

"As the Chief Executive, with responsibility for the preservation of an effective governmental framework, I felt that we were facing here a very serious situation. Russ was hopeful that he would settle this on the basis of commitment to reforms, but we now were settling into a situation where the demands were political, where they affected the whole structure of our government in the sense of recognizing a framework of law within which people could find freedom and could find personal security."

I was sure in my own mind that the rebel leaders would negotiate no more with the governor in the Administration Building at Attica than on the moon. I was sure they would insist that he come right down through the DMZ and into D Yard. I was sure that many, if not most, members of the committee would plead with the governor to take that one more step.

I had tested the sentiment of the rebel leaders by recommending that they meet with me and with the observers on neutral territory. Always the answer had been negative. They said we would have to come to "the people" in D Yard. And, of course, I had already been into D Yard on three occasions without result, and I had been fortunate to emerge unscathed.

Now I felt the revolutionary leaders would like nothing more than for the governor to enter D Yard, in front of national network television and receive his orders from a crowd of rebellious convicts. And even then, there would be no special reason for the rebels to release the hostages unless and until we accepted their non-negotiable demands.

However, I recommended to the meeting that the governor come to Attica, in spite of these reservations and concerns, because I felt it would be harmful to him in the public mind if he did not come. This, of course, was public relations advice—not a professional recommendation in my field of special competence.

When I spoke to the governor, I recommended personally that he come to Attica for the reasons I have described, even though, as I told him, I did not think there was anything he could accomplish, given the present intransigence of the rebel leaders.

Governor Rockefeller replied that he had dealt in the past with people who were this intransigent, and it was his experience that they did not change and that nothing really substantive would be accomplished by his coming.

The governor then mentioned that if he were to come to Attica, there would be a danger that prisoners in other institutions might riot and take hostages in order to require the governor's presence. "Wouldn't it be a round-robin trip to places that are demanding to see the governor?" he asked. I agreed this was a real possibility, especially at this volatile time for prisons everywhere in the state.

The governor also felt that a visit to Attica would have national implications and that other prisoners in other states might riot in order to demand the presence of their chief executives. Thus the whole prison system of the United States might be thrown into turmoil—not for prison reform, but as the trigger point of a national revolution.

The governor had a further thought: To date, the rebels had not trusted the commissioner of the Department of Correctional Services, they had not trusted the Citizens Observer Committee, and now, if they did not trust the governor, would they next ask for the President of the United States? Trust? Well, trust enough to negotiate in good faith and make concessions. The governor said, "In any event, nothing has been resolved."

This was still the crux of the matter: We had made major concessions; the rebels had made none; three rebel demands were non-negotiable.

Shortly before 12 noon, Bob Douglass, Norm Hurd, Howard Shapiro, and I reached the reluctant conclusion that the usefulness of the Citizens Observer Committee was running out. The committee had been brought into existence as an impartial meeting ground in which meaningful negotiations might take place. But—we now knew the rebels were just as arbitrary and uncompromising with the committee as they had been with the state government.

We were still reluctant to retake the correctional facility by force if there was anything we might yet be able to accomplish by direct negotiations with the rebels. So I decided to send in a new message to the rebel leaders that was subsequently termed by the committee an "ultimatum," although it was not. It was an invitation to resume direct negotiations out of the channel of the committee. It read:

ATTICA CORRECTIONAL FACILITY
Sunday   September 12, 1971

As Commissioner of Correctional Services, I have personally met with you several times in areas under your control for the purposes of insuring the immediate safety of employee hostages and the safety of all others concerned during this current difficult situation. As you know food, clothing, bedding, and water and medical care have been available to you. You have been able to meet with outside observers of your choice and representatives of the news media. A Federal Court Order was obtained promptly to guarantee that there would be no administrative reprisals; your representatives have been able to ascertain that no mistreatment of inmates has occurred.

I urgently request you to release the hostages unharmed, now, and to accept the recommendations of the committee of outside observers, which recommendations were approved by me, and join with me in restoring order to this Institution.

Only after these steps are taken am I willing to meet with a five-member committee chosen by you to discuss any grievances you may have and to create a mechanism by which you can be assured that the recommendations I have agreed to are implemented.

All possible efforts have been made to deal fairly with your problems and grievances to resolve the present situation.

All good faith is embodied in the proposed agreement I signed which is in your hands.

It is in the interest of all concerned that you now respond affirmatively to this request.

Signed by *Russell G. Oswald*
New York State Commissioner
of Correctional Services

At 1:25 P.M., unbeknownst to me and to the radical members of the committee, four of the members made a direct phone call to Governor Rockefeller at his home in Pocantico Hills, New York.

The four were Tom Wicker, who placed the call, Senator Dunne, Congressman Badillo, and Clarence Jones. This was a well-intentioned move, and the governor listened to every word they had to say. The call was to last an hour and a half.

"All of them felt very depressed, very concerned," Governor Rockefeller recalled in an account of this lengthy conversation. "Tom talked first. They wanted me to come to Attica. They didn't see, any of them, how any of these last three demands could be acceded to. They thought we had given everything that we could give, but while they didn't say it, I felt that they did not want to admit defeat in this and see this thing just go back to the commissioner.

"So I said, 'Well, what do you think would be accomplished by my presence?' and their answer was, 'Well, we don't know; maybe two things: One, something might happen and two, we could buy time.'

"'Well,' I said, 'who do you want to buy time from? Are you worried that the prisoners are going to move and kill the hostages or are you worried the state is going to move?' And they said, 'We're worried about the state.'

"'Well,' I said, 'if it's more time you want, I can give you more time.' 'Well,' they said, 'your presence here would be a new element and we admit you can't go beyond the twenty-eight points agreed to, but maybe if you just come. . . .'

"I felt we had now moved into what I considered the political phase of this thing, but those who were pushing this, who were not interested in seeing the settlement or seeing a reform, what they wanted to do was to drag this out, preserve the theater for worldwide coverage relating to revolutionary forces and to get another round, and I said to them, 'Wouldn't you assume that if I got there, the first thing they would do was say we demand that the governor come into the yard?'

"They said, 'We couldn't do that; we couldn't agree to it.' Well, I appreciated it. I talked to them about an hour and a half, as I recall it. I felt myself that their position was one where, failing to see how anything could be done, they were reaching out for something that might find a solution, although they couldn't see what it was.

"I then called back our people at Attica. I told them of the conversation, and we then went over the statement which stated that we had done everything, the commissioner had, the observers had, and that we had made every concession in terms of prison reform we could and that we would now put this back in the hands of the commissioner and he would deal directly with the prisoners."

The governor's statement, issued that afternoon, read:

From the beginning of the tragic situation, involving riots and hostages at the Attica Correctional Facility which imperils the lives of many persons, including thirty-eight innocent citizens and dedicated law enforcement officers, I have been in constant, direct contact with Correctional Services Commissioner Russell Oswald and my representatives on the scene.

Every effort has been made by the State to resolve the situation and to establish order, hopefully by peaceable means.

I have carefully considered the request conveyed to me by the Committee of Citizen Observers for my physical presence at Attica, as well as the demands of the inmates that I meet with them in the prison yard.

I am deeply grateful to members of the committee for the long and courageous efforts to achieve a peaceful settlement. The key issue at stake, however, is still the demand for total amnesty for any criminal acts which may have occurred.

I do not have the constitutional authority to grant such a demand and I would not even if I had the authority, because to do so would undermine the very essence of our free society —the fair and impartial application of the law.

In view of the fact that the key issue is total amnesty—in spite of the best efforts of the committee and in spite of Commissioner Oswald's major commitments to the inmates—I do not feel that my physical presence on the site can contribute to a peaceful settlement.

Commissioner Oswald has offered twenty-eight major proposals recommended by the inmates and the Committee of Citizen Observers.

I fully support the Commissioner's proposals and concur with the considered opinion of the Commissioner that the inmates must now be offered a direct opportunity to respond to his offers.

I join personally with the Commissioner in an urgent appeal to the inmates that they now:

1. Release the hostages without harm;

2. Co-operate in the peaceful restoration of order; and

3. Accept the Commissioner's good-faith commitment to the twenty-eight major proposals offered to the inmates.

I am in full support of the Commissioner's actions and I will continue to keep in direct communication with him in his untiring effort to achieve a peaceful solution.

We were all becoming so frazzled from unrelenting pressure and from lack of sleep that we could not help but lose track of time. I had last slept, for a couple of hours, on Friday night. Before that, I had not slept since the previous Wednesday. I thought of my wife, in pain and under strict security guard at the Albany Medical Center. And in Schenectady, our only son, Kurt, was desperately worried about both his parents.

I was now moving to negotiate directly with the rebel leaders and I wanted to meet with them in neutral territory. Assemblyman Eve and a few other members of the committee had met briefly with Brother Richard at A Gate in the DMZ and there had been no incident. At least the idea ought to be thoroughly explored. But I found that the Citizens Observer Committee was furious with me. Moderates and radicals alike, they resented my sending my own statement direct to the inmates, and they felt I had misrepresented their position. In that statement, I had urged the rebels "to accept the recommendations of the committee of outside observers, which recommendations were approved by me." Certainly the members of the committee who had talked with the governor had clearly stated their support of the twenty-eight points.

But some of the members felt their usefulness as intermediaries had been critically weakened by my statement. They felt the inmates would regard them from here on out as little more than bearers of the commissioner's proposals. "Man, you've just signed my death warrant," Arthur Eve said to me. He was angry and fatigued.

Nonetheless, I decided to let a subcommittee of the Citizens Observer Committee re-enter D Yard for another meeting with the rebel leaders. I wanted the subcommittee simply to explore the possibility for a meeting on neutral ground. I thought this was a risk worth taking, even though the subcommittee included Jay-

barr Ali Kenyatta and Thomas Soto, in addition to William
Kunstler and the two Young Lords, Juan Ortiz and José "G.I."
Paris.

Arthur Eve was going in, and Clarence Jones said he would go
in if Tom Wicker would, and they both did. They were all joined
by a TV man, Roland Barnes of WGR-TV Buffalo.

I required that the subcommittee people sign a waiver of liability for the State of New York in the event that any harm came to
them.* This was the first time that I had requested a waiver. I did
it at this time because I was worried about the hardening and
violent mood of the prisoners.

The formation of this mission had caused enough trouble—and
I ran into a great deal more. Mr. Douglass and Dr. Hurd now
said it would be dangerous and counterproductive to let the radical committee members back into the yard. There was also the
suggestion that some of the radicals might even join the rebels, as
voluntary hostages. It was at this point that I clashed with the
governor's advisers on the issue of who was running the show—but
the clash ended quickly. They made it perfectly plain that they
were giving advice—not challenging my authority. On the other
hand, I did mean it: I had to be in real command on the scene or
else we would have chaos.

When it came to a decision of the nature of whether even to let
the radical committee members into D Yard at this volatile point,
I did intend to make that decision. The fact that the meeting in
D Yard turned out to be an even greater disaster than Mr.
Douglass and Dr. Hurd had feared is, of course, germane. But so
was the fact that I had to find some new opening for the negotiations, and the try for a meeting on neutral ground was the most
hopeful avenue to explore.

It was bad in D Yard.

Arthur Eve knew there was trouble as soon as he got to A Gate

* "I, ———, residing at ———, as a member of the ad hoc committee of
citizens concerned with settlement of the differences between the inmates of
Attica Correctional Facility and the New York State Department of Correctional Services, aware of the potential physical dangers to me personally by
my voluntary participation in negotiations with the inmates, do on behalf of
myself, my heirs and estate, hereby release the State of New York and any
officials thereof from any and all liability for any and all physical injuries or
damages to me personally which may result from my voluntary participation in
these negotiations.

(signed)———"

in the DMZ—and the trouble was my statement to the inmates. Brother Richard was at the gate in person, and he said to the subcommittee, "There's guys in there who would love to kill you." Halfway across rebel territory at a door through a corridor-tunnel, before the subcommittee reached D Yard, it was stopped. The members were led through the door in pairs, with a longish, unexplained wait between each pair.

William Kunstler, who with José Paris had persuaded Brother Richard they had not known of ¬y statement, was frankly apprehensive at the wait. He later described how "I had visions of guys having their throats cut as they went through the door. The men were so frustrated and bitter, I felt they had already condemned us."

Arthur Eve was primed and ready as he rose in D Yard and addressed the throng. (His words were recorded by the news media and on a tape now in the possession of the state government.)

The Citizens Observer Committee, Arthur Eve began, were "solid, united," and pledged to get the story out to the people. "They have tried to divide us. We were together with you to oppose bondage. That's why Oswald sent that letter in.

"Bobby Seale was here because *my* secretary sent him a prepaid ticket . . . The Young Lords were here because *my* secretary sent them a prepaid ticket. We are mad, and we are with you one thousand, one hundred thousand per cent!

"We wanted complete amnesty. The men told me to be determined, and I am, and we want it, and we want the governor here *now!* We were able to get Senator Dunne to agree to this, and Reverend Walker and Emery to agree to this, and Tom Wicker, our brother from the New York *Times,* to agree with this, and I say to you now that this is a reasonable request and we must get the governor here *now. Now!*

"And all of us, and I say here, we, this is what the Observer Committee is now. As of last night they came, all of them, and we are saying 'we.' Some of the brothers and some of the observers were saying 'I, I, I,' but as of today, early this morning, they were saying 'We,' and that's what Oswald became very frightened about.

"Now, I don't know what's going to happen, but I can tell you that you have had a profound effect on the whole world. And when we told Oswald, and Bob Douglass, we told them, 'We don't want to see our brothers die. We want to see this thing resolved, and we want you to meet their demands.'"

Mr. Eve then told a story about when he was having breakfast that morning in his hotel, a woman walked up to him and said, "They ought to kill all of you."

"And we came back and we related this to everyone, because we had to bring everyone together on what this struggle is.

"And that the request for amnesty . . . amnesty is not unreasonable because of the hostility of the people who serve in these institutions with no training whatsoever in human dignity.

"We're going to continue to work. We're going to stay here and we're going to get the governor to come. He's got to come. Now, I say here you got to get this message out. We got to get on the six o'clock news."

A man interrupted: "No way to get on the six o'clock news."

"Seven-thirty?"

"Good."

Arthur Eve continued: "Now, I'll make sure that as soon as this film is ready to go, we'll have a special bulletin put out and . . .

"I'm going to end now. But Reverend Florence says that we have a bond, a bond with you in here. And today many of us observers know that all of us are not the same kind of observer.

"Some of us are pro-prisoner supporters and the line is drawn, okay?

"We are here to help and do everything we can but I guarantee you the world will know, and I hope that other brothers and sisters all over the world, and especially in this state, in penal institutions, will be treated better because of your efforts. Thank you and God bless you."

Then William Kunstler followed Mr. Eve. A man asked him: "What's this I hear about foreign countries?"

Mr. Kunstler replied, "There are four Third World and African country people across the street from this prison, prepared to provide asylum for everyone who wants to leave this country for this purpose."

"I want to say one more word, because I think it's important that you know it. Bobby Seale called me at 4:00 A.M. and said he would be at the prison at 7:00 A.M. He met us in the room where we've been imprisoned until they let us in here.

"Mr. Oswald said to him that he wanted him to accept conditions that are not acceptable to you. Bobby Seale would not enter this compound today because he would not compromise you. He walked out of this prison, although he wanted to see you, because he could not bring himself, as a black man, to come in here and tell you what the Man wanted you to do.

"So Bobby Seale left, but he wanted you to know that, in every city with a black or Puerto Rican community, there are people who are watching Attica prison.

"The gringos talk about 'Remember the Alamo!'

"Remember Attica!"

Here in D Yard was thus heard an authentic voice of revolution —confirming what the tragedy of Attica was all about.

Messrs. Eve and Kunstler did not attempt to win acceptance of the twenty-eight points of prison reform nor even to try to get our hoped-for meeting on neutral ground. Instead, they hopped up the prisoners' emotions in a revolutionary binge. Not a word about the release of the hostages. Not a word about a meeting on neutral ground. Nothing but a hardening of positions and an inflaming of hostile attitudes. This was all profoundly horrifying.

As Clark Whelton commented later in the *Village Voice*, a weekly newspaper published in New York City:

"But members of the Observer Committee, no matter how emotionally or sincerely they identified with the justice of the Attica uprising, were not in the same perilous position as the inmates. The observers wore parachutes. They could always jump if Attica went up in flames, while the inmates had to stay behind to face the vengeance of the State Police. For key members of the committee like Eve and Kunstler, whose reputations gave them the most leverage with the inmates, to have let themselves identify completely with the prisoners' predicament could only have helped make a tragic and bloody conclusion inevitable.

"Rhetoric, removed from the necessity of facing the consequences it provokes, tends to escalate rapidly. Only a truly neutral committee could have had a chance of guiding the inmates away from the disaster which awaited them."

All of this was sadly true.

But, for history's sake, it was sadly fortunate that the impassioned shouts of revolution had emerged for all the American people to hear. The meaning of Attica was being proclaimed for those who would listen. And it would also be true that the State Police, far from exacting vengeance, would be the instrument of an aroused American majority that was *for* prison reform and *against* the revolutionary overthrow of our free society and way of life.

Mr. Kunstler explained to *Newsweek* afterward that he spoke about the Third World people only because he felt the inmates were as good as dead and that the Third World message "would make them feel better." To the *Voice* he explained, "I thought if they were going to die, at least they should know that people were with them all over the world."

Mary Breasted, a *Voice* colleague of Clark Whelton, produced an after-the-fact statement from Tom Wicker on the D Yard meeting. According to Miss Breasted, Mr. Wicker said: "I knew I should have gotten up and gone to the microphone and said they're saying things here that they may believe, but there's no hope that you're going to get complete amnesty. I didn't have the courage to say that to that particular crowd. I should have." He said much the same to others. This agonizing thought would hover in Tom's mind like a nightmare weeks and months after the event, plunging him into anguish.

That afternoon Tom Wicker, the involved newsman, came out of D Yard and went out of the prison gates, climbed on top of an automobile, and held an impromptu press conference. He described strong unity among the rebels, and he reported the results of interviews with five out of the thirty-eight hostages. Mr. Wicker said, "All five hostages, in summary, said they all requested strongly that full amnesty be granted the prisoners, that Governor Rockefeller come here."

There were angry shouts from relatives of the hostages who had been waiting day after day, night after night, by the gate. One man shouted, "Is there complete amnesty for murder?"

The father of one of the hostages said, "We have to go in and bring those people out. Wet-nursing those convicts won't do it. We have to get our son back or just bomb the hell out of the place. That's all that's left."

Meanwhile, members of the committee, led by Congressman Badillo, had issued a statement: "The Committee of Observers at Attica prison is now convinced that a massacre of prisoners and guards may take place in this institution. For the sake of our common humanity, we call on every person who hears these words to implore the governor of this state to come to Attica prison to consult with the Observer Committee, so we can spend time, and not lives, in an attempt to resolve the issues before us." Actually, the whole committee did not authorize this statement, but about two dozen of the thirty-four members did.

Inside rebel territory, the TV camera was still rolling and the on-camera and off-camera voices spoke from the heart of the tragedy.

An amplified voice was shouting, "Take any of the men that belongs to us off the roof and any of the troopers out of here, because if you get these shaky guys shooting off, or shooting up in a flivver over something, somebody's gonna get excited and then we're all gonna pay.

"Now, this is no joke. This is not a—some kind of little tea party we've got here. Now, you've read in the papers all these years of the Mylai massacre. That was only 100-some odd men. We're gonna end up with 1,500 men here if things don't go right, at least 1,500."

A chorus of voices off the microphone: "Thirty-nine."

The amplified voice continued, "Now, and thirty-nine, right. There's thirty-nine or maybe more than that, maybe more."

Then the amplified voice called out: "Sergeant Cunningham."

Now, the TV camera was playing on the face of Sergeant Edward Cunningham, fifty-two years old, who had won the Bronze Star with cluster with the 43rd Infantry Division in the Second World War. Sergeant Cunningham had been taken hostage in the industrial buildings on the morning of September 9. The interview began, "Now, would you give us a message for Governor Rockefeller?"

"I certainly would—one of the recommendations is—and, if he says no, I'm dead."

"Do you think he should come?"

"No, he has—he should come. His refusal to come here is a monstrosity, because what he is saying is, 'Kill these men. I have no concern.'"

Another hostage, Corrections Officer Michael Smith, twenty-three years old, said, "And I just hope the commissioner and the other people on the committee that they've gathered together can come up with a solution to solve these people's problems, and ours."

And again, "I'm Sergeant Cunningham, down here at Attica prison. Now, as far as Commissioner Oswald is concerned, I'm speaking for all thirty-eight of these hostages. We haven't seen him, we haven't seen anybody, we haven't seen a damn thing around here.

"In fact, we're just a forgotten people as far as they're concerned."

Another man came on camera: "Excuse me—I'd like to make a statement, now, on behalf of the Five Per Centers [the Puerto Rican radical group smaller than the Young Lords]. We are not giving up any names. Only thing we're gonna do here is die. So I want you to understand one thing. If them people out there come in here, and if they're jiving, we'll just have us some more hostages."

Captain Pappy Wald went on camera to say that the hostages were now being treated solicitously. He said the hostages' situation had made it easier for them to understand the prisoners' situation and this might come in handy in the future. In a grim reference that was also very brave, Pappy Wald commented with a smile:

"It'd be a shame to waste a group of educated people like that."

Soon afterward, at 5:30 P.M., in an incredible and almost unbelievably hideous episode, inmate Kenneth Hess, his throat slit, appeared at a third-floor window in D Block and yelled for help: "They've cut my throat. Help me." He was promptly dragged back out of sight. He would later be found dead with two other inmates. They had more than twenty stab wounds in each of their bodies.

Through all of this clamor and emotion, I held as hard as I possibly could to my lifeline to the renewal of negotiations—my direct request to meet on neutral ground. As the subcommittee returned from the yard, I was told I would have my answer at 6:00 P.M.

At 6:00 P.M. I was there at A Gate in the DMZ waiting for the answer. Waiting with me were eleven members of the committee.

Fifteen minutes later, word came that the answers would be ready in another ten minutes.

At 6:25 P.M. I was urged by Clarence Jones, Arthur Eve, Robert Garcia, José Paris, Juan Ortiz, Tom Soto, and Franklin Florence to walk through A Gate and walk one half of the way down the corridor to get the rebel answer. At once I was warned by Buzz O'Hara and Walter Dunbar that this looked like a trap in which I would be taken hostage. But I said I would go inside to get the answer if that would help save the lives of the hostages. I did *not* think they were forgotten men.

This time I worked it out with Buzz O'Hara and Walter Dunbar that if an attempt was made to seize me at the edge of rebel territory, I would drop to the floor. I would be covered by armed personnel and the gate would remain unlocked.

More minutes ticked by—there was still no answer. And none came. The rebels resented the armed force on our side of the gate, and they would not give a formal answer. Instead, a rebel leader called out to Clarence Jones, "Jones, you already have our answer. You give it to the commissioner." It was odd that Mr. Jones and the committee members, as well as the rebels, wanted me to go inside the gate when, all the time, Mr. Jones had the answer.

Clarence Jones then indicated to me that the rebels' answer, as he understood it, was negative. The leaders would meet with me only in D Yard. "Mr. Commissioner, the next move is up to you," Clarence Jones said to me. I replied, "I've given everything. I've gotten nothing in return. It seems a little one-sided to me."

After this episode I was sure I was marked to be the next hostage. I was even surer that it would be madness for Governor Rockefeller even to consider entering D Yard, as the rebels would inevitably demand.

Meanwhile, the committee itself was getting out of hand. I now knew that some members of the committee had been taking messages out of rebel territory and telephoning movement sources on the outside. I was also fairly certain that several radicals had been sending messages to radio outlets and that answers were being relayed back to the prison in code messages that the rebels would pick up on their transistor radios.

At that point—whether I was overreacting or not—I felt I had to intervene. I had a deep responsibility to the police rescue mission that was in preparation for the contingency that the nego-

tiations might be unsuccessful. I had to think about security—
and I did not want Sam Melville and the others to find out how
we planned to go in, from what directions, at what time, using
which weapons.

So I ordered all further entry into rebel territory to be closed
off forthwith. And at 7:20 P.M. I ordered the telephones in the
Citizens Observer Committee room to be disconnected immediately.

This harsh decision really terminated the relationship between
the committee and the representatives of the New York State
government. There was no more meaningful contact, even though
I still hoped the members might be minimally useful in any new
move to propose a meeting on neutral ground.

At 9:25 P.M. Sunday I went along with Walter Dunbar to the
committee room on the second floor of the Administration Building for the last meeting of this astonishing organization. We had
been through torment together and I had no hard feelings. Yet
this was to be the most tempestuous meeting of all.

I began to stress my last hope: "I'm adamant not to negotiate
in D Yard, but I will in any location other than D Yard. I'll guarantee the inmate committee's passage to and from a neutral negotiating site."

Then came the tempest. Mr. Eve and some of the others began
to complain about the racial slurs and discrimination they had
encountered in the town, in the prison, from the corrections officers, and so on. I knew about this and I regretted it, but it was
obviously not my fault, and I did not see why they brought it up
now. State Senator Thomas McGowan, a member of the committee who had served ten years on the Buffalo police force, defended his constituents. He regretted the incidents and denied
there were racist feelings. He commented that the rebels in D
Yard were, when all was said and done, convicts—and convicts
were in prison for good reasons, especially in these days of probation and parole.

Assemblyman Eve then reiterated that I must reach the governor to persuade him to reconsider his decision not to come to
Attica. "Tell him to come. Others have. If he does not, he's not
fit to be governor. The results will be on the governor's hands."

Herman Badillo cooled things by arguing only that additional
time was needed for negotiations.

William Kunstler then spoke at some length about complete amnesty, the central issue to him. He said the chief executive of a state could grant effective amnesty by the route of executive clemency. This would mean a prior commitment that, in this case, the Attica rebels would go through the judicial processes with the knowledge that their sentences would be commuted at the end. This was much too slick a maneuver, it seemed to me, and no governor would tolerate it, and neither, of course, would the courts. Mr. Kunstler pointed out that the British government had arranged to release imprisoned Arabs in exchange for hostages held in hijacked airliners by Palestinian guerrillas in the fall of 1970—which was scarcely relevant to the situation at Attica.

I said that I had received not a single compromise offer in our negotiations with the rebels—nothing—whereupon I was circled by Franklin Florence of FIGHT, the anti-poverty organization in Rochester, and by William Gaiter of BUILD, the anti-poverty organization in Buffalo. They walked around me jabbing their fingers at me. Mr. Gaiter shouted that we had conceded the inmates "nothing . . . nothing!" But black people had been "dying for centuries" and it would be criminal if we could not let the committee have more time. Mr. Florence said the inmates wanted no violence, but they did want amnesty. If they could not have it, did we have to go in and murder them?

Once again, Mr. Badillo tried to cool things, and he asked how much time there was left. I asked him, "What avenue do you wish to explore?" Mr. Badillo said he wanted to explore amnesty. "The governor says amnesty is wrong. I want to talk to the governor. The issue is human lives, and the authority to commute would be amnesty." So the moderates as well as the radicals on the committee were now moving toward the rebels on the non-negotiable amnesty demand.

Mr. Badillo said, "We need the day." I asked once again, what for, what really did he have in mind? Then I grew angry about the committee's willingness to criticize when it had accomplished so little on its own. I said, "A committee as powerful as this ought to have been able to swing that group of inmates around."

Franklin Florence said President Kennedy and Chairman Khrushchev both needed time in the Cuban missile crisis. Many people at Attica were now scared to death they were going to be killed. William Gaiter suggested that we negotiate with the rebel leaders by two-way radio. Arthur Eve criticized the governor's statement of the afternoon. Tom Wicker said the governor had never given any indication that he would come.

Jaybarr Ali Kenyatta said that if we attempted to take back the institution, there would be a holy war. Mr. Kenyatta, Mr. Eve and several others said that if the prison was retaken by force, there would be street fighting and many deaths in the ghettos of many of the cities in the state, and it would bring on violent reactions in all of the large cities. I was even cautioned about bloodbaths.

Clarence Jones said there was a relationship between time and humanity and that nothing was final. Robert Garcia said everybody was too tired and should get a good night's rest and look at the problems again in the morning. Mr. Wicker said the committee had made its plea and needed time.

Tom Wicker was then kind enough to say that "few of us in this room will ever have to go through what Commissioner Oswald is." I appreciated it. Mr. Kunstler agreed with Mr. Wicker, but he added, "Everyone dies if they come in." I said, "All of us choose life, but the pressures are tremendous."

Walter Dunbar received a telephone call from one of the first two members of the committee, Professor Herman Schwartz of the University of Buffalo, who had slipped somewhat into the background. Mr. Schwartz suggested that we talk to Mr. Kunstler about a proposal just made by Mr. Schwartz's wife: The governor's hand should be forced by persuading the wives of the hostages to demand of the governor that he come to Attica to see them. Now the wives were to be used.

At 10:35 P.M. this final meeting of the Citizens Observer Committee broke up at the Attica Correctional Facility. The committee dissolved itself and said it would "toss the whole problem back to the governor and Oswald."

But the committee died hard: A group of nine said they would like to stay in the prison overnight, just in case they could be of some use. I consented, but, for security's sake, I told them they would have to stay overnight in the committee room and in the half-corridor leading to the bathroom. And I insisted that their phone would have to stay disconnected. If any members wanted to leave to get some sleep and come back in the morning, they would be let back in to the prison, but they would have to stay in the committee room.

Julian Tepper and his associate, W. O. Fitch, wrote in their diary:

"10:35 P.M.: We are now confined to one room and a half-corridor.

"Midnight: Still raining.

"2:05 A.M.: An absolute downpour. We sleep, rest, sit, talk on the floor, tables and chairs."

It was Monday, September 13, 1971, and, as one of my prisoner correspondents would write me from Attica, God must have been crying, for it was raining hard.

Into the early hours, those of us who represented New York State government* and key state legislators on the Citizens Observer Committee deliberated on one last proposal. The new proposal was this: We would let the rebel leaders know, directly, that the governor would come to Attica, but only *after* the release of the hostages. Then he would meet with a small committee of the prisoners and hear their grievances.

The attraction of the proposal was that, if the rebels wanted the prestige of a visit from the governor, they might have it if they released the hostages. But we would not in any event grant the three demands for complete criminal amnesty, transshipment of the leaders to "non-imperialistic" countries, and the removal of the superintendent. And no one really thought, after four and a half days of dealing with such determined adversaries, that mere prestige was their objective.

Under the new plan, no counterproposal would be accepted. The defunct Citizens Observer Committee would not be used as a channel. There would be limits on any renewal of negotiations —in which the governor might be counterpressured to come to Attica *before* the hostages were released, and pressured again to go into the yard.

* In the room in the Administration Building were Mr. Douglass, Dr. Hurd, and Mr. Shapiro, General O'Hara and also Major General John C. Baker, the current commanding general of the New York Army National Guard; Chief Inspector John C. Miller of the New York State Police, State Senator John Dunne, and Assemblymen James Emery and Clark Wemple. On hand from Correctional Services, in addition to myself, were Mr. Dunbar and Mr. Mancusi.

But there was not a man in the room who thought that the rebels would give up their hostages—their bargaining power.

State Senator Dunne shot down the new idea fast and hard—and he was one of the four committee members who had been urging the governor only the previous afternoon to come to Attica. Now he said the governor, in coming to Attica under the new plan, would serve no useful purpose. He expressed the view many of us held—that the rebel leaders did not really want a peaceful settlement and would try again to force their three conditions.

These three conditions?

I must admit it would have been quite a scene, quite a victory, from the movement point of view: here comes the governor down to the yard; now it is complete amnesty—all the rebels rejoicing in the collapse of the law; there go the leaders, striding out of Attica, clenched fists held high, on their way to the plane to Algiers. How to make the United States look utterly weak and foolish in the eyes of the rest of the world. How to spread the word that violent radicalism is sure to succeed—the example is set; all must follow—and how only a few hundred well-trained convict cadres can make the country crawl.

At Attica, in September 1971, nobody walked the extra mile toward peace, moderation, and justice more often than the representatives of the New York State government. On our final idea for the governor to come *after* the release of the hostages, even though we had a roomful against it, we nonetheless telephoned the governor in the middle of the night and put it to him, point by point. We also told him our latest news from D Yard: the rebels were now intensifying their weapons production and preparing to electrify their barricades. In the end, the governor repeated that he would not come to Attica.

The governor decided against the new proposal, as he had decided on Sunday morning, because the rebels were holding for the non-negotiable demands. We had agreed to everything regarding prison reform while the rebels remained adamant on the political demands. It was now abundantly clear that we were dealing with not just an uprising over prison conditions, over prisoners' grievances, to obtain prison reform. We were dealing with a very sophisticated and determined coalition of revolutionaries who were trying to exploit public sympathy to achieve their political objectives, to trigger a chain reaction undermining authority everywhere.

This obviously was an intolerable situation, not only in terms of the lives of the hostages but also, in a broader view, in terms of preserving a democratic society dedicated to the freedom and security of all citizens.

State Senator Dunne proposed—and almost everybody approved—that the rebels be given one last chance in the morning to respond to a direct appeal from me to release the hostages. I had already privately decided to do this. We would not use the word "ultimatum" and we would not consider it one. We would give the message to the rebels at approximately 7:00 A.M. If an hour passed with negative or no reply, then we would move to recapture the rebel-held sections of the correctional facility.

We continued to hope that at the last minute they would agree to my request.

In the early morning hours of Monday, an inmate named Ronald Lyons staggered into our territory, suffering from a puncture wound in his lower right chest wall that required six stitches. Taken to the infirmary for treatment, he said he knew who stabbed him, but would not say who it was because he was afraid of future retaliation.

Then he confirmed that the rebels were working all night on weapons and were ready to fight in the morning.

"They all intend to die if need be, but not alone," Mr. Lyons said.

He disclosed that they would fight the state troopers as long as they were able and, at the last, they intended to kill all of the hostages.

He said the rebels had heard on the radio that the State Police would go in in five-man teams. They hoped to be able to wrest the weapons away from the troopers in the five-man teams and use them in the fight. They were expecting us to come in from the flank and rear, move onto the roof of rebel-held D Block, and use rifles from there. The rebels then expected to surge up through D Block to the roof and try to capture the rifles. But Mr. Lyons would not tell us about the rebel weapons and defenses.

On the Monday morning, not long before my final decision to retake the Correctional Facility, I felt it my responsibility to raise the question once more with the governor. Should he come to

Attica? After all, we were on the eve of a battle and men would probably be killed, and we would all have to live with our consciences. I felt we all had to be absolutely, unmistakably sure. I asked Nelson Rockefeller on the telephone, "Have you thought any more about the point we were discussing yesterday?" The governor said he had not changed his mind. As he explained later, he felt his coming would have undermined my own authority over the prison system as a whole—and would also undermine public confidence in and respect for law and order.

The truth at Attica was still that the rebel demands were not acceptable in a free society.

CHAPTER 13

The Battle of Attica I:
Attack—with Minimal Force

At 7:46 A.M. on Monday, September 13, I went down to A Gate in the so-called "demilitarized zone" of the Attica Correctional Facility with Walter Dunbar and Buzz O'Hara and asked to see the man I believed to be the most influential of the leaders of the four-and-a-half day rebellion. This was Richard L. Clark, known to us all by now as Brother Richard.

Within minutes Brother Richard appeared, dressed neatly in prison fatigues, his face worn from lack of sleep, as mine must have been, his eyes flickering carefully from one of us to another. "Well," I said, "I've been giving much thought to the whole situation all night, and I want to give you a memorandum I would like you to discuss with your people." His face tautened as if he believed he was now to be handed the final ultimatum from the New York State government demanding the release of thirty-eight hostages and the surrender of 1,281 rebel inmates.

I did not deem this an ultimatum, however; on the contrary, I was still hoping and praying that we could resume direct negotiations, but on neutral ground, not susceptible to the mob pressures that had wrecked our previous meetings with the rebels. I said to Brother Richard:

"Apparently, you remain adamant in your feeling that you will not meet with me on neutral ground. Nor will you appoint a committee to meet with me.

"I'm frankly having trouble understanding how we can ever get anything settled with a group as large as your whole body.

"Mr. Clark, I earnestly implore you to give the contents of this memorandum your most careful consideration.

"I want to continue negotiations with you."

I gave Brother Richard the memorandum, which I had signed

in advance in the superintendent's office of the Administration Building, and he took it in his hand without reading it. He said formally, and not unpleasantly, that a matter of this kind would have to be referred to what he called the People's Central Committee. He added: "I'll take it back to them right now."

I said, "I will expect the answer within the hour," to impress him with the urgency of my proposal.

If the rebels accepted it, I would not act to recapture the correctional facility. The note was not a charade. Here is the memorandum I gave Brother Richard:

ATTICA CORRECTIONAL FACILITY
Monday   September 13, 1971

For four days I have been using every resource available to me to settle peacefully the tragic situation here at Attica.

We have met with you; we have granted your requests for food, clothing, bedding, and water; for medical aid; for a Federal Court Order against administrative reprisals. We have worked with the special Citizens Committee which you requested. We have acceded to twenty-eight major demands which you have made and which the Citizens Committee has recommended. In spite of these efforts you continue to hold hostages.

I am anxious to achieve a *peaceful* resolution of the situation which now prevails here.

I urgently request you to seriously reconsider my earlier appeal that:

    1. All hostages be released immediately unharmed; and

    2. You join with me in restoring order to the facility.

I must have your reply to this urgent appeal within the hour.

I hope and pray your answer will be affirmative.

Signed by *Russell G. Oswald*
New York State Commissioner
of Correctional Services

When Brother Richard turned back toward the rebel "nation" in D Yard, I still hoped that somehow he would be able to accept the memorandum and to persuade the coalition that at least acceptance might be preferable to assault. It is important to stress that when I met Brother Richard at A Gate in the DMZ that Monday morning, we were not committed to use force.

Walter Dunbar, Buzz O'Hara, and I returned to the superintendent's office, and I reconfirmed that we had all the time we might need to negotiate. The National Guard helicopters, from which we planned to drop large quantities of disabling CS gas, were ready to fly. But the CS gas had been prepared for use at any time before 3:00 P.M. or so that day. Of course, we did not have to use it at all if we restarted negotiations.

The CS gas was the controlling factor. With it, we could hope to recapture the facility with minimal force from rebels who had been disabled but not permanently injured. Without it, as would have been the case if we had invaded the rebel sections on the Thursday or Friday, we would probably have had to use firearms. We would also have to overcome hand-to-hand resistance from determined men armed with hundreds of weapons of all sorts short of firearms.

In sum, we had an infinitely greater chance of rescuing the hostages if we had to move in by going under cover of CS gas.

"We can call this off any time," General O'Hara told me after we returned from the meeting with Brother Richard. Several New York State Police officers reaffirmed that it was still a matter of making preparations at this point.

So—we were continuing to attempt a negotiation with the rebel leaders, and I had offered them the way in which they could do this without "losing face." All they had to do was to meet with me, not in D Yard, but in neutral territory.

As I had throughout the days and nights, I thought of Jane. After returning from the meeting with Brother Richard, I telephoned her at the hospital. After a brief chat I told her of the memorandum I had just given the prisoners. I asked her to join me in praying that they would release the hostages and meet with me. Then I told her that if this did not happen, I would have to order the take-over of the institution. We both ran out of things to say. I am certain we both began to pray.

At 8:29 A.M. Mr. Dunbar walked down the corridor and gave a copy of my memorandum to the fourteen or so members of the Citizens Observer Committee who had spent the night in their office or had arrived at the prison very early. Walter Dunbar told them the building was being cleared, but the members said they wanted to stay on, even though gas masks were not available. José "G.I." Paris of the Young Lords said, "If people get hurt, it will be on your shoulders." Clarence Jones said he would stay and help in any way he could.

At 8:30 A.M. I was back down at A Gate, almost straining for the first glimpse of Brother Richard turning the corner. With me once again were Walter Dunbar and Buzz O'Hara. We waited ten minutes and then Brother Richard walked up and told me, "We don't know what you're talking about, that you have approved the demands. What demands have you approved?"

For heaven's sake!

I told Mr. Clark these were, of course, the twenty-eight points—we had said we would accept the twenty-eight points if the hostages were set free and the rebellion terminated. I said, "These are the major demands that Mr. Jones discussed in detail with all of you on Saturday night." Brother Richard looked at me and said, "I don't think you have ever approved them."

I had approved them and so had Governor Rockefeller, and the governor had announced this in his statement to the people of New York. Brother Richard knew this because the rebels were tuned to outside events on their radios. I said sharply, "We did approve them." And I added, "I signed the demands with a note of approval."

Brother Richard paused and said, "Well, I just can't remember them."

I said, "I don't know what we'll do. You say you haven't seen them." This seemed to be a delaying tactic, but I did not know what for, and because men's lives were at stake, I thought I would make doubly sure. "Well," I said, "you'll have to stand here while I get you a copy of the twenty-eight points."

A sudden thought flashed to me, and I turned to Mr. Dunbar, "Walter, you don't happen to have one with you?"

Walter Dunbar is the kind of person who does carry most things in his overflowing pockets, and he said, "Let's see." And he looked and said, "I have one in my pocket." He brought out a copy of the twenty-eight points, signed "Russell G. Oswald, Commissioner of Correctional Services" beneath the word "Approved."

I gave the rumpled, incredibly important piece of paper to

Brother Richard, and he took a quick look. "I don't remember these," he said, and then, "I'll have to discuss them with the people."

I asked him, "How much time do you need?"

He said, "A half hour."

I said, "Make it twenty minutes," and Brother Richard said, "All right."

If this was the "summit meeting" at Attica, I did not want it to end quite that perfunctorily, and I said to the rebel negotiator: "Now, be sure to tell them that this *was* discussed with them in detail," and, *"Please*—release those hostages, and let's sit down and talk and get order restored here."

Brother Richard said, "Well, I'll see you," and off he went.

Now I returned to my office, leaving Mr. Dunbar, with a two-way radio, waiting beside A Gate for the final answer of the rebel leaders. General O'Hara went up to a high floor of A Block. From there he could survey the tactical detail of the yards, the corridor-tunnels, and the cell blocks we still hoped we would not have to take by storm.

It was not quite 9:00 A.M. For the second time that morning, Governor Rockefeller was brought up to date on the telephone on the final negotiations and the final plans for the take-over. I told the governor it seemed to me that I was no longer able to negotiate with the rebel leaders because they refused to meet me anywhere but in D Yard, and I would not go there again for obvious reasons. This meant that I was no longer able to continue negotiations unless they released the hostages. But the final answer from Brother Richard and the rebel committee had yet to be received.

A fragile light of hope still showed through the crack in the door. But the door was swinging shut.

We had set the attack strategy we might have to use as follows:

1. The prison must be retaken and the hostages set free with *minimum* use of force, and hopefully with minimum loss of life.

2. This was to be accomplished by the sudden helicopter-drop of large quantities of CS gas to render the rebels incapable of prolonged resistance.

3. The forces that would enter rebel territory under CS gas cover

would use only *minimal* fire power and only to protect their own lives and the lives of the hostages.

4. The forces were to be led by the New York State Police, highly trained and skilled in the use of minimum force.

5. The spearheads would be backstopped by reserve forces of New York State Police, a second line of professionals trained in the use of minimal force.

6. The corrections officers of our own department were not to form part of the first line, because it was feared they might have become emotionally involved in the rebellion in which so many of their comrades had been injured by the rebels and might seek to exact summary reprisal.

7. The National Guard would supply sufficient strength outside the prison to constitute a strategic reserve, if needed, to make victory certain; also, to handle any attempt that might be made even at that late date by friends of the rebels to interfere from the outside.

New York State Police Superintendent William Kirwan had delegated the Attica operation to two of his ablest officers, Chief Inspector John Miller and Deputy Chief Inspector Robert Quick, who had flown with me to Attica on Thursday, September 9. They had refined the capability of their striking force, and kept it lean, during our lengthy negotiations. Never once did they indicate impatience to me; never once did I doubt they would be ready in the sad eventuality that we might need them.

Who was to lead our field forces in the recapture of the Attica Correctional Facility? The New York State Police officer given this responsibility, perhaps the largest in the state on the morning of September 13, was Major John Monahan. He was the Troop A commander from nearby Batavia who had sprung back so rapidly from the rebel successes of September 9 and had recaptured A, C, and E Blocks with only 100 corrections officers and State Police. Major Monahan now decided to accompany the State Police into rebel territory in person. He delegated the mission of communications officer and over-all co-ordinator of the assault to Captain Hank Williams of Troop A, who was also a veteran of the Criminal Investigation Division. He designated Captain A. T. Malovich to lead the second spearhead into Attica.

Major Monahan's battle plan was bold almost to a fault. Against probably most of the 1,281 rebel inmates in D Yard, Major Monahan planned to commit 187 men. Because Chief Inspector Miller and Deputy Chief Inspector Quick would elect to accompany the men, the attack force would total 189.

This certainly was *minimal* force—with the numerical odds better than six to one against us.

Whenever I hear the slur today that the New York State Police went into D Yard on a turkey shoot, I seethe with indignation. Never did men risk their lives intending to inflict as little harm as the 189 men at Attica on September 13. Instead, I think all of our people ought to be proud of the New York State Police, their dedication to duty, their objectivity, their fairness, and their moderation. They are professionals—and where would we be without them?

At 7:00 A.M., September 13, in the mail room of the head clerk's office in our section of the prison, Major Monahan held his briefing. The specifics of the plan will unfold during my telling of the story of the engagement itself. But the outlines were that the State Police would move in two task forces of eighty men apiece from A Block and C Block into rebel territory. The spearheads would move along the corridor-tunnels and along the roofs of the corridor-tunnels. At Times Square they would sweep to right and left, respectively, and occupy the commanding positions overlooking D Yard.

Then a hard-driving rescue force of twenty-seven men would pile down three ladders from a corridor-tunnel roof into D Yard and make straight for the hostages to release them. They would be covered by sharpshooter teams on the roofs of A Block and C Block. This part of the plan was changed just before the battle to meet a sudden emergency.

Tactically, the idea was to let loose a sudden bolt right into the rebel heartland. Ideally, the rebels would be disabled and thrown off balance by the helicopter-drop of the CS gas. The State Police would suddenly erupt into their midst, freeing the hostages, seizing the vital centers. The rebels would be stunned into surrender.

This was how Major Monahan and General O'Hara envisioned a victory with minimal force. But in the event that the going got much rougher and the rebels were able to put on a clubbing, stabbing, hand-to-hand resistance, with the discipline and ardor they had shown on September 9, then larger forces would be needed.

The State Police therefore mustered four reserve forces of sixty-five, seventy-five, twenty-five, and twenty-five men around the perimeter to serve as reinforcements wherever they were needed. These forces would also be well positioned to resist any rebel countermove out toward the walls of the prison. There would be an additional 146 State Police troopers in reserve near the main gate.

Major Monahan briefed his officers and non-commissioned officers on the specifics of this plan, and then he laid down very sharp orders for the minimal use of force. Firearms were only to be used in self-defense or in defense of the hostages. Firearms were only to be used according to the judgment of responsible officers in charge of each detail. Rear echelons were not to fire at all for fear of hitting front echelons. Fire from the sharpshooter teams was to be ordered through the officers commanding the teams, who would designate individual targets to individual marksmen. So it went on—every conceivable situation; only minimum force to be applied.

Major Monahan, in his mail-room briefing, concluded on this note:

"All supervisors must be advised that we do not wish to be placed in the position of being accused of turning this facility into a shooting gallery or, in slang terms, being accused of 'shooting fish in a barrel.'"

General Baker gave his orders for the two main National Guard missions at Attica with the same emphasis. The first mission was the all-important helicopter-drop of the CS gas. There were two National Guard helicopters—one to air-drop CS gas canisters, the other to spray CS gas over a wider area. There was a State Police helicopter equipped with a bullhorn through which the inmates could be passed instructions from above. There was also a helicopter from the Department of Environmental Conservation loaded with water for putting out fires.

The second main National Guard mission was on the ground—and 621 Guardsmen were on hand after call-out by proclamation of the governor. Among the Guardsmen were the 221st Task Group, Riot Control, of the Connecticut Street Armory in Buffalo; the 27th Armored Division at the Masten Armory in Buffalo;

and the 152nd Unit of the Guard, an engineering support group. There was as yet no sign of outside intervention—hence the ground units would be used for evacuating casualties, security patrols, and minesweeping and weapons search details.

General Baker stressed the New York Army National Guard orders that made a situation parallel to that at Kent State University, Ohio in 1970 virtually impossible. He ordered that the National Guardsmen at Attica carry their own live ammunition—but they were not to load their weapons, for the most part M-1 and M-16 rifles. These orders were so meticulously followed by the Guard at Attica that, according to one officer, "*All* pistol and rifle ammunition issued to the Guard was returned unexpended."

Deputy Superintendent Leon Vincent of the Attica Correctional Facility briefed our own force of corrections officers—they were told their mission was primarily custodial. They were to stand by within our cell blocks and move out only when the rebel sections had been retaken. They were also a backup reserve if they were needed. Then they were to search prisoners and process them for removal to secure accommodations.

Wyoming County Sheriff Dalton Carney briefed the sheriff's deputies of no fewer than fifteen counties who had rallied to the scene. He told them they were to be placed in the grounds just within the main entrance and behind the Administration Building, also for use as a backup force if necessary.

Mr. Douglass once again re-emphasized to the State Police officers the critical importance of making it absolutely clear to the troopers that firearms must be used only to save the life of a trooper or hostage.

The strategy of minimal force would thus govern the movements of 555 New York State Police troopers, 621 National Guardsmen, some 200 corrections officers, and some 300 sheriff's deputies, plus 100 or so additional specialists, technicians, and command personnel. There were almost 1,800 men under command at Attica—but only 189 men would assault rebel territory, with only twenty-seven men launching the rescue thrust to save the hostages.

Major Monahan, General O'Hara, and the other commanders could perceive through the drizzling rain the shape and strength of the rebel defenses. There were now barricades in the corridor-tunnels between A and C Blocks and Times Square at upper and lower levels. This was precisely where our men intended to charge.

These barricades consisted of steel and metal tables, benches, partitions, link fencing wired to railings, the lot festooned with metal prongs on which the troopers might be impaled. The link fencing and other elements of the barricades could be electrified—as we had been warned they would be.

Near each of these barricades there were Molotov cocktails and fifty-gallon drums filled with inflammable liquids. Mattresses were being soaked with these fluids, presumably to be ignited if and when we launched an attack.

There was a long, shallow slit trench, dug during the rebellion, protecting D Yard from any attack launched from the corridor-tunnels. This was another of our planned directions of advance.

There was an additional barricade, an individual barricade, for the urban guerrilla who had put this whole thing together. On ground level, behind Times Square, out of line of fire from any of the surrounding roofs, was a steel and metal barricade for Sam Melville, the Mad Bomber. This was an admirably central position, right up to the front line, but there could be no escape from a position that far forward. Sam Melville obviously meant to win or die.

There were also special weapons—we did not really know what —fashioned by Sam Melville and his production people in the metal shops the rebels had captured on September 9. There was a large and almost incredible projectile launcher, with propellants devised from fire extinguishers and acetylene-gas cylinders. The idea seemed to be to use this as a rocket launcher which could theoretically hurl projectiles upward against very low-flying helicopters, but the contraption was not yet ready for service. The rebels also had their own depleted supply of tear gas.

Our State Police officers had watched these and other developments through their binoculars and had heard reports about them from inmate sources, some of them true, some doubtless exaggerated. Nobody on our side on the morning of September 13 knew quite what we would be up against—yet there was no amendment to our governing strategy of force used sparingly. Almost all of our men were routinely equipped with rifles, shotguns, revolvers, and standard issue of ammunition. All wore riot helmets and gas masks.

By 7:45 A.M. Major Monahan and the other officers of the other forces had completed their briefings. By 8:30 A.M. all assault forces were in position, ready to go. This was the moment I was down at A Gate waiting for my last meeting with the rebel leader, Brother Richard, on the eve of the battle of Attica.

Behind its barricades, set apart from the rest of the world, D Yard Nation was beginning to disintegrate. In the mud, in the debris of the littered tents and negotiating tables, the end was coming nearer.

There were 1,250 or so of the rebels, not counting the sick and disabled in the makeshift dispensary, and the catatonic ones wandering about aimlessly swearing they were going to die. The rebels kept moving in and out of the cell blocks, almost as if they could not make up their minds whether to grapple in the yard or seek shelter in the cell blocks. When Brother Richard left to meet me at A Gate, there were only 500 or 600 inmates in the yard. But there was virtually a full complement when he returned.

The rebels had long since eaten up most of their looted supplies, and the last meal they received from the State of New York was a meal of 1,400 roast beef sandwiches and 1,400 oranges and apples, served with coffee at 4:00 P.M. on Sunday afternoon. The rebels had also served a hot meal of goulash and noodles, and the solicitous Black Muslim security guards made sure the hostages ate first. Since the previous night's oratory, there had been a steady, drenching rain, and many of the rebels who slept in the yard out of sheer pleasure at being out of the cell blocks had reluctantly gone back inside. The others slept in their tents.

After Brother Richard returned to D Yard, the rebel leaders recommended the rejection of the memorandum he brought from me. This was ratified by a vote of "the people." There was a listless response of "Yea." In fact, there seemed to be a lessening of zeal in D Yard. Perhaps it was because there had been too much rain. Perhaps, as is often the case in confrontations, the other side was even more tired than our own.

The rebels had believed during the weekend that they would win because we would be too soft to retake the prison at the risk of losing the lives of the corrections officers—and there was no question about the rebel intention to do away with the hostages if need be.

The rebels had also rapped about their fantastic goals. One of the goals, overheard by a hostage, was to "get Rockefeller here" and then abuse him the way they had abused me. "Then get

Nixon in here and kill Nixon with the hostages." A bloodbath in D Yard—and all of it could be on television!

Some of the rebels believed that if the State Police came in, great crowds would riot in the cities and the ghettos and foment civil uprisings everywhere in the country. They said the United States Army, desegregated, was now 50 per cent black. Black soldiers would revolt and take over the Army. Then a new nation would be created in America. But there now seemed to be little of this optimism, even though one inmate shouted that it was time to raise the new nation's flag.

There was perhaps an emotional letdown in the D Yard Nation in the fifth day of a sustained ordeal characterized by high points of excitement—of appeals made perhaps too often to "die like men." As one inmate said afterward, "Nobody did nothing—we wasted time hollering. We was angry, angry, from too much suffering."

The rebels did *not* know our plan—and they even maintained nostalgic hopes that our men would come in only with batons for a good old-fashioned hand-to-hand rumble, as one inmate later put it, "them with the clubs and us with the knives." The man added—"But unfortunately, they fire from the roof."

However, the rebel leaders began to whip up enthusiasm. The spokesmen began to shout, "Prepare for war—prepare for war!" A low growling of mixed-up exhortations began. Militants moved among the rebel mass, saying again and again, "Prepare for war!" The shouts grew louder and began to fuse. The noise began to echo down the corridor-tunnels, across the barricades, to our own side of the lines. Then one of the rebel leaders gave one of the last orations of D Yard Nation: "They will come in with helicopters and try to bluff us. Stand your ground. These pigs ain't got no heart.

"Don't kill the hostages, the pigs, until I give the word."

The rebel leaders, having rejected my memorandum, now prepared to play a trump card. They transferred control of the hostages away from the Black Muslims, the security men, and gave the hostages to other rebels, known as "the soldiers." The soldiers were to be "the executioners."

Every executioner was assigned a single hostage to kill on orders. One of the inmates shouted, "Give me one!" The rebel leaders said, according to hostages, that the hostages were not to be killed until a hand-to-hand fight was over or shots were fired. It was to be the last act. But the rebel leaders now ordered that eight of the hostages were to be separated from the others and prepared for a special exhibition.

The leaders did not pick and choose their eight special hostages —it did not matter who. The soldiers went among the hostages and pulled out eight of our corrections officers and civilian employees.

They were preparing a horror show—whether to fire up the morale of their own men, whether to appal our onlooking forces, whether to make us give up any plans to retake D Yard—who knows? And horror show it was. Whenever today I hear sympathy expressed for the rebel leaders, I am almost overcome with disgust.

One of the eight hostages chosen was Corrections Officer Frank Kline, a man in his mid-fifties, who had been the last to surrender at C Block on September 9. Mr. Kline recalled, "I was blindfolded in the morning after the commotion resulting from early negotiations that morning with the administration. I felt a showdown was imminent. The inmates were going fanatic. 'Take eight of them,' they shouted.

"They removed me from D Yard, took me to the top of the tunnel while I was still blindfolded, on the outside of the Times Square cage. I was led upstairs . . . and I could see a little bit under my blindfold which gave me some orientation.

"While I was in the Times Square tunnel area, an inmate was on my right with a knife against my ribs, and an inmate was on my left with a knife against my throat. I believed I was facing C Block at the time."

Corrections Officer John Stockholm, who had been concealed for twenty-four hours on September 9 and 10 by friendly inmates, said, "We were blindfolded. They took me and tied my hands in front of me with a lead rope and took me to the top of a tunnel, I believe to the Times Square area.

"They pushed me up against the screen at Times Square tower. I then felt a liquid poured on me. I believe it was gasoline. I was moved toward B Yard, I believe. An inmate had a knife to my throat. I felt it. I smoked a cigarette and was told to spit it out when I had finished it. Not to move my hands."

Senior Account Clerk Ronald Kozlowski was sure he was going to die—he and some other hostages had previously accepted last rites from priests on earlier visits. Even if the rebel demands had

been met, according to Ronald Kozlowski, the hostages were sure
they would be killed just the same. As he later reported: "On Monday, I was dressed in civilian clothes. My hands were tied in the
yard and I was taken with seven others to the tunnel roof. My
guard, an inmate, asked me if I was an officer, and I said, 'No, I
was a civilian,' so he cut the ties on my wrists. My executioner
combed my hair, and gave me a Tum and a cigarette and said he
wanted me to look pretty to die. He had a night stick and apparently something sharp.

"Before being taken to the roof, the inmates poured gasoline
into a pit and said that if there was shooting, they would throw
all the hostages into the pit and set them afire. They didn't."

Captain Pappy Wald, who was with the majority of the hostages
in D Yard, recalled, "Oswald had given them one hour to make up
their minds. They took a vote, apparently decided to shout 'Prepare for war!' At this time, they got us up, tied our hands and feet,
and blindfolded us . . .

"I smelled raw gasoline in the area. I heard they intended to
throw us in the trenches and light it. The executioner I had was
much shorter than I was, apparently in the Muslim faith. He had
a knife in my neck—it was in there pretty good.

"Once in a while, he'd take the knife away from my neck and
wipe it on my eye bandages. He said, 'I want to make sure there
are no germs.'

"At that time, it was raining. It had rained all night. He said,
'As long as there is rain, it promotes life and growth, and, also, it's
a good day for death.'

"We stood there alone twenty-five to thirty minutes with all of
this happening. The inmates were working themselves into a
frenzy. Then—there was a long shout—'Here they come!'"

It was 9:05 A.M. and all around the perimeter at Attica our men
watched with horror and incredulity as the first two hostages were
brought on to the top of Times Square in the drizzle, their executioners beside them, in full view.

Walter Dunbar, still waiting at A Gate for Brother Richard's
final answer to my memorandum, reported on a two-way radio to
me that each of the hostages was blindfolded, with hands tied and
an inmate at his side.

Major Monahan, waiting to lead the assault spearhead from A

Block, saw the hostages brought out at Times Square, at the very point he intended to strike. He reported they were bound hand and foot, blindfolded. They had sharp instruments pointed at their throats.

Deputy Chief Inspector Quick, waiting to go in from C Block, saw several inmates behind the barricade. "It appeared that they were standing next to and holding hostages, but visibility was poor from the ramp level and the barricade obstructed the view. One inmate appeared to be holding a spearlike weapon."

When I received Walter Dunbar's report in my office that was now a command post, I got in touch with Buzz O'Hara, who was in a position to see everything. I checked out Walter's report with General O'Hara and ordered the State Police to prepare to launch the assault.

At 9:12 A.M. a prisoner yelled down the corridor to Mr. Dunbar, "If you want us—you know what we want—come and get us."

At 9:15 A.M. fires were lighted in the barrels near the barricades.

Also at 9:15 A.M. the rebels were seen bringing several more blindfolded hostages out of D Yard with prisoners holding knives at their throats. Upon hearing on the two-way radio that the rebels had done this, I said, "We have no choice now."

At 9:16 A.M. there was mass yelling in D Yard.

At 9:20 A.M. there were three hostages on top of Times Square with their executioners. Others were being moved there.

At 9:22 A.M. we received our answer from the rebel leaders. A prisoner shouted down the corridor over a loudspeaker: "If you kill any inmates, we will kill the hostages. We want the Citizens Committee in D Block Yard. There are hostages on the roof. It's up to you. Come in now with the Citizens Committee and Oswald."

Walter Dunbar shouted back that the message should be repeated, and it was. Then he shouted back, "Release the hostages now, and Commissioner Oswald and the Citizens Committee will meet with you." They asked him to repeat the message, and he did. Then came the end of the negotiations at Attica: "Negative."

Mr. Dunbar asked for the repeat, and it came:

"Negative."

Walter Dunbar reported the exchange to me on the two-way radio.

Having previously been given approval by the governor, I now gave the order to retake the facility. As I recall, the exact words I used were:

"I hate to do it, but we must go in now."

I said this to Captain Hank Williams, who was handling communications for the State Police.

Captain Williams said, "Yes, sir," and he passed the order to the New York State Police to recapture the Attica Correctional Facility.

The appearance of the hostages and the executioners at Times Square meant that we would have to make some rapid changes in the attack plan. We were still for use of minimal force. We were still basing our plan on the helicopter-drop of the CS gas, and it took an agonizingly long several minutes for the machines to warm up their engines, take off, and hover across the concrete walls of the prison.

Major Monahan had planned to fire tear gas projectiles from both A and C Blocks into the barricades on top of the corridor-tunnels and also at Times Square. He now cancelled the fire plan on Times Square and instructed his men to fire the tear gas shells only into the barricades at knee level, so as not to do serious damage to the hostages if they were brought even closer to us.

Much more important, the mission of the State Police sniper teams was completely revamped, all in a matter of a few minutes. Instead of providing covering fire if needed, they were given one of the most sensitive assignments of the battle.

Captain Malovich of the New York State Police, who had been slated to go in from C Block, was one of the first officers to grasp the fact that the rebels were making a mistake. They might well be producing an opportunity to save the hostages at Times Square. The New York State Police snipers had .270 rifles with telescopic sights, and the troopers might be able to stop the executioners before they could cut the hostages' throats.

Captain Malovich said laconically afterwards, "This was discussed telephonically with the troop commander and it was agreed upon that the members [of the State Police] utilizing .270 rifles on the roof tops were to observe inmates holding hostages closely and, at the first hostile act, they were to dispatch any such inmate with rifle fire, but only upon command of the detail leader."

Major Monahan at once relayed instructions to the sniper teams in A Block and C Block. He instructed the officers in command of the sniper teams to assign a target to each sniper—the target being the inmate with the instrument at the throat of each hostage. But the officers would control fire.

Chief Inspector Miller, in touch with both Major Monahan and Captain Malovich, advised that no shots were to be fired until the first hostile act was taken by an executioner against a hostage. Should the executioners take hostile action against the hostages, then the riflemen were to shoot the executioners.

Even though we had now given the orders to retake the prison and were committed to the assault, we *were* still going to use minimal force. This required waiting for the helicopter-drop of the CS gas—and the disabling of the rebels around the majority of the hostages who had not as yet been brought out on display.

Then the 189-man assault against the 1,281 rebels would begin.

Disgusted though the State Police were by the executioners they could see through their telescopic sights, they were too well trained to open fire prematurely and throw off the whole battle plan.

The State Police radio crackled word to and from the sniper posts:

"A-1, are you ready?"

"Ready, sir."

The same question and answer to A-1 through A-4, then B-1 through B-4, then C-1 through C-4, and then D-1 through D-4.

Then, from the Command Post:

"How many of the subjects [hostages] do you think we could clear out [set free] if we used the personnel [snipers] discussed?"

"Oh, about fifteen."

At 9:42 A.M. the electrical power was cut off throughout all parts of the Attica Correctional Facility—thus wiping out an important element of the defense. The barricades, in a single stroke, could no longer be electrified.

At 9:45 A.M. the engines of the National Guard helicopters were heard, and they grew louder and louder in the rain, until the chop was almost deafening. A helicopter pilot's voice was heard on a radio:

"There's a 200-foot ceiling. The low stuff is coming in from the west. It'll be about 100 feet."

CHAPTER 14

The Battle of Attica II:
Victory—at a Tragic Cost

The New York Army National Guard CH-34 Choctaw helicopters clattered across the thirty-foot wall of the Attica Correctional Facility. They dipped low across the cell blocks and made observation passes over D Yard. The skies were dark and lowering, and there was a steady drizzle.

"Look—we called their bluff," one of the rebel leaders shouted to the hundreds of inmates in D Yard, when the helicopters passed over and dropped nothing. He screamed, "We've won!"

The rebel executioners guarding the hostages in D Yard forced our men to their feet, blindfolded, their hands and feet tied, and they pulled our men's heads back so the helicopter pilots could see the faces. The rebel executioners guarding the eight hostages singled out for exhibition on the roof of Times Square held their blades poised at the men's necks.

As Corrections Officer Dean Stenschorn later reported it: "The man behind me had an instrument at my throat. A flat blade of some sort. This man knew how to choke. He was holding the blade with both hands, his knee in my back, forcing my head back. I was going, but the leader told him to ease up.

"They thought Rockefeller was in the helicopter. They told us to hold their heads up. As far as I know, I was in the front rank. I did not seem to be moved. I felt I was facing A Block because they turned me to the right a little.

"The man was using my body as a shield. You're God-damned right he was. He was right tight behind me.

"Helicopter—Rockefeller. Hold their heads up. This guy just pulled me over backwards on top of him. The order came. Stand the hostages up. They kept me up. They were all around my legs.

Then somebody pulled me down. 'Kill the pigs, kill the pigs!' Then somebody, 'Don't kill 'em!'"

Corrections Officer Stockholm, one of the eight men on top of Times Square: "An inmate had a knife at my throat when the helicopter came over again. I smoked at another cigarette. The inmate asked me, 'Do you know judo?' Then I sat down and my hands were untied, and I was told, 'If you move fast, I'll kill you.'"

Then the rebel leader on the loudspeaker shouted that the helicopters might be back—"they might harass for the next half-hour —but stand your ground—they might drop some gas and pepper bombs." They did not believe until the very end that we were serious.

Now the National Guard helicopters swung back low over D Yard, spraying CS gas and unloading canisters all over rebel territory. There was a loud popping and thunking, and a choking fog of gray CS gas enveloped the defenses. The rebel inmates swarmed about the yard, shielding their eyes, clutching their stomachs, as they brandished their spears, knives, and clubs against enemies they could no longer see. There was little chance they could put up an effective resistance for the next several minutes. The effect of the gas was overwhelming.

In the acrid clouds, some of the rebels ran toward the hostages in D Yard, hoping they would be safer the nearer they came to our men. The prisoner "soldiers" beat them off, inflicting injuries. Some of the rebels ran towards our sections of the prison, hoping to find shelter there—and also in a few cases hoping to give up without further trouble. Some of the militants ran after these men, and the effect was that of a fragmented banzai charge in our direction just as the New York State Police were about to move in. Most of the rebels huddled low, in an attempt to take cover from the gas.

Lieutenant Robert Curtiss was the corrections officer who had courageously decided to confront the troublemaking Company 5 of the inmates at the first moment of the uprising on September 9. Now, close to the end of the rebellion, he was held in D Yard as the helicopters made their passes. As he recalls it: "There was a hell of a lot of activity. I could hear, 'Pig, you're going to die.' I could see one hostage out of the corner of my blindfold. This hostage was bent over. His assailant said, 'Look at this, Pig, go ahead and pray, Pig, you're going to die.'

"I reached over—my hands were tied—and shook Sergeant Cunningham's hands. His were tied in a cross position, same as mine, and I said, 'This is the big one. Good luck.' I said the same thing to Ed Miller."

Lieutenant Curtiss stood ramrod straight, having decided that if he was going to die, he would die like a soldier. He was resigned and ready for death. After another pass, and no gas drop, his executioner told him, "Lieutenant, you've got a lot of heart."

Then Lieutenant Curtiss heard the helicopters circle around and a murmur among the inmates, "They're dropping gas." He heard the popping. But he decided to stay on his feet.

On top of Times Square, what was probably the first overt, lethal act of the battle took place. The executioner guarding Corrections Officer Kline must have thought the popping of the gas canisters was rifle fire or else he was simply confused. At any rate, the killer holding Frank Kline shouted, "The pigs will kill you first!" He then swept his knife across Mr. Kline's neck, nicking Mr. Kline under the chin on the first sweep, then slashing him twice, severely, against the throat on the left side. Mr. Kline fell, believing his jugular vein had been cut. He would later have to have fifty-two stitches in his neck.

Then, Mr. Kline recalls, "I heard gunfire."

At 9:45 A.M. I was in the command post and I was to stay there throughout the engagement. Walter Dunbar was at A Gate. General O'Hara was on an upper floor of A Block. Major Monahan and Captain Malovich were ready to lead in the State Police spearheads, respectively, from A Block and C Block. Captain Williams, the communications officer, keyed the jump-off to the helicopter-drop, "Zero in on targets. Do not take action until the drop."

Then another voice answered on the State Police radio, "The drop has been made. Jackpot One has made the drop."

At 9:46 A.M. Captain Williams ordered, "Move in, move in. The drop has been made."

The battle of Attica would surge within the gas clouds for the next fifteen or twenty minutes in three phases, which overlapped but nonetheless patterned the engagement. This is my summary appraisal of the reports, made to me, at Attica and afterwards, on the fighting I did not personally witness.

SHARPSHOOTERS VERSUS EXECUTIONERS

New York State Police Lieutenant W. L. Shurter commanded Post R-A of sharpshooters on the roof of A Block, seven men all told, armed with six .270 rifles fitted with telescopic sights. The troopers were posted toward the corner of A Block and D Block, their line of fire across Times Square, so that any missed shots would travel not into D Yard but into an unoccupied yard in the opposite quarter of the quadrangle.

Zone Sergeant K. E. Gellert commanded Post R-A3 on the third floor of A Block, overlooking the corridor-tunnel to Times Square. There were six men all told, armed with five .270 rifles with telescopic sights.

Lieutenant G. K. Elbel commanded Post R-C, on the roof of C Block, with line of fire across Times Square into another unoccupied yard. There were seven members of the State Police there, with six .270 rifles equipped with telescopic sights.

Zone Sergeant T. N. Kruk commanded Post R-C3, on the third floor of C Block, overlooking the corridor-tunnel leading to Times Square. There were six men in this post, armed with five telescopic-sighted .270 rifles.

The sharpshooters opened fire on their assigned targets between 9:45 A.M. and 9:47 A.M., when the executioners seen through the telescopic sights appeared to be slicing at the hostages. The executioners sometimes presented as little as six square inches of head or chest as targets as they hung very close to their victims. But every single one of the executioners was killed or wounded within a few seconds. The .270 bullets, powerful enough to split an automobile engine block, bowled back executioners before they could cut the hostages' throats. Two of the hostages, tragically, were killed by gunfire at Times Square. The sharpshooters saved the lives, without any doubt whatsoever, of the six other hostages on the roof.

It was a desperate race, with the knives moving as the bullets slammed into the executioners. Corrections Officer Kline was already down, with deep cuts in his throat, when his executioner was taken out. Mr. Kline remembered only, "I was in a daze, lying on the tunnel roof."

Senior Account Clerk Kozlowski said, "I heard a shot. The inmate was behind me, using me as a shield, and at the shooting I was cut by him, trying to slice my throat. He fell backward, and I fell to the floor. Bullets were everywhere, chipping concrete." Corrections Officer Stockholm: "No more knife at my throat. When the firing started, I played dead." His executioner was down.

Afterward, when I was confronted by press criticism of the sharpshooter action at Times Square, I could hardly believe it. What did they want us to do—let the executioners cut the throats of the hostages and ask for complete amnesty? And provide transportation for the executioners to other countries?

The accuracy of the shooting, through the gas cloud and drizzle, was high. Between ten and twelve executioners, presenting extremely small targets, went down and six out of eight of our men, who would otherwise all have been killed, were returned to their families.

THE CHARGE ALONG THE CORRIDOR-TUNNELS

At 9:48 A.M. Major Monahan sent in his first thirty-man spearhead from A Block along the roof of the corridor-tunnel, with Captain W. K. Dillon in command, and Lieutenant M. K. Halloran in assistant command. The leading five men wore personal armor sets and all wore riot helmets, gas masks, and raincoats. They carried 12-gauge shotguns, six fire extinguishers, two pike poles, three tear gas fogger units and tear gas grenades, and a 2½-inch charged fire hose line. Sergeant R. J. Dwyer commanded a ten-man barricade-removal team, equipped with fire extinguishers and four pike poles.

Captain Malovich led the second thirty-man spearhead striking from C Block along the roof of the corridor-tunnel leading to Times Square. His lead five men also wore armor, and the whole force wore riot helmets, gas masks and raincoats and were primarily armed with shotguns. They had six fire extinguishers, two pike poles, three tear gas fogger units and tear gas grenades, and another 2½-inch charged fire hose. Captain Malovich was assisted in command by Lieutenant K. S. Crounse. Zone Sergeant P. P. Zelinski commanded another ten-man barricade-removal team moving out of C Block along the roof of the corridor-tunnel. His men carried fire extinguishers and four pike poles.

The pike poles had been obtained from local fire companies for the breaking down and levering away of the barricades. Insulated gloves had been obtained from a local utility company, and bolt cutters were also available for the handling of any obstacles that might somehow be electrified, even after the main power had been cut off.

Major Monahan decided to travel with the spearhead from A Block along the tunnel roof to Times Square. Altogether, he was committing eighty men against this objective on the upper level. After reaching Times Square, the men from A Block were ordered to swing right toward D Block, and the men from C Block to swing left toward B Block. They would then take up new positions overlooking and commanding D Yard.

Captain G. R. Tordy was in charge of a twenty-man force that charged through A Gate, through the DMZ, and down the tunnel to Times Square. He was assisted by Lieutenant J. C. Moochler, the man who had led the scratch force of troopers in the recapture of E Block on September 9. This strike group was also equipped with riot helmets, gas masks, and raincoats, 12-gauge shotguns, tear gas equipment, three fire extinguishers, and five emergency lights. Sergeant J. B. Cornell commanded a backup of five men with three emergency lights at the end of the tunnel.

Similarly, Lieutenant B. Muthig led a twenty-man strike force along the tunnel from C Block to Times Square, assisted by Lieutenant D. O. Parr. They had riot helmets, gas masks, and raincoats, shotguns, tear gas equipment, five emergency lights, and three fire extinguishers. Sergeant J. J. Patterson led the backup of five members of the State Police, with three emergency lights, at the C Block tunnel.

Major Monahan was committing fifty men to the tunnel attack on Times Square.

Major Monahan finally mustered A Recovery Team, fifteen men under Sergeant D. O. Ellis, directly behind the A Block rooftop spearhead, and C Recovery Team, fifteen men under Sergeant E. M. Byre, directly behind the C Block rooftop spearhead. The sharpshooters, of course, were covering all these movements.

Through the gas clouds and the rain, the spearheads hurtled along the roofs and through the tunnels toward Times Square. Tear gas projectiles were fired into the barricades, a foot or so above ground level. There was no opposition on the roof—the executioners there were all dead or wounded and the rebels could not stand to the barricades amid that much gas. The troopers reached the barricades, wrenched them apart, and then charged on.

Along the tunnels near A Block, as one of the troopers recalled, "There was a figure in the doorway. He threw a bottle that landed about ten feet in front of us." The bottle was apparently a Molotov cocktail but it did not go off. The trooper said, "Someone, I think it was the man next to me, let him have it." An inmate ran out into A Yard and raised his hand to throw a spear. He was shot down.

In the choking gas, no rebels were able to make an effective resistance in the tunnels any more than on the roofs of the corridors. The CS gas was the decisive weapon.

On the roofs of the corridors Major Monahan's spearhead from A Block and Captain Malovich's from C Block rounded Times Square in less than a minute and swung to their right and left, respectively, as per orders. They charged toward D Block and B Block. Then they stopped. They did not attempt to force entrance. They were fewer than 100 State Police and there were 1,250 or so of the rebels to overcome. The troopers had been ordered not to overextend themselves in the first phases of the battle. They turned inward and peered down into D Yard.

Major Monahan tersely reported the success of the charge: "I accompanied the group going on to A tunnel roof, from where I could observe the activities of this group and some of the activities of the group on the C tunnel top. Both groups were able to effect passage through the barricades."

He added: "Upon arrival in the Times Square area, a number of casualties were observed on the tunnel roof, and base was contacted by radio and requested immediately to send in medical assistance."

Chief Inspector Miller left the Command Post and followed the spearhead from A Block. He said, "I observed the State Police detail move out on to the walkway on top of the A Block corridor, go through the barrier toward Times Square and the walkways toward B and D Block, and then I moved out myself on the walkway, leading from A Block.

"Initially, visibility was somewhat obscured from the gas being dispersed by the helicopters. The gas mask did not obscure my vision, but it restricted communication. I observed several inmates, whom I believed dead, lying on the walkway behind the barriers and in the Times Square area."

Deputy Chief Inspector Quick followed Captain Malovich's men down the ramp to the center of the yards where the four ramps converged in the area known as Times Square. His men turned to the left onto B ramp and lined up overlooking the yard where the prisoners and hostages were. He said, "At no time did I observe any members of this detail fire any shots after they had cleared the barricade on C ramp."

Corrections Officer Stockholm, one of the hostages on top of Times Square, was one of the first to be liberated: "I was playing dead. Shortly afterward, I was shaken by a state trooper, told to get out, and I went to C Block. I recognized Ron Kozlowski, a civilian hostage, with his throat cut. I identified him to State Police. I saw [Corrections Officer] Art Smith running behind us with his hands tied behind him. Art Smith, Ron Kozlowski, and I were the first hostages at Warsaw Hospital."

Ronald Kozlowski said: "The shooting stopped, the gas got bad, real bad, and a trooper grabbed me and helped me to an ambulance. My throat was cut about 2½ inches long and deep, and I had a thin cut from one ear to the other ear. Thirty-some stitches were required to sew me up." Frank Kline recalled, "I heard voices which said, 'This is an officer.' Someone took my blindfold off and took me out on a stretcher through A Block. I recognized Nurse Monihan, who put a compress against my throat. I was taken to Warsaw Community Hospital where Dr. Hanson sewed me up with more than fifty-two stitches."

THE TWENTY-SEVEN-MAN RESCUE TEAM'S STRUGGLE

Pounding right behind the A Block spearhead came the rescue detail of twenty-five State Police troopers accompanied by two of our Department of Correctional Services employees. They were under command of Captain J. W. McCarthy, assisted by Lieutenant Joseph P. Christian. They were equipped with riot helmets, gas masks, raincoats, and primarily with shotguns. Their objective was to climb down ladders into D Yard and head straight for the main body of the hostages.

The plan was to lance through to the rebel center while the

rebels were still disabled by the gas and shaken by the assault, to rescue the hostages, identify them, and bring them back to our section of the prison as rapidly as possible. This mission was to be accomplished, as far as possible, without direct reference to the rest of the battle.

Corrections Officer Bob Hulshoff, one of the two employees selected to go in with the rescue squad to identify the hostages, was crouched on the steel stairway leading to the roof of the corridor-tunnel when the order came to go in. He was so ready to go he almost climbed over the men in front of him. He burst out of the door, running at top speed along the roof top. Then the battle was all around him. As he later recalled to the New York *Daily News:*

"I was running along the roof, past the troopers and all the bodies, and I could see the prisoners [in D Yard] jumping out from behind the barricade they had built there . . . some of them with long clubs, others with spears, others with knives."

Several state troopers at this point opened up with shotguns at what looked to them through the loom of gas and rain like a banzai charge. A grim figure was seen in the murk, emerging from a barricade in the corner behind Times Square, hugging four Molotov cocktails in his arms. Suddenly this man began to rush toward one of the fifty-gallon tanks—known by the troopers to be filled with inflammable liquid. He was shot to death.

The dead man was Sam Melville, the Mad Bomber.

The twenty-seven-man rescue team traversed Times Square and lowered three ladders into D Yard. For an instant, as the small rescue force passed through the bottleneck created by the need to climb down ladders, there was one State Police officer facing the hundreds of prisoners—then two, then three, then six, then nine, and so on until the twenty-seven-man strike force was in D Yard—facing forty-five times their numbers and with the lives of some thirty hostages depending on the success of their charge into the melee. There was also the danger that the rebels could capture the firearms of the first State Police officers into D Yard and use them with deadly effect upon the rescue mission.

Here is the answer to questions asked later as to why the rescuers carried shotguns instead of handguns or batons: Against such odds, in such a crucial operation, only the shotgun commanded the respect and if necessary the firepower to deter or to prevent seizure of State Police weapons by determined inmates who escaped the more disabling effects of the gas. Within moments, the danger of such a weapon seizure—as well as the risk in using such a weapon—became apparent.

The first rescuers into D Yard charged across the slit trench the rebels had dug during the negotiations. They headed hard for a group of hostages in the midst of the rebels. It was difficult for the troopers to tell the difference between hostages and inmates; they were covered with mud and the prisoners had changed clothes with the hostages. It was a tough problem anyway, trying to see through the gas masks and the clouds of gas.

In one strip of the slit trench was Jerry Rosenberg, the jailhouse lawyer, one of the rebel leaders. His eyes were blurred by the CS gas but he said later he could remember the first wave of troopers charging across the trench toward the hostages. He and other occupants of the trench were ordered by a second line of the troopers to lie still.

Lieutenant Christian, second-in-command of the rescue squad, was the leader of the charge toward the hostages. He ran through the gas, rain, and gunsmoke toward our men. He saw one about to be clubbed by an inmate and told the man to drop the club. Then he ordered all the inmates and hostages in the area to drop to the ground.

Now came the single event causing the most casualties at Attica. One of the rebels grabbed Lieutenant Christian by the leg, and Lieutenant Christian lost his balance and fell. Somehow he managed to twist himself in falling and he was able to land on top of his shotgun. At all costs, our firearms had to be kept out of the hands of the inmates. As he lay on the ground, he was struck on the head with a club; fortunately, his helmet protected him from injury. One of the rebels yelled jubilantly in what must have been their first success of the day, "I got one of them!"

At once, a fellow officer opened fire to protect Lieutenant Christian, killing the man who had downed him. One or two other troopers overlooking D Yard opened up in support. But each of the shotgun shells was loaded with ten pellets, and they had a spray effect on the crowd of inmates and hostages in D Yard. Lieutenant Christian himself was struck twice, in the arm and the leg. He was one of six state troopers wounded in the assault.

Here, then, was the vortex of the battle, with gunfire now coming in from several directions into a densely populated target area. The rebels making their strongest stand and the hostages attempting to break free were all now in deadly danger. Here it was, from shotgun and other gunfire wounds, that seven of our hostages were killed—and another would later die of his wounds. Many of the hostages, injured during the uprising, were wounded again. Many of the twenty-nine inmates killed on September 13 fell in this brief and savage encounter.

But here it was also that most of our hostages were rescued. It was heartrending that we were to lose eight hostages in this phase of the struggle. But we saved twenty-two hostages in this same D Yard melee—and that was almost miraculous in the circumstances.

There was no way our sharpshooters could have picked off executioners in the crowded yard as expeditiously as they had done at Times Square. If they had found their marks, then other rebels would have surely killed the hostages where they stood. There was no other way—a rescue squad had to move right into D Yard to save our men.

Inevitably, perhaps, the very lead officer moving against hundreds of men, disabled even though they were by CS gas, was going to meet resistance. This one man was the pinpoint of the whole rescue mission. His life was saved by his comrades. His weapon was also saved. If the rebels had obtained a shotgun, they would have been able to knock out others in the rescue squad, take their shotguns, and inflict heavy casualties on the troopers.

All this happened within four minutes of the jump-off. Now the rescue of the hostages was at last at hand. As Corrections Officer Hulshoff in the rescue force said, "You see guys like this every day, with their suits and white shirts and ties, and clean-shaven, and here they are, like pigs. They've been out there three or four days, they've got a growth of beard, just an old pair of overalls. It was hard. And then you're turning people over, the blood and everything, and all of a sudden there's seven of your buddies lying there, that you're never going to talk to any more."

Captain Pappy Wald recalls, "We could hear the helicopter. The first gas canister went off. I heard a shot. The man holding me pressed the knife into my neck and suddenly he was gone. The bullet went right past my neck—missed it by an inch. There was a loud explosion. I don't know what it was, but whatever it was, it hit me a blow on the back of the head, knocked me down, and I lost consciousness.

"I was out about five minutes. I woke up in the middle of it all. I was still blindfolded and tied. I could hear voices. Thought the inmates were all around me. I thought they'd kill me if I moved. I moved the bandage off my eyes and saw the biggest trooper. He said, 'My God, we've been looking all over for you.'"

Industrial Superintendent Robert Van Buren, the senior civilian hostage, said, "The man behind me, my executioner who had a hold of my back, said he'd stop my feet from shaking soon. He tapped me on the back three or four times with a weapon. I heard the leader order not to kill anybody until one of them died. 'If we die, you die.' After release of the gas, this leader's same voice said not to get excited, it was only gas.

"Then there was this noise and shooting, and I heard a few groans behind me. Then I was knocked to the ground after being hit in the side, probably by gunshot.

"After I got hit, somebody kept tugging at me, trying to get me up on my feet. He did get me up on my feet. My hands and feet were still tied. He straightened me up. I felt a knife sawing away at the binding between my hands and my feet. I can only assume this was an inmate.

"As soon as the bindings came apart, I stood up, leaped forward, tried to push myself out of there still blindfolded. I must have traveled about fifteen feet. Somebody grabbed me from behind, yanked my blindfold off—then I saw the brightest and shiniest boots I ever saw—a trooper.

"I identified Sergeant Cunningham, who was quite dead; Carl Valone, who looked dead to me, and Gordon Knickerbocker, he was next to me. When I got hit, Knickerbocker was down and I felt his shoes against my arm at right angles to the ground.

"At this time, I felt blood running down my legs. A trooper asked me to drop my pants. He said I'd been shot."

Corrections Officer Dean Stenschorn reported: "A stick at my throat. Gas. Blindfold off. Stick came off my throat. I heard somebody saying, 'I'm stabbed.' State troopers arrived. Said lay down with your hands on your head. I identified myself. I saw Red Whalen lying there. I thought he was dead. His mouth was open, blood coming out. Dick Lewis looked as if he was dead. Sergeant

Cunningham was laying on the mattresses. Prave was holding his side. He was bleeding. I could see he had an open wound."

Corrections Officer Elmer Huehn, the A Block hall captain who had risked his life to help Lieutenant Curtiss at the beginning of the rebellion: "I was in the front rank, dressed in an inmate shirt, buttoned, with officers trousers, shoes, blindfolded, hands tied in front, and my feet tied. I was standing with an inmate behind me, with his hand on my throat.

"There was the blast of the gas. The inmate told me to drop. I stayed put on the ground, my blindfold partially pushed up. I saw three troopers and yelled for help, and they cut me loose. I went with troopers to help identify hostages. I climbed the ladder to the roof and walked all the way to the ambulance."

Afterwards Mr. Huehn told the Rochester *Democrat-Chronicle*: "My man—the one assigned to cut my throat, was a Puerto Rican guy I had known before this all started. I figured this is it. But the inmate placed the knife at my neck and whispered in my ear, 'I don't have the heart to do it. I'm only going to prick you.'"

Corrections Officer Richard Fargo told *Newsday* his executioner only nicked him with a knife and said, "There, don't tell them I didn't cut you." Then the executioner was shot.

Gordon Knickerbocker, the senior stores clerk who had been standing next to Mr. Van Buren, was down on the ground when the crunch came. His executioner tried to force him to stand, but Mr. Knickerbocker refused. The executioner tried to lift his hostage himself but could not do it. Mr. Knickerbocker reached his hands over to one shoulder and then suddenly he felt a sharp pain at the tip of his little finger—he thought it was as if a firecracker had just gone off at the end of his finger. Then the sound followed the pain, a whizzing noise, and a thud as the executioner dropped.

But Gordon Knickerbocker was himself wounded in the back of the head and, when he regained consciousness, there was a state trooper leaning down to take him to safety.

Industrial Foreman Fred Miller was blindfolded, his hands and feet tied, and his executioner was twisting a towel around his neck, holding him tight. The executioner was unusually vicious, and he kept showing Mr. Miller a 2½-foot length of pipe and told Mr. Miller this was what was going to be used to kill him. Mr. Miller's executioner used his body as a shield. Then, as Mr. Miller recalled:

"I heard the helicopter and explosions and I got hit—a blow in the center of the head—perhaps three or four times. I fell down, dazed. I was kicked in the shoulder by an inmate. After my rescue, I was put on a stretcher and removed from the yard."

Industrial Foreman Ed Miller: "An executioner was at my back and jabbed something into my back. I was sure they were going to burn us up. Something started hitting the ground as a helicopter passed over, and I threw myself on the ground, and my hands became loose and I removed the blindfold.

"Someone hit me on the head and dazed me, but I saw an inmate trying to pull me up and he had a pipe, and I grabbed it from him and hit him on the head, and he went down.

"I then saw a trooper and identified myself, and I was helped out of the yard. I had received a hairline fracture of the skull and a broken rib."

Corrections Officer Lynn Johnson: "I was retained in the center of the yard when the attack started. A little Puerto Rican knocked me down, jabbed and poked me, and threatened to cut my throat.

"When the firing started, my enforcer fell on me, and apparently a trooper killed him with a shotgun, because when my blindfold was removed, I noticed the man behind me with his back blown out.

"A trooper took off my blindfold shortly afterwards, and I went over the tunnel through A Block and was quickly sent to the Genesee Memorial Hospital, where I was shortly released. My only problem now is that I cannot sleep nights."

Gary Walker's hands and feet were tied together, so that he was unable to stand up. The corrections officer's executioner had specific orders to kill him if shooting was started. The executioner had a knife at his throat. Mr. Walker somehow managed, however, to roll and dive over a bench in front of him when the shooting began, and he rolled under a bench. After his rescue by the State Police, he went back to the place where he had expected to die, and he found the body of his executioner.

Corrections Officer Dean Wright, who had been sick and feverish all his time in captivity, was hit in the stomach by his executioner and he fell down, but survived the attack. Afterwards, he came down with pneumonia.

Philip Watkins, an officer whose arm had been broken by a man with a shovel on September 9: "I was left in D Yard. One man was behind me. I don't know if he had a knife or not, but he had a big iron bar. I could see under my blindfold a little bit, and I noticed that it was one of those big ice choppers in his hand. At the time of the attack, the man behind me pulled me down. I did so with difficulty because my hands and feet were tied. I was used as a shield, I believe. He accidentally pulled my blindfold off at one time.

"I untied my hands and ran like hell. Two troopers told me to lie down, and I argued with them, but they continued to tell me to lie down and I did. Some time elapsed before I left the area, because at first they believed I was an inmate."

Corrections Officer Frank Strollo told *Newsweek* that he was hit on the back of the head with a length of pipe when the firing began: "Whoever did it, he sort of got on top of me. I heard guys saying, 'Don't kill him, don't kill him.'"

Albert Robbins, the garage supervisor, said he thought that the radical groups argued among themselves about the final memorandum delivered from the New York State government, and he believed that two inmates who had wanted to accept the memorandum were taken away and taken care of. He said it was the radical rebel leaders who decided to take eight of the hostages away to Times Square and execute them when the first shot was fired. He added that all of the hostages left in D Yard were given to understand they too would be executed once the firing had started. He survived the attack when his executioner pulled him down to the ground and hid beneath his body.

Lieutenant Curtiss, still standing, suddenly felt a terrific jolt right in the center of his back. This knocked the wind out of him, and threw him to his knees, and at the same time a voice behind him shouted, "They're shooting—I'm shot." When he heard this, he pushed up his blindfold, looked back, and saw a man's hand on his shoulder with a hole in the back of the hand.

Then he saw the New York State Police—"the men from Mars, and God Bless them." They were still some ten feet short of him, so Lieutenant Curtiss dove toward them, his hands and feet still tied, and he rolled over on the ground until he was safe.

Sergeant Gerald Reger fell forward, away from his executioner, rolled forward some more, and lay still. Then he was rescued by the state troopers.

THE SUPPORT MISSIONS

The New York State Police mustered four major support missions on September 13. The first was Post Fence Southwest, in charge of Lieutenant R. W. Jones, and ranged from the southwest corner of A Block to the west wall of the institution. This force numbered sixty-five members, and it was there to prevent a rebel breakout in that direction. Post Hill South, under Captain R. F. Orr, deployed seventy-five state troopers from the south perimeter of the inner fence to the south side of the maintenance shop. The Power House Post, with twenty-five state troopers, was under command of Lieutenant C. J. Henderson. B Block Rear Post, in charge of Zone Sergeant G. F. Hoffman, was also twenty-five men strong and ranged to the rear of B Block.

This encircling force was 190 strong, as large as the assault force. An additional 146 members constituted a general reserve at the west wall of the correctional facility.

These New York State Police forces were not used in the offensive, but their mission would have been very important if hundreds of rebels had suddenly moved out of D Yard and descended on any one of these State Police posts. With so much CS gas used, however, such a countermove would have been difficult for the rebels to execute.

Finally, the New York State Police posted four members in each of four towers along the walls, one man in each team armed with a .270 rifle with telescopic sight and the other three with shotguns.

Deputy Superintendent Leon Vincent of the Attica Correctional Facility ordered the 200-plus corrections officers to stand by within the cell block areas and to move out only after the rebel sections had been secured to perform their primary custodial function. Since then, it has become apparent in reports made to me that many corrections officers exceeded their instructions and took part in the battle.

Corrections officers, many of them armed, some even with their own weapons, took post in the upper galleries of A Block and C Block. From there they could obtain a fairly long view into the rebel crowds in D Yard. They were armed so as to be able to fulfill their backup mission if they were called upon—but they were very specifically ordered not to use these weapons unless they were formally directed to do so by the State Police officers in charge. These orders were issued in written form and were signed by Superintendent Mancusi. There was no question that the corrections officers, who had viewed the grisly scene when the executioners brought the hostages out on top of Times Square, were by now extremely emotional. They had seen and heard their friends brutalized for the past four and a half days and now the execution scene must have been horrifying and overpowering.

General O'Hara was viewing the battle from one of these galleries, and he noted that the corrections officers stationed there had their weapons pointed out of the windows. He asked the officer in charge to tell the men to take their weapons out of the windows.

Inspector Quick, as he advanced with the State Police spearhead along the roof of the tunnel-corridor from C Block, heard what he believed to be numerous shots, from a variety of different weapons, fired from the galleries above and to the side of the ramp. He said, "I am of the opinion without having actually seen anyone firing from these galleries that there was gunfire from these areas."

Chief Inspector Miller said it was possible that some of the corrections officers in these galleries did fire, and most probable that corrections officers in other areas fired their weapons into the yard area. He reported: "There is no question that corrections officers were tense and angry at the initial takeover action of the inmates, the beatings, with one death as a result, that other guards received from inmates, threats against the hostages, and actual viewing of hostages being held with knives at their throats at the time of the police action."

Subsequently, I was told that some corrections officers did open fire without State Police direction to do so. I have not been given the names of these individuals, which might be difficult to ascertain. If these allegations are true, they are not only incredible but indefensible. Of course, we had to await the findings of the Wyoming County Grand Jury before we could move forward with any administrative investigation.

The sheriff's deputies, briefed by Sheriff Dalton Carney of Wyoming County, were placed on the grounds behind the Administration Building for use as a backup force. However, I was

informed at a later date that several of these sheriff's deputies
had been seen closer to the action.

The Army National Guard, as detailed in the previous chapter, was 621 men strong, and they were the strategic reserve. They
were able to backstop the forces inside the prison. There were no
outside attempts at intervention. The National Guard also flew
the CH-34 helicopters and helped in the medical evacuation of
many of the wounded. With metal-detecting mine sweepers,
guardsmen uncovered hundreds of weapons concealed by the
rebel inmates.

THE RECAPTURE OF D AND B BLOCKS

At approximately 10:30 A.M. Major Monahan prepared for the
final phase of the recapture. With the yards secured and hundreds of prisoners being herded out of the dead D Yard Nation, he
gave orders for retaking D Block and B Block. The initial instructions had been not to overextend, not to move into the cell blocks
until the yards were secure.

Mr. Douglass told Chief Inspector Miller and Major Monahan
that, if possible, gunfire should be avoided and only tear gas used
in the recapture of the two cell blocks. Major Monahan gave the
order to the leaders of the new assault force—with Robert Douglass standing beside him—that no further gunfire was to be used
unless it was necessary to save the lives of their men.

The spearhead that had moved out of A Block, past Times
Square, now moved hard into D Block with tear gas cover. The
spearhead that had moved out of C Block, led by Captain
Malovich, stormed into B Block. There was no further resistance.
No weapons were fired, several hundred prisoners surrendered,
and the rebel strongholds fell without a scuffle.

As early as 9:50 A.M., when Major Monahan's assault spearheads
were rounding Times Square and when the twenty-seven-man
rescue squad was lowering the ladders down into the gas and
gloom of D Yard, a State Police helicopter began to circle and
hover above. From this helicopter, a companion to the National
Guard helicopters from which the CS gas had been dropped, loudspeaker instructions were now boomed down to the rebels:

"Place your hands on top of your heads and move to the outside of B and D Blocks. Do not harm the hostages. Surrender peacefully. Sit or lie down. You will not be harmed. Repeat, you will not be harmed."

The State Police helicopter with the surrender message followed —rather than preceded—the National Guard helicopters in order to maintain the obviously necessary element of surprise. Frankly, we never thought of repeating the message in Spanish—but there was no question everybody in the yard knew we were demanding a peaceful surrender.

Hundreds of inmates surrendered within the next few minutes to the State Police, some of them kneeling and begging for mercy, others lying still and pretending to be dead until they were sure they were safe, others simply walking slowly toward our men and giving up. Lieutenant Parr, who had taken his men from C Block down the tunnel to Times Square in the first attack, began to accept surrenders. He said, "They were told to sit down and put their hands over their heads. They were told to walk slowly toward a guard. They were taken through the double doors on B corridor to another yard where there were not so many men.

"They were placed face down, stripped right there, and taken by a guard into A Block. They were very, very quiet. I think they were rather scared, and I think they knew that if they did anything, the guards would take retribution."

The corrections officers assigned to the custodial mission now came down from the galleries and helped bring the men out of D Yard toward A Block, which our men held. The custodial mission was to begin, once resistance had been overcome. There was a people jam at the entrance to one yard, and one of the helicopters had to assume "traffic control duty," passing down orders to broaden a perimeter around a doorway into one of the yards so all the rebels could be brought through.

Then the corrections officers began to get rougher, according to subsequent word brought to me. Several sheriff's deputies were in the yards as well. Some men formed a loose double line as a "corridor" back to the cell blocks, and the rebels, once they had been stripped, were run along an impromptu gantlet. The corrections officers prodded them along with batons, more in the manner of an old fraternity hazing than a beating, but many of these inmates said later that they had been brutalized.

Obviously, I did not expect nor would I have sanctioned, even a fraternity hazing during the return to the cell block. Even now that I have heard about this, I condone it in no way, but would be less than honest if I were to say I could not understand it. There have also been allegations that some of the corrections officers beat certain prisoners and broke many wristwatches and dentures in the yard and on the way back to the cells. Again, I have no documented evidence that this took place. If true, I would consider such conduct highly reprehensible—and I would hope that any persons involved will be dealt with by the Grand Jury.

Chief Inspector Miller of the New York State Police checked to see that his men did not get too close to any of the inmates, even in surrender. He did not want to risk the possibility that inmates might seize firearms even at this late stage of the proceedings. One of the inmates did attack one of the guards, and he was knocked down with a baton.

Chief Inspector Miller rechecked the surrenders twenty minutes or so later after the recapture of D and B Blocks. This time he saw and heard the next groups of inmates told to lie down when they were brought into A Yard, in the corner between D Block and A Block. Then he saw and heard the rebels told to crawl across the yard toward A Block, and the rebels were moved along as they crawled by brusque shouts and some prodding by corrections officers and sheriffs' deputies. Some State Police personnel appeared to be involved in this—although they had no batons and were doing no prodding.

Chief Inspector Miller intervened at once to stop the naked crawl, ordering the troopers around him to take no unnecessary physical action against inmates. He ordered State Police officers to instruct the men to stop it or to leave the area at once.

Superintendent Mancusi later testified in federal court in Buffalo that he relieved eight corrections officers of their duties because of their emotional condition. He said, "I wanted to make sure that no officer would be in an emotional state which would result in mistreatment or mishandling of inmates."

Walter Dunbar himself intervened to stop one corrections officer "overreacting" against a surrendered inmate. Mr. Dunbar reprimanded the corrections officer, who acknowledged his mistake in acting the way he did and who said he now had himself under control. This incident was also observed and reported by Chief Inspector Miller.

Inspector Quick concluded about his troopers: "Our men conducted themselves in a professional, well-co-ordinated manner without any extreme overreaction to what had been confronting them for the period of time before this action was taken.

"There are always different feelings and emotions between different individuals, but the action of our men was a well-disciplined and controlled action without any outward evidence of emotional involvement in the issues at hand."

Subsequently, I heard that a surgeon with the National Guard reported—but not to me, nor to any member of my staff—that when he went into the hospital section some distance from the cell blocks, he heard some screaming. When the surgeon opened a door, he said he found several corrections officers beating an individual whom they thought had emasculated a hostage. When the surgeon allegedly told the men to stop, he was told he had no right to be there and to leave the room. I would now certainly hope the surgeon can identify the corrections officers he said were involved and that, if he has not already done so, he will make a signed complaint for the district attorney.

Where were the rebel leaders? Sam Melville was dead, shot as he ran with the four Molotov cocktails toward the fifty-gallon tank of inflammable liquid. Elliott Barclay, the fearsome L.D., advocate of release and transshipment to "non-imperialistic" countries, had been seen in D Yard by another inmate with a knife in his hand. L.D. had taken a single bullet wound in the back, fired from a distance, and he was dead.

Jerry Rosenberg, after his capture in the slit trench, was stripped along with the others and an "X" was painted on his back, according to his story, to mark him as one of the leaders. He claimed he was beaten as he ran back to A Block. Roger (Champ) Champen testified in federal court that he had been in D Yard when the State Police came in and surrendered according to orders, but, "As I was crawling, I was snatched by my collar and kicked in the throat and hit in the head by an officer," he said.

Brother Richard and Brother Herbert were non-violent. They had a non-violent day of it and gave themselves up to our men undamaged. They were not seen in the struggle in D Yard by any of the participants. As for Charles H. (Brother Flip) Crowley, the phrasemaker of the D Yard television spectacular—"if we have to live like animals, then at least we can die like men"—Brother Flip had been long gone from D Yard when the big trouble came on Monday morning. He had made his way to our side the previous Saturday afternoon, reported into the infirmary for medical treatment, and asked for a protected cell in the hospital. As I have said earlier in this book, his arrival was not reported by the corrections officers—unbelievable though it may seem—neither to me nor to any member of my own, nor of the governor's staff.

All told, more than forty inmates believed by the authorities to have been leaders or associated with leaders were segregated in Housing Block Z, there to ponder the causes, the follies, the betrayals, the miscalculations that had brought such a bloody denouement.

The rebels' most critical error was their misjudgment of the determination of the state.

More than 400 weapons were found in the first search of the correctional facility. There were dozens of Molotov cocktails, shears, spears, and table knives; steel and metal pipes with taped handles; swords well made from flat steel with handles; wire bolos, some with razor blades attached; straight razors, clubs, and baseball bats with extended spikes. During the next few days, hundreds more weapons were located by the mine-sweeping squad of the National Guard and by our corrections personnel. There were also the two tear gas guns and projectiles, captured on September 9, and various propellant mixtures. And there was the half-completed rocket launcher of the late Sam Melville's dreams.

From 9:22 A.M. on September 13, when I took the decision to retake the Attica Correctional Facility, to 9:45 A.M., when the first helicopter drop of the CS gas was made, to 10:00 A.M., when the battle was won, I kept post in our command headquarters in the second floor of the Administration Building. It was the longest thirty-eight minutes of my life.

We followed the advance of the spearheads from A Block and C Block on the State Police radios and in the direct reports I was receiving from Walter Dunbar, Buzz O'Hara, and Inspector Miller. I heard the exploit of the twenty-seven-man rescue squad on the radios live, so to speak, and the bulletins conveyed the drama and the urgency.

"A rescue unit in the center of the yard."

"Expedite."

"Expedite."

"I've got an officer down."

"D Yard. Expedite the medical assistance, will you."

At 9:57 A.M. resistance was almost done.

The radio again: "I need a stretcher, for God's sake, a stretcher."

"Clear the door in D Yard—they're trying to get out."

"Jam that door up. Jam it up."

"Force them into B Yard."

"Anything that's interfering with the gathering of the prisoners, clear it away. You need more assistance in the yard?"

"Yeah, in D Yard, where the negotiations were going on."

"Should I commit the reserve to join you in the yard?"

"Send in help. I need help to clean up that tent-city area."

"Ground your birds. Just be ready. Stand by for evacuations."

"Cease fire. Cease fire. Easy. Do not overextend your positions."

In his office down the corridor Bob Douglass was on the open line to Governor Rockefeller in New York City. He reported the deliverance of each hostage, dead and alive. There were eighteen safe . . . then nineteen . . . then twenty. . . . Bob Douglass could hardly believe we were rescuing so many of the hostages, and neither could the governor.

I was praying, there in the Command Post, and once the State Police were committed to action, that was all I could do. I wanted to be out with the men, but my proper place was in the Command Post, where I could put into effect any changes in the plans that might have been needed. Then it was all over so fast that the comment was made to me almost offhandedly that the facility had been retaken. I am not even sure who told me.

I think the State Police, probably Captain Williams, the communications officer, simply said that all was secure. Then came the heartbreak of the battle scenes—people bringing out the injured to ambulances, people splattered with blood, badly beaten and cut.

I was astonished that we had been able to save the hostages at Times Square with the executioners right behind them, with the knives at their throats. I talked with one of the New York State Police sharpshooters right after he came down from his post, and it turned out this was the man who had saved the life of Ronald

Kozlowski. I had never before seen a man more shaken, yet more thrilled to have saved a life, to *know* that he had saved a life. He told me he had a target of less than six inches to shoot at, and his aim had to be that good.

I also spoke to Mr. Kozlowski, among other hostages, and saw the cut in his throat. Contrary to press speculation and contradictory reports there *were* throats cut at Attica. I saw them for myself. The other victim, Corrections Officer Kline, was already on his way to the hospital for his fifty-two stitches.

The scene outside the gates was harrowing in the extreme. A corrections officer came out and shouted the names of hostages who had been saved. Mothers, fathers, children, relatives, friends ran up, tears streaming down their faces in relief and agony, to find out to which hospitals the hostages were being taken. There were hundreds of reporters out there, trying to talk with the relatives, being shoved back by angry friends, and some were ordered away by a deputy sheriff at the point of a gun. One compassionate reporter, Bill O'Brien of the Rochester *Democrat-Chronicle*, wrote:

"And nothing anybody said meant anything at all when you looked at the mothers and the kids who didn't hear their names called out."

The television crews picked up the static of political polarization in the atmosphere. One of the young National Guardsmen who went into the prison later in the day said the surrendered inmates were being brutalized, that it was sheer racism in there. A group of our men was shown on camera rejoicing in the rain about "White Power."

Later in the afternoon a young doctor came out from treating wounded inmates and shocked the television audience some more. "Yes," he said, "there was a lot of blood. There were a number of deaths right in front of me. It was very depressing. It resembled the aftermath of a war. That's the only thing it can be compared to."

Many members of the Citizens Observer Committee were on hand. State Senator John Dunne was taken into the prison to observe the results of the 10:30 assault, even before the recapture of D and B Blocks was completed. He was accompanied by Howard Shapiro, and they saw naked prisoners being herded into A Block —prodded, but not beaten.

Why were the men stripped? For three reasons: to save time, to avoid the danger of frisking for hidden weapons, and to remove clothing that had been saturated by gas.

Assemblyman Eve criticized the governor once again for not coming to Attica. Then he broke into heavy sobs. Congressman Badillo said the committee had wanted the governor to come and "talk to us to get the benefit of our experience before he made a final and irrevocable decision. As far as I'm concerned, there's always time to die." State Senator McGowan said there had been no other choice but to recapture the facility. William Kunstler said this was "a monstrosity," and he went off to address a public meeting in Buffalo the same afternoon.

At 1:15 P.M. Julian Tepper and W. O. Fitch, still on hand, were asked to leave the prison immediately. They wrote, wryly, in their diary: "We leave the prison and, for our own safety, are escorted by the State Police to the Buffalo airport." Several members of the Observers Committee asked for safe passage out of the town of Attica and we provided a State Police escort.

For the mood of the community of Attica and the corrections officers in the prison was almost at a breaking point. For days, our men had heard, had feared, what was happening to the hostages at the hands of the militants. Now they had seen the dead, the cut, the beaten, and the wounded, and for every single thing they saw, they were ready to believe, or conjure up, a thousand more.

The community believed almost to a man that the hostages had been killed by the rebels. They thought the hostages had all had their throats cut. The first hostages to be seen leaving the prison indeed did have their throats cut. The other hostages had been blindfolded, and the blindfolds had slipped down around their necks, soaked in the blood of gunshot wounds, cuts, and beatings. Many of the other hostages who were brought out had bloody throats, often from these bloody blindfolds.

Then one of the hostages was brought out with a gunshot wound in the lower abdomen. He was in bad shape and his coverings were bloody. To those who saw him, here was "confirmation" of the rumor that had gripped Attica throughout the rebellion —that one of the hostages had been emasculated.

I was talking with a reporter from the BBC or maybe it was an Australian—I forget—but I was describing how the sharpshooter had fired and had, in a split second, saved the life of Ronald

Kozlowski, the hostage. I lifted my finger to my throat to show how
the executioner was slicing Mr. Kozlowski's throat. Some other reporters there—standing some distance away and not within hearing distance—thought I was explaining how the hostages had been
killed. So because they thought this, they reported it. However,
after I had called the attention of the press to the fact that I never
made any statement about slashed throats, the press acknowledged
this was the case.

Walter Dunbar had seen with his own eyes the men on top of
Times Square with the knives at their throats. He had also viewed
the hostages being carried out with their bloody blindfolds on
their necks, and he assumed they had died by having their throats
cut.

Mr. Dunbar must have been completely exhausted, as were all
of us, because he passed on to reporters, on a tour of the prison,
not only the assumption that the hostages who had died had their
throats cut, but also the emasculation rumor. He even pointed out
a prisoner said to have done the emasculating. A hostage released
earlier made statements about throat-cutting which were picked
up by at least one newspaper. The rumors in general were running rampant. All of us heard from many sources that throats
had been slashed and that there had been an emasculation.

The reporters, for their part, did not check out these stories nor
attribute the sources of other stories. The sensations spread out
of Attica through the rest of the day. When the truth was gradually revealed as the autopsy reports came out, the result was an
enormous credibility shock in the public mind.

In the first day after Attica, the decision to retake the prison
was widely regarded as wise. In the second day, the headlines were
almost as large with the word that the hostages had not been
killed by throat slashings, as state government representatives had
said, but by the gunfire of our own men. The decision was instantly
rendered wrong—or at least intensely controversial.

In the recapture of the Attica Correctional Facility, however,
the event surpassed the aftermath and left lessons for us all.

As early as 10:40 A.M., September 13, even before we had retaken D Block and B Block, I pleaded for perspective in the context of history. I made this formal accounting also for my own
conscience of my decisions at Attica. I said at a conference with all
media:

"For the past four days I have been doing everything humanly possible to bring this tragic situation to a peaceful conclusion.

"My main concern throughout has been for the safety of the hostages, the corrections officers, the State Police, National Guard personnel, local law-enforcement personnel, and the inmates as well.

"As you know, during this ordeal I have personally met with inmates on several occasions in areas under their control. I brought together a Citizens Observer Committee, most of whom were requested by the inmates, to assist me in bringing a peaceful resolution.

"I understand and am sympathetic to many of the grievances expressed by the inmates and have demonstrated my commitment to deal with the issues they have raised by accepting twenty-eight of thirty-one major inmate proposals in addition to progressive steps in programming already undertaken and implemented during my eight months in office.

"A federal court injunction demanded by the inmates to guarantee that no administrative reprisals would be taken was obtained overnight.

"In spite of all these positive efforts towards peaceful resolution on my part, the inmates have steadfastly refused to release the hostages and meet with me on neutral ground for a final settlement.

"It became apparent to me that the situation was seriously deteriorating and that the inmates, many of whom are confined to this maximum-security facility under life and long sentences, were not going to participate in reasonable negotiations. Tensions within the walls have steadily increased.

"Saturday a correction officer, who had been subjected to a savage beating, died. Last evening one inmate was stabbed in the abdomen after a fight with another inmate.

"The inmates who are in possession of tear gas projectiles and knives have continued to fashion other weapons, have prepared booby traps and electrically wired barricades, and have spread gasoline extensively.

"This morning I made a final attempt to resolve the situation without resort to force. The inmates were requested to release the hostages unharmed immediately and to join with me in restoring order to the Attica Correctional Facility.

"Additional time was asked for by the inmates, and the request was granted. It proved to be only a delaying tactic this morning. The leaders never returned, but callously herded eight hostages within view with weapons at their throats. This is the way they chose to give me their decision.

"That behavior was not different from their behavior on the street, where several were convicted of serious assaults, manslaughter, and murder.

"A few moments ago State Police troopers moved into the unsecured areas of the institution to restore order, under specific orders to only use force to meet force, to protect the lives of the hostages. At the same time a riot-control gas was dispersed by helicopters in an effort to immobilize persons in the unsecured areas.

"The action now under way was initiated with extreme reluctance, only after all attempts to achieve a peaceful solution failed.

"To delay the action any longer would not only jeopardize innocent lives but would threaten the security of the entire correctional system in this state.

"Armed rebellion of this type we have faced threatens the destruction of our free society. We cannot permit that destruction to happen.

"It has been an agonizing decision."

And it had been.

PART IV

"Why is it, that for all our professed
ideals, our hopes and our skill,
"Peace on Earth is still a distant
objective, seen only dimly through
the storms and turmoils of our
present difficulties?"

U THANT

CHAPTER 15

"The State Is Guilty of Murder!"

At 4:30 P.M. on Monday, September 13, in Lafayette Square in downtown Buffalo, an angry crowd of more than 200 people gathered to protest our recapture of the Attica Correctional Facility after four and a half days of armed rebellion. The crowd swarmed toward the Soldiers and Sailors Monument, stalling rush-hour traffic, shoving aside workers leaving their offices for the day. They waved banners that read:

WE CHARGE THE STATE WITH MURDER

INDICT ROCKY AND OSWALD FOR MASS MURDER!

On hand to address the demonstrators was Attorney William M. Kunstler. Mr. Kunstler had stated there would be uprisings across the country if the rebellion was put down by force, and there he was, not six hours after the last quenching of resistance in D Block, ready to pour on some of his oratory.

"They kill them behind stone walls where no one can see," Mr. Kunstler said, and, after applause and shouts of approval from the demonstrators, he added, "There are more decent people in jail than there are outside."

Mr. Kunstler blamed "the government" for the loss of the lives of the hostages and the inmates. He made a few more brief remarks and then the crowd began to chant *"Remember Attica! Remember Attica!"* This was the inflammatory slogan to which Mr. Kunstler had given birth during a fiery speech to the inmates of D Yard in mid-rebellion, when he had noted how "the gringos" had their slogan—"Remember the Alamo!"—and William Kunstler had flung down "Remember Attica!"

At this dangerous moment, Buffalo city policemen, no more

than fifteen, decided to intervene. Mr. Kunstler and the demonstrators had not obtained a permit to use a public-address system. So the fifteen Buffalo policemen quietly moved into the disorderly crowd and told them to move along. Most of them did.

One participant was knocked about eight feet off the monument steps and landed upside down in some shrubbery. He was handcuffed, arrested, and charged with disorderly conduct. A nineteen-year-old youth was accused by a detective of the robbery squad, who had joined the uniformed policemen, of attempting to heave him over a metal railing. "Instead," said the detective, "I pushed him over the railing." The youth was not injured but he was charged with resisting arrest and obstructing government administration.

In the brief scuffle ten men and one woman were arrested, and the whole thing was over within twenty minutes.

Was this minuscule affray really the beginning of the nationwide uprisings in the streets so confidently threatened by radical leaders throughout the Attica rebellion?

The day after Attica, a crowd estimated at only 150 people demonstrated in Los Angeles, the nation's third largest city. In an orderly rally in ninety-degree heat, they vowed support for "the Attica 1,200" and for renewed efforts to win release of Angela Davis and Ruchell Magee. One speaker at Los Angeles depicted the Attica rebels as "heroic brothers . . . laying down their lives for human dignity."

At the University of Oklahoma, in Norman, Oklahoma, a racist cast was given to an Attica demonstration that might have troubled the interracial leaders of the Attica rebellion. Approximately seventy-five black students blocked a one-way street for about two hours and chanted, "There is one way . . . the right way . . . but it ain't the white way." These demonstrators carried a sign that read, 30 BROTHERS DEAD AND THINGS GO ON AS USUAL.

And at my home in Schenectady our son Kurt sat dejected and angry on our steps in the rain, having just received yet another threatening telephone call. He was thinking of me at Attica, of his mother at the hospital, and of his responsibility to watch over our home and his wife and home.

But still—what of the uprisings in the streets?

On Saturday, September 18, a "big" demonstration was called

for Union Square in Manhattan. Among the sponsoring movement groups were the Vietnam Veterans Against the War, the War
Resisters League, the Harrisburg Defense Committee, and a new
Ad Hoc Coalition to Protest the Attica Massacre. Above the throng
was wagged an effigy of Governor Rockefeller. This was a dummy
plastered with dollar bills, with the head of a pig and a rifle in its
hand.

John Froines, one of the "Chicago 7," told the crowd in Union
Square flatly that Governor Rockefeller could have granted amnesty to the Attica rebels by the route of executive clemency. This
had been a tragically erroneous notion of Mr. Kunstler's during
Attica that would have made a plaything of the courts, not to mention the rule of law. David Dellinger, another member of the
Chicago 7, said our recapture of the correctional facility had been
an inexcusable "search and destroy mission." Jim Noonan, of
Vietnam Veterans Against the War, tried to tie Attica to the
peace cause. He said Attica was "another Mylai."

"There's no difference in my mind between the words 'prisoners'
and 'gooks,'" Mr. Noonan added.

But no more than 300 people were on hand for the "big" demonstration at Union Square.

In the first week after Attica, the all but unbelievable fact was
that fewer people had demonstrated from coast to coast than had
rebelled inside the correctional facility.

The so-called fragmented groups of United States society—the
poor, the young, the blacks, the pacifists, the disadvantaged—were
refusing to follow the militant lead of the rebels of Attica.

On Sunday, September 19, President Nixon, Governor Rockefeller, and I were tried in absentia for murder by a "people's tri-
bunal" in New York City. We were found guilty as charged. Bobby
Seale, in another statement put out somewhere else in New York
City, said President Nixon, Governor Rockefeller, and I should
be indicted for "first-degree murder and conspiracy."

At last, almost two weeks after Attica, the movement managed
to turn out 1,000 people for a rally in the state capital of Albany,
New York. This one was co-sponsored by the Students for a Democratic Society, the Prisoners Solidarity Committee, the Peoples
Anti-Fascist Resistance League, and the Progressive Labor Party,
all formed beneath an umbrella organization entitled the Peoples
Coalition for Peace and Justice. Now they marched three miles

through Albany, chanting "Rockefeller—Murderer," and "Attica means—Fight back." When the procession approached the State Capitol building, they shouted, "Fee, fie, fo, fum—Rockefeller here we come." Another of the chants was, "Attica rebels lead the way—Gonna make the bosses pay." And a third chant was, "People of the world are picking up the gun—Run, Rocky, run, Rocky, run, run, run."

David Dellinger delivered a keynote address to these marchers, who were supposedly offering some sort of alternative to the United States way of life. He said, "We weren't kidding when we said Rockefeller should be indicted. Only by indicting him can we wake up the people of America."

But this was the first and last rally of any size. The uprisings in the streets had simply not happened. The revolution proclaimed at Attica had won scant outside support—and this was a fact in historical terms of the utmost importance.

On the other hand, a noisy national debate was beginning to erupt about Attica amid the clamor of political extremes. I shall let the Attica debate swirl about without personal comment—the pros and cons, the truths and lies, the half-truths and half-lies, the self-seeking and the disinterested, the warm and the cold, the cruel, the understanding and the humane.

Governor Rockefeller said on Monday, September 13: "Our hearts go out to the families of the hostages who died at Attica. The tragedy was brought on by the highly organized, revolutionary tactics of militants, who rejected all efforts at a peaceful settlement, forced a confrontation and carried out cold-blooded killings they had threatened from the outset. We can be grateful that the skill and courage of the State Police and corrections officers, supported by the National Guard and sheriff's deputies, saved the lives of thirty-two hostages—and that their restraint held down casualties among prisoners as well.

"It was only after four and a half days of patient, round-the-clock negotiations with the prisoners by Commissioner Oswald and the Citizens Committee, exploring all possible means of peacefully securing the release of the hostages, that the State Police went in to rescue the hostages and restore order.

"I have ordered a full investigation of all the factors leading to this uprising including the role that outside forces would appear to have played."

After Monroe County Medical Examiner John F. Edland confirmed that the hostages had been killed by gunfire and not by throat-slashings, Governor Rockefeller said, "The new facts that have been uncovered . . . just go to deepen the tragedy of the whole Attica affair. My views are the same as everybody else's— one of tragedy. You know, under the heat of the situation that existed, tragedies do develop."

Tom Wicker, the member of the Citizens Observer Committee who was also a columnist for the New York *Times*, commented as follows:

"After the massacre at Attica, Governor Nelson A. Rockefeller issued a statement that began with this sentence: 'Our hearts go out to the families of the hostages who died at Attica.'

"Much of what went wrong at Attica—and of what is wrong at most other American prisons and 'corrections facilities'—can be found in the simple fact that neither in that sentence nor in any other did the governor or any official extend a word of sympathy to the families of the dead prisoners . . .

"That is the root of the matter; prisoners, particularly black prisoners, in all too many cases are neither considered nor treated as human beings. And since they are not, neither are their families . . .

"Dead hostages, for another example, were sent to the morgue tagged with their names; dead prisoners went tagged 'P-1,' 'P-2,' and so on.

"That is an almost unbearable fact to those who heard an eloquent prisoner shouting in the yard of D Block a week ago Friday night: 'We no longer wish to be treated as statistics, as numbers. We want to be treated as human beings, we WILL be treated as human beings!'

"But even in death, they were still just numbers . . ."

Pete Hamill, the liberal columnist, wrote in the New York *Post*: "The Nelson Rockefellers of the world will never understand the men of cell block D. Nelson Rockefellers don't heist gas stations. Nelson Rockefellers don't have sisters with rat-eaten faces. They don't have sons with brains gone soft from licking lead off ghetto walls. Nelson Rockefellers don't get laughed at when they shape up at the ironworkers hall; they don't get humiliated by stupid teachers who scorn them for speaking only Spanish; they don't have to live in Hunts Point or Brownsville or Bed-Stuy. Nelson Rockefellers don't feel the rage gnawing at the gut, the constant daily savagery of institutionalized despair."

Mayor John V. Lindsay of New York City implied that he differed sharply with the governor: "We know from long experience firearms under those circumstances are very dangerous. When we took the institutions in New York City not a single firearm was used. I went to both institutions and I appealed to the inmates myself. I felt it was required of me—there were lives at stake and it was a tense situation. I had no choice but to be at the scene."

United States Senator Edmund S. Muskie of Maine, then a leading contender for the Democratic presidential nomination, said that "the Attica tragedy is more stark proof that something is terribly wrong in America . . . We have reached the point where men would rather die than live another day in America."

Governor Ronald Reagan of California countered that Attica confirmed "the new revolutionary tactics of taking revolution into the prisons and attacking the system there."

United States Congressman Herman Badillo now said as spokesman for seventeen members of the thirty-four-member Citizens Observer Committee: "Official intransigence was responsible for the bloodshed on Monday morning. No individual observer adopted any position which prevented or hindered a peaceful resolution of the crisis."

Five-term United States Congressman John W. Wydler, Republican of New York, Fourth District, covering part of Nassau County, a Phi Beta Kappa from Brown University and an Air Force sergeant who served in the China-Burma-India Theater in the Second World War, issued a rebuttal in a letter to his constituents:

"In the gaggle of public figures, state, local, and federal, who have been sounding off on the Attica revolt, few, if any, have called for public appreciation and understanding of Governor Rockefeller—the one man who had the awful responsibility and met it on behalf of the people of the state. The terrible on-the-spot decisions were his to make, and he made them on behalf of the people outside Attica prison who have a right to expect him to act first and foremost in their behalf. . . .

"Those in prisons are owed no apology by the governor or the people of the state. They were in prison because of crimes they committed and because they were dangerous and in most cases violent men.

"There are some who say that Governor Rockefeller should have gone personally to Attica. It would have been good TV. But it would have made it harder to take the action he had to take and would have encouraged other prisoners, in other prisons, to demand his presence. If the governor had given into this demand it would have cost more lives and more riots, then and in the years to come . . .

"I want to see our prisons made more secure and also see our prisoners treated decently.

"I do not want to see public officials who make hard decisions on behalf of the public called evil while the law-breakers are idolized and used for personal and political advantage. Attica could have been a prison 'Munich.'

"Governor Rockefeller deserves the thanks of the people of the state for acting when others would have turned away from their responsibility."

The New York *Times* editorialized: "Americans have to ask themselves whether they want every evidence of malfunction in their society—a street demonstration by political dissenters, a campus rebellion, a slum riot, a prison revolt—suppressed by official violence. The moral rationale for putting violent, undisciplined men in prison is that the larger society is observing higher standards of human behavior. If that society is violent, the power to incarcerate remains, but what becomes of the moral authority?"

WCBS-TV said, "Attica was an epic tragedy in the Greek sense. Men were caught hopelessly in the web of their own fate: prisoners trapped by unforgivable crimes and non-negotiable demands; hostages trapped by circumstances; negotiators drawn from a who's who of liberal and radical politics and letters who found, ultimately, that there was nothing to negotiate; and, above all, the tragic figure of Corrections Commissioner Russell Oswald, a reform-minded man who tried to save lives but ended up giving the orders that resulted in the massacre of inmates and hostages alike."

The *Wall Street Journal* editorialized: "We see a great many excellent reasons for prison reform. If the recent prison riots lead to more serious efforts in this direction, it will prove that an ill wind can blow some good. Having said that, we must add that in fact we see almost no relationship between progress with such reform and the incidence of the type of prison riot we have witnessed at Attica and San Quentin."

The Amsterdam, New York, *Evening Recorder*: "When armed rebellion threatens the freedom and order upon which our society rests, then society must make its stand somewhere. It was made at Attica."

The London *Daily Telegraph* wrote: "The giant which grew from infancy to manhood on a diet of idealism and freedom struggles in apparent impotence with a host of snares entangling every movement. Yet history shows that the American nation possesses immense powers of recuperation from what might appear fatal setbacks and dangers. We do not believe these powers are absent now. This great country will surely see its troubles out."

Perry B. Duryea, Jr., Speaker of the Assembly of New York State, said, "Inmates of this or any prison are in no position to make 'non-negotiable demands' on society.

"It is difficult to assess how much efforts at improving the rehabilitation program in our prison system have been set back by the outrageous acts on the part of those inmates responsible for this carnage."

The American Correctional Association reaffirmed its guidance to corrections people:

"Demands of inmates that they be permitted to negotiate only with the governor, or some well-known news commentator, should be bluntly refused. The advisability of a governor entering into such a situation is probably unwise, except as a most extreme last resort. To do so inflates the rioters' egos and lends encouragement to a repetition of the same show on another stage."

The New York City Patrolmen's Benevolent Association likened the governor's leadership in the Attica riot to "heroism equal to that called for by the hazards of service in the ranks." The PBA praised him for acting decisively "to protect the fundamental democratic concept of government by law and accepting the burden of that decision with unflinching honor."

John J. Bouck, Republican party chairman for Cayuga County, along with approximately 230 guards at Great Meadow Correctional Facility, asked that I be dismissed for "giving the convicts at Attica the right to negotiate."

The Syracuse *Post-Standard* editorialized under the headline OSWALD DELAYED ACTION TOO LONG:

"A heavy share of the blame for the tragic climax of the revolutionary uprising of convicts at Attica State Prison must rest on the shoulders of Russell G. Oswald, state corrections commissioner.

"It was Commissioner Oswald who chose to negotiate with the felons rather than permit state police to put down the rebellion as soon as it developed.

"Obviously, the commissioner was thinking of the safety of the thirty-eight hostages, but he also mistakenly believed that 'decency' would win over the toughest of criminals.

"As soon as Commissioner Oswald sat down to listen to the prisoners' complaints, it was apparent—to them and to everyone else—that these convicted murderers, rapists, and burglars had the upper hand.

"Traditional roles had been reversed, and the rioters had won a great psychological victory."

Clayton Defayette, who headed the corrections officers union local at Clinton, said that "a lot of employees don't understand the position of Oswald." He indicated that many corrections officers there would prefer having as their leader a man who had come up through the ranks.

Jim Lambert, shop steward of Local 1264, Council 82, American Federation of State, County and Municipal Employees (AFSCME), said that most corrections officers wanted me to resign. He endorsed John Zelker, superintendent at Green Haven in Dutchess County, for the job. Mr. Zelker was depicted as a man who rose through the ranks. "He's fair, but he's also firm," said Mr. Lambert.

In the village of Attica itself, Frank Mandeville, for many years the owner of Timm's Hardware, told *Time* magazine: "Oswald was at fault. If he had gone in right away, some lives might have been lost, but not on the tragic scale we have now." Mr. Mandeville told *Time* he still doubted the story that hostages were killed by gunfire, and he said, "Political pressure caused Oswald to change his story." But he thought the assault was justified: "If the troopers had to kill some of the hostages, that was their job. I give them all the credit in the world."

A letter-to-the-editor writer typical of many during this period wrote: "So some poor woman is all bent out of shape because her son looks as if he's been mistreated at Attica. He's serving a term for first-degree murder. What did his victim look like when found? And how about the victim's mother?"

An unnamed corrections officer's wife at Attica wrote the Batavia *Daily News*:

"Seale . . . [has] called Rockefeller, Oswald, and Mancusi murderers because forty men were killed. The inmates held out for complete amnesty once they knew Officer Quinn had died, and, after being granted twenty-eight demands in return for the freedom and safety of the thirty-eight hostages, they still refused to give in.

"There could be no other course of action but to take the yard by force. Now there is the question of who gave the orders to open fire.

"Weren't they supposed to try to kill the executioners assigned to each hostage?

"Or were they supposed to stand there and negotiate some more.

"Personally, I think the troopers did a marvelous job. I only wish every hostage's life could have been spared."

Harriet Van Horne wrote in the New York *Post*: "Rural, ignorant, corrupted by the authority of their clubs and guns, Attica's security officers undoubtedly played a considerable role in the unrest that led to the riots . . . The climate of upstate New York is traditionally reactionary, repressive, and hypocritical . . . The state troopers who referred to the convicts as 'niggers' and 'barbarians' are hardly exceptional. I remember bank presidents and Eastman Kodak executives who talked that way too."

Max Lerner wrote in the New York *Post*: "This [development of two prison societies—inmates and guards] may help explain why the riot broke out, but doesn't excuse the early stripping and beating of the guards, nor the refusal to end the riot when State Corrections Commissioner Oswald had granted every demand the convict leaders had made bearing on prison conditions. To understand that refusal, one must understand that, however the riot may have started, it became political very soon, and remained political to the end."

United States Senator Edward W. Brooke, Republican of Massachusetts, said that prison conditions everywhere in the United States were "almost universally deplorable" and had a "dehumanizing effect."

An editorial in the New York *Daily News* summed up the conflict, under the headline THAT'S TELLING 'EM, YOUR HONOR:

"Brooklyn Civil Court Judge Fred G. Moritt the other day received a plea from the notoriously far-left National Lawyers Guild for a contribution to a fund for setting up an NLG legal office at Attica prison.

"The NLG says its Attica establishment will 'service inmates, litigate prison conditions, and provide defense coordination' for indictments expected to grow out of the Sept. 9–13 riot that left 43 dead."

Judge Moritt answered in part as follows (if we could improve on his language we would, but we can't):

> . . . May I ask whether your establishment is soliciting money:
>
> A. For the Attica guard who was murdered before the 'negotiations.'
> B. For the families of the ten murdered guards.
> C. For the medical bills for injuries sustained by the surviving twenty-eight civil service guards who were kidnaped by some of your clients in Attica.
> D. For the forgotten victims of the convicted murderers, burglars, thugs, thieves, and other assorted felons for whom you are so concerned and for whom you are soliciting funds.
>
> The silent tears are not heard above the wild roars of the rioters. When you decide to raise funds for the victims of the rioters, please do not hesitate to solicit me.
>
> Let this courtesy of a reply to your letter in no way, shape, manner, or form indicate to you the measure of my concern that all decent citizens have not only for prison reform—but also for the peace officer whose very life he puts in jeopardy, night and day, so that you and I can exist.

The Saratoga *Saratogian* editorialized under the headline OS-WALD'S WORK MUST CONTINUE:

"Second-guessers are busy these days dissecting the tragedy at Attica state prison.

"At one extreme are the supertough, who contend that state officials should have immediately tried to rescue the hostages by force, that no negotiations should have been conducted.

"At the other end are those superliberals who believe that negotiations should have continued indefinitely, that forty lives were lost needlessly because of the state troopers' assault on the prison.

"We reject both extremes.

"We disapprove of any attempt to victimize State Corrections Commissioner Russell Oswald by the growing number of 'Monday morning quarterbacks.' Here is a man who has consistently showed that he is striving toward prison reform and improvement in rehabilitation programs.

"His decision to storm the prison has been correctly likened to a battlefield 'command decision.' His closeness to the prisoner demand negotiations and the obvious flout of the ultimatum that fateful Monday, well equipped him to follow through on such a course of action.

"The work well begun by Oswald before the riot to correct prison conditions for those inmates who want and need to be rehabilitated to take their places again in law-abiding society should be continued, not stopped because of the Attica violence or Oswald's part in the riots.

"In such ways, perhaps there can be solace for the grieving families and friends of the Attica dead, both hostages and prisoners, and hope for something better than today's prison life."

Jim Fain wrote in the Dayton, Ohio, *Daily News:*

"Oswald is tough enough to hang in and continue with the kind of reforms he was bringing to the system before Attica. I hope the public will support him. To veer toward brutal suppression in our revulsion against what some prisoners were doing would be not just inhumane; it would be self-defeating. We cannot afford to be vengeful or bloodthirsty, whatever the provocation. We have to get on with putting society's house in order."

WAST-TV (Channel 13) in Albany editorialized:

"We commend State Corrections Commissioner Russell Oswald for his agonizing decisions and actions. His decision to storm the prison was a reluctant one for it had to mean that men were to lose their lives. TV-13 believes that more would have died if the decision would have been delayed any longer.

"It is our feeling that Oswald's decision to use force was not the one that determined the fate of the dead men. We feel the decisions that cost the lives of the guards and the prison inmates were made months ago by militant revolutionaries who desire to destroy our society. They consider themselves victims of a racist society and it is not difficult to sell prison inmates on the idea that they are also victims or political prisoners innocent of any wrongdoing but held captive by our system.

"We believe Commissioner Oswald sincerely tried to head off disaster but the confrontation had already been set. Peaceful settlement was steadfastly rejected and the killing pre-ordained.

"The uprising must be doubly tragic for Oswald who talked often of his plans to improve the prison system in New York State. Oswald spoke of the black militant as a new kind of problem prisoner who considers himself innocent of wrongdoing and the victim of racist society. Oswald said, 'We have to find ways to reach these people.'

"We agree."

In contrast to the sharp thrusts of the national debate, which seemed to come at the governor and me from left and right, day and night, almost all the time, our mailbag was overwhelmingly favorable. My own mail was running more than two to one in my favor, and so was the governor's.

As far as we could judge it, in these early days, public opinion as a whole was running better than five to four in favor of our basic decision to recapture the correctional facility. I believe this support would have been stronger but for the disastrous reaction to the misstatements about the deaths of the hostages by throat-slashings. On our controversial decision to negotiate in the first place, public opinion was overwhelmingly on our side—by more than two to one.

In the same spirit in which I presented the national debate, I now offer some excerpts from the governor's and my own mail response.

Austin MacCormick, executive director of the Osborne Association, a highly regarded organization of citizens interested in prison reform, wrote to Governor Rockefeller:

"I was disturbed and indignant over the unjust and unwarranted criticism you received for not going to Attica. In a correctional career of nearly fifty years, I have probably had more experience in dealing with prison riots than any other individual in the field. On the basis of that experience, it is my firm conviction that you were right in not going.

"On the question of amnesty you were right in saying that you had no constitutional power to grant amnesty to the rioters and were courageous enough to say that, if you had, you would not use it. The question of immunity was clearly non-negotiable.

"On the question of whether or not you should have gone to Attica, the most obvious reasons why you were right in declining to go are these, in my opinion: that, with all due respect for the fact that you know more about the operations of the state departments and agencies than most governors do, you are not a prison expert; that you had at the head of the Department of Correctional Services two of the ablest and most experienced correctional administrators in the country, Commissioner Russell Oswald and Executive Deputy Commissioner Walter Dunbar; and that the grave decisions which had to be made as the long negotiations came to a stalemate were properly left to them, with your concurrence on basic policies.

"In addition to having long experience in dealing with prisoners, both of them are humane men and their chief concern, as was yours, was to save lives.

"In addition to the above, there were reasons of prime importance to which I have never seen any reference in the comments on your decision. The urgent requests, amounting to demands, that you come to Attica came from the so-called Committee of Observers and the other volunteer 'negotiators' who swarmed into the prison and made rational negotiation well-nigh impossible.

"I'm not criticizing Commissioner Oswald for permitting them to enter the institution. He leaned over backward in his efforts to be fair to the prisoners and to the racial and civil rights groups whom most of the observers represented. His fairness should bear fruit in the future at Attica and at the other institutions . . .

"If you had gone to Attica, you would inevitably have found yourself cheek-by-jowl with Mr. Kunstler and Bobby Seale, and some others little better than they. You would have been smothered by publicity-seekers, and by the forty or more reporters, TV men, and photographers who lay in wait at the prison entrance. Statements would have been demanded when you entered the prison and when you came out, with serious danger of distortion of what you said . . .

"Finally, the prisoners would undoubtedly have demanded that you speak to them over the institution radio and would probably have insisted that you show yourself. If you did not say—as you could not—that they would be granted immunity, my opinion is that it would have stiffened their already stubborn resistance.

"I am not implying that you would have shrunk from these contacts. I mean only that they would have resulted in harassment and possible humiliation to which you as an individual and as governor should not be subjected, and would perhaps have ended in frustration and failure."

Dr. Asher R. Pacht, who had served with me in Massachusetts and who is now director of the Bureau of Clinical Services in the Division of Corrections in Wisconsin, wrote me:

"No one who knows you can ever doubt your sincerity, your conscientiousness, your compassion or the personal anguish you must have suffered (and still must be) in agonizing over the decision that had to be made. For those of us who were fortunate to have worked with you, these attributes of your personality combined with your tremendous drive to institute change were evidenced daily.

"What you taught me still serves as my guideline for what I would like to see take place in our field. I seriously doubt that I would have remained in the field were it not for your leadership and guidance in my early correctional years."

Robert J. Moore, superintendent of the Massachusetts Correctional Institution at Walpole, to which we had moved the prisoners from the ghastly old jail at Charlestown, wrote me:

"Just a few lines of encouragement for a very courageous decision we all know you had to make under terrifying conditions and agonizing tension.

"In my judgment, and in the opinion of all your friends in Massachusetts, you have been the top man in the field of penology in this country for many years. You have always been very intelligent, dedicated, progressive, humane, and God-fearing. What better attributes can any leader profess than these?

"I know how you must feel in regard to the loss of life but try to remember that, at times, this is a soldier's game. Decisions must be made, and when the ball bounces the wrong way, casualties can occur, and good men can get hurt through no fault of our own."

Rear Admiral Robert J. White, a retired Navy chaplain who had also worked in corrections in Massachusetts, wrote me:

"Several people who knew of our past relationship have asked my opinion of you. I have replied, 'In my judgment, Mr. Oswald is the most intelligent, most progressive, and most compassionate administrator in the field of corrections.'

"I have read all of the many press accounts and found many of them inaccurate, slanted, and venal. When the press can persuade readers that confirmed brutal and violent criminals are 'political prisoners,' then hope for law and order grow dim.

"Your conscience will be your silent but sustaining strength and consolation. With my prayers, dear Russ."

Governor Rockefeller wrote me:

"During these days, you have borne a responsibility almost beyond human endurance. That you met this responsibility with unfailing courage and good judgment is clear in the lives of twenty-eight men saved and order restored in the wake of the worst prison riot in the nation's history.

"I know personally and intimately, as perhaps few others do, the unbelievable pressures you faced, the infinite patience, understanding, and reasonableness you demonstrated, the agonizing decisions you had to make, the enormous hope you harbored, until no realistic hope remained, that order could be restored without force and that tragedy could be averted at Attica.

"I know, as well, that you met this responsibility bearing the added anxiety of having your wife, Jane, seriously ill and in the hospital during this period.

"I have said publicly, and to you personally, and I repeat now, that you did what had to be done and you acted when you had to act. I fully support your conduct, your decisions, and your handling of this unprecedented situation.

"I share the deep personal anguish you are suffering at the lives lost. Such complex situations always have to be placed in balance and judged accordingly.

"In making that judgment, I remain convinced that, by your actions, more lives were saved, bloodshed on a far greater scale was averted, the idea of social change through violence and coercion was rejected, and the necessity for preserving a lawful society was upheld."

Mrs. Ann Valone, the widow of Corrections Officer Carl W. Valone, wrote me:

"I thank you for your letter of sympathy and to assure you that your presence at the funeral would not have been an embarrassment to me. I felt that you were trying your best to obtain the release of the hostages. I also thank you for this.

"My problem is my grief is difficult for me because I am confused about many things.

"I spent nineteen hours in the Attica Correctional Facility parking lot watching men go in and come out of the prison. I did not feel that some of those men belonged there or would be helpful as I know you felt also.

"If we had a chance to go back in time again I imagine there are a number of things that would be done differently but at the time only God knew the outcome.

"I resent those who have so much to say and could solve it all now that it is over.

"I feel strongly now that I have to know and understand everything that happened there in order to be at peace with myself. There are so many questions and conflicting things that are upsetting to me—more so than the truth I am sure would be.

"I have one strong criticism that I must write. My husband and I talked about the prison. He felt some things needed improvement [for the prisoners], but he felt strongly that there was great need for improvement as far as the corrections officers job was concerned too. He worried about the corrections officers difficulty in recent years maintaining order in the prison and the safety of officers who were helpless if order could not be maintained.

"I cannot understand how our laws can be turned against us in our efforts to be fair and unprejudiced.

"How can intelligent and educated men make a mockery of

justice. If things had turned out differently I do not think I could have felt that some of the demands allowed were just."

In the midst of the national debate, the village of Attica was tranquil and desolate. Flags flew at half staff, voices were hushed, and there were repeated parades of corrections officers for the funerals of the hostages. Often, the funerals were made even more tragic by the sad necessity of taking the bodies back for further autopsies so that the causes of death could be determined beyond question.

"Until nine days ago," said the Reverend Charles Williman of St. Paul's United Church of Christ in a sermon at the funeral of one of the hostages, "we could believe we were sheltered from the rest of the world, separated as we were from the problems of the people in the city and the ghettos and the rest of the world.

"If we did not know it then, we know it now. Attica is part of the tragedy that is the world. Time will heal the loneliness and grief we feel now. But Attica can never return to the Attica of nine days ago.

"We shall never be the same."

Auxiliary Bishop Bernard McLoughlin of Buffalo concluded at another of the funerals of Attica: "On an occasion such as this, words are inadequate to express our true feelings."

I did not attend the funerals in view of the tension that had prevailed with the corrections officers during the rebellion, and I did not wish to seem to intrude. I did exchange correspondence with the families, however, and as weeks passed, I wanted to do more.

Not until the middle of November did I feel it was appropriate for me to visit the families, and then I asked Lieutenant Reger, the Sergeant Reger who had been one of the hostages of September, newly promoted, to contact the families and ask if I would be welcome. Of course I would be, he said.

So I returned to Attica on a Tuesday pilgrimage that we tried to keep secret. Arvis Chalmers of the Albany *Knickerbocker News* learned about it and he reported my visit tastefully.

I felt I had never seen a more courageous group of women in my life. They still seemed stunned, lost almost, but with a minimum of despair. They asked me over and again, "Why did it have to happen? What brought it about? What can be done?"

Many of the older children blamed the courts for being too liberal in their decisions and for engendering excess permissiveness in our society. Once I was asked why the courts did not take more into account the previous records of people sent to prison. There was criticism of the observers who had been brought in to help but who, in the families' view, had aggravated the problems and inflamed the situation. The younger children said they missed their fathers.

On more than one occasion, wives of the hostages showed me pictures of their husbands and, in view of the nationwide comments about prison brutality, asked me, "Does he look like the kind of man who would beat inmates? Well, he wouldn't."

Above all, the wives searched for every final detail on their husbands' last days in D Yard—what their husbands might have done, where they slept, how they wakened, what they said or thought.

Lieutenant Reger and I visited one of the surviving hostages, a young corrections officer still in the hospital in Batavia, still in serious condition from bullet wounds. This young man said to us:

"It's not just me. It's all of us. We've got to bring about a better correctional system for everyone."

CHAPTER 16

Three Secret Meetings

It was 10:00 A.M. Friday, September 24, eleven days after Attica and one day after the collapse of "nationwide uprisings in the streets." Amid the rancorous clamor of the national debate, the New York State government now attempted to shape the aftermath of Attica—as best we were able—and to set our cause of prison reform once more into forward motion.

Governor Rockefeller convened at the Executive Mansion at Albany the first of three long weekend meetings—all of them secret until now, as I write—in which we set principles and priorities, framed actions, and obtained the first of our needed financing. Less than an hour before, the New York State Capitol had been cleared because of a bomb scare. An augmented security guard patrolled in the brisk, autumn sunshine outside the mansion as we exchanged civilities and got down to business.

Governor Rockefeller and I were at one end of a long table, flanked by the senior elected officials, Lieutenant Governor Malcolm Wilson and Attorney General Louis Lefkowitz. Away from us along the right-hand side of the table sat Hugh Morrow, the governor's Director of Communications; General O'Hara, Superintendent Kirwan, and Chief Inspector Miller; along the left-hand side sat Deputy Attorney General Robert E. Fischer, Mr. Douglass, Mr. Whiteman, and General Baker. The man at the other end of the table, facing me directly, was the man who had led our assault, New York State Police Major John W. Monahan.

Governor Rockefeller opened the meeting by congratulating all present for courageous and effective professional performance at Attica. "It's a miracle we got so many of the hostages out alive. When I was on the phone to Bob Douglass and he kept telling me how many more we were rescuing—*you* were rescuing—I could hardly believe it. And, of course, there was more at stake even than saving lives. There was the whole rule of law to consider. The whole fabric of our society, in fact. And I want you to know how profoundly grateful I am for all you have done."

That said, Governor Rockefeller switched to a tough, interrogatory role as he put all of us through a detailed reconstruction of what had taken place. He looked through a pile of photographs of the wreckage in D Yard, pored over a map of the facility to refamiliarize himself with the tactical features, and seized upon the precise priority that had led me to order the assault.

"How can any of these critics say it was a turkey shoot?" the governor asked. "The problem was the executioners—there they were—and they had to be rendered harmless."

The governor signaled Major Monahan to detail the actions I have already described in this book. "Why didn't you go in and take the rest?" he asked, after the officer had described the first countermoves taken on Thursday, September 9. The governor knew of course about our shortages at that point of manpower and CS gas, and, after this had been rehashed, the governor ordered: There has to be a greater capability for a more rapid build-up of State Police forces using new lift techniques. There has to be CS gas on the spot for immediate use if needed at maximum-security institutions.

"How were they able to take over the prison in the first place?" the governor demanded. We summarized the reasons why—and the governor spelled out some new security measures he envisaged for our maximum-security institutions.

"How were so many of the hostages saved from getting their throats cut on the thirteenth?" the governor asked. Several of the state officials then expressed sharp objection to news reports indicating that the rebels had treated the hostages well for days and had spared them, and were then fired upon by the rescue mission. The officials stressed that the executioners were not "nice guys," but killers who had been incapacitated by the sharpshooters, disabled by the CS gas, and overwhelmed by the State Police just in time.

Attorney General Lefkowitz asked a series of questions that added up to one: Was our use of force at Attica *really* minimal? He stressed, "That's all I want to know," and he kept asking the same thing in different ways as the State Police officials retold the highlights of their battle of September 13. There was no question that our policy—and our orders—had been for minimal force, but the casualties had not been minimal.

At that point, Chief Inspector Miller tried to satisfy the attorney general's concern. He described the melee and the loss of life in D Yard after the rebels had brought down Lieutenant Christian. The governor turned to the attorney general and said, "This really *was* a fantastic operation—and it's a miracle that so many were saved." Mr. Lefkowitz patted me on my left arm and said, "It was due to this man's courage."

A little earlier in the meeting, Governor Rockefeller had turned to the tall, dark deputy attorney general who was now making his first appearance in the Attica drama. Robert E. Fischer of Binghamton, New York, formerly a judge and a friend of Mr. Douglass, had made a mark as head of the New York State Organized Crime Task Force. The press had dubbed him "supercop." Now Mr. Fischer was in charge of the New York State investigation of any criminal offenses at Attica.

Governor Rockefeller cut into Mr. Lefkowitz' questions about minimal force and asked Robert Fischer bluntly: "When your investigation is concluded, will you be able to tell me where and how many were killed, and why?"

Mr. Fischer and his associates had already been interviewing Attica participants for several days, and so, of course, had we. Now Mr. Fischer nodded his head to the governor and said he would be able to do this. And out of inquiries other than Mr. Fischer's, and at risk of violence to the chronology of this narrative, we were proving able to explain the volume of fire on September 13.

The New York State Police, in the first line, with orders to fire to protect their own lives and the lives of the hostages, expended a total of 364 rounds, as closely as we could judge it. This included sixty-eight rounds of .270-caliber ammunition used by the sharpshooters and others, twenty-seven rounds by .38-caliber revolvers, eight rounds by .357-caliber revolvers, and more than 200 rounds of .00 buckshot.

New York Correctional Services department officers had been positioned in the upper galleries of A and C Blocks in their backup role and New York State Police officers had heard sounds of firing from there. After the event, as far as we could judge it,

approximately sixteen corrections officers had fired in excess of
seventy rounds of various types of rifle and shotgun ammunition
during the brief battle, including rounds aimed at the executioners holding the hostages on top of Times Square.

Our specific investigation of the casualties appeared to confirm
our original post-battle reports. Of the ten hostages killed on
September 13, two were killed at Times Square and on the roofs
of the corridor-tunnels, one by a ricochet from a State Police
.270-caliber bullet, the second by a single shot from a .44-caliber
magnum rifle; this second hostage had also been cut in the back
of the neck by his executioner. The other eight hostages had all
been killed by gunfire in D Yard, five by shotgun fire and three
by .270-caliber rifle fire.

Of the twenty-nine inmates killed on September 13, eleven
were killed at Times Square and on the roofs of the corridor-
tunnels. Three were killed by a combination of .270-caliber rifle
and .oo buckshot shotgun fire, two by .270-caliber rifle fire alone,
and two by .oo buckshot shotgun fire alone. One was killed by
.357-caliber revolver fire and three by weapons as yet unidentified.

All the other eighteen inmates were killed in D Yard—nine by
.oo buckshot shotgun fire, five by .270-caliber rifle fire, one by a
combination of .38-caliber and .357-caliber revolver fire, one by a
combination of shotgun and .38-caliber revolver fire and two by
as yet unidentified weapons.

At the September 24 meeting, Mr. Fischer added, to Governor
Rockefeller, that he would also be able to produce information
on the deaths of the three inmates who had been killed during
the rebellion by their fellow prisoners. "Medical reports show they
each had more than twenty stab wounds in their bodies," Mr.
Fischer said to a hushed audience. One of the governor's associates commented, "Who said these prisoners were nice guys?"

Then there was some classified discussion about the methods
used by movement people to bring information into and out of
maximum-security prisons and about our own classified countermoves.

Governor Rockefeller's final series of questions focused on the
fact that Attica was only one of our maximum-security institutions. Actually, since the events at Attica and perhaps even in
harsh part because of them, things had been calmer at the other
prisons than might have been expected. At Auburn and at El-

mira, the normal routine had been cancelled for September 13 only, and there had been a deployment of additional security personnel. Elsewhere—rumblings, but no overt problems.

The governor's last question left us all with that all too familiar feeling. He asked, "How are things going to be this weekend?" And he swung his head to another group, "And the weekend after that?"

That afternoon, Governor Rockefeller spoke at the dedication ceremonies of the new State Bar Association center in Albany. I consider this one of his most statesmanlike addresses—made as it was in an atmosphere of spreading tension, polarization, and danger. Attica, said Governor Rockefeller, was only "another symptom of the deep-seated illness of our society.

"The tragedy of Attica is that we can no longer hesitate to diagnose and heal the truly fundamental problems.

"There is no escape from facing the sad fact that these stem as much from the failures of our society and government as from the actions of those small groups which would exploit legitimate grievances.

"The event dramatizes the need for firmness in dealing with the dangers from those who have given up hope of improving our civilization by peaceful means and are bent on changing it by force and destruction."

Governor Rockefeller said weaponry was not the solution— "nor can we accept the concept of those who would save our civilization by force alone, without change." There would have to be reforms, from safe streets through the courts to the correctional facilities, in which the rights and the dignity of the inmates and the corrections officers must be properly respected. And—after Attica:

"There never has been a moment when the American people were more tragically aware of—and receptive to—this necessity than they are today."

Governor Rockefeller and the leaders of the New York State Legislature were initiating Attica investigations other than that to be led by Mr. Fischer. At the governor's request, Presiding Justice Harry D. Goldman of the Appellate Division, Fourth Department, New York Supreme Court, had agreed to name a panel to report on the transitional period at Attica so that the public would know the constitutional rights of the inmates were being protected.*

Justice Goldman had indeed come up with some highly regarded observers: Clarence B. Jones, publisher of the *Amsterdam News* and member of the Citizens Observer Committee at Attica; Austin H. MacCormick, executive director of the Osborne Association; and also Donald H. Goff, general secretary of the Correctional Association of New York; Louis Nuñez, national executive director of Aspira Inc.; and Robert P. Patterson, Jr., of the law firm of Patterson, Belknapp & Webb.

Chief Judge Stanley H. Fuld of the Court of Appeals and the four presiding justices of the Appellate Division of the New York State Supreme Court would subsequently name nine members to a citizens' panel created at the request of the governor and the state legislative leaders. This panel was empowered to investigate all elements of the Attica situation for a report to the governor, the leaders, and the public. The nine members appointed, by an executive order signed by the governor, were:

Chairman: Dean Robert B. McKay, dean of the New York University School of Law and chairman of the Citizens' Union; the Most Reverend Edwin Broderick, bishop of the Roman Catholic Diocese of Albany; Robert L. Carter, an attorney and former counsel to the NAACP; Mrs. Mariano Guerrero, president of Friends of Puerto Rico; Amos Henix, executive director of Reality House Inc.; Burke Marshall, deputy dean of the Yale Law School and chairman of the Vera Institute of Justice; Walter N. Rothschild, Jr., chairman of the New York Urban Coalition and formerly president of Abraham & Straus; Mrs. Robert H. Wadsworth, president of Neighborhood Health Centers of Monroe County; and William Willbanks, a student at the School of Criminal Justice at the State University at Albany.

The McKay Commission set about the job of putting law students and others into interviewing 3,000 people in preparation for public hearings in 1972. They elected to give confidential status to any material given them by prisoners or staff. This of course made their ability to get alleged information much easier than was the case for other investigating officials who could not offer this status without offering immunity from prosecution. This

* See Appendix G, the Goldman Panel report.

makes the unchallenged statements made by many people to the McKay Commission far less acceptable as evidence under the circumstances. As such, this information must be weighed with extreme caution by those seeking the truth about Attica.

The thrust of the initial interrogations from the law students led many to feel that they had ignored the state of anarchy as it had existed at Attica. If the whole commission did indeed come in with a report lopsided in favor of the rebels, then its end result would have to be termed superficial. Anarchy, any way it is dissected, is chaos—and almost all of our people in the United States do not want to live like that.

Governor Rockefeller even formally requested the federal government to investigate allegations that the civil rights of Attica inmates were being violated. Usually state government is reluctant to tolerate federal investigation of its functions, let alone invite it. United States Attorney General John Mitchell was surprised by the governor's request. But the governor asked that the Civil Rights Division of the Justice Department look into things—"to assure public confidence in the objectivity and fairness of the entire Attica investigation."

The district attorney of Wyoming County, Louis James—the man who gave the pancake breakfast during the Attica crisis to three members of the Citizens Observer Committee—was also conducting his own investigation, and Wyoming County was soon to have its grand jury impaneled.

The United States Congress in the persons of Representative Claude Pepper of Florida and Representative Charles B. Rangel of New York was probing at Attica long before the September 24 meeting. And it would be the House of Representatives Select Committee on Crime, headed by Mr. Pepper, that would first get its open hearings off the ground.

The second secret meeting was held on the afternoon of September 25 in my temporary office in the bombproof underground bunker of the state civil defense organization on the outskirts of Albany. We had moved from our own offices downtown after a bomb had gone off on the ninth floor. Now I called in many of the deputy and assistant commissioners to our new quarters.

Down the steel staircases, below the pressure doors, amid the electro-alarms and the emergency water and electricity supplies came the veterans of Attica. There were Walter Dunbar, Gerald Houlihan, Wim van Eekeren, Robert Fosen, John Van De Car, William Baker, and Vito Ternullo, Director of Education and Vocational Training. On the agenda was the current situation at Attica—but I also wanted to sense the mood, and to express my own, in the privacy of our embattled group. Of course, the violence of the national debate was getting to us, and we needed to re-evaluate our objectives.

The situation at Attica itself, considering the $5 million damage done by inmates in the worst riot in our prison history, was recovering from its low point. Even on the Monday evening of September 13, all the inmates had living space, crowded three to a cell in A and C Blocks. The first night had been rough for the inmates, as they were often awakened for head counts that might or might not have been necessary. Day by day until September 22 we had transferred men out of Attica to other correctional facilities until we had reduced the population to 1,250. By Thursday, September 23, all the remaining inmates were housed once again in single cells.

By September 20 these inmates were provided with writing materials for correspondence. Incoming inmate mail was being distributed, and outgoing mail was being processed. Tobacco and toilet articles were issued. Laundry services were in operation. The facility kitchen was back in shape, and on September 20 three inmate meals were served as per pre-riot schedule, replacing the sparse but inevitable sandwich-based diets in the cells. Inmate clean-up crews, working under the close supervision of corrections officers, carted off the debris left by the rebellion but not from Cell Block D. Deputy Attorney General Fischer had placed D Block off limits until he reached an interim point in his investigation.

Security at Attica was improving somewhat—and there were new armed posts established on the roofs of A Block and C Block and manned by September 21. An inventory of dangerous substances and fluids was completed. Additional and repeated mine-sweeper searches uncovered hundreds more weapons, buried or hidden, obviously, for "the next time."

The sharpest argument was raging on the medical front, or so it seemed. There were hurtful charges that we were not doing enough for the inmates who had been injured during the Sep-

tember 13 engagement. On that Monday an emergency call for
medical assistance had gone out to Dr. W. G. Schenk, chairman
of the Department of Surgery at the University of Buffalo Medical School and chief of surgery at the Edward J. Meyer Memorial
Hospital. Dr. Schenk and surgical teams, including fourteen surgeons, operating room nurses, residents, anesthetists, and emergency room crews moved out to Attica. Three National Guard
surgeons were already at work. In fact, five complete operating
suites were moved from Meyer Hospital to Attica. Blood was
transferred from Rochester and Buffalo blood banks and blood-
matching personnel from Meyer Hospital were also rushed to the
correctional facility.

Dr. Schenk said that when his teams left Attica on the Monday night there were no recognized major injuries left untreated.
Many of the more serious cases had been transferred from Attica
to Meyer Hospital.

All that afternoon and evening, groups of medical personnel
from New York City and elsewhere began to arrive and demand
access to the prison, as requested by Attorney Kunstler, among
others. They were even reinforced by a court order, but access
was not granted.

Early on the Tuesday morning twelve surgeons from Meyer
Hospital again toured the whole Attica facility, providing post-
operative care, transferring two cases that had developed complications to Meyer Hospital.

All the rest of the week, some fifty to sixty physicians, medical
students, and hospital personnel worked on at Attica, and Dr.
Schenk said the correctional facility's thirty-bed infirmary, operating room, X-ray equipment, and laboratory equipment were adequate for the needs of a prison community of fewer than 2,500
inmates. But there was a rising protest among medical personnel
about the adequacy of health care. The first-year and second-year
students of the University of Buffalo Medical School voted overwhelmingly in favor of the school's taking over complete medical
responsibility for Attica.

A confrontation came on September 16 when dedicated but
outside medical professionals made a bid to take over some of our
correctional responsibilities. Dr. Le Roy A. Pesch, dean of the
School of Medicine, and Dr. Albert C. Rekate, director of the Edward J. Meyer Memorial Hospital, wrote that the School of Medi-

cine would "offer immediately an expansion of its present surgical program . . . to include general medical care. Additional professional staffing will be provided on a volunteer basis starting immediately." They added: "We recognize that the legal responsibility for medical care to the inmates must remain with the State Department of Correction," but further offered "the provision of comprehensive care at the Attica correction facility on a long-term basis."

Dr. James D. Bradley, medical director of our Department of Correctional Services, made a formal statement: "We are providing adequate medical care. We would like to have continued medical assistance and co-operation such as you are now providing and have provided in the past.

"We are unable to comply with your request that the faculty of the University of Buffalo assume control of the hospital at the Attica facility. We do have the situation under control and we are charged by law with the responsibility of providing medical care to inmates, which in fact we are doing."

I am not a medical man and I assumed that the specific charges and the complaints that had previously been made against the prison medical personnel at Attica would be proper subjects for the forthcoming investigations. It was certain, however, that no hostage, no inmate, lost his life from lack of medical care.

These were indeed ugly charges about the medical situation at Attica—and my associates and I were even more deeply troubled about the whole basic situation.

"Prison reform," I said to my associates at the start of our own secret meeting. "Is it really out of date? Do people really want it?"

"You mean prepare men to return to a normal life?" Mr. Dunbar asked. I said, "Yes, middle-class values, if you like, all that." Walter Dunbar said, "That's the normal life the revolutionaries consider abnormal."

I continued: "A good home, a stable job, a decent leisure life—it's the last thing these people want. They say they're not criminals—they're just victims of the system. But this is simply not so. They've had criminal records going back years and years before revolution even got talked about. The immediate issue is to identify these people and get them locked up."

Walter Dunbar asked with a smile, "Are you going to build

another Alcatraz?" I replied, "Of course not, no, no, no. But we are going to take our existing institutions and remodel them and replan them so we can handle the problems right now. We can't wait to put up a new institution."

Dr. van Eekeren said he had just come from a meeting with the state budget people and some of the leaders of Council 82 of the AFSCME, the corrections officers' union. He said the corrections officers' representatives were calling us "phonies" and "faggots" and one man had even shouted that "Rockefeller threw the hostages to the wolves."

Wim van Eekeren said it was typical that the corrections union was not only pressing for more riot guns, but was demanding to know who was going to choose them, and what type. "Their whole thrust is to *make* the correctional services department officials listen because we *have* to," he added. "There was nothing but hostility at the meeting. It was like being in the yard at Dannemora."

"Now we're dealing with the extremists on the other side," I said. "During Attica, many of the guards cursed and denigrated me for my liberalism. I'll never forget it. But we must have adequate security for the guards and safe and secure operations in which an effective correctional program can be carried out."

Mr. Dunbar and the others stressed that living conditions for the inmates also had to be improved right now, and I interrupted, "Sure, we need proper protection for the guards, too, and radio equipment, helmets, gas masks, and so on. But we've got to get to the attitudes of the white staffs of the prisons and we've got to teach them in a humanistic way. No matter what these people think a prison ought to be like, they've got to realize that the inmates are human beings with dignity and unless they realize this, we're not going anywhere."

Walter Dunbar insisted on his point. "Right now, it's how we handle the living problems. There must be a nutritious diet, a better balanced diet, more tasty food, that is, with proper balance, and there's got to be much better medical and dental care and more recreation." There was at least a $3 million repair job at Attica, and the provision of adequate programs would cost millions more. "What are we even offering the inmates as far as rehabilitation is concerned? It's still so bad it's a big deal whether a man gets a shower a week," I commented.

Mr. Dunbar said there should be a supervisor of food services at Attica who cared about attractive service and preparation of dishes as well as diet balance. He proposed that Attica take on an instructor in the culinary arts, in baking, and in correct meat-cutting—all this not two weeks after the Attica rebellion. With what seemed like half the country shouting for our blood and half the country shouting for the inmates' blood, here we were in our underground bunker talking about correct meat-cutting.

Education Director Vito Ternullo cut in, "Yes, we must address ourselves to living conditions—but including political conditions. Programs are O.K., but the same trouble will persist—I mean the revolutionary trouble—unless we view this realistically."

I said, "Mr. Mancusi wanted me to ship out the five or so most notorious troublemakers, but they would only have landed on somebody else. Let's face it—a lot of people want to hear about Mao and they want to hear about the new proposals being made.

"Even if we do isolate the troublemakers, we've still got to find ways to get to the minds of all the others. Revolutionary literature is not the only literature. Where's our literature—and where are our answers to the problems? We're showing them nothing—so our inmates are picking up the turnkey, the screw, attitude of the guards they see around them as representative. All too often, that's a fact.

"But Vito's right—for example, constitutional law. The men want to know about the law because of their own cases, and that's at least a start. There must be plenty of ways in which we can teach them how to respect the law—even what the rule of law is, and why it offers security to people.

"Look—if we can show the inmates there really is an opportunity structure in America, that in our society people really can get ahead, then maybe we will have more answers than we have right now.

"In the meantime, of course, the public is demanding protection from the radicals. They expect us to provide it and as long as I'm commissioner they're going to get it."

Dr. Fosen said he had great hopes for a new kind of "GI Bill" for the retraining and rehabilitation of inmates, even though there was little enough state money around for aid to schools and mental hospitals, let alone correctional services. I said I still plumped for basing prison reform upon the community, but I added, "The militants don't want the constructive people from the community. And as for the non-movement people, the good citizens, they don't really want to come in to help so much any more, and who can blame them?" A memory of Attica: "They might get taken hostage, even."

There was discussion about the long-recognized need for the increased recruitment of black corrections officers and for busing them into white communities such as Attica; also for the grant of some prison powers to chosen inmate councils, all of which would require detailed work-ups.

That afternoon, however, after the most grueling days of our lives, I suspect what we were all really asking ourselves was "Why carry on?" Yet we wrapped up the meeting with some new thoughts on how to negotiate with Council 82 of the AFSCME. Walter Dunbar said to me, "I'm going to need you to handle the next labor meeting. Talk about you being mercurial, think about me!"

Everybody laughed, but I decided to end the meeting on a more serious note: "Let's see now. No matter how things go, we're taking up this challenge, and maybe we can still get some advantage from it. It's sad that a tragedy like Attica has to bring things about—and people have been turning their backs on prisons and prison reform for years. Now, perhaps, we have a new opportunity. So whether it's the inmates with their pounding, or the corrections officers with their pounding, or even our pounding with the governor and the legislature—out of all this welter of controversy, let's hope something good can come out of it."

Then it was upstairs and out into the open air. The scene was deserted. Security was excellent. Mr. Dunbar smiled to me as he got into his small sports car. "The Panthers have put me on the list," he said. "They're threatening to kill Rockefeller, Oswald—and Dunbar."

Then I drove home to Schenectady in my more sober black sedan, to be greeted by Jane, who was now safe home from the hospital. The press had pushed her for a comment on my going into the Attica yard. She told them that "it was such a bad dream—and I will carry the picture in my mind the rest of my life. However, I was very, very proud of his courage and faith, and he still has a great deal of both left." On my decision to launch the rescue mission, she said, "He did what he had to do—what he thought was right. He is a very gentle man. I know what the situation must have done to him. He had such great plans, so many things he wanted to do. Now it may all be set back."

At 1:00 P.M. Monday September 27, Governor Rockefeller convened the third secret meeting of the long weekend in an executive suite in the heart of Manhattan. There the governor and I briefed the leaders of the New York State Legislature on Attica—and on how we wanted to move ahead. Specifically, the governor wanted to obtain an allocation of $4 million from the state emergency fund to repair damages at Attica and to purchase additional security equipment for corrections officers everywhere in the state. But we needed more—we needed a meeting of minds. The national debate was getting to us and we were under intense pressure.

The governor began the luncheon meeting with some informal remarks that I had not expected. "I think Russ has done a fantastic job under trying circumstances," he said.

Then something else happened that I had not expected. All around a circular table, from Republican and Democratic state legislators, from members of the governor's staff and my own staff, there came for me the first applause I had received since Attica.

The governor continued: "Russ did everything possible up there to avert loss of life. He went into the yard up there three times, and he only just got out the last time. There was danger to his life all the time. His faith in the democratic process is exemplary. He got that citizens committee in there and the twenty-eight points were negotiated. But then Bobby Seale came in—and the others. The three unacceptable demands had been made. These were the amnesty, the release of prisoners to a 'non-imperialistic' country, and the removal of the warden. These were not acceptable—of course.

"So Russ has gone through right down the line with amazing courage and perception. Then he took the action—and I want to say to you all right now that he has my 1,000 per cent endorsement."

There was more applause. I replied: "I want to say that throughout this tragedy, I haven't lost my faith in people. I still believe the majority of these inmates involved can be reclaimed. I am

sure we can do it. I think we have been able to bring to this state
the best men in corrections in the whole country. We have a first-
rate operational team. So things were really beginning to move
along in New York when, unfortunately, a small segment of the
inmates saw that change was coming and that we were actively
preparing to move into the mainstream of care.

"These reform developments did not fit their plans and we had
the problem we're here to discuss today. In any event, there were
compelling reasons why we didn't go in the first day, and there
were compelling reasons why we negotiated with these people,
and, finally, there were compelling reasons why we went in."

After some discussion about the monies that would be needed
—these would include $800,000 for additional security equip-
ment; $3 million for repairs and restoration of essential functions
at Attica; $200,000 for interim expenses of all the Attica investi-
gating committees and groups—I was ready for the question-and-
answer period that might or might not lead to a meeting of minds.

Assembly Minority Leader Stanley Steingut said he was tremendously concerned about the problems of the corrections
officers and the dangers they faced as they went about their jobs.
I spelled out some of our new security measures, but did not attempt to hide the realities. "There was great hostility on the
part of corrections officers who had seen friends and colleagues
and relatives beaten and threatened and in some cases killed. At
the same time, there is the hostility continuing on the part of
the militants.

"The corrections officers are badly outnumbered everywhere in
the state, and when they get home at night, they often learn their
wives and families received threatening phone calls during the
day.* The attitudes of the corrections officers are tremendously

* Yet another media squabble of the Attica crisis had erupted around my
own home in Schenectady, New York. After my life was threatened, we
changed the telephone numbers, of course, and the State Police maintained
constant patrol. Then television station WGY-WRGB showed my home to
the viewers in a gesture that prompted a letter to the editor of a local newspaper from a Mrs. Antoinette Makuc, of Scotia, New York:
"I was astonished and stunned by the display of irresponsible television
journalism . . . It is inconceivable to me that at a critical time, and a difficult time, in the life of Commissioner Oswald and his family, that a television
station would flash photographs of his home on the television screen, and not
only invade the legitimate privacy of the Oswald family but possibly jeopardize
his person and his property. There is such a thing as good judgment and dis-

important in the holding of mutual respect between corrections officers and inmates."

State Comptroller Arthur Levitt then asked some questions about financial matters at Attica and Attorney General Lefkowitz some questions about Superintendent Mancusi's background. Speaker Duryea asked: "What is the extent of outside political influence in the state prisons, especially top-security institutions?" I answered by summarizing information on this point that is familiar by now to readers of this book, and I added: "We look longingly for some facility in our system that is top-security right now. It's that insecure."

Then I talked for a while about my concept of segregating troublemakers so that the rehabilitation of the majority of offenders might proceed at greater speed. "The problem is so urgent," I said, "that we cannot wait for construction of a completely new facility. We will have to adapt existing security institutions for this purpose. Then we can juggle around our population."

There was a murmur of assent around the table. State Senate Majority Leader Earl W. Brydges asked how the troublemakers would be selected: "By degree of crime, or what?"

I replied: "These troublemakers ought to be selected by criteria including their willingness or unwillingness to conform to reasonable modes of conduct. I would not doom these people. They should be able to earn their way out of a maxi-maximum-security institution by good behavior and an improving attitude. Not even the most militant are hopeless. As we learn more about them, we may be able to move even these people and do things with them."

Lieutenant Governor Malcolm Wilson commented on the professional procedures we used in the classification of prisoners and

---

criminatory news reporting, but this was a demonstration of sick television journalism."

To which Donald Decker, Manager, News, WGY-WRGB-TV, replied to the same newspaper:

"Mrs. Makuc never mentioned why we used the film. We said the commissioner's home was under guard after numerous threats were phoned to the Oswald family, and we showed the film of the house as we reported these facts. We reported this just as we reported that some people felt Mr. Oswald was a murderer because of Attica, and that some, such as President Nixon, thought Mr. Oswald had done all he could at Attica. This is our job—to report. As far as invasion of privacy is concerned, the right of privacy simply does not exist with respect to news coverage and certainly Mr. Oswald and the Attica situation were extremely prominent news matters."

parolees, and he said that competent people really were able to keep their case studies under surveillance long enough, and thoroughly enough, to make sound recommendations. His point was that fair and objective criteria were not impossible to determine—as some held. The selection of men to be sent to maximum-maximum-security institutions could be surprisingly specific and sensible.

Comptroller Levitt then threw in an explosive question: "If the twenty-eight demands presented at Attica were acceptable by the state immediately, then why the hell could this have not been done before?" Mr. Levitt said he was addressing his question to "the system." Minority Leader Steingut said, "They are addressing it to all of us."

I replied that the Attica situation had been a crisis—we had accepted the twenty-eight points rapidly in order to try to save lives. We were in fact already actively attempting to obtain most of the twenty-eight points and we were adopting "traditional" prison reforms wherever possible everywhere in the state. But there were now substantial questions that had to be answered. For example, under pressure to save lives we had accepted a minimum wage for prison labor, free political activity within correctional facilities, and no censorship of mail—a prime conduit of the militant movement. I asked: "Did the state legislature want these changes to be made? Would the money be available? Would the public support them?"

I had accepted the twenty-eight points, but there were so many bugs in these three that I would have been happier with twenty-five points.

When Arthur Levitt bored in, I said if we had put all twenty-eight points into effect in all of our institutions right now, there would have been a great deal of trouble. "There would have been riots," I said. "The staff is not ready for us yet, for another thing, and the staff still look on us as lax and lenient." In general, however, I was delighted that Mr. Levitt and other prominent Democrats were so strongly for the twenty-eight points and I thought the momentum would be beneficial.

Governor Rockefeller then asked me to characterize the over-all situation at all of the major institutions. I said the problem was that we now had troublemaking prisoners unlike any I had ever known in my career. I said, "They are revolutionaries. They want to tear down the whole place—anything to do with the system."

The governor said, "So you are sitting on a tinderbox?" I laughed and said, "I was a lamb led to the slaughter." Mr. Douglass interjected, "Like an admiral put in charge of a burning ammunition ship."

Senate Minority Leader Joseph Zaretzki then raised the question of the different investigative commissions and asked, "Which one of these commissions is empowered to investigate the rights of inmates against other inmates?" The governor said, "That is a very good question," and indeed it was. It might be possible for inmates who wished to rehabilitate themselves to obtain formal protection from militants who might be construed to be violating their civil rights. Robert Douglass stressed how important this matter was because three of the prisoners killed at Attica had been slaughtered by other inmates.

Governor Rockefeller and Speaker Duryea drew upon various parallels from other states in which the rights of inmates to protection from other inmates had been critical. Speaker Duryea commented upon the Mississippi system of using trusties—prisoners with special privileges—and Governor Rockefeller said that in Arkansas trusties "sit in towers and watch over the inmates." They were empowered in some cases to shoot to prevent escapes.

Then Comptroller Levitt told a case history of a man who had been serving time for fraud, who had complained of callous treatment from a prison doctor and from corrections officers. Once this man's pills had been seized during a pro-forma search for narcotics. Arthur Levitt said, "Do prison doctors view these people in prison in the conventional relationship between doctors and patients, or are prisoners to be held at arm's length?" Walter Dunbar and I explained how the prison medical system worked.

But Mr. Levitt kept on coming: "What kind of guy is a prison doctor?" I joked, "He's a guy in private practice who works two hours per day for us and expects to get paid for it." One of the governor's aides said, "That is a candid comment."

Robert Douglass told an Attica story about how an inmate had walked out of rebel territory with a gut wound inflicted by a fellow inmate, "and he asked for the prison doctor. He asked for help from the very guy the others were trying to get kicked out of his job."

Governor Rockefeller now focused the meeting: "Really, what's been happening is that we have been doing a holding operation in our prisons for a long time. Now it's time for us to move ahead."

Mr. Levitt asked the governor if he thought the people of the state would vote for a bond issue for prison construction. There was some discussion about this, but nothing definitive. It was, of course, a major new idea.

Senator Brydges then supplied another important focus: It was important, he felt, to separate the immediate needs of the crisis— and the longer-term needs of our prison programs. He was very concerned that if new programs were seen to be the result of the Attica uprising, then "people will say the action by the inmates was justified." There would be an apparent incentive for new disturbances. In time the new programs ought to be good enough to run of their own volition, and not in response to a rebellion.

"The situation of the guards *must* be considered," Senator Brydges added. "Their work just isn't safe right now and we can't ask people to work in these conditions. The emphasis must be on making these places more secure."

"Attica was not really a secure prison when this thing started," Governor Rockefeller replied. "And now I'd rather leave the windows out, and the chapel destroyed, and all the other damage not cleared up, and restore the security of the prison first. I want to see the guards protected. This is the priority right now."

"The only way we can really provide security in the long run is programs. We must move out the troublemakers so that others can move ahead," I commented.

Mr. Levitt asked, "How does Attica compare with other prisons elsewhere in the United States?" I answered, "Better than most. But in the federal system, they've got the pacifists, the white-collar guys, the embezzlers, and so on, and because their prisoners are so different, their problems are almost irrelevant. Their reforms are almost irrelevant."

There was a pause and, in an apparent hiatus, Malcolm Wilson said:

"We've got to give Russ the flexibility he needs to handle the revolutionaries.

"The radicals and the press might criticize us.

"And the people will be all the way for Russ Oswald."

There was a murmur of assent around the table, and Arthur Levitt asked me, jokingly, "How did you get into this business? You could have been a senator or something."

Then the governor and the others discussed the need for a certificate of necessity for the use of the $4 million of emergency funds. The governor said, "I don't think the public is going to sit by for a year. We want action now."

It turned out that the governor wanted the certificate of necessity before the leaders left the room—and Governor Rockefeller got it.

Stanley Steingut, in an impressive intervention, said, "We're only kidding ourselves if we only talk about capital construction. We need the reform programs, too." He talked for some five minutes in the true vein of penological progress, and he concluded, "We can accumulate all the studies we need. We can bring in the best brains in the country—which we have right now. But the more we delay action on the programs, the greater our problems will be."

The governor said, "You are absolutely right, Stanley. We are going to have to come up with a budget that involves these new concepts Russ has been working on."

Out of this meeting there sprang yet another body—a fifteen-member state committee assigned to recommend improvements in the state-wide penal system. Governor Rockefeller and the legislative leaders named as chairman Hugh R. Jones, the fifty-seven-year-old president of the New York State Bar Association. The governor's other appointments were: Richard J. Bartlett, another lawyer and formerly chairman of the state's Penal Law Revision Commission; Major Mary C. Davis, director of women's correctional services for the Salvation Army; Howard A. Jones, chairman of the State Narcotic Addiction Control Commission; Richard A. McGee, president of the American Justice Institute and one of the top prison reformers in the country; the Reverend Earl B. Moore, pastor of St. Paul Baptist Church in New York City; and Angel M. Rivera, regional director of the Office of Economic Opportunity.

Senator Brydges appointed Senator Thomas McGowan and Senator John Dunne, both former members of the Citizens Observer Committee at Attica. Speaker Duryea nominated Assem-

blyman Clark Wemple, another Attica observer, and Assemblyman Dominick L. DiCarlo of Brooklyn.

Senator Zaretzki nominated Senator Robert Garcia, an Attica
observer, and Senator Joseph L. Galiber of the Bronx. Assembly
Minority Leader Steingut nominated Assemblymen Thomas W.
Brown of Albany, and Mark T. Southall of Manhattan.

Governor Rockefeller said the Jones Committee would make
"a searching examination into the problems affecting our correctional system . . . [and] make recommendations for improvements in the system along with short- and long-term priorities."

The eventual recommendations of this very able committee
made few sensational headlines but they were translated into a
1972 prison reform program to finance construction of new
facilities, upgrade existing facilities, improve correctional programs,
expand work-release programs, create a furlough program, expand
job opportunities for former inmates, and correct inequities in
parole eligibility.

These had all been areas of concern of the Jones Committee.
A key bill passed by the New York Legislature and approved by
the governor provided $12,022,600 to the Department of Cor-
rectional Services for improving our programs and administration
along these lines.

Two of the new bills would broaden employment opportunities
for ex-prisoners by removing unnecessary restrictions on their
employment in premises licensed to sell alcoholic beverages for
off-premise consumption, such as supermarkets, and by expanding
the category of criminal offenders who might obtain a certificate
of relief from disabilities that bar their employment on account
of their previous convictions. Any criminal offender who had not
been convicted more than once of a felony would be eligible for
the certificate of relief. Another bill enabled carefully screened
inmates to leave prison unaccompanied for the purpose of seeking
employment, attending educational or vocational training programs, obtaining medical care, and for compassionate reasons such
as visiting a close relative during a terminal illness, attending a
close relative's funeral, or tending to important family matters.

This meeting in Manhattan was a welcome contrast to the
divisive national debate. Here hawks and doves alike were viewing
Attica as a crisis that demanded unity if our society was not to
be further polarized. Governor Rockefeller said, smiling as he used

the cliché, "This thing is bigger than all of us." And he added, "It is a very real test—and opportunity—for the democratic process."

Outside the meeting, some people were discussing the same theme. One woman said, "Of course, they're right. Something's got to be done." Another said, "This used to be a wonderful country, but now it's like you're not safe walking home any more." A third woman said, "Anything they can do against crime, I'm for—and so's everybody else I know."

CHAPTER 17

On with Prison Reform

During October and November 1971, we began to recover from the Attica rebellion with increasing momentum. In our three secret conferences we had obtained augmented security, a meeting of minds on correctional philosophy, and emergency appropriations. Our debt to Governor Rockefeller's drive and humane concern was immense. We could now at least attempt to shape the aftermath that followed.

SEPTEMBER 28–OCTOBER 4
COMPLETE FIRST PHASE OF TRANSITION AT ATTICA

On September 28, the day of our Manhattan meeting, and September 29 the first Board of Parole hearings were conducted at Attica since the rebellion. This led to a deep sense of relief among the prisoners who had not participated in the rebellion but who feared, nonetheless, that they would be treated as if they had. On September 29 routine visits to inmates from 9:00 A.M. until 3:30 P.M. were resumed, in place of the visits that had been improvised amid the disorder of the postrebellion period.

On October 1 the industrial shops were completely searched and the last of the metal weapons unearthed. Inmates were assigned once again to industrial duties and the first group would report to work twelve days later. On October 4 the first group of twenty-seven new corrections officers assigned to Attica arrived at the correctional facility. They went into in-service training the same day.

Eventually, Mr. Van De Car of the Division of Manpower and Employee Relations would be successful in obtaining approval for the appointment of forty corrections officers, twelve corrections sergeants, and three corrections lieutenants to Attica. The in-service training programs included work in behavioral sciences. The prisoner population at Attica had meanwhile been virtually halved by transfers to other institutions.

OCTOBER 5–OCTOBER 7
AGREEMENT WITH THE CORRECTIONS OFFICERS UNION

The bitterness of our negotiations with Council 82 of the AFSCME reached new levels in the first week of October. The council now threatened a "lock-in" of all prisoners everywhere in the state for October 7 unless we went along with their demands. But with the assurance of the emergency funds from the state, and with federal funds for previously committed programs rolling in, I felt we ought to accentuate the positive. So on October 5 I summarized a series of proposals in a letter to William Ciuros, Jr., president of Council 82 and a man who, I might add, bore little resemblance to the rabble-rousers.

First, I said I had recommended to the governor that a commission study what benefits ought to be available for the hostages —the injured hostages and the families of the hostages who had been killed. These ought to go far beyond the usual disability benefits.

Second, I agreed to include representatives from Council 82 in selecting our sorely needed maxi-maximum-security institution. Council 82 had argued very hard for this new kind of prison for troublemakers—it was virtually their key demand.

Third, I stressed to Mr. Ciuros that I had now been authorized to fill all vacant custodial positions in the system and to rehire all men laid off during the state austerity program earlier in the year. I also had an additional $912,000 available from temporary funds to hire an additional ninety custodial officers. I had certified 160 narcotics corrections officers for employment. Sixty corrections officers would be trained each three-week period until the end of 1971.

Fourth, I said we were accepting bids already for $800,000-worth of additional security equipment. I had already ordered 4,242 more gas masks, 3,218 more riot helmets, and 695 more sets of face shields and goggles. New radio communications for our institutions would include a base station and trans-receivers and control points for twenty-four-hour operations, standardized for emergency use on a state-wide basis. We already had installed this radio security system at Attica. There would also be improved telephones, additional firearms, CS and CN gas supplies, ammunition, and two metal detectors for every correctional facility in the state.

Fifth, I said that the first fourteen correctional lieutenants would begin training at the New York State Police Academy the following week for new assignments as "training officers." They would be the first beneficiaries of a new federal-funded $1.6 million program to supply seventeen hours of advanced training in behavioral as well as custodial sciences to every corrections officer in the state.

Sixth, I promised improvements in the food, clothing, and sanitation available to inmates in all our institutions, which the union wanted as much as we did. I promised that "shower facilities are to be remodeled and relocated. Shower schedules are to be adjusted to facilitate showers as frequently as needed, daily if necessary." I said I was requesting $689,000 of the state planning board for the preparation of meals in prisons on the basis of a nutritious diet, $134,000 for a new clothing ration at Attica, and the beginning of an estimated $2 million that would be needed to make drastic improvements in the material, styles, tailoring, and laundering of winter and summer issue prison uniforms.

Seventh, I was able to tell William Ciuros that the New York State Police Academy would be available for corrections officer training. Once again, our comrades of the State Police had come through for us when we needed them. Also, I was requesting an additional $200,000 of the state planning board for a start to be made on a permanent corrections officer training academy of our own, a long-sought goal of Governor Rockefeller.

Eighth, I confirmed we were reviewing all of our custodial post assignments after Attica, and I confirmed I would consider recommendations made by Council 82 in this regard. They felt, and so did I, that we were generally under strength, and that our authorizations were insufficient. Never again ought a prison to be overwhelmed as easily as was Attica on September 9.

Ninth, I advised Council 82 to redirect any request for reallocation of corrections officers titles, with salary increases, to the Division of Classification and Compensation of the Department of

Civil Service. In July 1970 Council 82 had agreed to a two-year contract with the state providing starting salaries for corrections officers of $8,500 per year and $10,800 per year after fifteen years' service.

Just before 12:00 midnight on October 6 Governor Rockefeller's office, my own, and Council 82 announced an agreement along these lines. There would be no lock-in. In these negotiations, sterling work had been performed, in my opinion, by New York State Budget Director Richard L. Dunham and State Employee Relations Director Abe Lavine.

Council 82 President Ciuros accentuated the positive as he saw it: "For the first time, a labor union has induced a state government to institute major reforms in its penal and correctional system." The fact is that everyone knew we had charted these movements earlier and no one had to force us into them.

SEPTEMBER 26–OCTOBER 9
THE SHOWDOWN WITH THE NEWSPAPER
REPORTERS ASSOCIATION

On September 27 Governor Rockefeller received a formal letter from John Shanahan of the Associated Press, president of the Newspaper Reporters Association. Although we had agreed to admit press representatives to the negotiations with the rebel leaders in D Yard, we had not permitted press coverage of the rescue action, and we were not now permitting access to the inmates pending further progress in the multiple legal investigations under way. Mr. Shanahan made the documentable point that:

"News of developments at Attica state prison during and after the retaking of inmate-held areas September 13 was confusing and, as we have seen, inaccurate on some major matters. This came about largely because newsmen were not in a position to see what was going on during the assault. . . . It is only fair to the public to give newsmen full access to news sources and developments. This would protect the press and the public against hasty, faulty, misleading, and confused statements."

When the governor sent this letter to me for comment, I did not deny the fact that inaccurate statements had been made by our department personnel: "Perhaps we accepted too well our responsibility to inform the public and succumbed, as mentally, emotionally and physically exhausted people sometimes do, to the incessant pressures for answers." Reports from all classes of persons who would talk with the media were given credibility and reported. Anyone who would talk seemed to have "the facts."

But the deployment of "war correspondents" with our surprise gas attack and pinpoint rush into D Yard was absolutely out of the question—and for other than our own security reasons. I wrote the governor, "Psychologically, reasonably, and rationally, there are certain areas in which professional judgment must be left to the professionals. Attica was not a carnival. It was an agonizingly desperate attempt to save lives—hostages and inmates alike. As such, it transcends the immediacy of the 'public's right to know.'"

Needless to say, the newspaper reporters hardly accepted this answer as definitive.

OCTOBER 9–OCTOBER 12
PHASE TWO AT ATTICA

It was now one month after the rebellion.

On October 9 the commissary reopened for business.

On October 12 the industrial shops went back into business, and vocational training programs, in-cell study programs, and recreational programs got under way again.

On October 13 the contractors moved into the correctional facility to translate our patch-up repairs into something more permanent.

I scarcely believed it possible that so much could be accomplished in such a brief period amid continuing tension.

OCTOBER 26–NOVEMBER 17
THE REBEL LEADERS ARE HEARD FROM

The *Village Voice* left its competitors far behind and printed a long letter from inside Attica, and from none other than Richard L. Clark. Brother Richard made his most telling points, as usual, by focusing upon prison conditions—"each and every day upon waking from a restless slumber, not knowing what atrocities the day will bring. . . ."

"In reality, what we are surviving on [in the segregation block] is bread and water with two or three discriminate pieces of fruit thrown in. The corrections officers serve this garbage, and we say garbage because the men who work on a disposal truck are more conscious about hygiene and cleanliness than those serving our food. Since we don't eat pork, no means of substitution of pork items has been imposed—either you eat the pork or starve. . . .

"There are forty-seven men here [in segregation] and we haven't been charged with a thing.* Yet we are being treated as though we have already been charged, convicted, and sentenced. We are continuing to be intimidated and dehumanized by a testicle and anal search whenever we come out of our cells for a lawyer or family visit. . . .

"We, the Attica Brothers, urgently request that the people unite in their effort, because this is what the brothers in Attica, those living and dead, struggled for."

On October 27 Herbert X. Blyden was heard from in the letters to the editor column of the New York *Times*. Signing himself Minister of Information, Attica Liberation Faction, Brother Herbert wrote: ". . . If the system is antiquated, then who is to say that there exist no political prisoners.

"I am one who is innocent, and if given a chance to get out of America, I will."

On November 16 Richard Clark and Roger Champen along with four other inmates of HBZ were interviewed in Attica by Fred Ferretti of the New York *Times*. One of the inmates' lawyers on hand for the interview was Herman Schwartz of the University of Buffalo, the Citizens Observer Committee of Attica, and the veteran of our "night ride to Vermont." Mr. Ferretti wrote a descriptive paragraph:

* The *Village Voice* ran with this letter the first list of Attica prisoners held in HBZ. They were Gilbert Bates, Herbert Blyden, James Brown, Peter Butler, Roger Champen, Richard X. Clark, Richard L. Clark, Pedro Crispin, Edward Dingle, Craig Fowler, Frank Goddard, Mariano Gonzales, Alcinius Hardin, Gary Richard Haynes, Francis Huen, Milton Jones, Raymond Jordan, Lawrence Killibrew, Charles Locicero, Frank Lott, Ronald Lyons, Willie McCullough, Philip Myhand, Tuco Wilson Sanchez, Donald Noble, Kenny Orr, Michael Lewis, Robert Lee Robinson, Armando Rodriguez, Jerry Rosenberg, Philip Shields, Michael Smith, Samuel Walls, William Walls, William Wesley, Donald Weiss, Anthony Williams.
Also: Frank Noble, John Boyd, David Smith, Vernon Smith, William Outlaw, James Moore, Alvin DeLong, Frank Irons, Nicholas Reighn, Juan Soto, Frank Smith, William Ortiz, Bernard Strobel, Carl Jones-El.

"Each of the men interviewed wore white zippered coveralls and thin cloth sandals. Two wore socks. None exhibited outward signs of maltreatment but all complained that they had been beaten, that they were not eating properly and that they have been subjected to psychological and physical abuse on a regular daily basis."

Brother Richard was asked why the rebel inmates had not returned the hostages after the granting of the twenty-eight points during the rebellion. "They weren't agreed to by Oswald," said Brother Richard. "I don't care what they told you. He never agreed to them. Oswald was a puppet. Rockefeller pulled the strings."

Champ said that Governor Rockefeller's appearance at Attica could have "changed things. He would have saved lives if he would have had the inclination to come down and see the people who he directed."

Mr. Ferretti checked with Superintendent Mancusi on the claims of Mr. Clark and Mr. Champen that they were being forced to use experimental soap and dentifrice. On the soap, said to be lye-based, Mr. Mancusi said, it was the same formula as a popular commercial brand. Mr. Mancusi said the experimental toothpaste was a popular toothpaste without the label.

NOVEMBER 16
REPORT OF GOLDMAN PANEL

On November 16 the first of the investigative panels turned in its report, and very workmanlike it was indeed. This was the panel named by Presiding Justice Harry Goldman, and the co-chairmen were Austin MacCormick of the Osborne Society and Clarence Jones of the *Amsterdam News*. It read:

"It is the panel's conclusion that, although the scars of Attica are still self-evident and although the ill-feelings between the inmates and correctional officers still smolder, the resumption of normal routine for over 80 per cent of the present population marks an end to the transitional period contemplated. . . .

"The danger of harassment of inmates continues, however, and the likelihood of unjust and inflammatory acts in parole and other areas still remains."

The Goldman Panel found there had been no physical abuse of

inmates since the day of the State Police rescue mission, that the notorious HBZ actually provided better accommodations than routine cell blocks, especially as far as shower facilities were concerned, and that the panel's own suggestion of a medical "inventory" of all the inmates had discouraged both mistreatment and false claims of mistreatment.

The Goldman Panel thanked our correctional services department personnel for co-operation to the fullest, and, indeed, we felt we had nothing to hide from these professional ombudsmen or from anybody else. Their findings were a timely corrective to the new wave of propaganda from the resourceful rebel leaders in HBZ.*

NOVEMBER 25–NOVEMBER 27
THE RAHWAY RIOT

On Thanksgiving Eve approximately 500 inmates watching a film entitled *Making It* in the auditorium of the seventy-six-year-old New Jersey State Prison at Rahway put on an epilogue of a different sort. They grabbed six corrections officers, knocked down, kicked, and lightly stabbed Warden U. Samuel Vukcevich, and barricaded themselves in two wings of the maximum-security institution. Then they hung out the window a bedsheet scrawled with the fatal slogan coined by Mr. Kunstler, REMEMBER ATTICA.

But these inmates wanted no Attica. They wanted prison reforms, not revolution, and their petition of grievances stressed rehabilitation. The Rahway leaders wrote: "We are sincerely trying to correct the mistakes we have made in the past against other people. We not only want to correct the mistakes but we wish to prevent mistakes. The help must come from you and we are desperately asking for your help."

New Jersey's Governor William T. Cahill negotiated from a school in nearby Woodbridge. And Governor Cahill said, "I would not compare Rahway with Attica." He held back a planned State Police assault, granted the same kind of pledge against physical reprisals we had granted at Attica, and promised to consider the demands for prison reforms. And at Rahway the rebels quickly accepted these proposals and set the hostages free.

* See Appendix G, "Report of the Goldman Panel."

As opposed to media which contrasted virtually bloodless Rahway with Attica, to Governor Rockefeller's and my discredit, the Albany *Times-Union* commented:

"The Rahway revolt was more or less spontaneous. The rebels came up with demands for better treatment which made good sense. Most important, they displayed a reasonable attitude which gave Governor Cahill the opportunity to arrange an honorable truce. . . .

"Governor Cahill and his advisers most assuredly are to be commended for averting a potential tragedy at Rahway. The point is that they had a chance to do so.

"Governor Rockefeller and his fellow officials, on the other hand, had no choice but to order the violent confrontation made inevitable by Attica's defiant revolutionaries."

I was particularly impressed by the manner in which Governor Cahill handled the media. He kept almost all of them out. The Troy *Record* defined the situation:

"Governor Cahill says . . . there are times and situations in which the press and TV have no business. The inmates involved in a prison riot know they can get attention by setting fires and supplying other spectacular grist for the TV mill. TV news feeds on itself. Presence of TV cameras invites spectacular actions. This condition created, what can the cameras do, but cover it?

"Then it is broadcast to the TV screens, more emotions are aroused, more trouble is likely to occur, and on and on it goes, self-perpetuating emotionalism and violence.

"TV news has two dimensions that the printed word does not have—sight and sound. These awesome potentialities carry an awesome responsibility. Newsmen in that media would do well to keep that in mind."

NOVEMBER 29–DECEMBER 2
THE PEPPER COMMITTEE HEARINGS

On November 29 Superintendent Mancusi was the lead-off witness in Washington before the first public hearings of the House of Representatives Select Committee on Crime. Congressman Claude Pepper of Florida and his fellow committee members kept Mr. Mancusi on the stand for three hours.

Vincent Mancusi ascribed the blame to the Marxists and Maoists, the conditions of unrest, the inflow of radical literature, the "increase in that segment that wants to destroy the system." But Mr. Mancusi also discounted complaints about prison conditions and he placed little emphasis on prison reform. However, when Congressman Charles B. Rangel of New York suggested that Mr. Mancusi might be using "troublemakers" as a cloak for his own anti-black sentiment, Mr. Mancusi countered that he had been the one at Attica to institute a black studies program.

After my own testimony, when I was questioned on the same point, I de-emphasized the political aspects of Attica because I did not want the Select Committee to develop tunnel vision leading away from the improvement of prison conditions and prison reform.

Walter Dunbar testified to the Select Committee that he had in good conscience, given what proved to be inaccurate reports about the castration and about more throat slashings than had actually occurred at Attica. He said, "I honestly said this because I believed it. If I erred, I erred as a human being."

The soundest counterargument against my insistence on a maxi-maximum-security institution was put during these Pepper hearings. New York State Senator John Dunne thought the institution would end up as a black concentration camp, since most of the militant leaders were blacks, and this might prove to be both a destructive force—and an undesirable element in our free society. Clarence Jones in his testimony agreed with this estimate.

Congressman Rangel of the Select Committee had previously argued: "The establishment of such a prison would only confirm what many prisoners already say—namely, that they *are* political prisoners whose punishment is measured not by their crimes against society, but by the militancy of their political beliefs. I hope the citizens of New York see this special prison plan for what it really is—a political cop-out and not a constructive response to the Attica tragedy."

But I had to consider the prompt rehabilitation of *all* of the prison population—untroubled by militants and others—and I did not want prison reform to be further delayed, or discredited in the public mind.

DECEMBER 3–DECEMBER 7
CONFERENCE AT WILLIAMSBURG

On December 3 I was astonished when a Federal Court of Appeals enjoined us from further "abuse" of the inmates at Attica, and I took the rare step of criticizing a court ruling in public. I said the court finding was in contrast to the report of the ombudsmen of the Goldman Panel and also contradicted my own sources of information at Attica. "I would never tolerate abuse or mistreatment of any inmate," I concluded, "and brutality and excess of any kind are repugnant to me."

On December 6 and December 7 I attended the first National Conference on Corrections at Williamsburg, Virginia. This was a four-day affair sponsored by the federal Justice Department, attended by more than 300 professionals in the field of crime prevention and corrections. Attica appeared to be on everybody's mind, and I was often congratulated by complete strangers who came up to me and said I had saved our rule of law.

Not long after Attica, a European magazine commented that Attica was the point at which an aroused America decided that the permissive society had gone too far and had to be turned back. From this point, so went its thesis, the country could move ahead to greatness once again. I was sure, however, that these thoughts were not in my mind during Attica.

Attorney General John Mitchell, in a prison reformist speech, announced plans for a new national corrections training academy: "I believe that it will be the most effective single means of upgrading the profession and assuring that correction is more than a euphemism for detention." Mr. Mitchell blamed recent prison riots on "a hard core of militants," and he added that he believed the disturbances themselves might "help speed the process of corrections reform, because of the public attention they have focused on the problems of the prisons."

Supreme Court Justice Warren Burger, in an admirable speech, said:

"If we tie a person in a chair for a long time, we can hardly be surprised if he can't walk when we turn him loose. Within limiting regulations necessary for basic order, inmates should be al-

lowed to think and walk and talk as we will demand that they
do when they are released.

"We cannot turn the management of a prison over to the inmates, but society as represented by the 'keepers' can listen to
what the inmates have to say.

"Those who would disrupt and destroy a penal institution must
be separated to protect those who are trying to learn and prepare
themselves for the future. Every inmate has a right to be insulated
from those who are bent on lawless acts.

"We should develop sentencing techniques to impose a sentence so that an inmate can literally '*learn* his way out' of prison,
as we now try to let him '*earn* his way out' with good behavior."

As we moved into 1972 I was able for the first time since the
Attica rebellion to re-examine my own criminological philosophy.
And it seemed to me that, to a surprising extent, we were on the
right course. Our "traditional" prison reforms were sound and
sensible in their own right, no matter how the political extremists
of left or right derided them, disbelieved in them, or sought to
make them unworkable.

We were correct to set the trend for most of the prisoners away
from the giant human warehouses, the old bastilles, and toward
community treatment centers with diagnostic facilities. We were
correct to want to tighten security for the troublemakers and the
incorrigibles. We were correct in our preference for probation and
parole and also in our moves to open up the prisons to community ombudsmen and social workers.

Of course we were on the right track toward work-release, study-
release, and family furlough visits, and our emphasis on vocational
and academic training inside the prisons was also correct. We
were right to upgrade the professional dignity and remuneration
of the professional correctional workers, including those from minority groups. We were correct to phase our programs with those
of the State Police and the courts in an over-all, co-ordinated approach to law enforcement.

Inevitably, the revolutionary pressures would have to be measured and met, and, in this, correctional work would also reflect
the attitudes and actions of society in general. There has been a
great deal of racism in the United States, and it has been difficult
for blacks, in their turn in the "melting pot," to obtain decent

housing, education, and jobs. There is a climate of rising expectations in which revolutionaries flourish. Yet here too, who is to say we are on a fundamentally wrong course?

In the last decade the employment of blacks in the professional, technical, and clerical white-collar occupations has more than doubled. Median family income for blacks is said by the United States Census Bureau and the Bureau of Labor Statistics to have risen by 50 per cent in the decade. The numbers of blacks attending and graduating from high schools, universities, and graduate schools has increased sharply.

I am not so naïve as to regard economic and social gains as a substitute for dignity and a sense of worth—yet the more we are able to show that the United States is in fact as well as in doctrine an open economy and an open society, the more all our people will feel at home in it.

I have emphasized throughout this book that the militant revolutionaries at Attica found minimal support—I would be tempted to say no support—from the larger black community. I am not about to join those who are charging off into their own fantasies of a black-versus-white confrontation that will bring the United States down into the dust. At Attica I said for all of us: "Armed rebellion of this type we had faced threatened the destruction of our free society. We cannot permit that destruction to happen."

It is, in fact, increasingly urgent for us to get our economy and our society into shape, because the revolutionary threat is fundamental. Listen to Angela Davis, in a personally copyrighted article in the New York *Times*:

"Prisons have recently witnessed an accelerated influx of militant political activists. In utter disregard of the institutions' totalitarian aspirations, the passions and theories of black and Socialist revolution have penetrated the wall. . . . Prisoners have recognized that their immediate objective must be to challenge the oppression which finds concrete expression in the penal system.

"It was precisely this new thrust which determined the content of the Attica prison revolt."

There it is. And this is why prison reform is no longer an option for us. It is a necessity.

The deeper problem of crime and criminality goes beyond even the competition between a humane society and a dynamic revolution. Lenin recognized crime to be as serious a concern for a communist as for a capitalist state. And just as we in corrections are in the front line of the political struggle, so must we also recognize the dimension of the psychological and related factors involved.

Who are the criminals and why do they become such? There are many theories of criminality and many modifications of the theories. Some have reduced crime to subjective mechanisms or to objective compulsions. The determinists have denied the possibility of responsibility and say there is only accountability. Others have ignored the role of influences and motivations.

The projection of responsibility for our actions upon things outside ourselves is hardly new. Homer voiced a reaction to it on the *Odyssey* when he wrote, "Look you now, how vainly mortal men do blame the Gods! For of us they say comes evil, whereas they, even of themselves, through the blindness of their own hearts, have sorrows beyond that which is ordained." Or, as Aristotle wrote, "Is it meant . . . that we act voluntarily in doing what is right, and involuntarily in doing what is discreditable?"

The criminal, like each one of us, is born with the ability to distinguish between good and evil. He has a sense of "oughtness," but the identification of good and evil values is largely inculcated through the primary social groups, the family, the school, the parish, the neighborhood, and so on. The social order being inculcated into the individual is then enforced by social sanctions. Violation is possible. The formulation of the norm presupposes its violation.

None of this gets to the root of violence in humans, of course, but never knowing all the answers lends a curious dignity to men.

In our corrections work, as Robert MacIver once said, "We heed a clear sense of direction, the warm light of a guiding principle, the sense of a goal toward which we move."

We must remember never to let chaos act as the umpire. We must not claim obedience when it is not due. We must not excuse the refusal of it when it is due. We must aim at justice with its *suum cuique*, "to each his own," but remember that justice without charity can be cruelty.

We should be more angry with theft than before, but kinder

to thieves than before. We must forgive the criminal but not excuse the crime. To excuse behavior, to deny some degree of responsibility (except for psychotics), to declare criminals to be inwardly powerless is not kindness but rather a more refined cruelty, since it denies and even defrauds them of an active role. Rehabilitation lies in an active will, not a passive one.

We need a balanced viewpoint, of course. We must declare responsibility when it exists and not where it does not exist. We must credit the influences from within and without and the responsibility shared by all of us in the community. Yet we must not also surrender our own human values at the demand either of doctrine or of circumstances.

How should we treat our criminals in the end, then? Should we treat them as they treat us? Should we react emotionally in a spirit of revenge and cry out against the criminals as they cry out against us?

Do we seek simplistic solutions, demand helplessly that something be done by someone, fret against uncomprehending priorities? Or do we rededicate ourselves to the patient, hard work which is neither soft for those performing it nor for the offenders upon whom it is spent?

Only hard work in corrections, specifically, and by our clients, specifically, can change anti-social habits. And we must always believe that men *can* change. Aristotle, again, suggested, "The law has no power to command obedience except that of habit, which can only be given by time." And we must admit that daring, imaginative, confident, capable leadership has not always distinguished the corrections scene in the United States—even while we pay tribute to the reformers and humanitarians who have led us a long way from the dungeon and the whipping post.

Those of us who are now privileged in the 1970s to work in this grim but historic field ought to feel honored that ours has been selected as an arena for new revolutionary struggle. We are honored to give of ourselves in attempting to bring about adjustments in our maladjusted brothers. Progressive penology has not been without its setbacks, and never will be. But our programs—there is that word again—do in fact do inestimable good every day of every week, reuniting families, restoring hope, patching a life, forgiving those who trespass against us.

To rehabilitate?

What does it mean?

Webster once defined it:

"To invest or clothe again with some right, authority, or dignity.

"To restore to a former capacity.

"To restore, as a delinquent, to a former right, rank, or privilege lost or forfeited (a term primarily of civil or canon law).

"To put on a proper basis, or into a previous good state, again."

The worst of Attica is now over.

We must move forward with prison reform at the highest possible speed—and with the utmost determination. Yet we must all never forget these tragic days—as we who bear the scars will never forget them.

We who have lived have gone through sorrow and agony—and those who cannot remember the past are indeed doomed to repeat it.

APPENDIXES

APPENDIX A

Letters to the Commissioner from Prisoners at Attica

Letters to the Commissioner from Prisoners at Attica

Dear Mr. Oswald:

Having been incarcerated in Attica Prison during the recent riot, I feel I must write you words of praise, respect, sympathy, and constructive criticism.

First and foremost I want to emphasize that you had no choice, but to do as you did! If it had gone on further you might have had all the hostages dead!

I was not in D Block during the riot, but I did know L. D. Barclay, Flip Crowley, and Champ personally and I can honestly state that they were avid, militant revolutionaries who would not have given up without killing the hostages! They were some of the leaders.

From talking to numerous inmates who were in D Block all during the riot, I can tell you that every preparation was made to carry out the murder of the hostages! I won't go into detail 'cause you will get that information from the investigators.

I admire your courage. It took great courage to enter D Block as you did and even greater courage, of a different type, to make the decision you made to send the troopers in.

It will be hard to face the adverse criticism of some, but you were the one who had to make the decision under extreme stress and anguish. You did it, and no one should second-guess you.

Hindsight is 20/20 vision so naturally, now that everyone knows what happened, they can all come up with a better solution. You didn't have those after-facts at your finger tips.

Let them criticize. Ignore them and go on and do the job you were trying to do.

The mark of a man is how he reacts to adversity. You have shown yourself to be a man so keep it up.

Now I will proceed with the constructive criticism.

When you are dealing with fanatics you can't bargain!!! Every concession you make will be taken as a sign of weakness! You must be firm and decisive!

Knowing many of the leaders of this riot and knowing that, at the most, only 10 per cent of the population was actually for the riot, I can honestly state this riot was not really against prison conditions. Prison conditions were the excuse. The riot was 100 per cent politically motivated! The leaders and their followers were mostly Black Panthers, Young Lords, and Sam Melville's group of white activists.

Those people never talked about prison conditions! They constantly talked about the violent overthrow of the "oppressive, capitalistic, imperialistic, and racist establishment" and, brother, that is a fact!

You cannot rehabilitate that type of person! They are convinced they have done only what the "system" has forced them to do. They brainwash each other.

It is terribly hard to admit when you are wrong, so they rationalize and blame their conduct on their reaction to the "system" when in reality they make the choice.

As long as you don't sort out the political fanatics and radicals of all ilk and isolate them from the general population, you will have serious trouble.

You are a progressive man, and to a degree that is good, but progress at any cost is no good.

What is rehabilitation other than a widely misused word?

Rehabilitation is when a man decides he has been a damned fool to lead the life he has led and sincerely makes up his mind to do better. It must come from within the person and at his will.

All the education, all the vocational training and removal of walls etc. will do no good unless you can motivate a man to want to change for the better.

I am all for the above but I don't see how they change a man's character. A man's character is what must be changed—not his educational level! We are putting the cart before the horse. I know a little of what I am talking about.

Men must be taught self-discipline, self-respect, kindness, integrity, etc. and then improve their education.

I want you to consider what you would do if you went to school in prison and got a high school education and some college credits only to find that you could not become a CPA, insurance agent, hotel manager, doctor, lawyer, bank teller, couldn't legally work in a supermarket, hotel, or restaurant where alcoholic beverages were sold, couldn't work in a store, hotel, gas station, as a salesman etc. where you needed to be bonded, couldn't work for the post office, be a male nurse, etc. etc. You too would be disillusioned!

What the hell incentive does an intelligent, young, ex-con have to better himself when everywhere he turns he finds obstacles? He has served his sentence but he has to pay for the rest of his life.

Extra-legal punishment is where the reform should take place.

As things now stand you cut a guy's legs off by giving him a felony, then you fit him with artificial legs by giving him an education, then you put up a buzzsaw to saw off his wooden legs by restricting what he can attain with his education.

Self-pity is the biggest handicap we cons must overcome, but that does not take away the validity of my criticisms.

Well, enough of that! My principal purpose in writing was to say that at least 65 per cent of the cons realize you did what you felt you had to and we could see no alternative. We hope you do not retire and we hope the Governor has the courage to stick by you.

We need you and the state needs you. I've had times, when I met the parole board, that I would like to have spit in your eye, but I admire a man of courage and compassion and you showed me you have both: courage by making the hardest decision of your life and compassion by waiting as long as you did.

God bless you.

Dear Mr. Oswald:

I am writing this letter to express my sorrow for the deaths of the employees here on Sept. 13, 1971. To those on the outside, these men were husbands, sons, loved ones, and fathers. But the people on the outside fail to realize that many of these men were father images to us who never had a father and all of them were counselors in the true meaning of the word.

There are some of us here at Attica who were not involved in the riot and feel that they are being treated unfair. Some of us here risked personal danger because they armed themselves and protected some of the employees in the area in which they are assigned.

In fact I and another inmate protected six civilian teachers and one officer with the only weapons that were available, which consisted of two thermos bottles of boiling water and a couple of broom handles.

Now that things are getting back to order, I find that all my personal possessions have been destroyed, including all of my legal papers.

These possessions were not destroyed by rioting inmates, but instead by the officers who went through the cells and stripped them bare. I come from a poor family and they cannot afford to replace the papers that were destroyed. The fact that I was not involved in the riot would seem that I merit some consideration.

While many people have belittled you for ordering the assault Sept. 13, 1971, I want you to know that I realize that you had no other choice and I am sure that your vast years of experience led you to that decision.

Instead of them condemning you, you should be commended. Many of us here all believed you and pray that whatever decisions you may make in the future be as just and fair as they have in the past. We know that you are for Penal Reform but we also know that a change takes time.

Thank you and may God bless you.

Respectfully yours . . .

Dear Mr. Oswald:

I am writing this letter to you to express the feelings of many of us who are incarcerated here. Much has been said concerning, What should be done to us, and with us, because of the dreadful event of September 13, 1971. Sir, very little has been said by various media regarding what was done by a great many of us, as a result of the past aid in rehabilitation by the many Officers and Civilians, including many who did [succeed in rehabilitation] and officials of this institution [who helped].

It may be true, that when our past performances in the Society that incarcerated us looks at our past records, they may feel justified in their attitudes. The past is exactly what it is, the Past. It seems that we are all thought to be sub-human animals, completely lacking in regard for the lives of Officers and Civilians with only self-serving interest in getting what we want, no matter who it hurts, abuse of Officers and Civilians, contempt for Society and law, and running to the Constitution for protection against retaliation by those we abuse. This may be true with some, however, not with all of us.

There are those of us who had great concern for the Officers and Civilians in our areas, at the time of the riot on September 9th. It did not take the thinking out as to whether or not we should help them. There was no time to reflect on their past dealings with us. There was just the human desire and need to aid someone whose life was at stake. We knew that we would suffer the possibility of serious harm, death, or future retribution from other inmates by our actions.

In many cases, many of us were hurt, some seriously. Many of us took up weapons, not against these people, but in defense of these people. Some of us spoke to the groups around us and dominated their will to oppose us in saving these people. Thermos bottles of hot boiling water were heated and given to civilian teachers where no other weapon was available, while outside other inmates were yelling for us to keep hostages. Some of us refused to accept the surrender and keys from Officers and enabled them to find a way for the safety of everyone including ourselves, which they did.

We feel a great personal loss in the fact that human lives were bartered, subjected to torture, and finally killed, plus those who were intimidated, beaten, and killed on the other side. Much is absent from our lives because of this sad event.

Much is said about first offenders being separated and given special treatment, without the insight nor the acceptance that first offenders are often those who just finally were caught and are being finally punished.

It in no way means that they have no prior history of anti-social or criminal behavior. There are men who are second and third offenders, who have gotten the message years ago, but time and punishment still continues for them. My first-hand knowledge is that it was in almost every instance, a second or third offender who did his utmost to protect the lives of Officers and Civilians and in most cases succeeded.

Rehabilitation is not a group or collective system by which a method is found that changes the thinking of individuals by its application. Rehabilitation is a method and state by which the individual desires to change his own set of circumstances, develop new values, and the adoption of ethical and moral behavior patterns. The fear of going to prison is not and should not be the reason that man does what is right.

Man should do right because he is motivated in that way. Certainly, this is no easy task. It requires study of both moral and civil law. It requires observation of those whose custody you are placed in, and above all it requires human relations with all to whom you have contact with, Officers, Civilians, and Inmates.

Now our real problem has begun. The deaths of the many Officers and Civilians represent a personal loss to many of us. I have known many of them for some years and while not perfect, they were fair and not brutal.

I have seen no brutality here. Each inmate has always been treated according to the manner in which he carried himself. Further proof of their lack of reason lies in the fact that they hurt Captain Wald, a man who was most sympathetic to inmate problems, always willing to listen to us and help. The same can be said of Lt. Maroney and many others. It is our loss also.

Do not think that we are proud of what happened here. Do not think that we take great pleasure in the fact that men died or suffered in the hands of some here, who would never have received that same or even the thought of such cruelty as they gave. There are those of us that question their demands for religious freedom when by their very actions, they showed a lack of Christian ideals.

We now suffer the stigma of this deed, and the curses and expressions of hate for what was done here, silently. We see the mistrust, fear, and hurt in the eyes of the Officers who still work here.

We imagine the turmoil of you, the Commissioner who had great hopes for better solutions, and lifted our hopes beyond our dreams, by your sincerity and desire for change. We turn our heads from the Warden and his staff who had already brought changes to our situation, because we all feel the guilt of the crime that has been perpetrated.

We also realize that many of them still do not know how we

tried to help and who we are. We are afraid, not of being beaten, not of being killed or abused by the Officers, that has never been our fear. We who hope to leave here, fit for society, hoping to be received as citizens without fear, fear for those who have a lot of time to go or that may come here in the future.

I watch the Officers, Civilians, and Chaplains continue to try to aid us, and wonder why so many lies have been told about their past actions, and realize that the society that failed us did so no greater than we failed ourselves.

We wonder now who will help us, who will we seek counsel from, who should even care. We suffer the restrictions, anxiety, and hurt that is imposed or felt here because of what was done. We pray that Justice will prevail where Justice is due.

Sir: I pray that God inspire you to continue your job, to remember that we all share your feelings and that we reject this means used by the others in the name of Justice. That we do not and will not ever subscribe to these acts.

We hope that you will not cease in your efforts to find a better way for us, and be guided by that which is fair and humane.

We wish that there was help for us who had no part in this thing, but, we all must suffer because of it.

Our only consolation lies in the fact that for this act we are innocent, and our choice for a better future is to merit our freedom, through honest, humane, and reasonable ways, for in fact, any other way freedom will always be an illusive bird.

Sincere hopes for the speedy health of yours.

Respectfully Yours . . .

APPENDIX B

The Hostages Who Died

The Hostages Who Died

EDWARD T. CUNNINGHAM, Sergeant, Corrections Officer
Born: June 17, 1919
Married (wife, Helen), two children
Education: High School, Yonkers, New York
Military: Sergeant in 43rd Infantry Division during World War II
Wounded, Purple Heart
Bronze Star Medal with cluster
Background: Appointed officer at Coxsackie Correctional Facility,
1949; while at Coxsackie took special courses in
human behavior, correctional group management,
and fundamentals of supervision

JOHN JOSEPH D'ARCANGELO, JR., Corrections Officer
Born: November 11, 1947
Married (wife, Ann)
Education: Liverpool Senior High School, Liverpool, New York,
September 1962–June 1966
Auburn Community College, Auburn, New York,
September 1966–June 1969, Liberal Arts
Background: Appointed to Attica June 1971

ELMER G. HARDIE, Industrial Foreman
Born: March 16, 1913
Married (wife, Elizabeth), eight children
Education: St. Mary's, Buffalo, New York
Technical High School, Buffalo, New York
Bryant & Stratton Business School, Buffalo, New York
Background: Native of Buffalo, New York; resident of Attica,
New York
Formerly a businessman
Appointed to Attica August 1968

HERBERT W. JONES, Senior Account Clerk, Industries
Born: January 4, 1945
Married, one child
Education: University of Ottawa, Ottawa, Canada
              Bryant & Stratton Business School, Buffalo, New York
              Sam Houston State Teachers College, Huntsville,
                Texas
Military: Sergeant in U. S. Air Force, 1966–70
Background: Native of Attica
              Appointed to Attica April 1971

RICHARD JAMES LEWIS, Corrections Officer
Born: August 21, 1929
Married (wife, Beverly)
Education: Batavia High School, Batavia, New York, 1943–47
Military: U. S. Army, 1951–53
Background: Appointed to Attica January 1959

JOHN G. MONTELEONE, Industrial Foreman
Born: November 2, 1929
Married (wife, Ardith)
Education: Perry High School, Perry, New York, 1944–47
Military: U. S. National Guard, 1947–51
Background: Appointed temporarily to Attica July 1967
              Appointed permanently to Attica May 1968

WILLIAM E. QUINN, Corrections Officer
Born: 1943
Married (wife, Nancy Ann), two children
Education: Attica Central School, Attica, New York
Background: Worked at J. N. Adam School, Perrysburg, New
                York; West Seneca School for the Mentally Re-
                tarded; Iroquois Gas Corporation
              Member of Attica Fire Department
              Attended Green Haven State Prison Officers School,
                March 1970–May 1970
              Appointed to Attica May 1970

CARL W. VALONE, Corrections Officer
Born: June 11, 1927

Married (wife, Ann L.)
Education: Batavia High School, Batavia, New York, 1940–45
Military: U. S. Army, 1945–47
Background: Appointed temporarily to Attica December 1962
Appointed permanently to Green Haven Correctional Facility January 1963
Transferred to Attica September 1964

ELON F. WERNER, Principal Account Clerk
Born: September 16, 1907
Married (wife, Ruth)
Education: Attica High School, Attica, New York
Syracuse University, 1947
Background: Member of Attica Fire Department
Appointed to Attica as Account Clerk, February 1959
Appointed provisional Senior Account Clerk, July 1961
Appointed permanent Senior Account Clerk, September 1961
Appointed provisional Principal Account Clerk, June 1965
Appointed permanent Principal Account Clerk, January 1971

RONALD D. WERNER, Corrections Officer
Born: December 3, 1936
Married
Education: Alexander Central High School, Alexander, New York, 1951–55
Military: U. S. Air Force, 1956–60
Background: Appointed at Green Haven Correctional Facility, February 1963
Transferred to Attica November 1964

HARRISON WILLIAM WHALEN, Corrections Officer
Born: July 9, 1934
Married
Education: High School Equivalency Diploma
Military: U. S. Navy, 1951–56

Background: Resident of Alexander, New York
                   Appointed at Attica 1958
                   Transferred to Auburn 1959
                   Transferred to Matteawan State Hospital 1959–60
                   Transferred to Attica 1960

APPENDIX C

The Hostages Who Survived

The Hostages Who Survived

Hostages Rescued or Released September 9

C.O. Raymond Bogard
C.O. Roger Dawson
C.O. Richard Delany
C.O. Donald Head
C.O. Kenneth Jennings
C.O. Gordon Kelsey
C.O. Donald Melvin
C.O. Royal Morgan
C.O. Paul Rosecrans

The Hostages Released September 10–12

C.O. James Clute
C.O. Anthony Sangiacomo

The Hostages Rescued September 13

Capt. Franklin Wald

Lt. Robert Curtiss

Sgt. Gerald Reger

C.O. Donald Almeter

C.O. Richard Fargo

C.O. Elmer Huehn

C.O. Lynn Johnson

C.O. Frank Kline

C.O. Paul Krotz

C.O. Larry Lyons

C.O. Anthony Prave

C.O. Arthur Smith

C.O. Eugene Smith

C.O. Michael Smith

C.O. Dean Stenschorn

C.O. John Stockholm

C.O. Frank Strollo

C.O. Gary Walker

C.O. Philip Watkins

C.O. Dean Wright

C.O. Walter Zymowski

Robert Van Buren
(Industrial Supt.)

Gordon Knickerbocker
(Sr. Stores Clerk)

Ronald Kozlowski
(Sr. Acct. Clerk)

Edward Miller
(Industrial Foreman)

Frederick Miller
(Industrial Foreman)

Allen Mitzel
(Industrial Foreman)

Albert Robbins
(Garage Supervisor)

APPENDIX D

The Prisoners Who Died

The Prisoners Who Died

WILLIAM ALLEN, Bronx, New York
Manslaughter, 2nd degree—4 years
Bronx County Supreme Court
Sentenced January 19, 1970

PREVIOUS CRIMINAL RECORD

6/19/67   Committed to New York City Reformatory
12/28/67   Petit larceny—suspended sentence

ELLIOTT JAMES BARCLAY, Rochester, New York
Forgery and parole violation

PREVIOUS CRIMINAL RECORD

None

JOHN BARNES, Brooklyn, New York
Attempted robbery, 3rd degree—5 years
Kings County Supreme Court
Sentenced January 16, 1968

PREVIOUS CRIMINAL RECORD

No adult convictions

BERNARD DAVIS, New York, New York
Robbery, 2nd degree—7 years
Robbery, 3rd degree—7 years
Queens County Supreme Court
Sentenced December 2, 1970

PREVIOUS CRIMINAL RECORD

1/24/67   Committed to Elmira Reception Center—3 years
1/13/69   Criminal trespass—conditional discharge

ALLEN DURHAM, Brooklyn, New York
                    Murder, 2nd degree—20 years to life
                    Kings County Supreme Court
                    Sentenced September 17, 1968

PREVIOUS CRIMINAL RECORD
Two juvenile convictions

WILLIE FULLER, Apopka, Florida
                    Rape, 1st degree—10 to 20 years
                    Wayne County Court
                    Sentenced October 31, 1960

PREVIOUS CRIMINAL RECORD
12/30/56   Disorderly conduct—90 days
5/10/58   Vagrancy—fined
10/3/59   Simple larceny—4 months

MELVIN DUVALL GRAY, Rochester, New York
                    Criminal selling of dangerous drug—15 years
                    Monroe County Court
                    Sentenced January 7, 1970

PREVIOUS CRIMINAL RECORD
7/16/67   Unlawful possession of narcotic drug—probation five
                    years

ROBERT FRANCIS JOSEPH HANIGAN, Valley Cottage, N.Y.
                    Murder, 2nd degree—20 years to life
                    Rockland County Court
                    Sentenced January 27, 1965

PREVIOUS CRIMINAL RECORD
1/14/61   Assault, 3rd degree—fined and 60 days suspended
                    sentence

KENNETH HESS, Binghamton, New York*
                    Grand larceny, 3rd degree—4 years
                    Broome County Court
                    Sentenced May 13, 1971

* Killed by fellow inmates during rebellion.

PREVIOUS CRIMINAL RECORD

2/19/66   Public intoxication—7 days
5/24/66   Disorderly conduct—30 days
7/1/66   Disorderly conduct—30 days
7/19/66   Assault, 3rd degree—10 days
8/2/66   Assault, 3rd degree—25 days
9/5/66   Resisting arrest and assault on a police officer—3 years

THOMAS HICKS, Queens, New York
                    Robbery, 2nd degree—7 years
                    Kings County Supreme Court
                    Sentenced June 5, 1969

PREVIOUS CRIMINAL RECORD

7/13/57   Petit larceny—committed to New York City Reform-
           atory
6/14/58   Disorderly conduct—fined
11/20/58   Unlawful entry—1 year
11/5/60   Robbery, 2nd degree—5 to 10 years

EMANUEL JOHNSON, Brooklyn, New York
                    Robbery, 3rd degree—5 to 8 years
                    Kings County Supreme Court
                    Sentenced May 24, 1967

PREVIOUS CRIMINAL RECORD

3/17/60   Attempted petit larceny—60 days
12/26/60   Assault, 3rd degree—committed to New York City Pen-
           itentiary
10/22/63   Assault, 3rd degree—time served
2/13/64   Assault, 3rd degree—6 months
12/4/64   Robbery, 2nd degree—2½ to 5 years

CHARLES LUNDY, New York, New York
                    Attempted murder—15 years
                    Robbery, 1st degree—15 years
                    Assault, 1st degree—15 years
                    Assault, 2nd degree—7 years
                    New York Supreme Court
                    Sentenced March 13, 1969

PREVIOUS CRIMINAL RECORD
9/19/62   Affray—fined
1/5/68   Disorderly conduct—bond forfeited
4/23/68   Petit larceny—conditional discharge

KENNETH IVEY MALLOY, Queens, New York
              Robbery, 2nd degree—3 years 9 months to 10 years
              Queens County Supreme Court
              Sentenced January 19, 1968

PREVIOUS CRIMINAL RECORD
11/4/60   Petit larceny—New York City Penitentiary
2/27/62   Escape from custody—6 months
10/15/62 Petit larceny—6 months
4/27/64   Robbery, 2nd degree—5 years

GIDELL MARTIN, Brooklyn, New York
              Attempted possession of dangerous weapon—4 years
              Kings County Supreme Court
              Sentenced April 20, 1970

PREVIOUS CRIMINAL RECORD
8/9/57   Auto theft—1 year
2/15/62   Disorderly conduct—90 days
5/23/67   Petit larceny—1 year

WILLIAM MCKINNEY, Brooklyn, New York
              Manslaughter, 1st degree—20 years
              Attempted assault, 1st degree—7 years
              Possession of weapon—7 years
              Kings County Supreme Court
              Sentenced January 26, 1971

PREVIOUS CRIMINAL RECORD
11/25/58 Assault, 3rd degree—committed to New York City Re-
              formatory
2/15/61   Attempted petit larceny—60 days
12/30/65 Violation of the Public Health Law (marijuana)—60
              months suspended sentence

LORENZO MCNEIL, Queens, New York
Robbery, 3rd degree—5 to 7 years
Queens County Supreme Court
Sentenced June 23, 1965

PREVIOUS CRIMINAL RECORD
9/28/57 Disorderly conduct—suspended sentence
9/24/59 Attempted robbery, 3rd degree—2½ to 5 years

SAMUEL J. MELVILLE, New York, New York
Arson, 1st degree—6 to 18 years
Reckless endangerment, 1st degree—2 years 4 months to 7 years
Assault, 2nd degree—2 years 4 months to 7 years
New York Supreme Court
Sentenced June 19, 1970

PREVIOUS CRIMINAL RECORD
None

JOSÉ MENTIJO, New York, New York
Assault, 1st degree—10 years
New York Supreme Court
Sentenced June 24, 1971

PREVIOUS CRIMINAL RECORD
12/23/53 Criminal possession of pistol—(committed to New York City Reformatory)
5/19/55 Possession of narcotic drug—30 days
6/14/55 Violation of parole—returned to New York City Reformatory
3/26/56 Possession of narcotic drug—60 days
8/1/58 Attempt to feloniously possess narcotic drug—1 year 6 months to 1 year 9 months
11/29/60 Unlawful possession of narcotic drug—6 months
2/26/62 Attempted criminal possession of a pistol—3 to 5 years
10/21/63 Sale of narcotic drug (Federal Court)—4 years (to begin upon expiration of New York State sentence)
2/5/71 Reckless endangerment, 1st degree—3 months

MILTON MENYWEATHER III, Buffalo, New York
                    Attempted arson, 1st degree—10 years
                    Erie County Court
                    Sentenced November 24, 1970

PREVIOUS CRIMINAL RECORD

Three juvenile arrests
9/10/68   Possession of dangerous weapon and harassment—6
          months
9/30/68   Criminal tampering—6 months

CARLOS JOSEPH PRESCOTT, Rochester, New York
                    Murder, 1st degree—25 years to life
                    Monroe County Court
                    Sentenced February 5, 1970

PREVIOUS CRIMINAL RECORD

None

MICHAEL PRIVITERA, Buffalo, New York*
                    Murder, 1st degree—25 years to life
                    Monroe County Court
                    Sentenced October 14, 1968

PREVIOUS CRIMINAL RECORD

1/23/50   Disorderly conduct and resisting arrest—suspended sen-
          tence
10/2/53   Assault, 3rd degree—1 year
5/26/55   Disorderly conduct—suspended sentence
 7/5/55   Possession of instruments used in administering narcotics
          —1 year
5/10/57   Attempted grand larceny, 2nd degree—1 year 3 months
          to 2½ years
7/26/62   Petit larceny—1 year
7/15/64   Attempted grand larceny, 2nd degree—2 to 4 years

RAYMOND RIVERA, Bronx, New York
                    Criminal possession of dangerous drug—3 years
                    Bronx County Supreme Court
                    Sentenced March 10, 1970

* Killed by fellow inmates during the rebellion.

PREVIOUS CRIMINAL RECORD

10/15/64 Possession of policy slips—fined or 20 days in jail
6/10/68 Criminally selling dangerous drugs—consolidated with
above 3-year sentence

JAMES ROBINSON, New York, New York
Murder, 1st degree—natural life
New York Supreme Court
Sentenced November 27, 1968

PREVIOUS CRIMINAL RECORD

4/9/61 Grand larceny of automobile—committed to Morrison
Training School, escaped
1/15/62 Interstate transportation of motor vehicle—3 years
10/24/64 Larceny of automobile—1 to 1½ years
1/18/65 Assault with deadly weapon—1½ years
10/9/67 Assault, 3rd degree, and petit larceny—9 months

SANTIAGO SANTOS, Bronx, New York
Burglary, 3rd degree—4 years
Bronx County Supreme Court
Sentenced June 12, 1970

PREVIOUS CRIMINAL RECORD

4/27/67 Petit larceny—7 months
7/26/68 Attempted grand larceny—10 months

BARRY JAY SCHWARTZ, Queens, New York*
Manslaughter, 1st degree—10 to 20 years
Attempted robbery, 3rd degree—5 to 10 years
Queens County Supreme Court
Sentenced November 22, 1968

PREVIOUS CRIMINAL RECORD

2/1/65 Leaving the scene of accident—60 days
10/11/65 Petit larceny—probation
3/25/66 Attempted burglary, 3rd degree—suspended sentence
and probation
5/10/66 Disorderly conduct—30 days

* Killed by fellow inmates during the rebellion.

7/5/66 Violation of probation—committed to Matteawan State Hospital

1/20/67 Unlawful entry—suspended sentence of 60 days

HAROLD THOMAS, New York, New York
Robbery, 1st degree (4 counts)—10 to 20 years
Robbery, 2nd degree (4 counts)—7½ to 15 years
New York Supreme Court
Sentenced May 14, 1968

PREVIOUS CRIMINAL RECORD

3/27/61 Proceedings in sanity following arrest for robbery—committed to Matteawan State Hospital

8/8/63 Petit larceny—1 year

7/22/64 Possession of narcotic drugs—60 days

RAFAEL VASQUEZ, Bronx, New York
Attempted assault, 2nd degree—3 years
Bronx County Supreme Court
Sentenced October 26, 1970

PREVIOUS CRIMINAL RECORD

None

MELVIN WARE, New York, New York
Robbery, 3rd degree—5 years
Queens County Supreme Court
Sentenced November 25, 1969

PREVIOUS CRIMINAL RECORD

2/3/61 Petit larceny—probation

1/8/62 Attempted assault, 3rd degree, and possession of weapon —discharged on own recognizance

8/26/66 Resisting arrest and disorderly conduct—60 days

WILLIE WEST, Buffalo, New York
Robbery, 2nd degree—15 years
Burglary, 3rd degree—7 years
Grand larceny, 2nd degree—7 years
Erie County Court
Sentenced November 19, 1970

PREVIOUS CRIMINAL RECORD

Three juvenile arrests

10/9/62   Assault, 3rd degree—suspended sentence

11/13/64   Drinking in public—fined

6/25/65   Possession of marijuana—sentenced to Elmira Reception Center

ALFRED L. WILLIAMS, Buffalo, New York

Manslaughter, 1st degree—20 years
Robbery, 1st degree—10 to 15 years
Robbery, 3rd degree—7 years
Erie County Court
Sentenced March 31, 1971

PREVIOUS CRIMINAL RECORD

1/15/57   Auto theft—indeterminate term in Ohio State Reformatory

10/28/64   Unlawful possession of stolen property—1 year

5/23/66   Assault, 3rd degree—1 year

4/26/68   Theft by breaking and entering—3 months

Breakdown by Crime of Conviction of Attica Inmate Fatalities

Murder or attempted murder	6*
Manslaughter	4*
Assault	2
Arson	2
Rape	1
Robbery	9
Sale of narcotics	1
Burglary	1
Possession of dangerous weapon	1
Grand larceny	1*
Possession of drugs	1
Other	1

* Including one killed by fellow inmates during the rebellion.

APPENDIX E

*Members of the
Citizens Observer Committee
at Attica*

Members of Citizens Observer Committee, Attica

David Anderson (former executive director, Rochester Urban League)

Congressman Herman Badillo

Alberto O. Cappas (connected with SUNY-Albany)

Reverend Marion Chandler (FIGHT, Rochester)

State Senator John R. Dunne (and his assistant James Helmus)

Assemblyman Arthur O. Eve

Assemblyman James Emery

W. O. Fitch (National Law Office, Washington)

Reverend Franklin Florence (FIGHT, Rochester)

William Gaiter (BUILD, Buffalo)

State Senator Robert Garcia

James Ingraham (*Michigan Chronicle*, Detroit)

Ken Jackson (Fortune Society)

Clarence B. Jones (publisher, *Amsterdam News*, New York City)

Reverend Jaybarr Ali Kenyatta (Sunni Muslim sect, Los Angeles)

William M. Kunstler

State Senator Thomas F. McGowan

Alfredo Matthew, Jr. (Superintendent, Community School District No. 3, New York City)

Juan Ortiz (Young Lords)

José "G.I." Paris (Young Lords)

Mel Rivers (Fortune Society)

Domingo Rodriquez (BUILD)

Richard Roth (Buffalo *Courier-Express*)

David Rothenberg (Fortune Society)

Herman Schwartz (University of Buffalo)

Reverend B. T. Scott (FIGHT, Rochester)

Daniel Skoler (American Bar Association, Washington)

Thomas Soto (Prisoners' Solidarity League; Youth Against War
    and Fascism)
Lewis M. Steel (National Lawyers Guild)
Julian Tepper (National Law Office, Washington)
Reverend Wyatt Tee Walker
Assemblyman Frank Walkley
Assemblyman Clark C. Wemple
Tom Wicker (New York *Times*)

APPENDIX F

General Rules Governing Parole
in New York State

General Rules Governing Parole

In accepting parole you promised the Board of Parole which voted your release, to faithfully observe the following conditions of your parole. These conditions are in effect until the expiration of your maximum sentence. A violation of these or any other conditions imposed by the Board may result in your return to the institution.

These conditions are as follows:

1. Upon your release, proceed directly to the place to which you have been paroled and within twenty-four hours, make your arrival report to your parole officer. When you make your arrival report, you must have in your possession the money you received at the time of your release, except necessary expenditures of funds for travel, food and shelter.

2. Do not leave the State of New York nor the community to which you have been paroled without the written permission of your parole officer.

3. You must carry out the instructions of your parole officer, reporting as he directs, and permitting him to visit you at your residence and place of employment. Do not change your residence nor employment without first securing permission of your parole officer. If, for any reason, you lose your position, immediately report this fact to your parole officer. Every effort must be made by you to secure gainful employment and you must cooperate with your parole officer in his efforts to obtain employment for you.

4. You must conduct yourself as a good citizen. You must not associate with evil companions nor any individuals having crim-

inal records; you must avoid questionable resorts, abstain from wrongdoing, lead an honest, upright and industrious life, support your dependents, if any, and assume towards them all your moral and legal obligations. Your behavior must not be a menace to the safety of your family nor to any individual or group of individuals.

5. You will avoid the excessive use of alcoholic beverages. You will abstain completely from the use of alcoholic beverages, if so directed by your parole officer.

6. You will not live as man and wife with anyone to whom you are not legally married and you will not have sexual relations with anyone not your lawful spouse. You will obtain written permission from your parole officer before you apply for a license to marry.

7. You will surrender to your parole officer immediately after release any Motor Vehicle License which you have and you will not apply for a Motor Vehicle License nor own an automobile while you are on parole without the permission of your parole officer. If, while on parole, you purchase a motor vehicle without obtaining permission of your parole officer, or operate a motor vehicle without a valid license, it will be a violation of parole. A valid license will be deemed to be one issued subsequent to release on parole after permission has been obtained.

8. You will not purchase, own nor possess firearms of any nature without the written permission of your parole officer. If you carry firearms of any nature without a valid license, it will be considered a violation of parole. A valid license will be deemed to be one issued subsequent to release on parole after permission has been obtained.

9. You will not accept employment in any capacity where alcoholic beverages are made or sold without the written approval of the State Liquor Authority and your parole officer.

10. You will not correspond with inmates of any correctional or penal institution without the written permission of your parole officer. You will not carry from the institution from which you are released or send to any correctional institution, whether in New York State or elsewhere, any written or verbal message, or

any object or property of any kind whatsoever, unless you have obtained specific permission to do so from the Warden, Superintendent or other duly authorized officers of both the institution from which you are released and the institution to which the message, object or other property is to be delivered.

11. You will reply promptly to any communication from a member of the Board of Parole, a parole officer, or an authorized representative of the Board of Parole.

12. You understand that any reports, either verbal or written, made to or submitted by you to a parole officer, which are subsequently found to be false, will be rejected by the Board of Parole, and will not be used in crediting parole time served, and in addition may be considered violations of parole.

13. Before being released on parole you must agree in writing that should you be arrested in another state during the period of your parole, you agree to waive extradition and not resist being returned by the Board of Parole to the State of New York.

14. If you were sentenced to a State Prison or if you were committed to a Correctional Institution for Mental Defectives after conviction of a felony or received an indeterminate sentence with a commitment to the Reception Center, you will not register as a voter and you will not vote in any primary, special or general election because under these sentences your right of franchise was revoked.

15. You will report to your parole officer each and every time you are arrested or questioned by officers of any law enforcement agency and you will give all the facts and circumstances which brought about the arrest or questioning by such officers.

16. In addition to these general rules of parole, the Board of Parole has the authority to impose additional or special conditions in any case.

APPENDIX G

Report of the Goldman Panel
Investigation of the Aftermath
of Attica November 16, 1971—Full Text

REPORT OF
THE GOLDMAN PANEL
TO
PROTECT PRISONERS' CONSTITUTIONAL RIGHTS

I. THE PANEL'S MISSION.

On September 14, 1971, the day after the riot at Attica Correctional Facility was brought under control, Governor Nelson Rockefeller requested Presiding Justice Harry D. Goldman of the Appellate Division, Fourth Department, New York Supreme Court, to name impartial observers during "this transitional period at the Attica Correctional Facility, to the end that the public at large may be assured that the constitutional rights of the inmates are being protected." On September 15, Justice Goldman requested the following five individuals to serve on the Panel, and they were appointed by the Governor: Donald H. Goff, General Secretary of the Correctional Association of New York; Clarence B. Jones, Editor and Publisher of the *Amsterdam News*; Austin MacCormick, Executive Director of the Osborne Association, Inc.; Louis Nuñez, National Executive Director of Aspira of America, Inc.; and Robert P. Patterson, Jr., member of the law firm of Patterson, Belknap & Webb.

It was understood by the Panel that constitutional rights included also human rights not specifically protected by constitutional or statutory provision and that, although the Panel's major mission was to safeguard prisoners' rights, in doing so it should also respect the rights of correctional officers and other personnel of the Attica institution and of the Department of Correctional Services.

The members of the Panel assembled at the Attica Correctional Facility on Friday, September 17. They had been informed that logistical and liaison information would be provided by Mr. Michael Whiteman, Counsel to the Governor, and Mr. Howard Shapiro, First Assistant Counsel. On arrival at the Prison, the Panel met with Mr. Whiteman, Commissioner Russell G. Oswald, Deputy Commissioner Robert Fosen, Commissioner Almerin O'Hara of the General Services Administration, and Superintendent Vincent Mancusi of the institution.

Mr. Whiteman discussed the mission of the Panel and estimated that at least thirty days would be needed to monitor the transitional period. He pointed out that the Panel was not an investigative group, since investigation of crimes committed before, during, and immediately after the riot was the responsibility of Deputy Attorney General [Robert] Fischer and his staff and that investigation of the riot and its causes would be the responsibility of another group. Mr. Whiteman suggested, however, that protection of the inmates' constitutional rights would mean that the Panel should look into the way inmates might be interviewed by the personnel of the State Police's Bureau of Criminal Investigation, working under Mr. Fischer. He suggested also that an examination should be made of prisoners' housing, medical treatment, and sanitary conditions, food and clothing, etc.; that a determination be made of possible physical abuses of inmates since control was established on September 13; and that the Panel should insure that the inmates had adequate access to counsel. The Panel's responsibility was deemed to begin at the time, on Monday, September 13, 1971, when the rioters had been brought under control and had been placed in cells.

The Panel members were then introduced to Deputy Attorney General Fischer, who said that an Assistant Attorney General would be their liaison contact in Mr. Fischer's absence. The Panel maintained close contact with Mr. Fischer and his staff throughout its tour of duty and conferred with them on many occasions.

Briefing of the Panel continued by Commissioner Oswald and Superintendent Mancusi, who gave the members a statistical and narrative picture of the situation before, during and immediately after the riot. They were then introduced to Dr. James Bradley, Chief Medical Officer of the Department of Correctional Services, Dean Pesch of the University of Buffalo Medical School, and Dr. Schenck, Chief of Surgery at Meyer Memorial Hospital in Buffalo. These physicians described the services which the Medical School had been giving the Attica institution prior to the riot, the providing of fourteen surgeons when control was established, and their treatment of the seriously injured prisoners, of whom eighty-three required surgical treatment. (For further details, see the Human Rights section of this report, under Medical Treatment.) The Panel was given further briefing on various events in the days immediately following the riot by Executive Deputy Commissioner Walter Dunbar of the Department of Correctional Services, and received a lengthy document giving information on the institution, the chronology of the riot, and other material of value to the Panel.

II. OPERATIONS OF THE PANEL.

Following the briefing, the Panel went into executive session and elected Mr. Clarence B. Jones and Mr. Austin MacCormick as co-chairmen. After a short press conference to announce the election and the initiation of its activities, it made a rapid and limited tour of the cell blocks from A Block along the guards' walks on the roof of the corridor past D Yard into C Block, which was still reeking of tear gas. The Panel returned to A Block, where those involved in the riot were housed, and to HBZ, the segregation section, where the presumed main participants were housed, and talked with these prisoners. The next day the Panel went to C Block to talk with prisoners, presumed to be non-participants, housed there and to the prison hospital to interview and observe treatment. These were the first of the several trips to all parts of the institution—cell blocks, hospital, segregation section (HBZ), industries, chapel, school building, storehouse, etc.— which the members of the Panel were to make in the following thirty days.

All conversations and interviews of inmates at this time and on all subsequent occasions for the next month were limited to events allegedly occurring after the institutional authorities regained control of the institution on September 13 and did not relate to the prisoners' activities before or during the riot itself. Several inmates, however, did from time to time make comments in regards to the actions of State Police and correctional officers during the time they were entering D Yard and inside Cell Block D on September 13, 1971.

To check on the condition of Attica inmates who had been transferred after the riot and to be sure reprisals had not been visited on them, the Panel visited and talked with Attica inmates in the Great Meadows Correctional Institution, Comstock, on September 24; Clinton Correctional Institution, Dannemora, on September 25; and Green Haven Correctional Institution, Stormville, on September 27. On the whole their treatment was found to be satisfactory, although hampered by the transfer of personnel records and other administrative difficulties. Inmates who had been seriously injured in the assault and transferred to Meyer Memorial Hospital in Buffalo were interviewed on September 19.

At the outset Governor Rockefeller and Commissioner Russell Oswald of the Department pledged the Panel complete co-operation and assistance from all agencies of the State government. This pledge was fully kept.

Throughout its entire existence the Panel had the full and complete co-operation of Commissioner Oswald, Executive Deputy Commissioner Dunbar and other members of the Central Office staff of the Department of Correctional Services. In addition, the staff at the Attica Correctional Institution gave it full and complete access to all parts of the Attica Correctional Facility and to all inmates who had been in the Attica institution during the riot, whether they continued to be housed in Attica or other facilities in the Department of Correctional Services. This co-operation and the Panel's right of private discussions with prisoners were essential to its task of protecting the prisoners' rights.

As with representatives of the Department of Correctional Services, the Panel received the full co-operation of Deputy Attorney General Robert Fischer and the members of his immediate staff, being advised daily of the status of various court actions brought against the institution and the investigation itself by attorneys representing the inmates. It received the same measure of co-operation from Michael Whiteman, the Counsel to the Governor, and members of his staff. The Panel throughout its existence was also in direct contact with attorneys representing inmates.

At its briefing session the Panel had been advised that it was expected to make reports of its progress to the public as well as to the Governor and Commissioner Oswald. The Panel was immediately concerned about this responsibility because of its awareness of the contemporaneous credibility gap which existed concerning all reports from Attica as a result of the earlier incorrect reports about the riot, e.g., the deaths of hostages by throat cutting. On the night of September 17, its first day, the Panel resolved to meet this gap by not avoiding press conferences on entrance to or exit from the institution and by answering all questions propounded by the news media.

At its press conference the following morning, September 18, an announcement of the Panel's findings on its first tour the preceding day and most pressing needs noted by the members was made. These were:

1. Severe overcrowding. The Panel members were quite disturbed at the housing of three men to a cell in A Block, and by the fact that the inmates had not been out of their cells since originally locked in on Monday, September 13. Alleviation of the overcrowding was given highest priority by the Panel.

2. The need for a medical inventory of all prisoners. The Panel discovered in its initial tour that only those inmates who

complained of injuries had been examined by physicians. Although the Panel believed that the medical treatment afforded all inmates after the riot had been good, it believed that under the circumstances it was important that a complete medical inventory of each inmate be made by an outside medical group to include Spanish-speaking as well as black doctors.

3. The need for monitoring in view of allegations by inmates of post-riot beatings. The Panel members were disturbed by the reports they had received from inmates of physical abuse and beatings alleged to have occurred after the rioters were subdued on the day of the assault and prior to and during the time they were being returned to cells.

4. Need for improvement of personal and human rights.

   a. The inmates had not had baths for over a week.

   b. Many inmates had no writing paper to write to their families.

   c. Toothpaste and personal articles. Many inmates had complained that they had lost their eyeglasses during the disturbance. Inmates were in need of shoes and socks, toothpaste, and tobacco.

   d. Food. Inmates were only receiving two meals a day in their cells.

   e. The need for greater access for counsel. Although the rooms provided for attorney interviews were excellent, the number of rooms or the time allowed for counsel to be in the institution was not in the mind of the Panel adequate under the present circumstances.

These announcements were the first reports on post-riot conditions of prisoners at Attica and the Panel felt the breadth of the findings and the promptness of their release to the public provided the Panel with a satisfactory credibility base from which to operate. During the many subsequent news conferences on its later findings, more fully described later, the Panel was not made aware of the existence of any credibility gap in connection with its relations with the news media.

In general the efforts of the Panel during the period of its existence fell roughly into two not mutually exclusive areas—those related to the protection of the constitutional or legal rights of the prisoners and those related to concern for the human rights of the prisoners. A detailed description of these efforts follows.

III. PROTECTION OF PRISONERS' LEGAL RIGHTS.

The Panel took the following actions for the protection of the inmates' legal rights:

1. The right to counsel involved an area of immediate concern to the Panel. On September 17, the Panel's first day at the institution, certain attorneys blocked the entrance to and exit from the institution for all visitors in protest of the institution's limitations on lawyers' access to inmate clients. A Panel member known to certain of these lawyers was able to indicate to them that it would be wise for the inmates' lawyers to agree on which of them had priority of entrance, and on a time limitation on each lawyer's interview, since the facilities and time for interviews would of necessity be limited.

The Panel examined the four rooms provided for lawyers' interviews that same day and concluded that they were all suitable for free communication between lawyer and client under the condition and circumstances at the Attica Correctional Facility. Review with institution authorities of the space requirements of the Deputy Attorney General and his staff and of visiting legislative committees indicated that no additional suitable space was available for the attorneys. The Panel was able to arrange for an extension of hours from six to eight hours each weekday and for six hours a day over week ends. This provided increased access for all attorneys.

The Panel also furnished the prisoners' rights group of the Legal Aid Society and lawyers associated with them and also with the names of over 100 inmates who indicated to the Panel that they wished help with legal matters or needed legal advice. These matters involved rights to appeal and rights to parole, as well as advice in connection with events of September 9–13.

Panel members arranged with officials of the New York State Bar Association to offer aid and assistance to the Fourth Judicial Department to supplement the efforts of local county bar associations so that the services of a sufficient number of qualified defense attorneys could be available to inmates to avoid conflicts of interest. In this connection, it was the Panel's belief that such conflicts were bound to arise due to the differing interests of the various inmates involved in the disturbance. This action sought to ensure that no inmate would be put in the position of fearing that the advice of a defense lawyer representing him was not independent but, instead, was affected by the interests of another inmate represented by the same defense lawyer. As far as civil legal redress for the prisoners was concerned, the

Legal Aid Society in New York organized a lawyer referral plan sponsored by four Bar Associations in the state.

2. The Panel also concerned itself with insuring the right of inmates to make complaints to authorities possessing the power to press criminal charges. In this connection the Panel was informed that Deputy Attorney General Fischer had co-ordinated prosecutorial powers with the District Attorney of Wyoming County and that within the State no other office possessed such powers. The Panel also determined that Mr. Fischer and his staff had responsibility for investigating charges against inmates in connection with criminal acts which occurred during the disturbance as well as for investigating charges by inmates against correctional officers and state troopers for actions which allegedly occurred after the disturbance was quelled. The Panel's observations led them to believe that Mr. Fischer's investigators were concerning themselves solely with the former responsibility and not with the latter and it was concerned about the conflicting responsibilities held by the Deputy Attorney General.

There followed an announcement by the State Police that Captain [Hank] Williams, who had participated in the quelling of the riot and was in charge of the detachment of State Police on the premises throughout the periods in question, had been named as chief of investigators under Mr. Fischer. The Panel brought to Mr. Fischer's attention the direct conflict of interest that Captain Williams brought to this position and asked the Deputy Attorney General to remove him from the assignment as chief of investigators, and to request the Civil Rights Division of the United States Department of Justice to undertake an investigation of the criminal charges which the prisoners were bringing to the Panel's attention regarding alleged crimes occurring after the riot had been quelled, i.e., alleged beatings, alleged running of gantlets, and alleged homicides.

Thereafter, on September 25, Deputy Attorney General Fischer telephoned and on September 27 wrote a letter to William O'Connor of the Civil Rights Division requesting, on behalf of the Panel, an investigation of these alleged violations of the inmates' civil rights. A member of the Panel kept in touch with the Civil Rights Division in Washington to determine their reaction to this letter and, when no action seemed to be forthcoming, the Panel requested the Governor to request the United States Attorney General to order such an investigation. The Governor complied with this request on October 5, 1971, and thereafter the Civil Rights Division, which so successfully conducted the Fred Hampton slaying investigation in Chicago, agreed to instruct the Federal Bureau of Investigation to initiate an investigation of the complaints of the prisoners of beatings, being forced to run through gantlets, and homicides. On October 20 the Attorney General (see New York *Times* of October 21) made public a letter which he had written Governor Rockefeller on October 19, stating that he had ordered the Civil Rights Division to make the investigation requested. The Attorney General said that representatives of the Division had already met in Albany with Deputy Attorney General Fischer. A Justice Department spokesman stated that Department lawyers estimated the investigation would take two to three months. Somewhat earlier Captain Williams had been assigned to other duties.

3. The Panel was concerned with the procedures followed by the Bureau of Criminal Investigation of the State Police and investigators working for Mr. Fischer when questioning the inmates. In this connection the Panel was told that constitutional warnings required by the Miranda decision were being given. After observing the questioning and making inquiry of several State Policemen, however, it became apparent that Miranda warnings were not being given. The Panel brought this to the attention of Mr. Fischer, who stated that he would give it his immediate attention. He reported back that, although oral instructions had been given, they had not been followed by the State Police, that he had ordered all questioning stopped, and that he was issuing written instructions ordering Miranda warnings in every case.

The Panel concerned itself with whether additional questioning of inmates was being conducted by correctional officers and other representatives of the Department of Correctional Services and was told that instructions were issued to halt all such questioning. In addition, the Panel pressed Mr. Fischer to inform all inmates that they had a right to counsel. Mr. Fischer then had the prison authorities distribute a questionnaire to each prisoner which informed the prisoner that he had a right to have his counsel present if he was questioned and permitted the prisoner to request assignment of counsel if he had none. He assured the Panel that each prisoner's request for counsel would be honored. The Panel had proposed that counsel be assigned to advise each prisoner prior to his being questioned. Whether the complexities of the unique circumstances now confronting an Attica prisoner are such that he requires the advice of a lawyer to waive intelligently his right to counsel, is a novel constitutional question currently awaiting judicial decision. Accordingly, this report does not deal with that question.

4. The Panel became concerned over whether the prisoners' rights to parole were being violated by the correctional authorities. Here it was found that some prisoners scheduled for parole were apparently being subjected to administrative charges of an insubstantial

nature to prevent improperly their parole. In those cases which came to its attention, the Panel informed the Board of Parole, which investigated the matter and ordered the prisoners' release. Because the Panel is going out of existence and in view of the highly emotional events which have transpired and the possibility of future unjustified retributive acts, the Panel advised that, as regards all administrative charges of misbehavior during the disturbance, the Department of Correctional Services should advise prisoners that counsel will be permitted at such proceedings and consent to appellate review of the proceedings. The Department has indicated it will follow this procedure.

5. Return of prisoners' personal property was a concern of the Panel. Most inmates had lost personal belongings during the riot. Many uninvolved prisoners had been made to clear their cells of all unauthorized personal property. These items ranged from leather-working tools and thermos bottles to aquariums and art work. Inmates formerly housed in Cell Block A lost virtually all their personal property when the contents of their cells were thrown out to make room for the rebellious inmates from D Yard.

On September 17, personal property in Cell Blocks B and D was in such disarray as to lead one to question whether much of it could be returned to its rightful owner. Guards blamed the disarray on the inmates searching for food and looting during the disturbance. Inmates blamed the disarray on retribution by guards in the aftermath of the disturbance. Sorting and bagging of articles for each individual prisoner was undertaken first in Cell Blocks C, E, and HBZ and later in Cell Blocks B and D, but the Department of Correctional Services determined that "unauthorized" articles would not be returned.

The Panel was especially concerned over the loss of prisoners' legal papers. In a number of instances an inmate's right to appeal was affected by the destruction or non-availability of the legal records which had been in the prisoner's possession prior to the disturbance. In connection with destroyed court papers, the Panel made arrangements through the Governor's office for the replacement of such papers without cost to the inmate and initiated procedures whereby each prisoner could notify the proper authorities as to which papers had not been returned to him. The Panel also arranged, at the suggestion of one of the Attica correctional officers, for the Public Defender in Rochester to provide for applications for assignment of counsel and appeal *in forma pauperis*, so that inmates could more rapidly obtain such assistance from the courts.

With respect to the return of other personal property to the inmates, the Panel was responsible for accelerating the sorting and bagging of prisoners' belongings in the cell blocks and eventual return of such belongings to the prisoners who had been relocated elsewhere in the prison or transferred to other prisons. It should be reiterated that the Department has ordered that only "authorized" property be returned to the prisoners and that "unauthorized" property has not been returned. Since "unauthorized" property included articles which had been acquired with full knowledge of the prison authorities, deprivation of such property might well constitute an unconstitutional deprivation without due process of law. For instance, many hobby work materials and other belongings were surrendered in cell blocks which were not involved in the riot as well as in cell blocks in the riot area. Thus, as a result of this departmental order, uninvolved prisoners suffered the loss of personal property which it had taken months and years to earn, collect, or create. At the request of the Panel the Department has ordered the prison authorities to return many articles to the inmate owners and with respect to the remainder to store same until their release or send them to the inmates' homes.

Replacement of eyeglasses and dentures was a very serious problem of which the Panel became immediately aware. Prisoners reported that they were lost during the riot or claimed that they were deliberately broken by correctional officers or troopers afterwards. The medical inventory disclosed these losses and made it possible for prison authorities to order new eyeglasses where the prescriptions were a matter of record. Eating and seeing involve fundamental human rights and at the Panel's urging the prison dentist is now making the necessary dental impressions and an outside optometrist is making the necessary eye examinations where prescriptions do not exist. Providing the missing dentures and eyeglasses should be arranged as soon as possible.

IV. PROTECTION OF PRISONERS' HUMAN RIGHTS.

In addition to protection of the prisoners' legal rights described above, the Panel was concerned with protection of what it has chosen to call their human rights although many of them also involve constitutional rights. Human rights are rights to which prisoners are entitled on the grounds of humanity and common decency, and under the policies and directives of the Department of Correctional Services. The human rights of American prisoners in general are spelled out specifically or clearly implied in the American Correctional Association's *Manual of Correctional Standards* and other literature of the correctional field. It should be borne in mind that the prisoners confined in the Attica Correctional Facility in the post-riot period, and those who had been transferred to other New York State prisons,

had not as individuals been charged with crimes relating to the riot at
the time when the Panel was functioning. They were, in their second-
ary status, prisoners detained awaiting legal action and theoretically
innocent of participation in the riot until charged and proven guilty.
Their rights, therefore, were those to which they were entitled in
their primary status: that of convicted prisoners serving sentence.

The main responsibility of the Panel was to guard against the harassment and physical abuse of prisoners in the period after control of
the institution had been established and they had been locked up. In
addition, the protection of the prisoners' human rights involved serving as a catalyst to stimulate and expedite restoration as quickly as
possible of the institution's normal services, programs, and activities:
Housing, Food, Clothing, Bathing, Commissary, Family Visits, Mail,
Yard Privileges, Industries, Religion, Education and Library, and Vocational Rehabilitation Program. The actions taken by the Panel in
each of these areas follow.

Prevention of Harassment or Physical Abuse. When the Panel
began its tour of duty on September 17, there were strong indications
that prisoners who were believed to have been participants in the riot
would be subjected to harassment and possibly to physical abuse by
correctional officers, especially during the night hours. The reports of
beatings in the immediate aftermath of the riot focused the Panel's
attention on this problem. The Panel immediately agreed on the
medical inventory by independent doctors described later. The Panel
also discussed the desirability and practicability of setting up a
monitoring system, with observers not connected in any way with the
Department or the institution patrolling at all times the tiers of the
cell blocks and reporting incidents which they had seen or that had
been reported to them. The administrative practicability, aside from
the expense, of adequate monitoring raised questions in some Panel
members' minds as to whether round-the-clock monitoring by an independent force was a wholly realistic proposal.

In response to the Panel's request, a limited program utilizing
mature and experienced parole officers was established by the Department. These men, usually three in number, patrolled the institution
during the day hours, talking to prisoners and making inquiries about
any mistreatment. Their daily reports were available to Panel
members.

Members of the Panel, less systematically, but perhaps more effectively, walked around the cell blocks and became well enough
known to the prisoners to be likely to hear of any serious abuse or
other mistreatment. They heard complaints of such harassments as

officers requiring a man to get out of bed and stand in the middle of the night for a "head count," or using insulting and provocative language to prisoners. All such harassments were promptly reported to the authorities. Supervisory correctional officers gave warnings to their subordinates that harassment of any kind would not be tolerated and would subject them to disciplinary action.

As for beatings or other forms of physical abuse after its appointment, the Panel received only a few complaints of this nature: a prisoner with a black eye and several bruises, one with contusions on his shins, and another with abrasions. Each had gotten into altercations with guards but it was impossible for the Panel to verify any acts of unwarranted force. It would appear that the medical inventory hereinafter described and its record of all bruises and other marks on prisoners' bodies may have had the effect hoped for: discouraging mistreatment which would show new bruises or contusions and, on the other hand, discouraging false claims of mistreatment with no new signs of injuries to uphold the claim. Although there were allegations reported in the press that physical abuse of inmates was continuing, the Panel believes such stories (1) were based on the same complaints of abuse in the immediate aftermath of the riot which the Panel had publicized at its first press conference on September 18 and (2) were an outgrowth of the highly emotional series of events which had occurred at Attica.

Medical Services. As was stated in Section I of this Report, on September 17, the Panel's first day at the Prison, the members were briefed by Dr. James Bradley, Chief Medical Officer of the Department of Correctional Services, Dr. Pesch, Dean of the University of Buffalo Medical School, and Dr. Schenck, Chief of Surgery at Meyer Memorial Hospital in Buffalo. Dr. Pesch reported that there were fourteen surgeons from the Medical School in the institution on the evening of Monday, September 13, immediately after the assault in D Yard, and that they proceeded to treat the seriously injured. A total of eighty-three prisoners required surgical treatment, not counting those treated for minor cuts and bruises.

On Saturday, September 18, Panel members visited the institution hospital and interviewed all prisoners there who were under treatment for wounds and other injuries. The medical care they were receiving appeared to be adequate. On the following day (Sunday, September 19) three Panel members went to Meyer Memorial Hospital, and interviewed all prisoners in the Security Unit, Recovery Room, and Intensive Care area of the Hospital. These were the most seriously wounded prisoners. The medical services rendered by doctors, nurses, and other medical personnel were excellent.

The prisoner-patients at Meyer Memorial Hospital had no complaints concerning their treatment except a few who were shackled by one foot to the bed frame. The correctional officer in charge of the security personnel said, in answer to questions by Panel members, that he had received no orders to shackle the prisoners, but deemed it necessary because some of them were large and strong, and presented an assault and escape risk.

Throughout the period of the Panel members' presence at the Attica institution, members from time to time visited the institution's hospital facility and considered the medical care and treatment adequate. Whenever a prisoner confined in the cell blocks complained to a Panel member of something which seemed to need medical attention, arrangements were made for him to be sent to the hospital for examination and, if necessary, treatment. Dr. Bradley, the Department's Chief Medical Officer, was also at the Prison during much of the Panel's stay and kept a watchful eye on the medical program.

Medical Inventory. Before the Panel members arrived at the Prison on September 17, medical examinations of all the prisoners had been made, its purpose being to discover any men whose injuries or other need of medical treatment had not come to light. The Panel discovered, however, that the instructions to have every prisoner strip and undergo a physical examination had not been followed, and that only those who complained of injuries had been given full examinations.

The Panel felt strongly that a medical inventory with complete examinations of all inmates should be made at the earliest possible date, with two main purposes: (1) to provide a complete record, as of the date of the examination, of all bruises, contusions, and other injuries on each man's body, regardless of whether or not they were alleged to have been inflicted during and immediately after the assault on the rioters in D Yard, and (2) to discover every prisoner in need of medical treatment or replacement of lost eyeglasses and dentures. This record could be referred to, if a prisoner claimed that he had been beaten or otherwise abused physically subsequent to the examination, and fresh bruises or contusions would support his claim.

In view of the allegations that the authorities were hiding continuous prison brutalities, the Panel believed the medical inventory should be made by impartial doctors who had no connection whatsoever with the Prison or any other State Department or agency. It also believed that the examining team should include black and Spanish-speaking as well as white physicians.

The Department authorities agreed with these proposals, and on September 19 the Panel members were advised by Dr. Bradley that arrangements had been made through the Erie County Medical Society to have the medical inventory on the following Saturday, September 25. The Panel protested that this was too long a delay, and it was agreed to try to accomplish the inventory on Tuesday, September 21.

The medical inventory began on the morning of September 21, and was made by a team of nine doctors (including four black and three Spanish-speaking doctors) who had volunteered through the Erie County Medical Society for this service without compensation of any kind.

Dr. Bradley took responsibility for instructing the doctors that each prisoner was to be stripped and examined either inside or outside his cell, and was to be asked if he had lost eyeglasses or dentures and needed replacements. The instructions were carried out with the exception of a brief time when Panel members monitoring the procedure discovered that, because of a misunderstanding of the instructions, a few prisoners had not been given a full examination.

At the conclusion of the inventory, Dr. Bradley and the Panel members questioned the doctors, confirmed that they were independent of any state influence and received opinions from them that all injuries found were approximately a week old. The Panel members then attended a press conference in the Superintendent's Office which Deputy Commissioner Dunbar had called. Dr. Bradley read a press release explaining the purposes and procedures of the medical inventory. He and the Panel members expressed their appreciation to the doctors for the notable public service they had rendered.

Housing. The Attica Correctional Facility has a total individual cell capacity of 2,466. At the time of the riot the inmate population numbered 2,243. The rioters initially obtained control of Cell Blocks A, B, C, D, and E. The institution later gained control of A, C, and E Blocks, leaving the rioters in control of B and D Blocks and D Block Yard. The institution never lost control of the Hospital or the Reception Building, in which HBZ, the disciplinary segregation section, is located.

When the riot was brought under control, it was found that B and D Blocks had suffered so much damage that they were not habitable. The damage to E Block was slight, but this is a medium-security building and, when repaired, could be used for low-risk inmates only. When the riot ended, the only living quarters, not counting the Hospital and Reception Building, available for the general run of the inmate population were A and C Blocks, with approximate capaci-

ties of 480 apiece. The prisoners housed in C Block were not involved
in the riot and their cells were therefore not available for housing the
prisoners, estimated at about 1,240 men, who were in B and D Blocks
and D Yard area when control was established, and were deemed to
have been involved in the riot in greater or less degree. The only
quarters available for housing them were about sixty single cells in
HBZ, and the 480 single cells in A Block, a total of 540 cells.

The institution, prior to the Panel's arrival, had started screening
both participants and non-participants for transfer to three maximum-
security facilities: Clinton, Great Meadow, and Green Haven.

When the Panel arrived at Attica on Friday, September 17, they
found about sixty rioters housed in HBZ, only one man to a cell, and a
total of about 1,200 in A Block, three to a single cell. It should be
made clear that while HBZ, the disciplinary segregation section, is
commonly referred to by prisoners as "the box," it is a modern cell
block with cells of standard size and the usual bed, wash bowl, and
toilet. There are no dark cells or so-called "strip cells" (cells with no
toilet facilities except an opening in the floor known as an Oriental-
type toilet). The HBZ section, in fact, has one advantage over the
other cell blocks, in that there are shower bath stalls in the section,
and it is not necessary to take prisoners to the bathhouse at the end
of some of the longest corridors to be found in any American prison,
as it is in most of the other blocks.

Panel members addressed themselves immediately to the situation
in A Block, where three men were housed in cells designed for one:
generally two men sleeping head to foot on a narrow bed, and the
third one on the floor, with a blanket and no mattress. These men
had not been out of their cells since control was established four
days before for a bath or any other purpose. They had shirts and
pants only and no shoes or socks. They were being fed two meals a
day in their cells.

The Panel was informed that a number of prisoners were being
transferred, that B Block would be made ready for occupancy in about
three weeks and then all prisoners would be housed one to a cell. This
delay in solving the A Block situation did not seem defensible to the
Panel. The authorities finally agreed, by stepping up the transfers and
other means, to a schedule where the three-man occupancy would
be brought down to two men by Sunday, September 19, and to one
by Wednesday, September 22. This schedule was met by a total transfer of about 1,200 men to the other institutions and in the meantime shoes, socks, underwear, sheets, and toothpaste were issued
as fast as they became available. Radio head-sets were also issued to
those lacking them.

Food. The institution's food services were badly disrupted by the large-scale looting of food supplies in the storehouse and the fires set there, and the danger of letting larger numbers of men go to the mess halls until the screening process had been completed. All prisoners, not just those considered participants in the riot, were being fed two meals a day in their cells. The Panel stressed the idea that getting food services back to normal as soon as possible would be a major step in the task of reducing the inmates' tension and improving their morale. Successive steps were taken in that direction: increasing the meals to three a day, letting selected prisoners go to the mess halls, and finally sending all of them except a small minority for whom it was not considered safe to do so. Normal food preparation and services, with those exceptions, had been resumed by the first week in October. The steward's office showed concern about the Muslim inmates' complaint about the pork content in the prison diet, and although pork continued to be served, the steward had taken steps to reduce (not eliminate) pork in the diet, e.g., ordering all-beef frankfurters and beef cuts.

Clothing, Bathing, etc. As stated above in the section on Housing, clothing that prisoners lacked was issued as quickly as could be expected. Clothing services were seriously crippled by the tear gas impregnation of clothing and shoes, the damage to the laundry equipment, and the non-availability of large amounts of clothing supplies in the institution. Bathing was delayed in resumption by the fact that the Attica institution had an archaic bathhouse in a remote section of the prison instead of the shower stalls on each tier of the cell blocks that are standard practice in better designed prisons and are to be installed by the present administration. A nearly normal bathing schedule, however, was also reached by the first week in October.

Commissary. Prisoners are allowed to purchase from the Commissary (canteen) supplementary supplies: tobacco, toilet articles, writing paper, candy, cookies, and some other types of food that is already cooked, up to a total amount of $40 a month. This is one of the prisoners' greatest privileges. Soon after the Panel's arrival it arranged to have the regular supplies issued to prisoners in their cells. By October 2, at the Panel's request, a temporary arrangement for the sale and distribution of tobacco and a few other commissary items was put in operation. This last item was clearly an unearned privilege, since the rioters had looted and burned the Commissary, but it was an important step forward in the efforts to restore the institution to normalcy.

Family Visits. Visits by members of prisoners' families were suspended for two weeks after control was established, but on September 29 they were resumed. The visiting room was not large enough to accommodate the number of visitors appearing on the first day, and it was necessary to limit the visits to one hour each. On subsequent days the numbers dropped to the point where the usual time limit of "all day" was restored. The Panel discovered that members of prisoners' families coming from the New York City area must not only go to great expense but also have transportation difficulties because of lack of train and bus services to Attica. This is a situation that should be explored with a view to ameliorating it.

Mail. In the first few days of its life the Panel had pressed for the early resumption of mail service in and out of the institution as a means of protecting prisoners' legal and human rights. The authorities then distributed to the prisoners writing material to advise their families of their condition and to communicate with their lawyers. Incoming mail and reading matter was also distributed although service was severely disrupted by the many necessary relocations and transfers of prisoners.

Yard Privileges. Three of the four exercise yards were cleared of debris soon after control was established, but D Yard was full of ditches and debris left by the rioters and was not cleared for nearly two weeks. Restoration of exercise periods in the other yards was resumed on September 25 for C Block, where the non-participants were housed, and gradually thereafter for all but two companies (eighty-two men) of the prisoners in A Block. A limited number of A Block men were let out at a time, and the exercise period was limited to twenty minutes for each group.

Industries. Some of the industrial shops were badly damaged by fire during the riot. The Wood Shop was almost completely destroyed, and the upper floor of a metal shop suffered damage requiring $50,000 to $75,000 of repairs. Plans for the speedy repair of this floor have been made and the funds are available. Fortunately, Metal Shop #2, the largest and most important of the industrial shops, suffered only minor damage. The work of cleaning out debris and checking over the equipment began on October 11. A list of men who formerly worked in the industries has been checked by the investigators, and those who have been cleared will go back to work as soon as the shops are ready. Allen Mills, the Department's Chief of Prison Industries, has been at Attica during much of the post-riot period, and has expedited the return to normal operation and production in every possible way.

Religion. Formal religious activities were severely handicapped by the fire that made the Chapel, which is also the auditorium, unusable. The roof over the stage was destroyed and will require considerable reconstruction. Plans to seal off the stage and resume use of the main floor are under consideration. For some time, however, the number of men allowed to go to the chapel-auditorium at one time will be limited for security reasons. In the meantime, the chaplains are being helpful in many ways.

Education and Library. The damage by fire to the interior of the School Building was extensive, and no part of it suffered more damage than the Library and its contents. There was no need for the Panel to try to expedite repair, refurnishing, and restocking this building, for it is part of the over-all restoration of the institution's damaged facilities for which $4,000,000 has been made available. Departmental officials and prospective contractors were appraising the damage and making estimates of costs during the first week of October.

Panel members discussed with the institution's Director of Education plans for activating the educational program, and encouraged him to go forward as rapidly as possible, even though the lack of facilities will necessitate more emphasis on cell study courses than usual. The Director, Mr. Dickinson, is also responsible for the Library, and showed initiative in providing some library services by converting the day-room on one of C Block's floors into a temporary Library, stocked with newly purchased books and others donated by "Operation Bookshelf" in Scarsdale, New York. He was planning to use the day-rooms on the other floors as classrooms. The possibility of erecting temporary prefabricated buildings for educational use is under consideration.

Vocational Rehabilitation Program. The vocational training and counseling program, financed by Federal and State funds, is housed in E Block, the medium-security building erected for that purpose in 1966. It has 200 cells or rooms of the outside type (i.e., each with its own window), and space for vocational training shops and classrooms. The program was necessarily suspended for about a month, but the damage to the building was slight and by October 11 men were being screened for return to the program. It was expected to resume in the near future with sixty men enrolled. Panel members gave encouragement to those in charge of the program.

V. CONCLUSION.

It is the Panel's conclusion that, although the scars of Attica are still self-evident and although the ill-feelings between inmates and correctional officers still smolder, the resumption of normal routine within the limits indicated above for over 80 per cent of the present population marks an end to the transitional period contemplated when the Panel was appointed. The danger of harassment of inmates continues, however, and the likelihood of unjust retaliatory and inflammatory acts in parole and other areas still remains. The Panel understands, however, that the Department of Correctional Services has agreed to take the further steps suggested herein. Accordingly, the Panel is hopeful this will constitute its final report. Because of the importance of a further cooling off if Attica is to function effectively and the hitherto co-operative attitude of the Department the Panel expects these steps to be completed in the next few days. A tense situation still exists, however, and the Panel stands ready to resume its task if necessary.

(*Signed*)
_____
Donald H. Goff
(*Signed*)
_____
Clarence R. Jones Co-Chairman
(*Signed*)
_____
Austin MacCormick Co-Chairman
(*Signed*)
_____
Louis Nuñez
(*Signed*)
_____
Robert P. Patterson, Jr.